Ottoman Refugees, 1878–1939

Ottoman Refugees, 1878–1939

Migration in a Post-Imperial World

Isa Blumi

B L O O M S B U R Y
LONDON • NEW DELHI • NEW YORK • SYDNEY

Bloomsbury Academic

An imprint of Bloomsbury Publishing Plc

50 Bedford Square	1385 Broadway
London	New York
WC1B 3DP	NY 10018
UK	USA

www.bloomsbury.com

Bloomsbury is a registered trademark of Bloomsbury Publishing Plc

First published 2013

British Library Cataloguing-in-Publication Data
A catalogue record for this book is available from the British Library.

ISBN: HB: 978-1-4725-1536-0
ePDF: 978-1-4725-1538-4
ePub: 978-1-4725-1537-7

Library of Congress Cataloging-in-Publication Data
A catalog record for this book is available from the Library of Congress.

Typeset by Newgen Knowledge Works (P) Ltd., Chennai, India

To Bahrain and Syria

Contents

List of Figures and Maps

Prelim images

Images in the text

List of Abbreviations

ACS	Archivio Centrale dello Stato
AHR	American Historical Review
AiT	Ambasciata d'Italia in Turchia
AMAE	Archives Diplomatiques de Ministère des Affaires Etrangères
AQSH	Arkivi Qendror Shtetëror
ASMAE	Archivio Storico del Ministero degli Affair e Esteri, Serie Affari Politici
ASMAI	Italian African Bureau
AUSSME	Archivio dell'Ufficio Storico dello Stato Maggiore dell'Escercito
BBA	Başbakanlı Osmanlı Arşivi
BEO	Bab-i Ali Evrak Odasi
CSSAAME	Comparative Studies of South Asia, Africa, and the Middle East
CSSH	Comparative Studies in Society and History
CUP	Committee of Union and Progress
DH.ID	Dahiliye Nezâreti Idare Kismi
DH.MUI	Dahiliye Nezâreti Muhâberat-ı Umumiye
DUIT	Dosya Usulu Iradeler Tasinifi
EIC	East India Company
FO	Foreign Office of British Government
HAT	Hatt-ı Hümayun
HHStA	Haus-, Hof- und Staatsarchiv
HR.MKT	Haricye Nezareti Mektubi Kalemi
HR.SYS	Haricye Nezareti Siyasi
IJMES	International Journal of Middle East Studies
IMRO	Internal Macedonian Revolutionary Organization
IOR	India Office Record

LON	League of Nations
MAE	Ministeri Affairs e Estare
MV	Meclis-i Vükelâ Mazbatakları
NAUK	National Archives, United Kingdom
PA	Politisches Archiv
PR	Political Resident
SAP	Serie Affari Politici
TFR.1	Rumeli Müfettişliği Tasnifi
TFR.1.KV	Rumeli Müfettişliği Tasnifi Kosova
TFR.1.ŞKT	Rumeli Müfettişliği Tasnifi Arzuhaller
USNA RG	United States National Archives Record Group
YA.HUS	Yıldız Tasnifi: Sadâret Hususî Mâruzât Evrakı
YA.RES	Sadâret Resmi Mâruzât Evrakı
YEE	Yildiz Esas Evrak
Y.MTV	Yıldız Tasnifi: Mütenevvi Mâruzât Evrakı
Y.PRK.MŞ	Yıldız Perakende Evrakı Meşihat Maruzatı
Y.PRK.MYD	Yıldız Perakende Evrakı Yaveran ve Maiyyet-ı Seniyye Erkan-ı Harbiye Dairesi
Y.PRK.UM	Yıldız Perakende Evrakı, Umum Vilayetler Tahriratı

Preface and Acknowledgments

As of March 2013, the United Nations reported that more than 1 million Syrians were stranded as refugees inside Syria or in neighboring Turkey, Lebanon, and Jordan. Such reports, despite years of experience in dealing with similar situations, continue to keep the abject conditions of the refugee camps out of the mainstream media. The refugee's very existence is predicated on her being a victim, nothing else. As a useful object for pity, the refugee's relationship with the world necessarily requires their abject poverty, a lack of privacy, and long sleepless nights. Without such conditions, the juxtaposition between the worthiness of "Western" support and the apparent evil of the regime that brought them to such a state would be useless. And yet, in spite of the generic anti-Assad narrative that implies a pathetic vulnerability and helplessness occupying these Syrian refugee camps, rather than being enclaves of passivity, they in fact are sites of intense power struggles that contradict every effort to homogenize their agency (or assumed lack thereof).

The battles for ascendency within these desperate places not only pit heavily armed factions made up of non-Syrian "jihadists" and other kinds of freelance soldiers hoping to infiltrate the lucrative civil war inside Syria. But local "host" communities themselves, forced to accommodate these refugees and their competing armed groups, invariably show signs of political mobilization. In the case of Turkish hosts living along the frontier, patience has long run out. As in many cases in the past, the conflicting needs of refugees and the opportunistic agendas of war profiteers, lurking religious proselytizers hoping to capture one heathen soul, the leering men looking to buy cheap temporary wives from desperate families compelled to sell one daughter to save the rest, or those glorified foreign "fighters"—some with idealistic aims, some criminally mercenary—constitute a volatile mix that has destabilized host countries like Lebanon, Jordan, and especially Turkey.

And, lest we forget, other "humanitarian" crises around the world continue to expediently drop off the mainstream media's radar. There are still millions of peoples displaced by years of violence in Iraq, Yemen, Somalia, East Congo, the Sahel, Burma, and Sudan, let alone the millions of Palestinians scattered throughout the world as a result of century-long depopulation campaigns. As seen in Mali in early 2013 with the conquest of much of the uranium-rich Sahel north, or the dozens of roaming militias in the Eastern Congo unleashed by war in Uganda, Burundi, Sudan, and Rwanda 20 years ago, refugees also have ambitions to forge a meaningful role in the world. As is the way with Euro-America's conflicted relationship with "human rights," these "other" refugee efforts to attract life-saving "Western" patronage often prove futile. Resources and diplomatic cover provided by the likes of US Senator John McCain and/or French "philosopher" Bernard Henri-Levy are apparently the kinds of priceless assets reserved for those able to serve larger geostrategic and economic agendas. This glaring disparity and the never-ending injustice visited upon these "other" refugees inspire the following study.

This study, however, could not be the simple product of inspired anguish over the injustices of the world. No matter how angry I am, I could not have done this book drawing from fury alone. With all sincerity, I express my appreciation for all those wonderful friends (and necessary foes) in my life who sustained me with love while I festered in rage. In the end, it was love more than hate that helped me through this project.

I start the ubiquitous list of acknowledgments with a deep appreciation for my mother and Dardane Arifaj's continued support despite the fact we had to again live away from each other during crucial moments of our respective lives. As in the past, my home, in Geneva or elsewhere, may yet be one day set, with a "Zog" and luvs forged with every glace de Gingembre at Café Remor or lasagne at La Cantinella.

Drawn from the same well is always the formidable love I feel for and from Kosova, the incubator of my tormented soul. This is largely the result of my amazing fortune to be so closely attached to my Kosovar family. I reserve a special thanks to Adrian Arifaj, whose dedication as a father and brother is truly unique and inspirational. Ardi, and not the gangsters who have taken over our country, is what we should be celebrating: A true burre. I write this book with Ardi's lovely ladies, from Naxhije, beautiful Sarah, and sweet Nora in mind; may we never, EVER have to go through the horrors of the 1990s again. Of course a great thanks to Visar (Kryetar Legjendar) for helping with the images and maps, again. And then there is Mom! Shume falemnderit for raising such wonderful children!

Far from being a single "home away from home," I have little use for maps when I pass through virtually incognito my various offices in Atlanta, Manila, Leipzig, Geneva, and Sharjah. The routine has been numbing as I set off again for another stint, in another town, with only my little laptop at my side and thoughts of Rrugac. But one thing that thankfully remains certain is my friends.

First and foremost, when it comes to my work as an historian, the irreplaceable Ebru Sönmez has remained my treasure of learning, guidance, and support. I will forever return to the gifts she has given me through her love of language and most things Persian and Ottoman. Of course there are others. For those of you still in my corner after sometimes years of no correspondence—from John J. Curry, Steven Hyland, Michael Hamson, Bettina Feller, Stacy McGoldrick, Ryan Gingeras, Jens Hanssen, Robert Baker, Carol Woodall, Tarek, François Burgat, Mogens Pelt, Catharina Raudvere, Lale Can, Sharifa al-Badi, Ahmed al-Qassimi, Saad Khan, Norah Salim, Francesco Caccamo, Alex Manevi, and Agon (urime sukses)—your simple presence somewhere in my life is all I apparently need to remain useful. Thank you.

I must shine the brightest light, however, on the sincere friendship built over the years with Joe Perry, who again offered to read portions of this book and is always ready to share a bottle and one more round of Roxy Music in celebration. And dear Joyce DeVries, the trip is always better with you in it. You two, along with Puss, are my anchor in Atlanta: thank you for many a wonderful night in East Point.

To my intellectual fellow travelers, especially Jon Schmitt, whose intelligence and diligent pen once again made for an amazing ally and friend, thank you. Then there is

Casey Cater, continuously giving and reassuringly intelligent, as always, thank you and your family as well. These two stars of Georgia State University provided not entirely uncompensated support in this book's finalization, a collaboration which would be a useful case study in determination and enduring intellectual companionship; a lesson for fine-weather friendships that easily fade in this academic world I increasingly despise.

And here then enters a new, amazing set of friends and no doubt, future colleagues. First and foremost, the amazing, no AMAZING, Joud AlKorani. It was Joud's sharp (dare I say brilliant) eyes and formidable intelligence that helped make my tormented rewrites become gratifying rethinks. Joud, I can only imagine where you are going with that intellect and wonderful choice of music. May there always be plenty for those road trips between the near and far over the next 32 years!;

From the same fortunate conjuncture of time and space I had the chance to meet Maryam "al-Bahraini." To Maryam I also send a deep thanks for making the process of living again civilized and meaningful. Your art initially helped me make a spiritual climb back . . . if only by the thinnest thread of hair.

But my time writing in Sharjah allowed me to meet so many more amazing friends. Perhaps unexpectedly to her, I want to first thank Asma al-Shamsi for her charming bullying tactics. They came at the right time and reminded me why I do all of this fighting, all of the time. I only hope that when we reach the final bell, we are on the same side. Then there are the wonderful companions I met while writing, whose diverse passions all converged at a common point. Indeed, I found myself surrounded by just amazing human beings while in Sharjah: Shamma al-Qassim, Aya al-Oballi, Sarah Zaben, Tamara al-Gunaid-Khamis, Dana Ahmad, Maysa'a Abu Hilal (you promised), Kevin Horbach, Munirah Eskander, Mehrdad Saberi, Aisha Ali, Oliva Jones, and Yara Ramadan. Thank you all for being wonderful friends and companions in this tormented world.

In academic terms, this book would not be possible without the generosity of my colleagues at the Centre for Area Studies and American University of Sharjah, who graciously tolerated my presence on (off) campus as I sought a quiet, relatively secluded place to finish writing this book. For this, I have to thank specifically Antje Zettler, Forrest, Geert, Markus, Martin, Steffi, Elisabetta, Nadine, Kristin, Sarah, and Matthais Middell at Leipzig for their support as I went off to write this book. In Sharjah I owe a special thanks to Stephen Keck for making my stay in the UAE comfortable and ultimately productive. Likewise, many thanks to Pia Anderson, Pernille Arenfeldt, Kevin Grey (and the moot, but certainly not mute, court gang), Ravi Sriramachandran, Angela Maitner, Thomas DeGeorges, and Yuting Wang for their support and occasional coffee/tea in "town." In this respect, I have to leave a special thanks to my friends I made while writing at the Caribou in Matajir. In particular I wish to extend a warm appreciation for the friendship and constant concern for my progress to Moses "Boss" Ubong Etim.

At the same time, my "home institution" at Georgia State University, while going through some painful transformations, has at least toward me, been very generous. It is not a comfortable position to be in as I watch from afar the poor treatment of people who are not only my friends but vital to the relative success of my departments. For their contributions to making my life manageable while on leave, I need to thank from the bottom of my heart Alta Schwartz and Michelle Lacoss. They deserved promotions and raises.

In addition, I have some especially supportive colleagues, among whom I single out Ghulam Nadri, Michelle Brattain, Larry Grubbs, Jared Poley, Christine Skwiot, Michele Reid, Douglas R. Reynolds, Nick Wilding, Hugh Hudson, and Larry Youngs. Thank you for remaining interested.

And then there was Bloomsbury Academic Press. Rhodri Mogford, has been most professional and very pleasant to "work" with during my hectic writing phase while Srikanth was as tireless as accommodating during the production phase. Thank you for your patience.

Finally, I wish to acknowledge the professionals who helped facilitate my extensive research throughout Europe/Middle East. In particular I want to thank the staffs at the Arkivi Qendror Shtetëror (Tirana), Haus, Hauf und Staatsarchiv (Vienna), Singapore National Archives, the Philippine National Archives (Manila), the Zanzibar National Archives (Stonetown) and a special thanks to Salim Najaf for introductions, the Politisches Archiv des Auswaertigen Amtes der Bundesrepublik Deutschland (first Bonn then Berlin), Centres des Archives diplomatiques de Nantes/Paris, League of Nations Archives (Geneva), Archivio Storico del Ministero degli Affari Esteri (Rome), the Başbakanlık Arşivi (Istanbul), the National Archives, formally known as the Public Records Office (Kew Gardens), the US National Archives (Maryland), and finally the Atatürk Library in Istanbul. Additional acknowledgment must be given to the organizations and institutes that have provided generous funding to help research this book: The Fulbright-Hayes Committee, American Council of Learned Societies, the American Research Institutes in Turkey and Yemen, CAORC, and the Social Science Research Council contributed generously to my research all over the world.

As is my "nature," I end on a tragic note. As possibly noticed by some, I dedicate this book to Bahrain and Syria, two jewels of our world now brought to ruin by a chauvinism and selfishness that was once reserved for the worst tyrants of the Middle Ages. Their fake piousness, disguising the greed and barbaric emptiness of an illiterate bigot, is now poisoning what was left of a beautiful way of life in my spiritual and cultural heartland. Both Syria and Bahrain, two incubators of humanity, where "different" peoples could unite in love, make beautiful art, and bear beautiful children, are now all but gone. O how we have let the white devil take our dignity, our faith, and finally our humanity away from us.

Maps

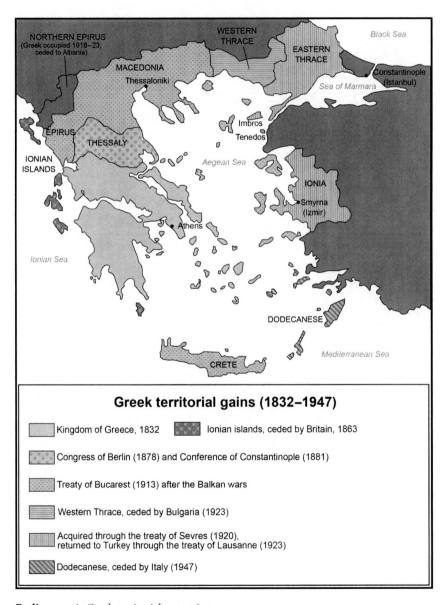

Greek territorial gains (1832–1947)

Kingdom of Greece, 1832

Ionian islands, ceded by Britain, 1863

Congress of Berlin (1878) and Conference of Constantinople (1881)

Treaty of Bucarest (1913) after the Balkan wars

Western Thrace, ceded by Bulgaria (1923)

Acquired through the treaty of Sevres (1920), returned to Turkey through the treaty of Lausanne (1923)

Dodecanese, ceded by Italy (1947)

Prelim map 1 Greek territorial expansion

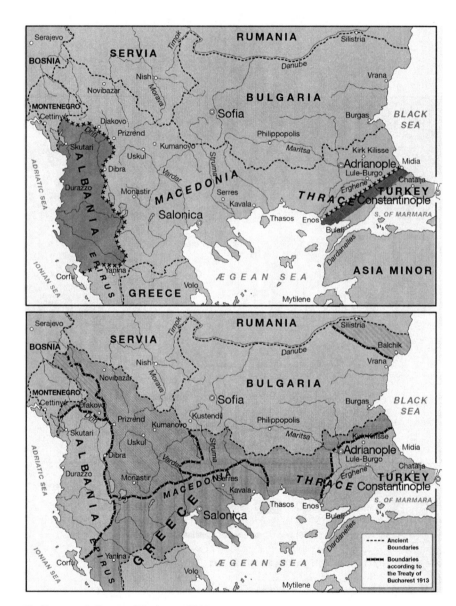

Prelim map 2 Treaty of Bucharest 1913

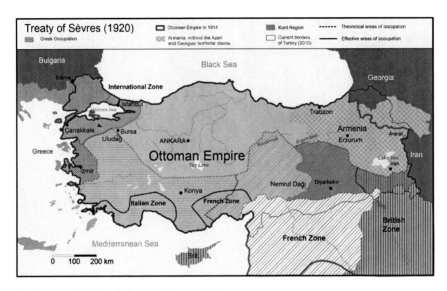

Prelim map 3 Map of Treaty of Sèvres, 1920

Prelim map 4 Map of Treaty of Lausanne 1923

Introduction

Having escaped, lost in exile
Constrained and incarcerated,
I ache with tears unabated
On the Elbe's shores, and Banks of Spree
To Where have I Fled, Leaving all Behind,
Impoverished Homeland, destitute nation
I lay unclean on the seashore
Remaining unseen in the sunlight
Starving at the dining table
Ignorant among the Learned
Naked and anguished
Sullen in body and soul . . .

Anës lumenjve (On the river's banks) by Fan Noli (1882–1965)

Introduction

It is the precarious existence of exile—whose life is haunted by the unabated beckoning of an ever distant homeland while left wanting in a foreign land—that leaves a collective anxiety in a national polity's memories. As a result of such anxieties lurking in the Balkans, the many Albanian children who memorized Fan Noli's beautiful, if complex dedication to an exiled national hero, may at times miss the irony of the author's own accomplishments as an activist, at times himself in exile.[1] As a teaching tool, the "diasporic" life engrossed in Noli's poem posits exile as a contradiction of human energy that historians, activist Bishops, and middle-school teachers far too often subordinate in favor of the evocative melancholy of the lost homeland. The refugee forced to live in exile, in other words, is a hapless shadow of history until she returns "home."

This is a book that aims to reverse these appropriations of artistic tropes for the purposes of telling a tragic, and largely subordinate national story. Its goals are as much driven by the wish to arm fellow researchers with new approaches to studying modern history as offering its own comprehensive revision of that recent past. At its core is a methodological drive to complicate through particularization and comparison the "inevitably" tragic experiences of specifically Ottoman refugees during a 1878–1939 transitional period. As explained throughout, the particular lives of refugees as migrants not only promise to offer a dynamic set of filters through which we can explore world histories in new ways, but it does so by way of challenging previous uses of Ottoman history that sought in their own way to tell different kinds of post-WWI stories.[2]

At the heart of this corrective study is the enduring question of who contributes to History. The manner in which the refugee in particular is mobilized to produce western "meta-history" proves emblematic of the larger methodological debates consuming the politics of memory.[3] As a result of being cut off, perhaps permanently, from the resources and support of his/her homeland, the refugee *appears* marginalized and thus bereft of agency. This vulnerability seems requisite to certain kinds of composite nationalist mythologies.

To the contrary, I will make the case below that refugees can become part of dynamic constituencies in a large range of settings and as a result, *do* influence history. In fact, these refugees contribute to History to such an extent that they may be at crucial moments considered a generative force behind, for example, forms of modern state bureaucracy, the emergence of institutions of violence, and even the ascendency of Western finance capitalism. As involuntary migration affects the world in many ways, dependent on context, the historian thus may need to avoid trying to define a monolithic migratory condition. Instead, refugees/expellees/poor migrants may in fact consist of individual and small clusters of groups that collectively act to, for instance, advocate for a common cause, often in the form of rioting over a lack of food and shelter. They also could organize, often with non-refugees, to lobby for their political integration into the new societies they settle. More interestingly still, it is suggested throughout that refugees can become an outright force of destabilization in those same host communities. This is to say, even if the generic refugee is forgotten in the wake of blinkered international aid, or through calculations of *realpolitik* is effectively "cleansed" from his/her homeland, he/she becomes a historical agent elsewhere in the world.[4]

To attempt this restoration, I will highlight the contributive force of refugees in a late Ottoman and then immediate post-Ottoman context (1878–1939) as it spread across the empire's entire geographic reach from the western Balkans, Eastern Anatolia, to Southern Arabia. This trans-regional scope will help make the argument that these historic peoples and the rapidly changing communities they regularly created (and broke apart), played a more significant role in the shaping of the larger modern world than is granted them by traditional scholarship.

To the observant reader, such an intervention may seem redundant. Considering the plethora of scholarship on the plight of many of the Ottoman Empire's refugees who were dispersed throughout the last 50 years of empire—from Jews, Armenians, Balkan and Russian Muslims, Albanians, Arabs, Greeks, and Bulgarians—it would seem this topic has been covered already.[5] As much as this appears true on the surface, however, the very manner in which the theme of "refugee" is mobilized in the scholarship needs closer scrutiny.[6] I believe that we need to question how the Ottoman refugee is referenced in transitional stories about the birth of post-Ottoman nations, and indeed about the role of the Ottoman Empire's collapse on the development of the "modern world."

Unfortunately, within the confines of Ottoman studies as they stand today, the refugee becomes an almost empty category of analysis with very little differentiation across temporal and geographic contexts. The refugee is, in other words, a monolith, a categorical point of reference made subordinate to a larger narrative about the trajectory of the empire and its successor ethno-national states.[7] When done properly, such studies largely succeed in complicating otherwise generic histories that focus on relations between states, the acts of political elites, and listing wars and the treaties that ended them.

The heavy focus on treaties and political elite is fully understandable in complex countries like Turkey, which is in fact one of the dozen or so post-Ottoman polities whose members were made up of refugees and internally displaced peoples (IDP).[8] Indeed, Armenia, Turkey, Greece, Bulgaria, Bosnia, Serbia, Chechnya, Syria, Iraq, Palestine, and Albania (Kosovo) all tell some version of the refugee story in their national histories. Unhelpfully, scholars tend to evoke the refugees in order to fit narrative conventions expected to reinforce the myths of the modern state's inevitability rather than providing a means to understand the complexity of social and economic change surrounding their experiences. In other words, the refugee story in the hands of the nationalist historian is a retrospective device by which individual and collective suffering are made to serve the ascendant nation.[9]

Extending this apparent nation-building role of specific national refugees even further, it is the horrors of "ethnic cleansing" that attract the most emphasis in the existing literature. In this regard, the collective suffering of "our ancestors" initiates an historic "process" deemed necessary to productively "break" from a premodern past.[10] That is to say, the "historically inevitable" violent collapse of the premodern multiethnic empire helps the nation shed its "backward," "Oriental" past and in turn permits it to become part of the modern world.[11] As such, being victimized castaways of the Ottoman "Islamic" Sultanate serves to "restart" a process that had been arrested by so many hundreds of years of "Turkish" (or Habsburg/European) imperial occupation.[12]

While this may in fact be the prevailing meta-narrative of "the nation," one that varies only slightly in each post-Ottoman society, it often completely distorts the complexity of historical events, and is especially prone to depict the protagonists (and antagonists) in ways that border essentialist racism. The central complaint lodged by this study is that it is impossible for such rigidly defined parameters to accurately reflect the dynamics around those peoples living in an Ottoman past. To redress this, we will position the refugee (loosely defined to the extent that I include immigrants coming from outside the empire, as well as economic migrants, and IDP) and her/his various experiences in indeterminate and complicated ways, allowing for a more intricate and perhaps more dynamic historic image to emerge.[13]

One way of accomplishing this is to look specifically at—and thus question—both the physical and apparent spiritual migration of various peoples toward the possibility of an Ottoman (at times Muslim) "universal" safe-haven. This angle has come relatively late in the process of writing this book and is inspired by recent breakthroughs in the scholarship. In particular, it was after reading the excellent new book on conversion (and apostasy) by Selim Deringil that it became clear the documents the historian uses to decipher the chaotic events of Ottoman collapse offer both barriers to "explaining" the violence of the empire's final years, as well as invaluable insights into what was possible for so many in these defining moments of survival.[14]

In contrast to any number of studies that necessarily "expose" the violence toward "Armenians" as Christians by way of "Muslim" or "Turkish" state (and thus entire society) policies of murder, dispossession, and ethnic cleansing, Deringil's approach to the study of religious conversion adds several layers of analysis to the dynamics at work in cases of wide-spread human suffering during imperial collapse. Following Deringil's welcome discussion on what is at stake when debating conversion, I am questioning further how religious and/or ethno-national "confession" operates as a categorical determinant of historical action. I will demonstrate throughout that if not placed into a number of contexts through which, in particular, the violence of imperial collapse takes place, the utility of categories of analysis like confession, ethno-national identity, and thus religious conversion proves misleading.

Paradoxically, Deringil's study demonstrates perfectly the need to carefully steer the analysis of any interface between competing empires and individual (or community) acts of desperation, cunning, deception, or love away from concepts derived solely from Western knowledge. As Deringil points out, too many scholars have left the story of "Christian" conversion to "Islam" trapped in the larger framework of variations of the "clash of civilizations" theme. In this regard, Deringil seems careful enough not to assert uniform conclusions to a "theme" of conversion in order to fit it into a normative "Great Game" or worse still "Pan-Islamism."

As Deringil partially points out himself, much of the reading of the tragedies that produced multitudes of Ottoman refugees misses several points. The fact is that these transitional peoples were not only physically uprooted, constantly mobile refugees; but they were also ideologically, culturally, and economically resilient in their transience. In other words, those deemed in the scholarship as the most vulnerable "victims" of imperial extension and/or collapse were also those displaced refugees who proved capable of adapting to rapidly changing events. Far from being helpless, the refugees flooding the Ottoman Empire in the late nineteenth and early twentieth centuries were very much itinerate agents of history.

Moreover, in their mobile state refugees constantly reorganized previously displaced communities. Often, out of their newly created publics, refugee collectives took the form of armed militias or social clubs, viable constituencies demanding institutional attention. In turn, their potentially disruptive activism led to new regional instabilities. Some good examples of the opportunities created by refugee activism are found throughout Anatolia and the Balkans in the mid-1870s—activism that proved the key window of opportunity for both Russia and the Habsburgs to enter these region's domestic affairs.[15]

The resulting 1877–8 Russo-Ottoman war actually instigated yet a new wave of refugees whose flight into Ottoman territories simply restarted the many different processes of adaptation, violent competition over resources, and political alliance-making. These new refugee constituencies had long-term consequences for the way the Ottoman state developed vis-à-vis its subjects and the larger world. What I bring new to those works that characterize the result of the post-1878 refugee wave as a "resurrection" of peoples whose violent revolts would serve the modern nation-state is that I find that these constantly adapting communities proved far more ideologically elusive.[16]

Instead of being unquestioning surrogates for ethnic hatred, persecuting others as they were once themselves persecuted, refugees emerging in the 1870s often proved to be the most stubborn Ottomans. In face of violence, often perpetrated by de-facto mercenary armies of "foreign" men who claimed to be "liberating" them, these stubborn Ottomans grasped at reformulating—and often successfully mobilizing—seemingly "outdated Oriental" sensibilities. Such gestures often amounted to protecting "Muslim" or "Armenian" or "Bulgarian" neighbors from the merchants of war who co-opted the useful lie about human incompatibility to help expand what I will characterize throughout as the potentiality of Euro-American economic hegemony. Indeed, it is this important face-off between resistant Ottoman-era values of cohabitation and the "ethnic entrepreneurs" of a new era of possibilities that animated much of the 1878–1939 period.[17]

A sensitive reading of the different, constantly shifting lives of refugees helps us expand on the entire, very violent, later stages of Ottoman rule in areas as diverse as the western Balkans, Arabia, and Mesopotamia/Eastern Anatolia. Moreover, what studying Ottoman refugees does to redefine the parameters of power relative to individuals and the institutions built around them can lend new urgency to the ethical engagement with the inherent complexity of present-day refugee catastrophes. To start this however, we must consider some of the conflicting agendas at play among those clusters of peoples straddling the political and commercial frontiers of the Balkan, Eastern Anatolian, and Arabian/Middle Eastern provinces of the late Ottoman Empire.

In these conflict-ridden spaces, purportedly separating ancient peoples and clashing civilizations, I maintain that the violence characterizing those events long associated with the causal sources of imperial collapse may more usefully be understood as a transitional phenomenon. In other words, conflict emerged from a historically contingent set of conditions reminiscent of other, equally vexed locales facing systemic violence.[18] We need to stop assuming the violence shaping the contours of refugee life (let alone the larger population) is endemic to these "non-Western" regions and their inhabitants. Instead, it is necessary to believe that the refugee experiences as linked to the Ottoman Empire is a living product of specific conditions introduced by, among other things, the transformative factors related to expanding finance capitalism and its associated methods of state rule.

Outline of book

The emergence of finance capitalism created a particular kind of refugee exposed to a form of exploitation that increasingly scoured the earth for cheap labor. With Greek, Armenian, Albanian, Montenegrin, and Syrian landless peasants loaded onto the increasing numbers of ships docking at Ottoman ports, merchants of human toil offered developers in the rapidly industrializing North America and the vast untapped agricultural wealth of Latin America cheap labor to join still virgin economies.[19] Many others joined these economic refugees, including peasants specifically targeted for forced expulsion, first by invading armies and then, through negotiation promoted by the ascendant Euro-American powers, in diplomatically sanctioned "population exchanges." By 1912, it became part of an operating logic that certain social associations characterized by creed or race were "naturally" incompatible with different neighbors and were thus necessary victims to service a larger international order seeking to both oversee how human labor, and other natural resources, would be "developed" and assure such exploitative practices remained fully regulated.

In the case of the human being as commodity, the negotiated process of forcefully separating now ontologically different "races" of potential laborers became the precursor to ethnic cleansing, mass murder, and ultimately genocide in the quickly conquered Ottoman lands from 1912 onwards.[20] Increasingly historians are beginning to link these disruptions in human communal life as the lucrative source of all kinds of new means to "securitize" human beings' labor.[21] What is not entirely clear to most who elect to focus on the savagery of this sordid period in Middle Eastern and Balkan history is that the same Euro-American powers, via diplomatic meetings or the League of Nations, imposing programs of forced population exchanges resulting in millions of Ottoman refugees by 1918, were in their own right the perpetrators of the worst kind of mass murder, forced migrations, and starvation elsewhere.[22]

What arose from those peoples being institutionally coerced to flee from zones of conflict were often fly-by-night operations erected to rationalize these now refugees' (re)settlement. Where our story about the Ottoman refugee diverges from this often well-told one is that these refugees did not *necessarily* contribute positively to the creation of our current, narrowly defined modern state. In this respect, it may be wise not to assume that the "natural" destiny of these temporarily dislocated peoples was to form homogenous, modern ethno-national, exclusivist communities. Instead, there may be evidence during these periods of violent transition to suggest that these former Ottoman subjects persisted in acting in decidedly "Ottoman ways" as much as the embittered founders of chauvinistic, exclusionary nation-states.

This itinerate sensibility that pervaded the refugee experiences is identifiable in, for example, Theodora Dragostinova's crucial revisionist work. Dragostinova explores tensions arising within targeted communities facing intermediate choices between exile/resettlement and living a "minority" existence in what became Bulgaria. To many, these options eventually materialized into ambiguous political niches inhabited by "political acceptable amphibians [who] navigated official expectations" and left state-building operations in flux as a result.[23]

Indeed, Ottoman refugees during the 1878–1939 period often forged alliances that cut across otherwise neatly delineated ethno-national, sectarian, and class lines outside forces constantly sought to impose. In these alliances, refugee communities resembled more a capacious Ottoman revival than the enforced ethnic homogeneity of the nation-state. Consider, for instance, Syria and Iraq under French and British occupation from 1917 until at least the 1930s (see Maps 1, 2, 3, 4). The otherwise "mixed" communities proved as much able to defy the international order as vulnerable to manipulation by the "divide and rule" tactics of "civilizing" missions sanctioned by the newly minted

League of Nations. In this respect, peoples throughout the former Ottoman Empire acted in ways that contradicted the pseudo-imperialist taxonomies that international interests eagerly sought to use in order to distinguish Shiite, Sunni, Kurds, tribes, Armenians, Assyrians, Druze, and Maronite from each other.[24] The same held true in the violent period of state-formation in Albania, Yugoslavia, and Turkey after World War I, a period when strident policies that criminalized "difference" often faced collective responses that revealed an ecumenical spirit that occasionally compelled the stream-roller of modernity to redirect.[25]

This rejoinder to an otherwise programmatic narrative of post-Ottoman nation-building is especially important in the context of the Balkans, Eastern Anatolia, and present-day Syria and Iraq. These are all regions which experienced well into the twenty-first century forms of state and extra-state funded violence aimed to (de) mobilize some form of population politics. This is modernity in its most negative sense, a by-product of struggles between Ottoman refugees in transitional settings— both physically displaced and ideologically marginalized—that ushered in a new world order by way of local ethnic and/or sectarian entrepreneurial intermediaries. To ultimately deepen our understanding of how this struggle takes place depends on our willingness to revisit a multifaceted intersection of forces during the 1878–1939 period. More importantly, this elaboration needs to take place outside the confines of the standard analytical categories that rule contemporary scholarship.[26]

For this reason I am steering this book on refugees away from merely repeating the recent scholarship that proves Muslim/Christian or Turkish/Arab hostilities did not always set the tone in post-Ottoman societies in the Balkans and Middle East, let alone during the empire's last years. These corrective narratives offer an abundance of examples of how productive relations cut across simplistic lines of distinction. These studies, however, tend to focus only on one set of cases, usually located geographically in a relatively small corner of the (former) Ottoman Empire. So while this book builds on the excellent work of colleagues, it expands the study to cover *comparatively* these hitherto singularly observed cases of a lingering cosmopolitanism and tolerance for the religious and cultural diversity. I look intermittently at how such processes compare and contrast in Bulgaria, Greece, Yugoslavia, Albania, Anatolia, and Mandate Iraq and Syria, as well as within several Ottoman diaspora settings around the world.

To contextualize these transitional processes, Chapter 1 studies the political economy of the late empire. A close reading of the role of international finance as increasingly dominated by a small group of banks, debt, and the evolving relationship with land as a commodity, for example, can initiate new ways of linking the politics of imperial collapse to a new found utility for dispersed, landless peoples as laborers. Perhaps ironically, these processes did not all automatically service the emergence of some form of ethno-national state throughout the former Ottoman territories, an emergence that was contingent and highly variable across post-Ottoman geographies. As such, the very dynamics of settling the refugee within a rapidly changing land regime and industrialization of finance must be compared across very different settings. I do this by first exploring how land ownership and the politics behind land use transformed during the course of the Ottoman Empire's last 50 years.

Tied to these processes are the structural changes transforming the way states interacted in the global economy. Throughout the first three chapters of this book I consider the Ottoman state as a mechanism that tried to productively settle these refugees (by and large displaced from newly lost lands in Crimea, Caucasus, and the Balkans) in order to further emphasize that land management issues directly linked with refugee agency in such times of turmoil. That being said, it is important to remember that the entire period of Ottoman reforms (conventionally understood to span the years 1839 to 1876) underwrote the post-1878 era of this refugee resettlement. By 1912 an *intact* Ottoman Empire was no longer as attractive to the strategic calculations of various financial interests as it had been during the nineteenth century.

This waning interest in a unified Ottoman Empire is crucial to start the larger argument of this book. A necessary precursor to the disintegration of the Ottoman Empire over the nineteenth century, therefore, was the *Tanzimat*, a period of reforms that introduced the kinds of transformations to Ottoman society that blurred the intentions of these reforms and left many at the time to wonder whom were they supposed to serve.[27] By taking into consideration that these proto neoliberal reforms reflect very much the kind of social disasters ushered in today by such massive, foreign imposed programs that prioritize exposing local economies to "global" markets, we can begin to rethink the terminology used to explain this crucial era. The Ottoman Empire, and crucially, large numbers of its subjects, many who either became IDPs or care-givers of refugees, were exposed to the exploitative forces of global capital.

The reasons for the growing political turmoil starting in the 1870s become obvious when adopting a political economic approach. The rewards for those who ruled—or influenced the latter—were great. There were personal emoluments for being pliable, incentives that included joint ventures in lucrative trading deals, and even potential for celebrity in European media. Similarly, those who wanted to stem the pillaging of their homeland out of patriotism (what has been called Ottomanism or unionism), needed to gain access to the decision-making offices of the imperial government and then securing them by legal or extra-legal means.[28] This too had political economy implications.

As these reforms launched socioeconomic reorientations, the consequences for displaced peoples were varied and profound. At times, and depending on the given context, those invested in the spirit of reform completely transformed the manner in which they interacted with their putatively destitute refugee brethren. Taking this into account allows us to challenge how we understand the effects a set of demographic transformations had on the primary stakeholders—the bureaucrats and reformers whose Balkan and Transcaucasian homelands were to be lost forever—and thus begin the task of inserting refugees into the modern history of the region.[29]

This can be done further in Chapter 2 by including questions about how the Ottoman state may have evolved into something far more akin to a modern one *because* of its attempts to care for millions of uprooted peoples. I suggest that part of the way in which reforms, resistance, and further transformations associated with the last century of Ottoman history can be studied is by investigating how the demands of provisioning for refugees were met. The need to feed uprooted refugees in times of political and economic collapse gradually clashed with a new calculus among a number of stakeholders aiming to profit from this "demand" to eat.

As such, provisioning for refugees constituted a moral threshold that marked the contentious fault lines refugee/internally displaced (post) Ottomans straddled. Moreover, refugees' productive, necessarily "fractious" interface with the agents of Euro-American capital created the conflict between the moral necessity to feed refugees and those "market forces" seeing value in high demand for resources. It is this conflict, I argue, that marked the ultimate point of origin for the modern world.

Struggles over the control and use of resources are the crucial points of reference to understanding when and where Euro-American hegemony begins and ends.[30] In other words, how the "provisional" agendas of the Ottoman state fluctuate in this context proves of elementary importance to understanding the dialectical relationship between being Ottoman and the new world order. To compliment (if not further complicate) these insights I offer in Chapter 3 a detailed analysis of how Ottoman subjects end up in neighboring states and principalities during the 1900–18 period. I do this in order to raise new questions about how we can actually understand the exiled refugee (in the form of "diaspora") experience in the larger context of the global transformations that destroyed the period's heterogeneous empires. Be they Albanian intellectuals in Romania or Egypt, Armenian radicals in Bulgaria, or Russian-born Ottoman "patriots" organizing in Paris and Cairo to "reunite" the Empire by way of reinstating the annulled constitution of 1876, these quasi-refugees living in neighboring safe-havens offer a valuable angle to this story.

In these translucent settings we find numerous Ottoman actors enjoying a unique set of conditions, conditions I frame as a "*proximate*" dynamic. By being proximal, in some cases literally contiguous to the Ottoman political space, these de-facto refugees straddle roles otherwise omitted in the post-Ottoman historiography. For scholarship that retrospectively fixates on a hero's rebellion or a political agency focused entirely on shaping a post-Ottoman world, the Ottoman refugee inhabiting this transitional space complicates the story. Indeed, this contribution by refugees on the immediate "fringes" of the Ottoman governed space problematizes the story by fluctuating from an intimacy with "domestic" Ottoman concerns to an ability to function outside the formal capacity of the state to dictate the parameters of action. This *proximate* dynamic, in other words, mediates between the political agent's exile and the relevance of these agents in a variety of settings, both inside the Ottoman Empire and these neighboring polities.

This migrant Ottoman story must at all costs be freed from the political intrigues of the era in which the foundational narratives to the present-day nation-state were forged. The fact that many of today's political parties claim legitimacy by associating themselves to "founding fathers" has required that historians focus on the political intrigues of individual men in Bucharest, Paris, Geneva, and Cairo. The problem is these men and the plots they schemed were hardly representative of the larger dynamism in the world around them. Considering how secretive these cells in Bucharest, Salonika, Geneva, and Paris were (all monitored by either the Ottoman secret police, with the occasional assassin at their call, or host governments actively persecuting these early forms of "terrorist" cells) they could not productively interact with their fellow Ottomans.[31]

Yes, their publications have become useful tools to analyze these early developments of anti-regime, and even anti-Ottoman, activism. But then again, how representative are they of the world in which members of such secret organizations operated within the *Ottoman proximate*? Exploiting these sources can lead to conclusions that are speculative at best. In this regard, Chapter 3 is careful to not fall into the trap of allowing overly secretive, and in many cases, violently paranoid, political activist groups to dictate how we should characterize the diasporic spaces of the Ottoman *proximate* refugee.[32]

The fact that so many of these groups operated in such self-isolating cells can help us speculate as to the kind of political culture these men carried with them after "victory" in the summer of 1908. As this "Young Turk" revolution brought temporarily into power many from the Ottoman *proximate* spaces, their subsequent descent into factionalism after taking power was predictable; rivalries were already evident while in exile as they often played out in the European press. Such earlier tensions were only exasperated by the intrigues introduced when they attained power, which in turn means their earlier exilic context is crucial to understanding the development of ideological orientations that transformed the empire after 1908.[33]

That many among these oppositional exiles demonstrated a tendency to keep meetings secret and they infuse their publications with abstract symbolism accessible only to members left many future "heroes" of the nation operating in circles beyond the specific concerns of individual Ottoman citizens. For the Free-Masons, whose influential role in the CUP is now beyond a doubt, the dynamics of Ottoman transformation bears consideration in the larger context of power circles throughout the Euro-American world.[34] Likewise, the introduction of Anarchism and Bolshevism animated internal oppositional politics in the Ottoman world, with the Ottoman refugee/diaspora most deeply affected by the rising tide of certain forms of polemic.[35]

To develop this story further, Chapters 4 and 5 offer a global perspective of refugee agency that can serve as a further layer of complexity to the story of Ottoman sensibilities which I believe persisted even when Syrians, Arabs, Greeks, Albanians, and Armenians lived thousands of miles away. By offering a preliminary survey of Ottoman activities as both settlers hoping to find meaningful employment in the Americas or Southeast Asia, and Sufi missionaries seeking to transmit a spiritual message to places as distinct as Zanzibar and Mindanao, I am offering yet another medium through which we can understand evolving Ottoman sensibilities, those composed and often vociferously articulated on entirely different continents.

It is in these Ottoman refugee diasporas, many of which outlive the actual empire, that a vision of the world, seemingly outdated by the violence of interethnic/sectarian wars and genocides that would ravage the Ottoman homeland by 1912, still proved stubbornly relevant. What comes out of these two chapters should be an appreciation for how different constituencies emerge with far different immediate and medium-term experiences within the process of global transformation that inflicted much suffering (and new possibilities) on these itinerate Ottomans. It should also become clear that these refugees of a transforming "land-based" empire had, just like their counterparts in the *Ottoman proximate*, a considerable impact on their host societies. In this respect, it bears remembering that most of these Ottoman refugees moved to important points of exchange, where the juxtaposition of vastly different political, economic, and social forces intersecting at crucial moments (as in Eastern Africa, the Americas, and the South China Sea) often turned to exploitation and even depredation. In this regard, not only must we begin to tell many different kinds of migrant stories through an Ottoman refugee filter, but in equal measure mediate the common story of European imperialist violence through the stories of Ottoman refugees serving as middlemen or collaborators.

My main characters are presented as far more varied than the conventional laborers seeking new sources of income in an increasingly cash-based global economy. At once spiritual as much as economic opportunists, political exiles and uprooted peasants, it is both their diversity and their distinctive associations with their new environments that make it impossible to fit refugees into a more general narrative. For our purposes here, narratives about those whom I see as diverse surrogates for an inarticulate, initial gesture of Ottoman spiritual colonialism, are drawn from within Ottoman refugee communities often consisting of no more than a handful of Sufi missionaries in tropical Central Africa or shop owners in a Mexican village. Many of these itinerate men of faith (and their requisite links to commercial interests exploiting the "New World") will prove useful in that they offer a much different perspective on how the "modern" world was made.

By opening up in Chapter 5 a tension within imperial state/administration theory and practices I suggest yet another role for the migrant/refugee to play in the modern world. After my brief history of how purportedly Ottoman state-led efforts at the (partial) institutionalization of religion in the nineteenth century unfolded, it will then be possible to offer a detailed rethinking of the causal factors behind *both* imperial policies dedicated to "Islam" and by revealing the internal dynamics behind "Muslim" missionary work in the Indian Ocean. As argued, the factors instigating the missionary work of a small group of itinerate, nominal Ottoman Sufis, stems not from state policy but an indigenous network of constituencies operating at the fringes of the Ottoman world.

While rethinking what possible role the Ottoman Empire played in the larger world it will be useful to study these small enclaves of Muslims, many originating from non-Ottoman lands and only having tangential, theological/spiritual/ideological associations with the empire. I demonstrate that it is the independent work of small groups of concerned merchants and Sufi scholars whose activism actually helped to redefine the "borderlands" of Islamic "modernism," inter-imperial rivalry, and even the future methods of Euro-American colonialism. From within this doctrinal diversity hundreds of itinerate Sufis would engage European power in ways that allow us to appreciate the possible integration of missionary-like operations into a larger discussion of the politics of empire and religion. To this reorientation of causality, we must insist that the context of these global processes remains along the contested frontiers of finance capitalism, not in the formal halls of government in London, Bombay, Singapore, or Istanbul. It is, in other words, out in Eastern Africa (and by extension Southeast Asia), where we begin to appreciate just how dispersed spiritually the so-called Muslim world was in the 1860–1900 period.[36]

As a result of their spiritual training and immediate, changing political context from which they came, Sufis from the Indian Ocean push the meaning of being a Muslim in entirely different directions than desired by any of the state institutions twentieth-century scholars have thus far linked to the larger period of "Islamic reform." In the end, rather than a reference to any rigid partisanship with Sultan, socioeconomic interest group, or even "religion," the itinerate Sufi was a missionary for much broader (and at the same time, narrower) concerns than the relative place of the Ottoman Empire in a world increasingly dominated by Euro-American standards of governance and commerce. To make this clearer, however, it is perhaps worth deconstructing the value of highlighting those "Islamic" institutions emerging at a time scholars expect to indicate the growing influence of "Western" thought and practice.

Theorizing the refugee in the context of modernity

Throughout this book we take this effort to undermine the ontological weight of these categories of analysis one step further by charting how post-Ottoman state and international administrations attempt to forcibly settle the refugees of imperial collapse through a complicated set of identity-building mechanisms. This takes place at different times in different locales. For instance, as discussed in Chapters 1, 2, and 3 it is already happening in the Balkans by 1878 (and more comprehensively after 1912), while intermittently during World War I in both Anatolia and the Levant. In both cases—Ottoman state officials seeking ways of settling refugees and foreign agencies compelling refugees to relocate in various, often entirely foreign conditions—there are underlying concerns that go beyond the simple need to bring order to otherwise chaotic post-conflict settings. The manner in which these peoples are identified bureaucratically becomes critical.

Highlighted by different national historiographies with the intention of convincing (perhaps even emotionally blackmailing) us that the quintessential antimodern evil, the Ottoman (Oriental) Empire, had to collapse for each of "our" peoples to enter into the modern world speaks to a rhetorical project that not only helped destroy the Ottoman Empire geographically, but continues to subvert different ways of thinking (and talking) about the world. That is, instead of lamenting the destruction of such an interesting, cross-cultural heritage that till today lingers in the way people eat, speak, and socialize, it was more objectively useful in history books to see the Ottoman Empire as an unnatural "mixing" of different races. Cast in these terms, living under the Ottoman Empire was a tragic story of Oriental "enslavement" of essentially "white" European Christians whose national ambitions could only be served when they lived in distinctive enclaves from "others" not of their denomination. The modern answer to these crimes was to aggregate religiously diverse peoples into national conglomerates—Pan-Hellenism, Pan-Slavism, Pan-Islamism, Pan-Turkism, a German Union or even Italy—that more accurately reflected their ethnic and sectarian "identity."[37]

This type of thinking reached its first peak in the late nineteenth century (specifically after the Treaty of Berlin in 1878) as "ethnic" wars broke out in the Balkans. Outsiders as diverse as Austro-Hungarian diplomats, former attorneys from the United States, and ethnographers from Switzerland began to propose lasting solutions to these seemingly intractable conflicts between different "races."[38] But as this book explains, through the filter of refugees expelled from, or passing through the Ottoman Empire, there is a more complicated set of processes at work that does not surrender easily to the reductive use of ethno-national, sectarian, and "ethno-biological" categories to explain events as a product of "difference."[39]

Considering all that was at stake with assuring that the Balkans (and by extension the Ottoman Empire) remain wealth-producing geographies, the European financial elite would not countenance this threat to their investment. As argued in Chapter 1, by the 1870s, the region as a whole was already integrated into the larger global economy, with a vast amount of European and North American money invested in seeing it produce hefty annual surpluses. Most of these investments were capital intensive, requiring the bond markets to play a heavy role in infrastructure—railroads, bridges, and ports—development.[40] This financial concern was threatened with Russia's sudden military victory over the Ottomans in 1877 and its imposition of a Greater Bulgaria. To the consternation of the Euro-American financial elite (and thus their diplomatic surrogates), Russia had taken advantage of Ottoman vulnerability as a consequence, first, of its reckless decision to default on debt payments to European private banks in 1875. The Russians then exploited the fact that the Ottoman Empire went through two palace coups—an outside hand cannot be entirely discounted—and endured a power struggle between the newly enthroned Sultan—Abdülhamid II (1876–1909)—and a powerful bureaucracy.[41]

The source of the financial powers' concerns was that Russia's sudden victories made any repayment of upwards of £200 million on direct loans to the Ottoman Empire (and countless millions of investor's money lent on railroads, lands, and ports) much less likely.[42] Such concerns led to a joint intervention by France, Britain, and Germany in the form of the Berlin Congress (1878). The subsequent treaty formally restored Ottoman oversight of some of its territories, including an autonomous (but geographically truncated) Bulgaria. Crucially, this "solution" immediately imposed "protections" that reinforced the new taxonomies of racial difference that brought violence to the Balkans. The Ottoman Empire—or at least those representatives allowed to negotiate in Berlin—agreed to surrender considerable power to local "autocephalous" Christian communities at the expense of their Muslim and Rum Orthodox counterparts.[43] What was newer, and most volatile, in this arrangement was that communities were loosely defined along constantly changing—and thus hotly debated—ethno-national lines.[44]

With so many millions of Ottoman Muslims—and the insolubly "mixed" demographics of the Eastern Mediterranean at the time—the fact that a former Ottoman administrative order in the region had been compromised by granting Slavic Christians extraordinary rights meant violence was always a possibility. As each older power structure faced obsolescence, a power vacuum followed, leaving new constituencies to struggle over the possibilities of "representing" these reconfigured communities. For those recognized in such settings as new "leaders" the rewards were considerable, including stipends, government positions, and outside diplomatic protections.

Obviously, the two major powers most interested in upsetting the British/French/ German imposition of balance in the region—the Austro-Hungarian and Russian

Empires—saw this as an opportunity.[45] With the ink on the Berlin Treaty barely dried, the two states, parties to the treaty, got to work crippling forever the Ottoman Balkans. Their staggered policies—at times cautious, at others recklessly aggressive—clashed with the spirit of the Berlin intervention that hoped to put the proverbial "genie/jin" of sectarianism back into the bottle.

In this respect, the events studied throughout are infused with a violence linked to an Ottoman political (and external financial) class who, as many rightfully argue, juxtaposed their notions of Progress and Modernity with a "native" (traditional) primitivism their reforms aimed to eradicate.[46] Entangled in Eurocentric thought, the way these Ottoman statist elite moved from an Ottoman ecumenical outlook to a "secularist," "positivist," and biological materialist worldview, where a modern order reigns supreme, did suggest a shift.[47] Indeed, the violence—as in genocide and ethnic cleansing throughout the 1913–39 period—perpetuated by certain institutions at certain times does vitally distinguish the different epochs of social and institutional organization covered throughout.

Where this book differs from other studies of this transitional process is at the point of avoiding the claim that the emergence of new forms of governmentality leading to violence is necessarily a product of Modernity. The direct linkage of new strategies of violence perpetrated by Ottoman officials to Eurocentric ideas of "secular modernity" is a dangerous ploy of epistemological colonialism.[48] The *quality* of Ottoman violence was—even when prosecuted by officials enamored with European statecraft—of necessity determined by the *specific historical conditions* created by the very fact of Ottoman refugees being *objects of that violence*. Thus, Ottoman violence must *qualitatively* differ from violence in *historically specific* European cases as in North Borneo, Oklahoma, or Bengal.

Put differently, linking these new, historically specific forms of Ottoman state (extra-state) violence to a generic "Secular," "Modernist" political sensibility dangerously perpetuates an epistemological colonialism of human beings' past. The many episodes of violence in the Ottoman Empire qualitatively differ from the variety (and thus diverse forms) of Euro-American forms of violence in that the internal dynamics accounting for the "unforgivable" in Eastern Anatolia, for example, must necessarily reflect the contingencies created by the presence of many different groups of interests, including Ottoman refugees.[49]

These tumultuous combinations were unique to their time and places and thus deserve to be studied as such. Failing to recognize this mires us in an ideologically gerrymandered version of history, one that treats as "criminal" otherwise familiar forms of secular state violence that merely reflect the attributes of an essentially false modernity grasped at by the quintessential "Turkish" parvenu. The insistence that Ottomans merely aped the ways of Europeans while performing the acts of "savages" simply perpetuates a project of the so-called victors of history incriminating others for the same crimes they themselves have committed.

One of the consequences of reducing the story of the refugee's role in telling the modern story is that such violence becomes the primary element shaping the experiences of most post-Ottoman societies. The danger is then in allowing this violence to dictate how we interpret relations between antagonists in very dynamic settings. It is perhaps not entirely accurate to frame the dynamics around the refugee in terms of hatreds that often replace deeper analysis of the events shaping the way in which the empire collapsed. Anthropologists like Goran Aijmer and Anton Blok argue, for instance, that understanding violence as a symptom of some type of societal dysfunction or as a "senseless" phenomenon expresses value judgments derived from normative notions of the state's monopoly over legitimate violence. So in some cases violence becomes irrational, a charge projected exclusively onto the acts of the colonized population or in postcolonial revisionist narratives that try to legitimize violence in terms of a relative heroic struggle for liberty.[50]

I would suggest that violence may be more usefully considered a form of interaction that reflects specific moments that warrant contextualization—what Blok terms a "thick description of cases of violence"—in order to avoid reducing assassination, expulsion, mass conversion, or starvation to something senseless, irrational or, on the other side, unequivocally heroic. That is to say, the goal with studying the violent refugee experience, be they linked to ethnic cleansing or a "state liberation" program, is to question the form, and thus meaning, of violence that constantly shifts in different socioeconomic, political, spiritual, and at times even geographic contexts.[51]

This paranoid European inscription of Ottoman violence as primitive, savage, and crucially, wantonly cruel demands that "Turks" and "Muslims" must remain qualitatively different in order that secular modernity's violence remains productive in the teleology of the Euro-American world. This not only results in the continued quest to colonize the "Oriental" savage's physical geography by way of post-Ottoman Mandates issued by the League of Nations, but to also make sure that we reinscribe the history of their institutions as perpetually barbarous vis-à-vis the equally imagined modernity still in the making.[52] Thus it is the double project of exonerating the victors of World War I from their own culpability to human suffering and rhetorically maintaining the neat divide between "secular liberalism" and the sectarian and ethnic hatreds that ruined the peoples of Anatolia, a vast "savage" land waiting the stern hand of modern European administration.[53]

Approaching the devolution of the Ottoman state as a contingent, heterogeneous process, a process that saw its final phase commanded by politicians who touted (often for self-serving, purely "political" reasons) the organic primacy of the nation-state, actually proves vital to the larger revisionist story of the modern world. Tragically, the project of nationhood too often became a project of chauvinistic "disidentification" with a still unclear set of "others" that required the use of violence to realize.[54] In this respect it is not entirely surprising that men who perpetrated the most horrific crimes were later heralded as the "modern" founders of Turkey. Crucially, they are remembered (and admired) in the Euro-American world precisely because they effectively (and violently) erased Ottoman (Islamic, Armenian Catholic, Rum Orthodox) heritage in order for Turkey to fully integrate with the modern world.[55] Ironically, what made it no longer possible for a still sizable contingent of loyalists to Ottoman values to resist the rise of the distinctive "Turkish" nationalism was the opportunistic invasion by the empire's Balkan neighbors in 1912.[56]

The resulting millions of dislocated peoples flooding into the "Anatolian" heartland created the opportunity to bring to the fore an entirely new sensibility which overwhelmed the tattered principles of Ottoman patriotism. In the place of "unity" and "justice" the "modern" concepts of race, population science, and nation reign supreme. Tellingly, as it played out in the Balkans, and for much of the Middle East under a post-Ottoman French and British occupation regime, generic sectarian and tribal categories became the tools of choice to perform the tasks of administration.[57] As already discussed above, while ubiquitous in the documentation, these tools of analysis utterly fail to help us understand just what was happening to the Ottoman refugee/migrant in any number of contexts.

Almost everyone writing on these difficult topics, especially regarding Armenians, constructs an Anatolian (or Middle East or Balkans) context that necessarily ignores the persistent "normality" of cohabitation and naturalizes the exceptional. Moreover, by insisting we study events by way of the invoking of generic "Armenian" and "Muslim" categories in ways that anachronistically assert *disidentification*—separation— processes leaves us with little space to operate. It is hoped that we could begin to feel an obligation to steer away from preordaining these events that were in fact built atop dynamics of multiple contextual factors intersecting at entirely unpredictable times and places.[58]

Invaluably, Taner Akçam's careful reading of newspapers and state-produced documents identifies an ideological turn whereby the "idea of a homogenous" polity becomes a possible supplement and eventual replacement of sensibilities of "union."[59] This was not, however, an inevitability. Ottoman union remained important enough that a majority of those on the "Muslim," "Christian," "Jewish" "sides" took to the streets in demonstrations in 1908 calling for "union" and indeed, died by the hundreds of thousands to protect it in the "decade of war" beginning in 1911. Far from the visceral chauvinism directed at ever-changing "enemies," the Ottoman world(s), or "Islam," or "*Rum* Orthodox Christians" of themselves do not provide the ingredients for modern holocausts. Violence, in other words, does not erupt because these societies are "mixed" and are just waiting for systemic break-down to unleash primordial hatreds pent up in the hearts of every patriotic Serb, Albanian, Arab, Turk. What does in large part account for the vicious turn must be put into intersecting contexts involving an entirely haphazard rise of certain kinds of ideological orientations from within the bowels of Euro-American Empire.

What studying the role of the global Ottoman refugees offers in this respect is a perspective of an individual's willingness to survive. The Ottoman refugee throughout this book proves her/his ability to straddle epochs when empire, once serving as a legal, cultural, and economic point of reference, transformed into a far more aggressive, bureaucratically interventionist modern state servicing at times external financial interests more than the needs of a diverse citizenry. As such, in the context of European imperialism, as intimately entwined with the interests of Euro-American finance capitalism, the period in which Ottoman refugees interface with these global historical forces resists being just a story of devastating alienation.

Prelude to Disaster: Finance Capitalism and the Political Economy of Imperial Collapse

Introduction

If one had to summarize how researchers account for Ottoman imperial collapse, the seemingly premodern social order of the larger society most fits the bill. Scholars working on the Balkans and Middle East long associated the linked social loyalties determining such orders with incumbent characteristics of "Oriental" (and violent) backwardness in mostly socioeconomic and ultimately implicit, if not explicitly used biological terms. Among the primary characteristics believed most crucial to understanding the disastrous social conflicts arising from such backwardness was the so-called "pre-capitalist" economy based on "subsistence production" and "limited external trade potential."[1] In this regard, Ottoman cultural diversity proved a detriment, not an asset in the modernizing world; worse still for scholars speculating on the causes behind Ottoman collapse, the forced integration of the Empire into the modern world unleashed inherent conflicting interests of hitherto "suppressed" ethno-national and sectarian aspirations. As scholars and contemporary diplomats alike claimed, it was these aspirations and archaic loyalties that ripped "premodern" social hierarchies apart and opened the door for the modern nation-state.

Beyond such normative sociological explanations, other scholars have tended to veer toward political economic accounts that emphasize the obsolescence of the exploitative system under which Ottomans supposedly lived. The most elaborate of these interpretations associate the unleashed ethno-nationalist aspirations of Ottoman peoples with their cumulative frustrations behind their being economically exploited. Ultimately, scholars stressing this aspect have embraced the notion that a litany of socioeconomic causal effects contributed to both institutional break-down and the incumbent violence between the empire's peoples. This violence ultimately brought down the empire.

While there is little dispute that violence, much of it domestic, contributed to the weakening of the Ottoman state, as this chapter will set out to explain, some other contributing factors have remained obscure to post-imperial observers. I account for this neglect the fact that there remains utility in emphasizing the same ethno-nationalist, sociological, and sectarian forces that are constantly mobilized in the twentieth (and still in the twenty-first) century to secure political and economic power for a set of vested interests. In other words, as seen today in analysis on the violence in the Middle East, reference to generic sectarianism or tribal rivalries substitutes for any deeper examination into social and structural change. Yet, as much as social scientists and Euro-centric historians insist ethnic, tribal, or religious "difference" remains at the root of almost all conflict in the "third" world today, there may be a need to return to those now considered "out dated" suspicions that "capitalist" forces also contributed to shaping the contours of modern violence. More importantly, investing some time to consider the manner in which Ottoman state reforms in particular, proposed and imposed by a group of Ottoman nationalists (Young Ottomans/Young Turks), may be a more useful way to analyze the processes in which the Empire and its refugees proved a global force of change rather than simple victims sitting on the peripheries of history.

Indeed, in the context of state-building reforms that are today universally known as products of the *Tanzimat* era, efforts by Ottoman patriots (and agents of external finance capital with conflicted loyalties) may have at once thwarted efforts to completely subordinate the Empire to the whims of capitalist expansionism while, paradoxically, actually serving as the incubator for what only later could be associated with "Modernity." That is to say, the social engineering and concomitant state-building agendas of Young Ottoman/Turk "unionists" differed little from counter-parts in the Euro-American world in that there was a core struggle between competing financial interests and hitherto entrenched indigenous sociopolitical interests.[2] Crucially, these tensions translated into the kind of productive "friction" that induced in rapid succession many new kinds of governing strategies among the most patriotic Ottomans and disloyal agents of international finance capital. The emergence of such constantly reconfiguring political, economic, and social constituent groups, and the necessary conflicting sets of interests they represented, ultimately manifested in politically significant events.[3]

Much as with the best of revisionist European historiography, our task here is not to anachronistically impose ethno-national or sectarian significance to these events but rather steer our analysis towards rethinking these events as parts of possibly contradictory, still indeterminate human community trajectories that at crucial moments intersected to produce specific moments that sometimes (rather than necessarily always) contributed to forces that link Ottoman collapse to the larger post-WWI story of "Modernity."[4] At this point it is useful to further elaborate on how various contradictory, and crucially, constantly modifying, sets of constituent interests interacted and disaggregated over the long nineteenth century; studying such engagements actually offers a more satisfying account for what transpires over the 1878–1939 transitional period covered throughout.

In order to avoid the determinism of previous accounts, however, we must always emphasize that the Ottoman relationship with the rest of the world (but primarily with emerging European empires) was complex. Such statements seem today self-evident, considering the vastness of the scholarship on the Ottoman Empire. But behind the veneer of so much detail, the underlying assumptions about Ottoman destiny—subordination to "modernity" and thus historical obsolescence—leave little room for nuance with respect to the kind of relationship Ottoman subjects shared with each other and their varied, often hostile "outside" world.

Other than clashing proto-nationalisms, the notion that the Ottoman's cultural complexity was a source of its demise applies most directly to the empire's economic relationships with the larger world. With the benefit of hindsight, the association of the more than 23 million diverse peoples living in the Ottoman Empire with economic marginalization vis-à-vis the juggernaut of Western Capitalism indeed seemed inevitable. The "obvious" collapse seems to justify the conclusion that such a composite of human diversity inevitably fell victim to the larger "modernizing forces" of the global economy and the magnetic appeal of Western liberalism. For the historian with a global, comparative perspective, however, such linear narratives unhelpfully obscure both the forces involved in this seemingly straight-forward process of "civilization's" ascendency and the principal agents involved.[5] One way to avoid such false conclusions is to recognize that the Ottoman economy dominated much of the Mediterranean world in the nineteenth century.

Revisiting Ottoman economic relations

As a correction this chapter reexamines the causes of imperial financial collapse and asks whether they truly reflect an intrinsic systemic failure unique to the Ottoman Empire. Ottoman "collapse," in other words, may rather hint at signs of calculated multidirectional attacks on a vital rival from hitherto exculpated sources. Indeed, far from being an impediment, the empire's strengths were in its human diversity, industrial innovativeness, and agricultural productivity. In fact, to some crucial outside interests, this Ottoman capacity to produce wealth proved both a long-term threat to their own expansionist aims and at the same time an attractive source of potential revenues if properly harnessed.

In this sense, among those responsible for Ottoman demise was an emergent Euro-American financial oligarchy. Private banks that were extensions of vast family networks in particular proved central to processes which ultimately led to the incremental disaggregation of the empire. This staggered process of land sequestration, forced migration, and labor exploitation often resulted in the brutalization of millions of people trapped in conflicts over increasingly privatized and commoditized resources, which in opportunistic ways were reframed in later scholarship as unique reflections of ethno-national (or sectarian) rivalry. In fact, this process needs to be studied as gradual and external to primordial "hatreds" between "different" peoples forced to live in close proximity. Social collapse marketed *ex post facto* as ethnic hatreds did not happen overnight, but followed several different trajectories that took their final shapes after considerable adaptation. In other words, Ottoman collapse(s) was contingent on a number of factors that as much reflect a variety of indigenous actors' interests informed by local processes as those of the banking houses in Paris, London, Frankfurt, Vienna, and Milan.[6]

Taking this last suggestion into account, it may be useful to revisit the intricacies of various sectors of the Ottoman economy in relation to the contested political arenas germinating within, along, and beyond the empire's borders. I suggest this because over the nineteenth century, the contours of political and economic interactions actually consisted of multiple layers, with Euro-American banking families being only one. At any number of intersections it is possible to see that the empire's dynamic regional economies were attacked, or in less pejorative terms, "integrated" by an often concerted, unified block of foreign interests. For example, in the reform period that evolved from an internal political crisis between the central state and insubordinate regional governors, the empire's relative economic stability increasingly hinged on the extent to which disparate, still competing groups of foreign financial interests devoted resources to either sustain or destabilize Ottoman socioeconomic life.

For much of the eminently important *Tanzimat* reform period (1839–76), such foreign pressure was mediated by an Ottoman administrative capacity to innovatively resolve local political crises. At a crucial point, however, a number of intersecting interests, both within and outside the empire, developed irreconcilable differences. This in the end resulted in a clash between legitimate Ottoman patriots, among whom were known Young Ottoman reformers, and an increasingly emboldened financial capitalist class by then fully in control of Euro-American central banks (and thus global money supplies).[7] Confrontations over who would control the resources of the territories still within Ottoman authority invariably led to an entirely new form of foreign interference in the domestic matters of the empire. This kind of interference could only happen with the cooperation of segments of Ottoman society.

To best capture how this contentious, often very violent (but productive) "friction" between a distinctive European "liberalism" and an "archaic" Ottoman polity translates into processes of historic import, this chapter interweaves refugees into the story of finance capitalism's penetration into the disparate Ottoman territories. This is done to stress again the key understanding of indigenous events as products of local initiative. As much as the story of Ottoman subordination to global forces depends on the role of "the West," the still missing link between Euro-American financial interests, their local surrogates among the Young Ottoman reformers or CUP statists emerging after 1908, and various refugee constituencies deserves serious consideration.

Possible candidates for this missing historical force are family-run trading houses. They include the Rallis brothers, known as the lessor Rothschilds. Having established a firm first in Chios, they expanded to Izmir, Istanbul, to Malta, Livorno, and then London on the back of major deals with British-based financial interests. Another group, the Armenian brothers Toumantiantz, started in the Caspian Sea and expanded to Odessa, Moscow, Vienna, and Paris.[8]

It is precisely at the point when we integrate the activity of such indigenous conglomerates that questions of how to label the principal actors thus become crucial: As much as racial, sectarian, and ethno-national categories have attracted the scholarly attention on modern identity politics, the ever-present "refugee" may prove to offer a set of alternative angles to understanding the transitional era that so much involves domestic and international finance. Adducing the formation of new, constantly fluctuating constituencies in the Balkans, Anatolia, and larger Middle East will radically problematize the narrative of straightforward financial domination and open space for historical actors that were formerly paralyzed by conventional narratives of "Modernity." What makes the story of these agents (or products) of change (destruction) in the service of expansionist liberalism more complicated still is that they became entangled with a new kind of socioeconomic order, one which can be clarified by a political-economic analysis of its constituent events.

A summary of the long nineteenth century

Ironically, the heart of the Ottoman Empire's problems in the late nineteenth century lay in the success of its regional economies over much of the early modern period. Indeed, by the turn of the nineteenth century, these regional economic accomplishments became the engine for the creation of powerful regional polities. In areas as diverse as Serbia (around Belgrade), Tunisia, Kurdistan, the western Balkans, and Egypt, a class of local notables (or *âyân*) emerged to reconstruct relations between the distant central government and the provinces.[9] As these regions developed new commercial relations with neighboring (non-Ottoman) polities, the emergent ruling elite (often a forgotten coalition of beneficiaries-cum-patrons of the "Great Men" including merchants, local bankers, and numerous international go-betweens, such as Lord George Byron, in the case of Yanya/Janina) often established diplomatic relations beyond the formal oversight of the Ottoman Sultan, technically still these ruling elites' sovereign.[10] As long as these powerful regional polities continued to pay their annual dues to Istanbul, however, their quasi-independent states were left alone to economically outpace the Ottoman state itself. In time, the economic wealth of these regions translated into greater ambitions for their ruling elite. The tensions over ultimate control of the regional state's revenue, as in areas north of Mosul, Egypt, or throughout the Balkans, constituted the classic interface between the Ottoman Empire and its regional subjects.

Generally treated as a negative, such relations also could be seen as an impetus to all kinds of reforms that allowed for new forms of cooperation. Such productive "frictions," in other words, laid the foundation for new polities to emerge. Derviş Pasha, for instance, after battles with Sıpki Communities (*Aşiret*) based throughout Erzurum and Van provinces, adopted polices that proved instrumental to infusing Eastern Anatolian regions with direct state rule. The nature of these struggles was how to best use the rich lands and access to their revenues.[11]

Similar "domestic" political relations affected the way power would be distributed. In the particular case of Mehmed Ali of Kavala and company, for example, they would not only reconquer Egypt in 1805 on behalf of Sultan Mehmed II—and then the holy cities of Mecca and Medina in 1811–12 from Wahhabi/Saudi fanatics—but would then use the opportunity to expand the Egyptian army to the point that it became a regional superpower. Using innovative (some insist "European") organizational tactics, Egypt's regime captured much of the Nile Valley (Sudan and parts of highland, present-day Jimma, Ethiopia) by way of a newly created, well-trained standing army.[12] With the accumulated wealth this effective governance generated in Egypt, the regime in Cairo became an expansionist power *par excellence*.[13] The resulting combined military and economic power ultimately led to a direct conflict with an increasingly weak Ottoman central state.

The subsequent challenge to Istanbul's rule culminated in the 1840s with the loss of much of its ability to exert influence over vital revenue-producing territories like Syria/Palestine—territories that by 1832 were under the governorship of Mehmed Ali's son, Ibrahim, and his tight circle of local allies.[14] At the heart of such a confrontation was the economic juggernaut that created the region's first industrial-scale agricultural projects. Such capital-intensive projects entailed the investment of many years of future annual tax revenue to transform the Nile, its vast delta region, and then much of the "occupied" Levant to service the production for export of as much wheat, sugar, and cotton as possible.[15] These massive physical works included the expansion of ports, and, in the case of Çukurova in present-day southeast Turkey, building a brand new industrial/farming zone for the production of cash crops.[16]

Conventional studies of this process focus almost entirely on the impressive institutional developments and the structural transformations linked to the growing power of the central state. There seems to be, however, some important issues not addressed by traditional narratives, namely, the epochal financial "evolution" initiated by Ottoman provincial actors. One useful, entirely new way of looking at these developments is to understand that Mehmed Ali's expansionist state was not only an early version of the modern colonialist state geared to expand capitalist interests far and wide, but may indeed have served as the model which European capitalists and the Ottoman *Tanzimat* reformers applied to their own state-led developments in both industry/manufacturing and military/policing sciences by the 1840s.[17] Whatever conclusion we reach concerning the impact Egypt's ruling oligarchy's state-building experience had on the future of European/Ottoman modernization, it is clear that their Egypt (as had the earlier regime of Ali Pasha of Tepelen in the western Balkans and its dangerous alliances with first Napoleon and then Russia or the Habsburgs) threatened a number of external interests.[18]

If we can understand what assortment of interests was affected by the rise of Egypt's regime as a regional, if not potentially global, power, it may then be possible to ask why such a fine-tuned wealth extraction operation needed to be stopped. It just may be that the Egyptian regime's expansionist power, at the expense of a clearly weak and fully exposed Ottoman Sultanate, may have had the *potential* to become the most powerful state in the region. As the regional superpower, Egypt by definition would then threaten the commercial inroads which various English and continental financial interests started to make in the western Indian Ocean world.[19] This is where a new orientation was imposed on the entire region.

The primary concern facing European lobbyist was a virtually incoercible Egypt-dominated Ottoman Empire that would likely have reversed recent concessions Istanbul gave to European merchants by scandalously opening its lucrative domestic markets to cheap imports. Most importantly, a powerful, reconfigured Ottoman state under Egyptian leadership would have halted any eventual drive to pillage the vast human and natural resources found in the blessed lands of the Ottoman realm.[20] In the end, the emergent financial cartel of Europe beginning to realize the potential for global hegemony would not countenance such a threat in this strategically important region. And while the joint intervention of European militaries—again, in the service of financial interests—did contain Egypt, this did not mean complete subordination of an empire that was still a decentralized, region-based cluster of polities.

By the time of the last great *âyân* of the late eighteenth and early nineteenth century, the Ottoman Empire constituted a fertile set of contradictory interests whose complex interactions transformed the way the rest of the world could both directly and indirectly act within its borders.[21] One aspect of this crucial transitional period was how it informed the needs of a rapidly growing finance capitalist sector in Europe.[22] While the agenda in retrospect was to capture larger and larger portions of the world's wealth, at the time, such ambitions may not have been fully formed. It was, as argued throughout, the manner in which individual, often competing coalitions of Euro-American financial interests, engaged different segments of Ottoman (and other) societies that explains the kind of "system" that emerged. In other words, the story of the rise of a new form of colonial/imperial enterprise and its codification as an order is told by the distinctive qualities of the interest groups most likely to profit from a changing world order.

The private banking families of Rothschild, Péreire, Baring, Warburg, Oppenheim, and Morgan were the primary beneficiaries of this global transformation. Their tentacles had, by the mid-nineteenth century, reached the inner halls of Euro-American political (and thus military) power. They also established crucial influence with banking families—eventually absorbing them—in Bombay, Japan, and most of Eastern Asia. At the same time, however, we must foreground this fact with the story of Europe's often violent relationship with the Ottoman Empire and its varied peoples. As will become clear by looking closely at the role refugees (or economic migrants) played in this complicated century-long interface, much of the violence afflicting the empire had a direct link to the manner in which the Ottoman state and its citizens were integrated into the still emerging global structures of finance capitalism. More importantly, such conflict had significant impacts on how these Ottomans accommodated the development of global finance capitalism. Crucially, this process lacked uniformity and thus resists any linear explanation; one must instead study different events at different times that took place in seeming isolation.

It was a result of the productive works of regimes around *âyân* like Mehmed Ali that the Ottoman Empire became one of the many jewels that eluded European private financial interests in the early nineteenth century. In this respect, the Ottoman Empire was the only major state to have never borrowed money from foreign banks, a distinction that lasted until the early 1850s. Until the Crimean War, the Ottoman Sultan and the state offices borrowed from multiple indigenous Jewish and Armenian bankers, such as Isaac Camondo and Antoni Pirianz. This situation would soon change, however, as European trading houses and private banks salivated over the possible earnings in, for example, the still untapped tax revenue potential of the empire. French observers, for one, realized some serious needs for fine-tuning the budget of the empire, seeing that so little of its potential tax revenue was ever collected. Clearly to those who reported back to French financial interests, the Ottoman Empire was a ripe fruit waiting to be picked.[23]

How private financial interests would harvest this imperial fruit depended on the extent to which they would leverage their positions against partnerships with local Ottomans. Indeed, it is hard not to connect the regular concessions granted to British and French commercial interests with the pledges to prop up the flagging Ottoman government against quasi-independent regional governors who continued to resist European economic predators.[24] To begin taking advantage of the new found leverage over the Ottoman Sultan, Paris and London-based financial circles sought to integrate targeted regions into their sphere of influence. One way of realizing these monopolistic ambitions was the introduction of new social organizational mechanisms that specifically favored one "group" over others. As a result of the concessions the besieged regime in Istanbul had to make to those who "saved" it from rebellious Egypt, highly productive areas around Adana and coastal Syria (regions recently developed by the Egyptian colonial regime) were partially subordinated to French-based investment interests. These concessions represent one aspect of the "opening" of the regional economy deemed crucial in the historiography.[25]

As a result of the flooding of imports protected from custom duties unconnected locals still had to pay, many Ottoman (mostly Muslim) merchant houses collapsed. This in turn contributed to a rapidly changing socioeconomic power dynamic in the region, especially in respect to who controlled land. Not only would a new kind of merchant elite emerge in soon-to-be booming port towns like Mersin, Jaffa, and Beirut, but the eventual commodification of the agricultural and mining sectors of these economies completely transformed the relationship inhabitants had with each other, their land, and the empire at large.[26] As we learn from numerous studies of this period, the tragic result in larger Syria was decades of intermittent civil war between newly constituted, and legally defined, "sectarian" (*millet*) groups.[27]

In the process of carving out this "sphere of interest," French-based bankers, in particular, insisted on instituting modifications to the way local "Levantine Catholics" (known as Maronites) interacted with the Ottoman state. As charted by Ussama Makdisi among others, this introduction of sectarianism in Greater Syria resulted in the eventual violent disaggregation of once "mixed" local communities.[28] The subsequent reterritorialization of the regional economy into "spheres of influence" made Syria (and the larger empire) into a kind of tribal, ethnic, racial, and/or sectarian "patchwork" that, like the Balkans and Africa later in the century, crumbled. At the forefront of this process were policies of intervention administered by a newly empowered "international order" informed by social scientific objectifications that asserted the modern world (and the civilization Europeans exclusively claimed) would not countenance the ontological "other" living in such close proximity.

Such abstract logics manifested themselves most prominently on Mt Lebanon and the Balkans (see Map 1.1). As elsewhere, these processes resulted in the alienation of peasants from their land, the rise of industrial-scale farming, and subsequent mass migrations first to regional cities, and then to the larger world. In what now reads as a perfect storm (in fact manufactured in Europe), the monetization of local economies with private banking paper added to the ruinous, conflict-inducing concessions granted to surrogates of French, British, and later German financial oligarchs. By 1840, under pressure from a number of outside interests, the Ottoman State decreed that all

Map 1.1 Western Ottoman Empire 1877 (prior to Berlin Congress).

salaries and, more importantly, all taxes due to the state, had to be paid in a central treasury-issued currency. Overnight, communities once thriving in circulating silver or gold coin originating from various sources, or even simply paying taxes in kind, such as wheat or livestock, became subservient to a money "system."[29] At its heart was the decision to monetize the Ottoman economy and force state subjects to pay taxes in this currency, which was de facto the private issuance of European banks.

It is often overlooked that this monetization of local economies constituted the backdrop of *Tanzimat* reform edicts. Crucially, a result of the enforced introduction of a state-backed currency (collateralized debt) was that many formerly autonomous economic circles were now, for better or worse, linked to the imperial treasury and the empire's debt obligations. With this fact in mind, the question then arises: Who actually controlled this money supply and what influence would this power have on inflation and the periodic "bubbles" that characterized the global economy going forward?[30]

Charting Ottoman state subordination to European financial interests

As suggested above, crucial to these foreign financial interests' initial successes was getting officials to rewrite Ottoman trade laws.[31] More important still, foreign interests sought to assure that liberal-minded reformers infiltrated the Ottoman bureaucracy. These reformers were expected to help enforce measures which would in the next century play a central role in the emergence of a distinctively modern form of state violence that would enforce the dispossession of so much of these regional peoples' wealth.[32] In fact, it was such a cadre of reformers who pushed through the destructive new free-trade agreements that made the empire's trade regime the "most liberal in the world."[33]

This formal alliance with factions emerging within the Ottoman bureaucracy did not yet, however, mean absolute control over regional economies. Indeed, challenges to early efforts to "liberalize" regional economies, such as tax revolts and land consolidation in regions as distinct as Prizren in Kosovo, Botan in Diyarbakır, and throughout Syria, reveal that such measures as much threatened investments in regional economies as opened them up.[34] Perhaps ironically to some today, the economic "liberalization" many of the Euro-American finance capitalists sought required greater direct state control of these disparate territories. This issue ultimately links back to enforcing monopolistic agendas, which, as already seen in Britain's enclosure laws and the Euro-American genocidal expulsion of native peoples in the Americas, required alienating people from their life-sustaining homelands and creating large numbers of landless peoples.[35]

Within the Ottoman bureaucracy, however, there were concerns that any termination of Ottoman government oversight, no matter how weak, would result in violent struggles between still competing European interests and large numbers of people capable of resisting European encroachments. In light of the thinking that the Ottoman Empire's long-term survival necessitated streamlining its coercive abilities and command over the economic production of still powerful regional interests, subsequent efforts to balance the need to "keep the peace" and please British and French representatives led to some rather unique forms of government.[36] To be sure, the *Tanzimat* Reforms, as such, were not uniformly applied, and certainly experienced very different receptions in the empire's vastly diverse territories.

As is well known now to Ottoman historians, this de-facto command economy, managed from state offices, was not entirely possible where the requisite "monopoly" of violence did not yet exist. Without this monopoly, Ottoman reforms would not only have to service the needs of outsiders, but continue to strive to find a balance between subordinating regions to the central state, and maintaining order by way of power-sharing partnerships.[37] This constituted the important dynamism in the Ottoman economy, where the bureaucratic elite must not be treated as an ideological monolith, but composed of competing factions whose conflicting designs for the Ottoman future were tempered by the relative ability of regionally based subordinates to work productively with locals, including refugees.

For our purposes, these often contradictory and frequently antagonistic sensibilities manifested themselves within the transforming Ottoman bureaucracy. Often, the debates among the governing elite were about schemes aimed at how to best rationalize the state's relations with the plethora of actors in the territories. As we see throughout the *Tanzimat* period, Ottoman policies entailed not so much the collective ambitions of newly formulated political factions, but the discursive (and thus imagined social and political) boundaries separating modern liberal values that denigrated "tradition." Such hostility to the lingering primitivism of so many who ended up refugees conveniently reinforced the doctrines of these "Westernized" Ottoman statesmen that the only hope to save an empire from this collective fate of demographic chaos was to "educate" its lingering "savage" rural population. By bringing everyone up to a basic standard of "civilization," the empire just might be saved from a destiny of socioeconomic upheaval and eventual destruction. This aggressive Social Darwinism was in some hands, modified into a patriotic "Ottomanism" that still motivated so many within the empire—Muslims, Christians, and Jews of various linguistic, geographic origin.[38]

In contrast there were still those who held onto a stubborn belief in an Ottoman sensibility that could offer citizens the sustenance to endure the at times horrendous individual and collective suffering. That is to say, there were still powerful divisions within the competing Ottoman elite over how to proceed with reform, but the goal was still to keep the empire intact. So on one side, would-be European liberals increasingly denigrated large parts of Ottoman society as backward, and thus leading to the application of "disciplinary" violence against them. They coupled this blatant adoption of European racist epistemologies with notions of "science" and "freedom" as linked to the corrective power of open markets, which led many Ottoman statesmen to advocate the unhindered integration of the Ottoman Empire into the global financial system.[39] In contrast, Ottoman patriots and many still entrenched communal leaders of "tradition"—from the *Rum* Orthodox Patriarch to self-identified Muslim intellectuals—stressed empathy, grace, and honor as enduring societal assets in face of the rapidly changing world.

This ideological war manifested in often contradictory ways throughout Ottoman society. The resulting schizophrenic relationship with the material accruements of open markets enjoyed by a few and the realization that the Ottoman Empire was being sucked into a dangerous dependency on European-supplied finance, translated into pathologies of social alienation among certain future leaders of the so-called Unionist movements.[40] These leaders would be entirely responsible for adopting the most "European" of characteristics in respect to using the modern state to assure the long-term development of society. Many among these "Westernized" bureaucratic elite believed in the edifying violent capacities of the state to instill "progress" into "backward" elements of society, identified by way of racist taxonomies evident throughout Euro-American discourses at the time.[41]

In hindsight, and for many of those refugees who lived through the consequences of this deadly fusion of Euro-American predatory capitalism and embrace of "Western" racist epistemologies, the end result was a violent disaggregation of a once formidable Ottoman Empire. As already noted, when the newly ascendant bureaucratic elite started to monetize the Ottoman economy, which by 1840 meant taxes could only be paid in cash, an Ottoman Empire that once could borrow gold/silver from local suppliers—mostly Ladino Jews, *Rum* Orthodox Christians, and Armenians based in Istanbul—increasingly proved helpless without direct foreign intervention. A resulting need to find additional supplies of gold and silver (to back state-issued treasury notes) led to the eventual capturing of the Ottoman treasury by largely unknown British, (and later French) investors.[42]

Below we focus on several regions of the empire where such processes manifested. The drive to convert hitherto peasant lands into more efficient agricultural factories—especially the conversion of farmlands into opium, sugar, wheat, and cotton fields—proved the most disruptive to regional economies. For our purposes here, the focus on especially large infrastructure projects, ones that required massive amounts of capitalization, reveals the extent to which the Ottoman Empire was quickly integrated into a global financial "system." As a result, the empire surrendered considerable power to investors whose capture of railroad, port, and road/bridge construction concessions marked a virtual subordination of the Ottoman state to private finance.

These infrastructure projects, deemed at the time essential to progress, gave cover for the predatory lending European (thus American) banks practiced around the Ottoman world.[43] The railroad and port-building projects that attracted the most attention from European investors were Ottoman ports like Salonika that would come to link the Macedonian hinterland (then extended deeper into the Kosovo province and Belgrade/Vienna beyond), and Adana, Mosul, and Beirut in the French-based banks' sphere of influence.[44] What made this process of domination halting at best, however, was the rivalries that existed between various financial groups, and even more crucially for the nineteenth century, the presence of Russia. Interests inside Russia clearly struggled to remain independent of those dominating Western and Central Europe.

One way this manifested was the Romanov regime's relationship with the Ottoman Balkans. Most studies of Russian interests in the Ottoman Empire focus on military concerns. In this respect, it was the strategic necessity of gaining access to the larger world's maritime (and later rail) trade routes, be it via the Black Sea or Adriatic, which shaped Russian policies in general. What remains neglected is how Russia's race to capture Ottoman territories at the expense of European finance capitalists also shaped the political economy of the nineteenth century.

Ottoman financial weakness in the 1840s likely accounts for much of the subsequent intrigue between the Habsburgs, Romanov, and later Italian empires surrounding the Balkans. Indeed, the struggles for "spheres of influence" created new strategic possibilities for the inhabitants of the region, especially in Greece, Serbia, Bulgaria, and Bosnia/Herzegovina. These regions soon became the focus of diplomatic and occasional military struggle as considerable investment was made in railroad and port construction, all assets that required "protection."[45] For those interests eager to thwart Russian ascendency, using the Ottoman Empire as the bulwark required a crucial intersection of forces at various times. For instance, much as happened in the case of Egypt's threat to Ottoman power in the 1830s, a similar coalition formed to assure victory in the 1850s Crimean War the Ottomans fought against Russia. One of the key concerns in this intervention was assuring that trade routes remained in reliable hands. By the 1850s, it was Russia that proved the more independent and like with Egypt in 1839, any ascendancy in the Balkans (and Central Asia) could threaten the monopolistic designs of various London/Paris/Vienna-based interests.[46]

As already noted, the financing of first the Ottoman war efforts and then the expensive implementation of a new generation of state reforms in this crucial period allowed some private bankers to gain considerable leverage over the decision-making mechanism of the Ottoman state. These influences immediately translated into the even greater "liberalization" of the Ottoman economy after the Paris Peace Treaty of 1856 ending the Crimean War. Put differently, what had still been a barrier to direct foreign ownership of Ottoman lands was lifted. While much of these lands formally remained in the hands of indigenous Ottoman landowners for the duration of the nineteenth century, in reality the international banks owned them. Ottoman "landlords," much like their counterparts in North America in this quintessential example of "globalizing" practices, got caught in a borrowing spree using their real (attractive) assets of rich, productive farm land as collateral. With the land privatization acts of 1856, 1861, and 1867, when foreigners were allowed direct ownership, a massive transfer of real wealth took place in the region, adding to the speculative dynamics that opened the window of opportunity for foreign bankers which included large-scale land development schemes in Basra, Palestine, and Macedonia.[47]

Private French banks, like Crédit Lyonnais, the Société Générale, and the Comptoir National d'Escomte de Paris in particular, took advantage of these new opportunities. Throughout Cilicia, greater Syria, and increasingly in Mesopotamia and the Balkans, these French-based financial interests aggressively invested in Ottoman territories.[48] By way of their heavy involvement early on, these French banks popularized investment in Ottoman debt, creating an industry unto itself. The corresponding creation of an Ottoman property market resulted in constructing new financial business niches that proved equally lucrative. As the Ottoman state grew addicted to the huge amounts of money European investors were willing to funnel into state coffers at rates as high as 6 percent, brokerage houses, insurance companies, and financial management firms rushed to join the finance bonanza. Prominent on the list of possible sectors in which outsiders could invest were infrastructure projects.

Within months of the Ottoman Empire floating its first loan with European banks in 1853, ostensibly to pay for war with Russia, a new calculus emerged, one that could link the inevitable insatiable Ottoman state need to raise revenue, with expensive "investment" that promised structural improvements and greater profitability. A vicious circle thereby materialized whereby the Ottoman state (and increasingly individuals) borrowed money to pay off previous loans while selling off greater amounts of the empire's economic future directly or as collateral.

In the hope of managing these growing debt obligations, local allies of foreign capital started to "farm" out these roles to outsiders; the eventual creation of the *Banque Impériale Ottomane* in 1862, for instance, resulted in the transference of all management of Ottoman debts and budgets to foreign "shareholders." In the process, the empire's coveted assets, including vast forests, untold mineral wealth, especially increasingly coveted hydro-carbons like coal and oil, fertile agricultural lands, productive labor, and strategic location would service the greed of a soon ascendant global financial oligarchy.[49]

Simply put, by way of borrowing heavily from European banks in order to initiate necessarily expensive reform projects, the Ottoman Empire constantly leveraged its future with the very lands on which Ottoman peoples lived serving as collateral. The exploitative conditions under which the utterly compromised Ottoman state borrowed money from European banks peaked in 1874, when out of the inordinate amount the government borrowed—238,773,272 Ottoman lira—a staggering 46 percent of the loan (111,653,052) went to pay the bankers supervising the loans in the form of broker fees and banking commissions.[50] The Ottoman Empire, in other words, was a classic debt slave, and its subjects suffered the consequences.

The kinds of pressures applied to the empire to constantly find new ways of generating revenue—just to pay the interest of these now out-of-control loans—pitted the competing factions within the ruling elite against one another. Many realized that their economic fortunes were being determined by the whims of foreign groups, a situation that no self-respecting patriot would allow; an important faction within the expansive bureaucratic elite put pressure (often with support from members of the military and loyal regional stakeholders) on the Ottoman state.[51] By 1875, it was agreed by a faction within the reformist camp that the empire would be better served by returning to borrowing exclusively from indigenous sources of finance and these Ottoman patriots promptly defaulted on their European-held loans.[52]

Those who ultimately steered the Ottoman state toward bankruptcy did not do so out of incompetence. In fact, there was much that led patriotic Ottomans to believe the empire was not entirely defenseless and could win military victories. Indeed, well into the mid-1870s, Ottoman forces could still militarily simultaneously suppress uprisings in Bosnia, Eastern Anatolia, and Kurdistan while territorially expanding into the Gulf and Yemen.[53] At least in Arabia, the Ottomans were in direct confrontation with British Indian forces for ascendency and successfully captured large parts of the Arabian coast both in the Gulf and Yemen at the expense of erstwhile European interests.[54] There was, in other words, plenty to be positive about in Istanbul. In this context, when the advocates for defaulting on European loans gained temporary power in 1875, state reforms were also accelerating state-centralization policies. It also seemed that operations early in the decade had successfully settled yet more refugees who had become productive citizens. In this context of a still formidable military and effective administration, after consultation with the still present Galatta banking families, it appeared feasible for the Ottoman Empire to default on the onerous, intrusive debt with which the previous generation saddled the state.

In the midst of this momentary audaciousness, however, two successive palace coups resulted in the installment of a relatively inexperienced Sultan Abdülhamid II in 1876.[55] As if to reward those with the most interest in seeing previous trends toward Ottoman financial independence reversed, the new Hamidian government immediately initiated policies aiming to consolidate the state's revenue base through an aggressive regime of direct taxation.[56] As such, the state's new revenue raising policies shifted most of the tax burden to the empire's peasants, with predictable consequences.[57] Already primed for revolt in response to regressive tax schemes promoted by lenders,[58] communities in the Balkans faced an even more devastating problem with the sudden flood of refugees displaced by the short Russo-Ottoman war of 1877–8.[59]

It is at the heart of this financial and diplomatic quagmire that the Ottoman power structure temporarily collapsed. As a consequence, a number of small-scale insurrections throughout 1876–7 led to large segments of the western Balkans and Eastern Anatolia/Caucasus being "cleansed" of their Muslim populations. Confronted by this human tidal wave, a series of bureaucratic bottlenecks emerged, exposing internal rivalries that sapped the empire's human and natural resources. Simply put, the internal order of the bureaucratic class had been broken, and by 1878 new power circles emerged as hundreds of thousands of people flooded into the shrinking Ottoman territories.

Having again "saved" the empire from partition, this time at Russia's expense in 1878, the Ottoman state had to begin a new era of "economic reform" pushed by

French, British, and German benefactors. These latest reforms further damaged rural economies—already burdened in some parts of the empire by hundreds of thousands of refugees—as much as they created new opportunities. For its part the new regime of Sultan Abdülhamid II would continue to play the role of putting the Ottoman Empire back into the good graces of the banking elite. The new sultan, for example, suppressed a patriotic parliament whose ambiguous relationship with the banks eventually led to the political demise of the great reformer himself, Midhat Pasha. Perhaps the sacrificial lamb for those looking to reassert themselves into the Ottoman bureaucracy, Midhat Pasha had proven still too principled for some interests, both in the palace and among the Sultan's foreign advisors. He was eventually exiled and then murdered.[60]

With the opposition of men like Midhat Pasha dispatched, the Hamidian regime made the fateful decision to reassure foreign bondholders through the complete surrender of future state revenues in key industries and even, as in the case of Cyprus, entire regions.[61] Another key concession granted early in the Hamidian era was assurance that a significant proportion of future Ottoman state revenues were set aside to pay bondholders.[62] In most Ottoman citizen's eyes, the establishment of the Public Debt Administration (PDA) (1881–1924) was cancerous to Ottoman political economy. It demonstrated the extent to which the Hamidian regime would collude with foreign lenders at the expense of the empire's long-term fiscal health. This was all made possible, of course, by effectively cleaning the state of its potentially cantankerous opposition by way of closing the newly established parliament. This accomplished, the Istanbul regime, with almost treasonous enthusiasm, surrendered authority over the empire's ports to a privately run, foreign agency that was charged to collect all duties on specific commodities traded in the international market.[63]

The role of the PDA in the development of government institutions and policy becomes especially important in addressing what I understand to be a significant local component to regional economic development. The PDA's aggressive measures to assure that regional economies be taxed paradoxically weakened its capacity to tax trade. As such, commercial patterns throughout the frontier territories of the western Balkans reconfigured in response to the new levies. A particularly rough issue for local traders was the PDA's direct involvement in the taxation of key commodities like salt and sugar, products that could not be produced locally and had to pass through port cities like Işkodra (Shkodër). In the end, government policies linked to the PDA pitted merchants, mule train owners, landowners working with state officials, and small, self-sufficient regional economies against increasingly threatening Ottoman state policies. With respect to the emergence of smuggling networks in response to these policies, looking more closely into how local landowners secured greater profits from their land helps reinforce the underlying theme discussed throughout this study.[64]

In addition to revenue from trade redirected to the PDA, as much as 30 percent of all Ottoman expenditures during the period were devoted to servicing sovereign debt.[65] Moreover, there was the creation of various monopolies that also siphoned off huge amounts of the formal economy's revenue directly to the European banking elite. As such, the acquiescence to bankers to create, among others, the tobacco monopoly *Régie Ottomane des Tabacs*, left a new kind of tension between a growing industrial work force and the apparently unbreakable stranglehold the Euro-American financial world held on the formal economy.[66] As these operations required reliable labor—preferably the type unlikely to unionize—the role of the indigenous intermediary became increasingly important.

In many ways, the Ottoman state facilitated this supply of cheap labor because it became a major benefactor for hundreds of thousands of refugees expelled from Serbia, Greece, and Montenegro. The state's crisis management policies, often at odds with more general economic strategies promoted by the central state, worked at the local level to assure that cereal production remained stable so that there was food for refugees.[67] The local administration therefore distributed seed, granted tax exemptions to producers, and extended cheap credit to locals at the same time they were granting railway construction concessions to European investors.[68] The problem with this form of state intervention was that it depended on a select group of producers who were capable of making demands on their patrons, demands that ultimately challenged the assumption by state officials that they were in control of economic policy.

This was particularly clear in the manner in which the state, with the encouragement of the PDA, hoped to stimulate new kinds of land use, especially the production of high-end agricultural products like silk, cotton, or tobacco for export.[69] In fact, a number of products from the provinces were identified as possible revenue producing resources of the state and measures were taken to facilitate their exploitation.[70] In the central Balkans, it appears that poppy fields, found within walking distance of the few rail lines linking Central Europe and the port of Salonika, were established after heavy state investment and subsidies to farmers for crop substitution.[71] These arrangements created a mutually dependent, three-way bond between the state, those locals expected to expand the production of valuable revenue-producing agricultural products, and ultimately the outside interests identifying such operations as potential investments. In time, something akin to an Ottoman "welfare state" emerged that relied on the finance offered by foreign capitalists attracted to such regions, with the indigenous landowner becoming an intermediary to the forces of modernity.[72]

Naturally, local landowning families with a vested interest in the direction of the transitional process from an era dominated by the bureaucratic ruling class wanted to be sure that the aggressive commercialization of the Ottoman economy did not undermine their interests. Indeed, monitoring how landowning families in Syria/Cilicia and the western Balkans tried to guide the regions over which they reigned through the most dangerous periods of economic transformation meant the difference between profiting from partnerships with finance capitalists and being expunged from the region's history forever. In this respect, a number of families from the southern Balkans adjusted and became crucial intermediaries between the now hegemonic representatives of foreign capital, locally based institutions meant to mediate the state's policies of reform as demanded by these foreign banks, and other stakeholders commissioned to assure regional stability—which often included refugee management.

How this all links to a discussion on the political economy of the refugee experience is, on some level, reducible to the balancing act charged to those responsible for mediating the exploitative projects of foreign capital and the need for domestic peace. The aforementioned intermediaries from the Balkans by and large came from families who, by the first half of the nineteenth century, had invested in infiltrating their sons into the heart of the Ottoman bureaucracy.[73] Indeed, the region of southern Albania—Toskalık—supplied the Ottoman bureaucracy with dozens of such liberal-leaning reformers in the Tanzimat era.[74] Some, like Ismail Kemal Bey (Qemali) became important conduits for both efforts to institute the many generations of "liberal" reform, and for assuring, by way of partnerships with foreign investors, that certain regions remained trading hubs.[75]

What stands out with such characters, however, was their tendency to involve themselves in the murkiest of politics. In time, the post-Ottoman state of Albania's "first" leader revealed his chameleon-like skills to successfully inculcate himself in many mutually exclusive circles that became the foundational political space for many of the events transforming the southern Balkans from the 1890s onwards. In this regard Qemali was heavily invested in forging political alliances with certain British political circles, which appeared to have influence on the activities of particular factions within the umbrella Committee of Progress and Union (CPU, later CUP). Such intrigues led rivals to eventually break the oppositional movement into two factions by 1902; as British authorities observed, the duplicitous actions of men like Qemali alienated many from the foreign-based opposition and made any effort to confront the autocratic powers of the conservative elite in Istanbul difficult.[76]

A neglected aspect of these intrigues was Qemali's shared investment interests with many of the factions with whom he conducted his political business.[77] As Qemali conducted business with the outside world, forging partnerships in mineral and timber concerns, he translated these close commercial relations into political capital, and was able to successfully navigate the volatile political scene within the inner circles of imperial power as well. Indeed, where his personal business interests (or those of his partners) began, and where his loyalty to the liberal cause ended was impossible for many to figure out.[78]

And yet, what proves most intriguing is the possible leverage Qemali enjoyed over his interlocutors because of his ability to command a sizeable peasant coterie for use as either laborers or militia. Qemali appears to have been able to garner, on demand, able-bodied men by the thousands. Stemming from this capacity, he could also market his autonomy from direct state threats. In short, such local landowners brought a range of assets to the table that made them invaluable to investors and to the staff of various European consulates.

As their regions became increasingly targeted for development over the last 50 years of Ottoman history in the Balkans, Arabia, or Anatolia, the local intermediary was crucial.[79] If it was not the lands and the various natural resources they could provide, it was the manpower available to these intermediaries that made them essential.[80] Their ability to command manpower notwithstanding, what proved especially important when business opportunities and/or political collaborations went sour, was these intermediaries' skill in peddling their ability to produce violence or more crucially still, *threaten* violence. This fact would hamper any efforts to bring stability to strategic areas like Macedonia. Well into the 1930s, roaming, autonomously operating clusters of armed men would write the tale of violent clashes between these loyalists to men like Qemali and forces of "rational" government in Serbia, Albania, Greece, Bulgaria, Turkey, and Mandate Syria/Iraq.[81]

The Macedonia crisis

It was in the immediate aftermath of the Berlin Treaty that the Ottoman Balkans and Eastern Anatolia witnessed perhaps the most intense period of violence in its modern history.[82] In many ways residents faced constant assault by the powers whose most immediate interest was capitalizing on any instability in the region. A part of this subterfuge was the cynical use of the ethnographic "sciences" to impose an acceptable "solution" to the Balkans intensifying "ethnic" and "sectarian" conflicts. What governments in Vienna and St. Petersburg devised over the next 20 years constituted the kinds of "schemes" that succeeded as much in further destabilizing "mixed" communities as in stemming violence. A brief survey of these "schemes" as the Austro-Hungarian and Russian diplomats (with the aid of scholars, journalists, and various *agents provocateurs*) rolled them out starting in the late 1890s will do much to set the ideological/diplomatic context against which the stories of Balkan refugees unfolded.

It was in part due to periodic violence in Macedonia and Anatolia over the entire 1878–1903 period that both the Austro-Hungarian and Russian empires demanded a new set of measures to assure the protection of Slavic and Eastern Anatolian Christians.[83] This concern for Christian "safety" against a putative Muslim threat emanated from newly minted social-scientific taxonomies that assumed different ethnically constituted confessions always clashed.[84] Curiously, practitioners of this "social science" chose to ignore centuries of evidence that contradicted its claims— namely, the relative interethnic/confessional harmony that prevailed under most Ottoman administrations. Regardless of this history, every outsider commissioned by some foreign interest to study the region saw the demographics of the Balkans in terms of distinct "ethnic" Christian groups—Greek, Serb, Vlach, Albanian, Bulgarian (and sometimes Macedonian)—and that the prevailing natural hatreds extended to each other as much as toward the "Muslim race."

In this way, various parties claimed throughout this period special "rights of association," a by-word for established "spheres of influence" that each major power could use to play the Balkans to their strategic tune. In this framework, each community needed both special protections and then, by 1903, strictly defined autonomously administered enclaves. These "racial" lines of separation would prove the single most devastating intervention to the well-established history of inter-communal politics in the Ottoman Balkans.[85]

This part of the story is crucial to the larger book, as such distinctly "modern" logics proved to be the fault lines for much of the period under study. Modernity's logics (or, as we will see, the logics of several modernities) accounted for most of the outbreaks of violence and help explain why this period in Ottoman history is so densely intertwined with the refugee. As will be explored in subsequent chapters, one of the consequences of poorly conceived "diplomatic" interventions using these dubious ethnographic categories to differentiate peoples was that policies intended to expunge unwanted "minorities" led to a global refugee crisis. Indeed, after the final settlement of the Berlin Congress of 1878, the central problem for the Ottoman Empire and its new neighbors in the Balkans was the constant small-scale violence breaking out on either side of newly established frontiers.[86]

Of particular interest are the Ottoman provinces of Kosova, Işkodra, and Manastır, which had the misfortune of having to accommodate by the beginning of 1878 at least 200,000 refugees from newly independent (or autonomous in the case of Bulgaria) neighboring states. While the details of this process are covered later, the broader argument is that this new reality created by the introduction of a new kind of "identity politics" forced the Ottoman state to adopt a series of state policies that needlessly pitted rapidly reformulating communities against each other.[87]

The nature of the violence that captured so much bourgeois attention did more, however, than simply put pressure on the Ottomans and their European counterparts to find a long-term solution to a recent Christian/Muslim problem. It also incited outsiders to invest in new kinds of political activism, such as the recruitment and funding of mercenaries to exploit economic opportunities created by the conflicts.[88] Such tactics prompted communities to organize "self-protection" units in face of unprecedented, seemingly random attacks—a trend formerly unheard of in these areas where codes of conduct were enforced by harsh blood vendettas that were never lifted.[89]

In this regard, the 1897–1903 period is one in which neighboring states (just recently separated from the empire) also initiated a process of expanding their influence into key districts of Macedonia, a region encompassing portions of the provinces of Kosova, Salonika, and Manastır.[90] This outsider involvement brought a new vigor to local and regional political life already animated by previous settlement issues raised by a flood of refugees after 1877. With the introduction of outside patronage, this often led to neighbors competing over extra-communal support. Today we assume the nature of these alliances with outsiders was predicated on "natural" categories of differentiation like religious sect or ethnicity, but as argued throughout, there were more complicated interweaving interests at work, interests that often led to "paradoxical" alliances.

The source of such conflicts that became the excuse for neighboring empires to impose "reform schemes" was not the revitalization of hatred between different faiths or members of competing linguistic groups.[91] Rather, violent conflicts in the Balkans were in large part created by the way outside powers operated inside these dynamic settings. The fact that the Great Powers would only deal with interlocutors who represented group affiliations the Great Powers themselves had prescribed greatly narrowed how Ottoman Balkan inhabitants, at times in desperate need of material support, communicated their concerns to each other, the Ottoman state, and the outside world. As discussed below, the manner in which Austro-Hungarian, Russian, British, and Bulgarian/Greek officials appropriated local conflicts to fit "ethno-national" narratives ultimately touched off larger regional conflagrations that pitted the "powers" against each other as much as locals.[92] The more outside patrons insisted on using certain categories to understand (and ultimately "resolve") local conflicts, the more some "ethnic entrepreneurs" in these communities exploited the wide and varied communal identity claims that locals and refugees were able to adopt. As a result, all these Ottoman societies faced the internationalization of their domestic disputes, which ultimately undermined the ability of the evolving Ottoman state to manage the Balkans.

The consequences of this shifting pattern of local politics were at first imperceptible to Ottoman officials. It would take the warnings from locals concerned with the direction events were taking to attract Istanbul's attention. Some of the more troubling trends reported were land acquisitions by foreign-funded religious organizations and raids on villages by pseudo-nationalist criminal groups receiving weapons from outside interests.[93]

With the benefit of hindsight, scholars claim the two principal powers involved in this intensification of local politics were Austria-Hungary and Russia. As already noted, both shared an interest in the outcome of developments in Macedonia and negotiated with each other to find a workable solution to what was determined to be the inevitable crash of Ottoman rule in the Balkans. As noted by the Ottoman Grand Vizier of the time, Said Pasha, Istanbul knew that the Russians and the Austrians had a direct hand in the growing violence afflicting Macedonia.[94] In response, they initiated their own reforms in 1902–3.

Outsiders' interests in investing in such an exercise, and in often patronizing patently brutal opportunists, were motivated by the wish to exploit the region's abundant natural wealth. For much of the period after the Ottoman Empire floated its first loan with private European banks, its rich farmlands, mines, and forests served as collateral. Part of this process meant Istanbul granted concessions to companies invested in Ottoman debt. Among these concessions were the rights to "development" projects such as the construction of rail lines and ports in order to more efficiently exploit this vast land.[95] Instructively, this process very much paralleled those in the Americas and Africa at the time; the corresponding violence against the inhabitants of these coveted lands thus deserves the same moral outrage directed at the systematic destruction of native peoples elsewhere in the world.

The eventual decision to simply expropriate these lands from "rival" communities (or Ottoman sovereignty altogether) offers a larger political-economic context to the ethnic violence so often noted in the scholarship on Macedonia (and larger Ottoman world). As in Africa, the Americas, and Asia, the nineteenth-century agents of capital, through local surrogates I identify throughout as ethnic entrepreneurs, eventually set the tone for seemingly interminable violence in the region.

Crucially, it was not only a diplomatic process or one predicated on the simple distribution of guns to willing mercenaries, but a discursive one. The operatives of finance capital, via ethnographers or diplomats, set the discursive parameters within which all policies in the Ottoman Balkans would be plied from the 1880s onwards.[96] In this context, the Ottoman state, already restrained from using decisive force because of the growing outside patronage of armed groups, was put on alert by the Great Powers that significant reforms were needed. Such pressures to manage often impossible situations did not result, however, in a single policy. Ultimately, a series of resolutions dedicated to resolving the Ottoman Empire's diversity "problem" were promoted, opening a new era of direct foreigner involvement in the Balkans that did not conform to sectarian or ethno-national criteria scholars often assume existed. Reading the subsequent events in this light offers us another way to explain what precipitated the crucial years leading up to the actual disintegration of the empire.[97]

In an attempt to counter such outside designs on Macedonia, the Sublime Porte initiated a series of "reforms" especially designed to stem the violence. In December 1902, Hüseyin Hilmi Pasha was assigned the task of administering these reforms.[98]

Initially, Hilmi Pasha's administration successfully confronted the problems and the regime was praised by outside observers.[99] The problem was that many of the "reforms" entailed using force against primary members of the local population in Kosovo, many who served as the key interlocutors for the Ottoman state.[100] As a result, these stopgap measures introduced a new rupture in Istanbul's relations with locals who had recently gone through an equally difficult time of settling tens of thousands of refugees. So while locals like Ibrahim Temo from Ohrid went along with the early reforms in recognition that they were key to securing peace in the region, many others adopted a more belligerent position, seeing an opportunity to secure greater rewards from those interested in Macedonia's instability.[101]

Over the course of these efforts, far from stabilizing matters, the reforms became a pretext for new upheaval. An entirely new set of actors had been slowly cultivated in neighboring countries and had intermittently been using various tactics, even violent raids, to create new conditions on the ground. As a result, a growing number of factions involved in challenging the ad hoc government institutions started to call for the outside "protection" of their beleaguered "ethnic minorities" in a classic spiral of violence. To policy-makers in Vienna and St. Petersburg, such events seemed to indicate the inevitable crash of Ottoman rule in the region on which they could both capitalize. Both agreed during secret meetings (some held with selected locals) to continue cooperating in the hope that any future contingencies might service their mutual interests rather than letting things get out of control between them.[102] Before this so-called Vienna Scheme could be realized, however, the spread of a new wave of violence led by unaffiliated "Bulgarian" factions sabotaged its implementation.[103]

What is notable about how these proposals were implemented on the ground is just how quickly locals adapted and began manipulating the sentiments behind them. Countless commissions sent by the powers met with "community leaders" who "enthusiastically" reinforced the categorical niceties of ethnicity and sect imposed by outsiders.[104] In full recognition of the immediate and possible long-term benefits to being identified a "Serb," "Greek," "Bulgarian," or just a Christian, those who manipulated the "reforms" inspired by yet another scheme in 1904—the Mürzsteg plan—finally began to tear apart hundreds of years of multiculturalism in Kosovo. Communities and their leaders, now reading into the importance of outside patronage, promoted themselves in a manner that gave them new power over their neighbors and spelled doom for the heterogeneous Ottoman Balkans.[105]

Importantly, it was precisely in terms of "sectarian violence" that the powers selectively understood events in the Balkans. Inspection of the materials produced at the time of the 1902–3 crisis demonstrates how identity politics found its way into the political and economic vernacular of all the actors on the ground.[106] As a consequence, many of the communities affected began to adapt to the diplomatic parlance and learned to use the language of ethnicity to secure outside patronage. In many ways, the period was a watershed in the systematic articulation of local realities in the terminology of ethno-nationalism, a crucial entry-point for war profiteers and ultra-nationalist politicians in Belgrade, Istanbul, Sofia, and Athens.

As already suggested, to deal with the messy world of the Balkans, an international commission sent in 1903 by the Great Powers proposed the establishment of a decentralized administrative regime that would permit "ethnic communities" to be governed by "their own" leaders, within recognized, ethnically pure boundaries.[107] The Russian delegation to this commission, in particular, insisted that the "rights" of separation be granted to "Serbian" and "Bulgarian" residents in the form of autonomously governed enclaves free of Ottoman (and Muslim) influence. It is in these terms that we begin to see the formation of local demands that satisfied the taxonomical logic of the Russians.[108] These early "innovations," I argue, proved crucial in later efforts by post-Ottoman states to play the identity card in the hopes of realizing new kinds of governmental power, power of the kind already being cultivated in the form of "reservations" in North America, "tribal homelands" in the Philippines, and "tribal kingdoms/nations" in Southern Africa.[109]

In order to enact the separation of communities along these entirely new "ethnic" lines, clearly defined administrative boundaries were needed. In the third article of the plan offered by the 1903 commission, for example, the Ottoman government was "... to re-arrange the boundaries of the provinces with a view to making regular groupings of different nationalities." The fourth article wanted to ensure that Christians would have access to their own judicial and administrative institutions as well as a gendarmerie that would be regionally based and also divided along communal lines.[110] Furthermore, within these definable, bounded areas, communities were to operate free of Ottoman state taxation, allowed to administer their own militias—with the assistance of outside "experts"—and be permitted to direct their educational and cultural lives free of Islamic cultural influence.[111]

By March 1904, the actual implementation of the Mürzsteg reforms created dozens of incongruent autonomous enclaves throughout the Kosova and Manastır provinces.[112] The frontiers of these enclaves, vaguely drawn to represent each newly configured community's limits, immediately caused problems as Christians made increasingly bold territorial claims on land inhabited by neighboring, mostly Albanian Muslim or Pomok (Bulgarian Muslim) communities. Protected by gendarmeries organized and led by participating powers like Italy, Russia, and France, a number of reports suggest that "Serb" and "Bulgarian" "communities" exploited their protected status and "raided" Albanian-Muslim (or Albanian-Christian) lands in search of property.[113] These actions exhibited a new sense of possibility that came with the fact that any subsequent clash between neighbors would be blamed on an Ottoman failure to curb its Muslim "fanatics."[114]

For their part, the Ottoman authorities delayed or obstructed the implementation of these reform projects knowing full well that such proposed modifications to the way these regions should be governed would result in certain groups advocating for the territorial separation of their Christian communities entirely. Furthermore, kicking Muslims off their lands accompanied this new agenda, guaranteeing an eventual violent eruption that would intensify the long-term dangers of complete societal collapse.[115] It was this fear that animated many of the cries for "union" coupled with "progress" by the antigovernment opposition finding its greatest domestic support in Macedonia itself.[116]

And yet, by 1912 the violence between the different "races" still trapped inside the Ottoman Empire took on aspects of "primordial" conflicts that could only be terminated by way of a lasting (final) solution.[117] Part of this solution to Balkan "savagery" required imposing "natural" borders that separated the "races" based on "social scientific" knowledge.[118] This plan, however, was not foolproof: many Ottoman communities were still inextricably "mixed," and bloodlines simply did not break evenly along imposed taxonomical borders.[119] This "unnatural" ethnic hybridity meant that sequestrations were rarely executed voluntarily, and that Euro-American "civilization" needed to use coercion in order to force different peoples to move to their allotted national territories.

Perhaps ironically, the Swiss ethnographer George Montandon proposed imposing such "natural" borders and forcefully separating ethnically "different" peoples by way of policies that could administratively make life impossible for those refusing to comply with the "internationally" backed compulsory migrations. As a precursor to a century of imposed "population exchanges" that utterly destroyed heterogeneous societies that thrived for centuries, Montandon advised that "minorities" who remained in districts from which they were expected to leave, should, as an incentive to migrate, lose rights including the denial of property rights and citizenship, an especially telling combination of punishments for being "different" considering the larger issues discussed throughout this book.[120]

Conclusion

All this is to say that as racial calculations animated the policies of Euro-American imperialism as a whole, refugees of Armenian, Bulgarian, Albanian, Greek, and Turkish nationalist lore were the "victims" of the very epistemologies that promoted the genocidal programs in Southern Africa, Palestine, and the Americas. Nevertheless, to many post-Ottoman historians, the origins of the genocide horrors accompanying Ottoman collapse were the "unnatural" permeation of "Islamic" mores into the lives of still—at their very core—pure ethno-national groups, instead of the ascendant post-Enlightenment creed that made diversity "unnatural," perverse, and ultimately "illegal." The tragic population exchanges agreed upon after 1912 by all the major leaders of "victim" nations and international powers alike were thus seen (and continue to be seen) as necessary sacrifices to finalize the liberation moment, and not the crimes that they were.[121]

In Anatolia, much like the Balkans, the amount of violence various constituencies could bring to the fore as these events unfolded shaped a great deal of political life. Among the most contentious spaces for such entrepreneurialism to take place were settings where a sudden rush in economic activity—such as areas with new rail road lines or bridges—could open up previously inaccessible opportunities to new economic, political, and social agents. One of the major contributing factors was the need for labor. These major construction projects, for instance, required the organization of laborers, a task often farmed out to local surrogates, thus giving many in the workforce supply chain the opportunity to gain new leverage. Such opportunities became arenas for new constituencies to emerge as migrant workers, often composed of refugees desperate for wage-earning jobs, comingled for weeks at a time.

Several places around the empire seemed particularly vulnerable to such forces. One of the more interesting was Adana, which saw important structural adjustments redirect the economy to produce more bulky goods for export—primarily grains, but also livestock and timber. With such assets on offer, the profitability of any future train line or industrial farm seemed assured, thereby attracting a number of potential investors, foreign and local. Indeed, rival investment groups placed bids for a newly listed railway concession that would link the relatively new port of Mersin to Adana and eventually Baghdad and Berlin. Such rival bidding spilled over into local politics, a major source of violence in the region never discussed in the larger issue of Armenian genocide.[122] As elsewhere, just how events unfolded suggested a rich patchwork of interests vying for potentially lucrative "finders' fees" invariably on offer. It also opened up windows of opportunity for those who could address the demands for wage labor.[123] There were rewards to those who could provide wage-earning jobs for local men and women, including the tens of thousands of "idle" refugees.[124] Perhaps more importantly, influence awaited those who could organize these pockets of laborers, be it in unions or politically active parties.[125]

The process was contentious and, over the course of the late 1870s and 1880s, a great many resources were expended by local bidders (who initially won the concession). Unfortunately, well-connected outsiders succeeded in undermining the financing of this initially successful project and forced a new round of bidding. The fact that British and French financiers ultimately succeeded in bullying two Ottoman subjects—Costaki Theodoraki and Mehmet Nahit Bey—out of the concession demonstrates the possible incentives for such "losers" in the development game to gain new forms of leverage by other means.[126]

What really brought this dynamic to the fore was the influx of so many hundreds of thousands of landless refugees. These potentially violent, destitute, itinerate Ottomans faced 50 years of intermittent conflict with local "host" communities, periodic famines, and heavy-handed government agencies. These peoples constituted the potential for building militias that would serve patrons keen on either capitalizing on the post-default chaos and forging lucrative partnerships with outsiders (like the French), or using refugee forces to protect their inherited assets from those same predatory finance capitalists coveting their land, forests, and water sources.

These issues are not properly explored in the literature on conflicts between communities, as those in Adana throughout the nineteenth century. Rather than asserting a natural proclivity for Turks, Kurds, and Muslims to attack their peasant, Christian neighbors, the issues of proper land use, especially with the arrival of Circassian refugees to these areas, dominated the concerns of civilians and state officials alike. The relative availability of rural farming work greatly determined the extent to which these refugee populations were assimilated or not. When not, groups emerged who took up banditry or pursued lucrative political rent-seeking by way of offering their "services" to assure stability in return for regular payments, be it from the state directly or through local community leaders.[127]

Well into the 1890s, the kind of influence needed to assure that investment projects like the development of various ports in the East Mediterranean and railroads succeeded to transform the productive lands in the western Balkans into agricultural factories, rested in the hands of constituencies created out of alliances between landowners and, in many cases, newly arrived, landless refugees.[128] This gambit to turn refugee destitution into political (and often commercial) success necessitated a convergence of forces that still left the future entirely up-for-grabs for any number of actors. One way of capturing this otherwise opaque struggle throughout the Ottoman Empire is to focus on first undermining the narrative cohesiveness of predominant themes and then identifying various sources of indigenous "agency" that may account to alternative circuits of change.

As suggested here, the "political economy" of the refugee is closely linked with finance capitalism; a relationship mediated by any combination of state institutions and/or semi-autonomous landowning elites. Understanding this relationship through these Ottoman cases may help future students of this era to center issues on complicated "indigenous" perspectives. This perspective has proven to be crucial to analyzing the institutional and sociological transformations that lead to imperial state, and associated community collapse (and reformation). In this respect, highlighting otherwise marginalized, seemingly secondary consequences of larger historical processes demands a rethinking of a number of intersections that rarely break through the standardized historical narratives of the period. In particular, the role of debt (personal, family, communal, imperial), competing conceptions of the utility of land and the "right to access them," and finally the influence of foreign banks (at the expense of indigenous sources of capital) in how communities in far more disaggregated terms related to the larger imperial dynamics may serve as a key corrective angle to studying Ottoman collapse.

In time, the strategies to increase the value of imperial assets likely induced the increasingly violent clashes between numbers of competing constituent groups spread throughout the regions absorbing refugees and the state. For those in government, especially liberals, such confrontations offered the opportunity to resort to violently ripping apart an Ottoman sensibility if it got in the way of "progress." In the aim of assuring social harmony within society, services providing for an ideally subservient government subject, especially affordable food, could be "farmed" out to service global finance capitalism, the arbiters of progress in that period. The Ottoman-era farmers on these increasingly valuable lands, or displaced, land-less peoples who would become part of the global workforce, thus all played their part. It is the latter group that proves especially interesting; we shall study further in Chapter 4 those hundreds of thousands of Ottomans who were compelled to join the millions feeding global capital's need for cheap labor in the Americas.[129]

And yet, the scholarship universally sacrifices the exploration of such local factors in its search for the "general" trends that can explain an "inevitable" outcome. The point of emphasis in the following chapters will be that contingencies like the flow of hundreds of thousands of refugees through, out of, and into the Ottoman territories may constitute a different set of causal agents that directly shaped the institutional developments later deemed requisite for Ottoman decline and/or reform. The underling focus here, therefore, may prove invaluable to stepping beyond the rubric of imperial collapse in the larger context of Western modernity. Perhaps narrowing (or perhaps it is expanding) the interpretive agenda to patiently explore the refugee phenomenon could offer new perspectives on how modern forms of finance capitalism itself transformed as itinerate Ottomans interweaved with immediate and medium-term socioeconomic forces. It is offered here that the complexities of the multiple refugee experiences spread over a multiplicity of territories constantly forced all major stakeholders in the subordination of the Ottoman economy, including foreign bankers, to address the needs of, among other constituencies, Ottoman refugees. This in turn completely transformed how local, regional, and international political agency was expressed, and within which governing institutions operated.

Indeed, even the most progressive of critics of the "Age of Capital" miss the opportunity to consider the variance in how forms of government, local commercial networks, rural polities, and European private capital interfaced in often counterintuitive ways. By simply citing statistics from partially complete sets of ministry records or banks (as if the "real" economy submits receipts to the government), the dynamic local contexts of expanding capitalism-as-modernity is lost. The end result is a skewed picture of a world dominated by formalities and hegemonic pretensions when in fact the peoples of the world in the late nineteenth and early twentieth centuries were nowhere near becoming subordinate to the whims of finance capital.[130]

As we proceed to explore in the next chapter how refugee violence after 1878 at once linked competing local political and economic interests with the multiplicity of stories of the Ottoman Empire's collapse, a few key issues require special attention. First, returning to the issue of what happens to people inhabiting these spaces increasingly deemed "investment-grade" strengthens the need to link how a number of stakeholders—landowners, foreign investors, refugees, and local government officials—made their evolving economic and political calculations. In this respect, following up on our initial attempt to connect various political groupings with the at times chaotic efforts to profit from building an Ottoman infrastructure requires returning to theorizing the role of otherwise forgotten "subaltern" causal agents to these volatile events.

Resettlement Regimes and Empire:
The Politics of Caring for Ottoman Refugees

Introduction

As demonstrated in the last chapter, Ottoman reforms during the 1839–75 period launched social reorientations whose consequences, while profound, also varied within disparate Ottoman communities. Much like their counterparts elsewhere in Europe, Ottoman reformers who imagined themselves "in power" could never fully harness "the state" as an exclusive agent of change in this period of reform. No matter how much was invested in streamlining the Ottoman state, and despite the historiography deterministically framing these measures as part of an epochal "process," contingencies were always possible.

Indeed, in a matter of two years this "Tanzimat Period" and the state assumed to have emerged from it all changed. The disasters visited upon the empire after the Russo-Ottoman war of 1877–8 completely altered the manner in which the political and economic elite interacted with their fellow citizens. Such adjustments in many ways entailed dismantling, or at best modifying, a half century's worth of reform. Crucially for us, the nature of these postwar adjustments often meant completely transforming the state's role in shaping local, political, and regional economies as its managers tried to service the needs of a new imperial demographic: the refugee.

Being at once the sanctuary for the Mediterranean's and Central Asia's political outcasts as well as opportunists fleeing periodic economic downturns throughout Eurasia, the Ottoman Empire frequently bore the burden of accommodating large numbers of immigrants. For much of the early modern period this was not considered an especially worrisome phenomenon as these people could be strategically useful to the imperial project of expansion and territorial consolidation. Often, these mostly Muslim migrants were resettled in the still under-populated hinterlands of the vast empire, helping bring both economic productivity and security to hitherto neglected areas. Otherwise, migrants simply assimilated into the empire's expanding cities.[1]

These tactics to accommodate these peoples, however, had to change as a result of a new set of pressures put on the Ottoman Empire after 1878.[2] Before large influxes of Tatars, Chechens, or Central Asian Muslims could have positive consequences after settling in sparsely populated areas of the empire. After 1878, however, expansionist neighbors grabbing large chunks of territory, coupled with the growing strains on raw materials necessary to build the infrastructure needed to accommodate yet more peoples, forced the empire's bureaucratic elite to adopt new, often inauspicious, counterproductive governing measures. Indeed, it is this last aspect that, with so much pressure to meet an unprecedented number of refugee demands, the relationship between the empire's diverse communities and the ever-expanding central state changed forever.[3]

By the 1880s, a new kind of political, as much as economic, entrepreneurialism emerged. Those Ottoman subjects possessing the ability to make or break the peace in the Ottoman realm became a very important political commodity. Indeed, with new constituencies emerging as a result of massive inflows of refugees from recently ceded Ottoman Serbia, Montenegro, Greece, and Romania, the elements requisite for "revolutionary" processes began to appear in abundance in the Balkans and larger Middle East. Such radicalization of domestic politics in response to the refugees made their full integration (and thus political neutralization) impossible.

In order to make sense of the resulting struggles to contain or exploit the opportunities made by these sudden change of fortunes, this chapter explores how such an influx of refugees into diverse regions of the Ottoman Empire after 1878 compelled various strata of regional, local, and imperial government to adapt. As explained below, amid the constant efforts by government officials to address these refugees' needs, measures taken to assure violence did not break out offered any number of those stakeholders involved—state authorities, refugees themselves, community leaders—opportunities to rise in prominence. In this respect, as much as the new Hamidian regime (1876–1908) needed to assure that the regions most affected remained calm, those expected to contribute to the stabilizing process often proved cunningly aware of the kind of leverage they gained under such crisis conditions. Their opportunities to act grew even further once the hardened "Great Power" determination to keep the Ottoman Empire (at least in the Balkans) intact began to change.

A regular figure in this mix of opportunists and surrogates of competing interests was the Balkan/Anatolian rebel. Known in the literature as a mixture of bandit, terrorist, and/or nationalist rebel, the *çeta/hajduk/kaçak* of Balkan/Anatolian legend (and a plethora of possible allies, patrons, and rivals) completely changed the relationship between the Ottoman state and communities inhabiting the Balkans and Anatolia from 1878 forward.[4] Their activities, fringed by the fluid refugee settlements established throughout, opened the door for a "micropolitics" of violence that is now understood to be a major historical force.[5]

These temporary exchanges between disparate actors created multitudes of temporary constituencies whose many, often violent actions at once centered refugees in imperial and interstate polices and equally externalized their demands as they became part of "criminal" activities supported by bandits and/or foreign-funded rebels. This "fluid" exchange ultimately left migrant Ottomans trapped in contested sociopolitical situations and the resulting battle for survival became the engine for much of the change in the empire's last 40 years. More importantly, such contentious, unstable sociopolitical conditions proved to be the Ottoman Empire's impossible governing situation. As much as the empire already demonstrated the administrative wherewithal to adapt to such influxes of refugees with the *Muhacirin Komisyonu* created in the 1850s, other factors made this period after 1878 especially transformative—and onerous—for everyone involved.

Adding to the dynamism of the era of course was that it overlapped with the Ottoman debt crisis discussed at length in the last chapter. Coupled with regime change in the form of a young Sultan Abdülhamid II in 1876, the (re)entrenched bureaucratic order was given a chance to push the Ottoman state onto a new, even accelerated path of modernist centralization, a direction seemingly ill-fit for a society suddenly exposed to such large amounts of perilously desperate refugees. Indeed, efforts to both steer the empire out of its crisis with Western financiers and deal with its refugees would at times result in a concentration of power that impacted how the state (and larger Ottoman society) could and/or would provide for refugees, a crucial ambiguity that played into the hands of hitherto obscure or even nonexistent "historical forces."

Making sense of an Ottoman provisional modernity

One of the primary tasks of the Ottoman state immediately after the start of its war with Russia and its Balkan allies in the second half of the 1870s was to assure the strategic settlement of "displaced" peoples who flooded these contested, recently created "borderlands." (See Map 2.1.) A manifestation of this was the creation of a General Administrative Commission for Migrants (*Idare-i Umumiye-i Muhacirin Komisyonu*) in 1878, which quickly branched out services to so-called Migrant Directorates established in each territory where refugees were received and resettled.[6] One of the immediate consequences of these stopgap actions was an unexpected transformation of the actual relationship refugees had with their "hosts." For example, many of those refugees receiving state assistance at these reception points actually ended up forming entirely new communities, often dominating the original inhabitants in the process.[7]

Just how this unfolds under the guise of an expansionist government resettlement scheme became highly politicized in the decades leading up to the upheaval throughout Central and Eastern Anatolia and the Balkan Wars of 1912–13.[8] During these years, a cycle of government action and reaction often pitted ambitious local surrogates of foreign interests against state officials' efforts to use any means necessary to keep the peace in their vexed homelands. It is especially at this kind of conjuncture that ethnic entrepreneurs in various parts of the empire and their foreign patrons exploited tensions arising over how local assets would be distributed to accommodate newly arrived refugees rather than indigenous communities. The resulting conflicts over access to communal forests, arable land, and water rights are but a few of the transformative flashpoints invoked throughout this book.[9]

Map 2.1 Ottoman Western Balkans 1878–1912.

Political activation and integration politics

At the heart of this churning human adaptability was the operating directive of the Ottoman bureaucracy—to provide care for these floods of destitute victims.[10] I call this a *Provisional Modernity* that will serve as an interpretive angle that deracinates events from tendentious contexts post-Ottoman historians imposed to serve the individual nation's story. As presented here, the flow of human beings throughout the Ottoman territories as a direct result of significant territorial loses after war complicated a slowly emergent, but still malleable, international liberal capitalist order germinating around the world. While shaped by legal standards, diplomatic principles, and "laws of civilization," this materializing "world order" proved contingent, subject to constant transformations taking place on the ground especially in the Ottoman Balkans, Anatolia, and even Mesopotamia, rather than in hitherto nonexistent national spaces.

The point here, in other words, is not to impose a single set of causal forces behind say the "rise of capitalism" or the "liberation" (or destruction) of a national people but to open up new interpretative spaces to appreciate what took priority at the immediate level for state officials and various Ottoman subjects. For instance, it may have been critical to relations between various Ottoman officials and representatives of outside financial interests that the massive population shifts—due in part to violence induced by famines in Eastern Anatolia and Arabia, as well as the result of a defeat at the hands of Russia—became the primary focus of Ottoman state reforms.[11] Such momentary shifts surely undermined some bankers' agendas as a consequence.

This conflict in priorities becomes increasingly important when we understand how strife within communities over access to key resources, such as water, land, and fuel leaves the entire structure of imperial order even more confusing from the perspective of investors. That we are dealing with the introduction of refugees in those fragile spaces disrupted by war, compounded by the fact that the Ottoman government was in tremendous flux (partially in response to the refugee situation), reinforces the claim that we can usefully consider explaining much of the transitional era through the prism of itinerate Ottomans.

Unfortunately, at these crucial moments when organization and generosity were most needed, there was often little the defeated government could do. War and occupation by hostile troops had strained those communities hosting refugees to the breaking point. With their supply chains cut off and their food stores depleted by raids, for example, regions directly affected by war were the least able (and least willing) to accommodate tens of thousands of refugees. In situations like this, the demands put on host communities to accommodate refugees, even temporarily, proved to disrupt—and in some cases destroy outright—indigenous political orders.

A primary source of such disruptions was the sudden clashes over the distribution of the basic necessities of life. For instance, we can observe in Kosovo that during this initial 1878–81 period a lack of provisions (often due to artificial "shortages" created by high market prices for grains and livestock and subsequent hoarding) left most communities straining to feed themselves, let alone refugees flooding these areas by the tens of thousands. The conditions were so bad in parts of Kosovo that throughout the winter and early spring of 1878, whatever government agency existed had to occasionally induce the large-scale transfer of already "settled" refugees to other locations.[12]

A kind of interminable uncertainty emerged in such settings. As a result, throughout 1878 the immediate needs of refugees were constantly frustrated. This failure to adequately care for temporarily resettled populations resulted in the realignment of relations between locals, the Ottoman state, and refugees. For their part, the refugees were not going to countenance enduring hunger, and many took matters into their own hands. One of the more spectacular examples of such determination was the raiding of known food stores in Kosovo and Manastır's towns. It is not hard to imagine the scene when reading the short reports about the sizable contingencies of Ottoman troops garrisoned in these towns refusing to stop the looting.[13]

More than simply an issue of feeding one's hungry and cold family members, the emergent refugee constituencies proved fully articulate of their rapidly adapting demands. In this respect they graduated quickly from being "refugees" to politicized refugee communities inside a larger post-conflict Ottoman Kosovo. Here lies the dynamic space of something we can call an *integration politics*, one obviously fraught with flashpoints that could redraw the contours of local society for years.[14] Indeed, as revealed below, refugee agency became the source of a productive volatility, an instability that necessarily rearticulated for many what in fact served as communal interests for years to come.

It was not just feeding refugees (or potential ones) that shaped the provisional arenas in which postwar societies (and the reforming state) operated. The underlying concern to cater to or prevent the movement of (potential) refugees for local officials meant that there were also complex patterns of community-building at play.[15] In this respect, viewing events with the benefit of hindsight, the observable "chaos" sprouting out of regions most afflicted by waves of refugees was not entirely negative, at least for certain actors. For one, it invited the kind of conflict that ultimately opened doors of opportunity for external powers and local ethnic entrepreneurs seeking foreign patronage. Furthermore, the lack of a coherent policy in dealing with the refugees not only changed the way people interacted with their neighbors, but also ultimately disrupted the traditional patriarchal structures that had allowed old landowning families to sustain their influence well beyond the transition from Ottoman to post-Ottoman rule.

As seen in the case of Mt Lebanon as early as 1840, this bastion of French direct interference witnessed a power struggle between "old-guard" community leaders with strong links to the Ottoman state and an emergent, radicalized group of activists whose sharpened sectarian identity claims strategically complicated previously harmonious inter-communal relations. At its source, the decades-long violence periodically rising out of these "mixed" communities thus proved an enduring struggle for ascendency in face of shifting land ownership and foreign power patronage.[16] At the heart of these tensions played out in similar fashion in Syria/Lebanon was the use by French consular staff of their diplomatic immunity and powers to "protect" Ottoman Maronites at the detriment of others. As these well-known events prove, most often, the gravest threat came from those men willing to side with the first outside interest capable of paying a stipend, issuing land, or offering the much-sought-after modern rifles.[17]

The Balkans immediately after the Russo-Ottoman war of 1877–8 proved to have fallen into such a quagmire. Any number of people emerged as active agents of change in the midst of desperate measures by the state to accommodate tens of thousands of Ottoman subjects (mostly Muslims) being strategically expunged from their lucrative lands in Bulgaria, Niš, Herzegovina, and Montenegro.[18] Specific to those regions on the "frontline" of this tsunami of potentially dangerous refugees was the newly recalibrated province of Kosovo. This vast region, spanning from Novipazar to the north to present-day Macedonia to the south, had long seen the influx of refugees. The fact that upwards of 200,000 largely Muslim Albanian and Slavic speakers flooded the Kosovo area (in which no more than 800,000 people lived) during the 1877–8 war meant the authorities trying to temporarily settle these peoples would always have to take into account that their homelands were within walking distance.[19] Ultimately, the phenomenon of refugee communities being camped literally within view of their old farmlands posed entirely different kinds of problems for the newly expanded government offices charged with caring for them. As such, the fateful decision (if the state even had a choice) to keep most of the Niš refugees relatively close by in the Kosovo regions of Drenica and Gjakova ignited a firestorm of conflict.

Known today in the local Albanian context as the *muhaxhir* (derived from Arabic, via Ottoman, meaning expellee or sometimes simply immigrant),[20] these "*Nish muhaxhir*," constituting a powerful sub-group in present-day Kosovo's domestic politics, were immediately positioning themselves to organize a way back home.[21] As I proceed to study this process, it is important to stress that the manner by which these refugees mobilized disproves the normative association of refugees with political vulnerability and dependency on the charity of others. For example, these refugees from Niš proved unwilling to rely on the modest capacities of their hosts in Kosovo to accommodate their needs, if that meant making them subservient to host (or government) political demands. In this respect, far from being paralyzed, these refugees quickly formed interest groups, constituencies that immediately forced their ways into local affairs.[22] Indeed, considering the extent to which their presence created the impetus for the three-year period of violence in Kosovo, known today as the quintessential era of Albanian nationalist rebirth or *rilindja*, it is probably safe to say that these *Niš muhacir* took over local polities.[23]

Facing an unprecedented amount of pressure, previously autonomous Kosovo Albanian communal leaders reached out to the Ottoman government to seek direct state assistance in face of the fully mobilized, and increasingly hostile *Niš muhacir* communities settling in their midst.[24] These overtures reflected a contentious coexistence between hardened camps with entirely different needs. The resulting political theater would transform local politics to the extent that the future violence in Macedonia—and incumbent foreign interventions—was most likely the birth child of this new order imposed on the Ottoman Balkans.[25]

As such, what the mostly Niš-origin (and Bosnia) refugees accomplished by reconstituting themselves within those Kosovar communities forced to accommodate them proves to be a crucial turning point in the region's modern history. By the summer of 1878, many were radicalized by their experiences of first expulsion and economic ruin, then the often hostile reception from local landowning elites forced to hand over properties and valuable supplies during the winter to accommodate them. In face of such local hostility to their presence, and the diplomatic process in Berlin still "under negotiation," Niš-community leaders took matters in their own hands; they basically pushed back at efforts by their hosts to exclude them from local council meetings held during the crucial spring of 1878 period.[26]

Evidence suggests that they not only forced their way into the debates with visiting government representatives that concerned their immediate and potentially long-term interests, but that they also, in several instances, circumvented the authority of local leaders in those areas they were forced to settle. In many ways, the Drenica (Rahovec, Suha Reka, Lipjan, Mitrovica, Klina) and Dukagjin (Peja, Gjakova, Prizren) sub-districts where most of these *Niš muhacir* settled (and still live) became the incubator for a rival, far more radical, often anti-state constituency. Indeed all evidence points to the conclusion that, within a few months of these *Niš muhacir* massive settlement, the domestic politics of a region long entrenched in Ottoman affairs as a reliable bulwark to expansionist Slavic neighbors, was torn apart. There is no better evidence of this transformation than the violent confrontations that took place, not with the Montenegrin and Serbian forces entrenched nearby on newly conquered lands, but with Ottoman state authorities and their local Kosovar Albanian (Muslim) allies.[27]

As these Niš refugees waited for acknowledgment from locals, they took measures to ensure that they were properly accommodated by often confiscating food stored in towns. They also simply appropriated lands and began to build shelter on them. A number of cases also point to banditry in the form of livestock raiding and "illegal" hunting in communal forests, all parts of refugees' repertoire.[28] At this early stage of the crisis, such actions overwhelmed the Ottoman state, with the institution least capable of addressing these issues being the newly created *Muhacirin Müdüriyeti*.

Ignored in the scholarship, these acts of survival by desperate refugees constituted a serious threat to the established Kosovar communities. The leaders of these communities thus spent considerable efforts lobbying the Sultan to do something about the refugees.[29] Such overtures tangentially led to the sharpening of regional interests as policies implemented to address local concerns impacted potential clients of these external powers. The long-term consequence was a deep divide within Kosovar society, one that strengthened the ties of the "conservative" regime in Istanbul (that included the Sultan as a "Muslim" and the *Rum* Patriarch whose support of a strong Ottomanism hinged on continued authority over Orthodox Christians) with once entrenched Albanian and Slavic landowning families now threatened by new constituent interests.[30]

While these *Niš muhacir* would in some ways integrate into the larger regional context, as evidenced later, they, and a number of other Albanian-speaking refugees streaming in for the next 20 years from Montenegro and Serbia, constituted a strong opposition block to the Sultan's rule.[31] It is chiefly from these reconstituted groups that the most active supporters of the future CUP would arise. It is important to stress, however, that not all *muhacir* grew to despise the Sultan. Bosnian and Chechen refugees would prove, by in large, the most enthusiastic supporters of the government, a reflection of the strategic thinking of the Ottoman state that settled these peoples amid the Kosovo/Macedonia quagmire in such large numbers.[32]

Perhaps the most emblematic (but often abused in the scholarship) manifestation of these tensions was the violent response to the Ottoman Empire's formal surrender of many of these peoples' homelands during the Berlin Congress of 1878. One particularly infamous event has been totally misrepresented by the nationalist historiography at the expense of considering the refugee impact on domestic political stability in Kosovo.

As local notables reached out to Istanbul to help negotiate a viable, long-term solution to the rapidly changing dynamics in the region, a delegation led by one Mehmed Ali Pasha arrived in Kosovo to begin a tour of the province and meet local notables. By the time his delegation reached the important trading town of Gjakova (Yakova in Ottoman) in western Kosovo, all the tension within this heavily afflicted region was at play.[33]

Gjakova and its rich lands had become a major destination for streams of refugees, especially from the highland Catholic communities being gradually eradicated by Montenegro. While it appears the Ottoman state tried to accommodate these virtually intact Catholic *Malësorë* (Northern Albanian highland) communities with lands they "purchased" or "leased" from local landowners, clashes over the rights of these lands stressed the region.[34] In many ways, local Albanian notables—Catholic and Muslim—were keen on seeing the state assert a new order to the area that would preserve what remained of their power.

It did not work out that way, however. Disgruntled refugees and relatively fluid local constituencies interpreted this open alliance between the Hamidian state and local landowners a long-term threat. The brutal attack on the house of Abdullah Pasha, the local Albanian notable who hosted the Ottoman state's representative Mehmed Ali Pasha, constituted an especially dangerous breach of all that was sacred in western Kosovo. A long-held tradition of respectfully hosting and providing shelter to guests (especially dignitaries sent from Istanbul) meant that this unprecedented attack on Abdullah Pasha by refugees ran afoul of an important mechanism designed to ensure the maintenance of local order. What seems to have developed in Kosovo as a result of the San Stefano and Berlin treaties was a sharply divided postwar social and political milieu.[35] And while the scale was never more than local outbursts of violence between a relatively small amount of people, this condition, as will be seen inside Kosovo's Macedonian territories within the decade, would have the cumulative effect of destroying the Ottoman Empire's ability to manage this transitional period. The murder of Mehmed Ali Pasha and his highly respected host, therefore, should not be understood only as a simple act of defiance of Ottoman order, nor as the sudden breakdown of local custom, but also as a usurpation of local power.[36]

Serbia's Niš settlement scheme

As a point of contrast, it may be useful to briefly consider just how differently Serbia managed its integration politics in the very Niš territories from which so many of these refugees upsetting the Ottoman Balkans came. The fact that lands recently conquered would remain culturally "mixed" posed a problem for some early nationalist state-builders in Serbia.[37] In an attempt to address this incongruent social reality, state bureaucracies in Serbia became the new political battleground as conflicting visions of the post-*Tanzimat* order clashed. On the one hand, politically ambitious liberals aimed to instigate new social rules to their uncomfortably heterogeneous societies. The subsequent struggle to secure these "rescued" homelands in face of resistance by those suddenly deemed "minorities" created several mutually exclusive narratives of modern statehood that mirrored the emerging factions within the new states' bureaucracies.[38]

Many within these governments (and without) capitalized on the apparent contradiction to create new narratives of fear, plans of colonization, and alliances with newly empowered religious institutions. In this context, the new border areas themselves became the domain in which questions of belonging, especially within state-sanctioned religious orders, surfaced in their most raw and violent form.[39] On the other hand, there were elements within all these regimes that frowned upon such politics of "difference." Fiscal conservatives in particular, in face of demands from Europe's financial elite to start again repaying the Ottoman's debt their new country inherited, feared the likely economic disruptions caused by any rise in ethno-sectarian chauvinism. In their attempt to preempt any outbreak of violence, factions within each government of Prince Obrenović promoted a flexible, accommodating regime in the economically productive lands that made up the new borders separating, for example, Serbia and Kosovo (the former Niš *sancak*), and the Adriatic from its hinterland (Işkodra *vilâyet*). The ensuing struggle to shape government policies thus pitted bureaucrats against local stakeholders, a constant in western Balkan history that would not change until the 1920s.[40] For those who saw the disruptive long-term consequences of permanently expelling "non-Serbs" from the newly awarded territories, which by most accounts was a majority non-Serb population prior to 1877–8, the biggest concern was the region's economic base. Simply put, placating Belgrade-based nationalists did not fit well with the demands Serbia's newfound independence made on the economy.

Recall that both Serbia and Montenegro inherited some of the outstanding debt from the Ottoman Empire and were thus expected to adopt strategies to repay it. As a consequence, Serbia and Montenegro had to expose their economies to European private capital, eventually floating new loans while establishing a national economy geared to paying back its debt.[41] In this setting, Serbia's hard-liner "ethnic" entrepreneurs were somewhat restrained throughout the 1880s as bureaucrats insisted that the country needed to maintain a balance between demands for demographic purification and the need to preserve the economic vitality of the Niš province and its many tax-paying districts (Pirot, Leskovac, Prokuplje, Vranje, and Toplica).

This all suggests that considerable energy was invested in adapting to the very different and diverse local conditions that had evolved over the course of the *Tanzimat*. At the forefront of this accommodating side of the new Serbian regime was the attempt to return this highly productive area of Niš to some form of economic stability. Much evidence exists to suggest that officials prioritized economic stability in the region, long dependent on agriculture and regional markets found in what was after 1878 in Ottoman Kosovo. As a consequence, many officials in Belgrade would have to adopt policies that encouraged continuity and reintegration, not destruction.

The most readily available example of this balancing the domestic political needs of radical nationalists with larger economic demands is the management of the so-called *Novi Krajevi* (new areas) of Niš recently transferred to Serbia.[42] In these areas, the Serbian regime actually attempted to protect the "minority" landowning class whose Muslim faith presumably disqualified them from living in the new principality. Rather than simply confiscating the land, as promoted by some, more pragmatic elements of the state bureaucracy developed mechanisms that advocated greater stability. For example, almost immediately after securing the regions around Niš and through the

Morava and Nišava river valleys in July 1877, experienced bureaucrats from Belgrade were sent to the region with considerable administrative power. Among other things, this cadre of administrators, under the direct command of the Minister of Education and Religious Affairs, successfully transferred governmental responsibilities in these areas from the army to civilians.[43]

In the process of first establishing a civilian-run provisional government and then adopting policies that formally integrated these southern territories into a larger Serbia in less destructive ways, an elaborate scheme developed around the standard of local-Belgrade collaboration. This proved somewhat inconsistent because of the diverse conditions facing officials sent by Belgrade. After all, these were formerly Ottoman territories with a vastly more diverse population that, no matter how effective Serb army's "ethnic cleansing" schemes were, was not fully eradicated.[44] Instead of seeking to "complete" the task of "purifying" Niš, however, it is clear that in many cases, considerable effort was put to not only keep "non-Serbs" from leaving but also encourage large numbers now living as refugees in Kosovo to return.[45]

One of the measures adopted to realize this goal was consulting with locals in drawing up plans to entice expellees to "repatriate." Such a strategy corresponds with evidence that the civilian government granted "non-Serbs" important roles within the municipal councils set up in these early years of integration. Such local participation greatly tempered the push by Serbs from the north whose attitude toward these "backwater" districts resembled more a colonialist than a "Serb brother." In these regions, as a consequence, far less economic exploitation took place. This distinction between more "integrated" districts and those remaining distant proves crucial to understanding the post-Berlin Congress Balkans in general.

In those municipalities and districts where locals retained the desired counterweight to Belgrade-based nationalist and army officials, considerable continuity from the Ottoman era to the Serbian is evident. According to a report to Belgrade, Vasiljević, the Serbian-government administrator preserved many of the Ottoman institutions, and, as much as possible, encouraged those who previously ran them to stay. He justified this by assuring his superiors in Belgrade that locals were accustomed to these institutions and would be willing to cooperate with the new regime if not faced with so much day-to-day change affecting their lives. In other words, the choices made by local administration reveal an underlying tension in the modern world: Serbian state rule would be acceptable, even to Albanians and other Muslims, if these old institutions remained in place.[46]

One can observe that in strategically important areas, the new Serbian state purposefully left the old Ottoman laws intact. More important, when the state wished to enforce its authority, officials felt it necessary to seek the assistance of those with some experience, using the old Ottoman administrative codes to assist judges make rulings.[47] There still remained, however, the problem of the region being largely depopulated as a consequence of the wars.

Miloš Jagodić tabulated that at least 30,000 "Albanians" had been forced to leave the towns of Niš, Prokuplje, Leskovac, and Vranje for Kosovo.[48] Belgrade needed these people, mostly the landowners of the productive farmlands surrounding these towns, back. In subsequent attempts to lure these economically vital people back, while paying lip-service to the nationalist calls for "purification," Belgrade officials adopted a compromise position that satisfied both economic rationalists who argued that Serbia needed these people and those who wanted to separate "Albanians" from "Serbs." Instead of returning back to their "mixed" villages and towns of the previous Ottoman era, these "Albanians," "Pomoks," and "Turks" were encouraged to move into concentrated clusters of villages in Masurica, and Gornja Jablanica that the Serbian state set up for them.[49] For this "repatriation" to work, however, authorities needed the cooperation of local leaders to help persuade members of their community who were refugees in Ottoman territories to "return."[50]

In this regard, the collaboration between Shahid Pasha and the Serbian regime stands out. An Albanian who commanded the Sofia barracks during the war, Shahid Pasha negotiated directly with the future king of Serbia, Prince Milan Obrenović, to secure the safety of those returnees who would settle in the many villages of Gornja Jablanica.[51] To help facilitate such collaborative ventures, laws were needed that would guarantee the safety of these communities likely to be targeted by the rising nationalist elements infiltrating the Serbian army at the time. Indeed, throughout the 1880s, efforts were made to regulate the interaction between exiled Muslim landowners and those local and newly immigrant farmers working their lands. Furthermore, laws passed in early 1880 began a process of managing the resettlement of the region that accommodated those refugees who came from Austrian-controlled Herzegovina and from Bulgaria.[52] Cooperation, in other words, was the preferred form of exchange within the borderland, not violent confrontation.

And yet, small-scale violence constantly broke out on either side of the established frontiers.[53] As seen in the case of the "Macedonia" problem 20 years later, unsettlement both mobilized refugees to organize to the point of becoming formidable political forces in their own right, and sustained a contentious socioeconomic space that allowed for all kinds of opportunity-seekers to thrive as bandit leaders, revolutionaries, state henchmen, and/or smugglers.[54] Part of the problem was the reckless behavior of outside powers not necessarily invested in seeing the kind of stable integration of these post-Berlin Treaty polities created by shifted boundaries.

For instance, while the Treaty of Berlin defined the legal status and guaranteed the rights and liberties of so-called minorities, especially Christians, Muslims in many of the newly "liberated" lands occupied by Bulgaria still suffered hardships. Those Bulgarian state authorities who were put into positions of authority during Russian occupation immediately got to work in denying those Muslim inhabitants refusing to flee Bulgaria's "liberated" territories the right to cultivate their lands. Indeed, in parts of western Bulgaria that was still populated by a sizeable "minority" of Muslims, forces were unleashed to actively terrorize those remaining pockets of Muslims (and Serbs) who would not take the increasingly popular measure of "converting" before an apparently active roaming band of Exarchate Bulgarian priests.[55]

Beyond forcefully converting Muslims and Serbs, officials made sure non-Bulgarians would be disarmed. At the same time, state officials armed those "Bulgarians," many who were themselves refugees, as a means of integrating them into areas once inhabited by Muslims, Serbs, or *Rum* Orthodox Christians further south. For example, officials seized Muslim weapons and passed them onto those "loyal Bulgarians" who were then charged with "keeping order" in the Zishtovi and Edirne regions. One General Gurko apparently added another 60,000 rifles to the region by passing out to Bulgarians located further south—on the Macedonia "border"—a policy of selectively arming civilians that had obvious consequences in the years to come.[56]

No longer capable of defending themselves from a mobilized, now politically empowered class of "unleashed" bandits-*cum*-nationalists, many Muslims had no choice but to move. What is crucial is that many did not end up as refugees in Ottoman territories, but clustered into areas within the confines of territorial Bulgaria where other Muslims either lived, or had earlier moved.[57] These "internal" displacements—which can only be seen as casualties of a new strategic calculus—often forced state officials to take new measures to assure these refugees were properly accommodated. For example, as with Serbia, new considerations about what to do with the potential assets of newly conquered areas also shaped Bulgaria's *integration politics*. In time, Bulgarian government policies no longer sought to use violence to summarily expel Muslims. Rather, almost all post-Ottoman states in the Balkans realized that the entire "depopulation" of areas inhabited by Muslims would not just destabilize countries, but impoverish them.

For newly created "national" leaders, a new kind of discourse formulated around action plans emerged. While the pursuit of demographic "balance" in the "liberated" regions of the former Ottoman Empire was important for the long-term political development of Bulgaria, Greece, Serbia (Yugoslavia), Middle East, and Turkey, the economic realism embraced by a liberal elite—men often first socialized in the late Ottoman world—staunched "final solution" level operations promoted by less-disciplined political forces. Economic stability, after all, was necessary as all post-Ottoman states inherited part of the Ottoman debt and were thus compelled to make annual payments to the same banks the Ottomans did. In this respect, these transitional governments were not entirely deaf to the interests of otherwise publically vilified Muslim/Albanian/Kurdish "others," all Ottoman subjects still living in those areas that would have to produce revenues and pay off inherited debts.

For their part, targeted Ottoman Muslims in Bulgaria did not stand idle. As a first step, some of the afflicted communities in western Bulgaria tried to petition the powers to address their fears of imminent expulsion.[58] If, however, such calls were not heeded, as would prove to be the case in the vast majority of time indigenous peoples begged European authorities for help, there were other options.[59] As would become clear in areas further westward, just in case soliciting outsider sympathies by way of evoking "universal" values did not work, local communities had a much older repertoire of tactics on which they could rely.[60]

Such manifestations of internal power struggles became distorted through the lens of Great Power diplomacy and of regional patrons struggling for power in their newly created post-Ottoman (or, in the case of Bulgaria, autonomous tributary) polities. Be they consular staff members writing letters to home offices in Paris, Berlin, Vienna, or London, or regional "informants" infusing those reports with calculated lies, distortions, or points of emphasis (at the expense of other possible angles of interpretation/representation), selected moments of violence (or cooperation) functioned to streamline otherwise "incoherent" Balkan politics. This constituted the kind of transformative window of opportunity that ethnic entrepreneurs and expansion-minded venture capitalists needed to transform the region after 1878.[61]

Over the next three decades, Bulgaria became itself a new dynamic force in regional affairs, joining the conflicted struggle between Serbian and Montenegrin (not to mention Habsburg and Ottoman) political actors to control a post-Berlin world.[62] In this new and volatile context, efficient management of land and resources became absolutely crucial if refugee communities were to be accommodated without further upheaval. Having proven their ability to violently force the state to grant them concessions, many refugees' tactics of threatening violence transformed the methods of rule in many parts of the Ottoman Empire, often upsetting the phase in Ottoman "governmentality" that some scholars today herald as a kind of "Ottoman colonial modernity."

What may be more useful at this point is to consider how these integration policies not only left a political imprint, but were integrated into a set of economic calculations that had lingering consequences on the way the major receiving areas of Ottoman refugees managed conflicts. In the end, the marginalization of community leaders from the daily administration of the region's self-defense mechanism was probably the most dangerous change introduced by the various agreements signed by the Ottoman state and outside powers on behalf of local, often Christian constituents.

Economizing integration politics

Another important factor in the relationship between refugees and their hosts was the regional economic climate just prior to the refugees' influx. Communities in diverse regions like Basra/Kuwait, Kosovo, Anatolia, and Işkodra were in the throes of widespread economic and social transformation before they became host to tens of thousands of refugees. In the Balkans, the changes caused by the sudden shift in regional trade following the redrawing of borders had immediately manifested in new frontier structures. Roads and bridges, for instance, were often redirected in order to fit the contours of the borders. This fact occasionally left parts of once well-connected regions suddenly isolated. Facing economic marginalization, these now frontier communities often became the centers for lucrative smuggling networks. As I previously noted, these unanticipated "consequences of empire" transformed the political careers of entire regions and their temporary political leaders.[63]

This also plays out in interesting ways in an area of northeast Arabia/Kuwait, where rival landed/property-owning elites faced a game-changing influx of refugees. Due to a sudden shift in local fortunes instigated by drought in the Hasa region further south, throughout the 1890s a large group of people were chased out by the resulting poverty and violence as people competed for water and food that was in short supply. This migration invariably led to Basra in southern Iraq becoming a major receiving point—a shift that compromised the effectiveness of Ottoman administration in larger Mesopotamia for much of the last 30 years of rule in the region. One of the results was a series of actions/counter-actions within the extended al-Sabah family on whose lands/farms many of these thousands of refugees settled.[64]

As peoples continued to escape the violent consequences of drought in Eastern Arabia (thus inducing peoples to seek refuge in securely administered Ottoman areas like Basra), regional leaders like Muhammad al-Sabah attempted to capitalize on new trading possibilities engendered by growing human traffic. These moves were at least partially motivated by the desire to economically marginalize Muhammad's younger brother Mubarak, whose activities proved destabilizing to Kuwait's domestic politics. In this connection, we observe grand "imperial-scale" projects/machinations being put to the service of a local sibling rivalry.[65]

As elsewhere, the region became an area of conflicting interests. The Berlin-to-Baghdad railroad in particular weighed heavily on the calculations of a number of stakeholders. It is through this same highly contested oasis and "empty lands" that the rail projects necessary to expand trade would have to pass. The influx of tens of thousands of destitute peoples thus lent new value to the project, both as an economic investment and in respect to its political importance.

As the project moved forward in the context of such demographic upheaval, the cooperation of local leaders capable of controlling these masses proved vital. This international project linking Germany to the Persian/Arab Gulf, in other words, needed local cooperation to assure lands once used for pasture, water extraction, or farming would be available.[66] Likewise, the project was considerably more feasible economically because these large numbers of destitute refugees could become an invaluable pool of "cheap" labor used to build the railroad.

Beyond the immediate need for labor, which, depending on the companies receiving land concessions, could have resorted to importing cheap labor from the Mediterranean or India, the dynamics put into place by so many refugees from Arabia meant an entirely new source of labor for not only European construction companies, but also Ottoman ones, emerged. As many of these refugees would have to "pay" for their right to use local water and lands, the interests of multiple actors in this period of transition were served by the new influx. Local landowners in particular were empowered as they gained new leverage. Such a redistribution of power ultimately compelled the agents of foreign financial interests and rival imperial states to solicit the assistance of these landowners in order to ensure that the region's land and human resources would be available for future capital-intensive development projects.

Perhaps the most adversely affected area by this massive influx of destitute peoples and the parallel struggle over concessions for the railroad was the port town of Kuwait. For one, it was the preferred terminus for any railroad from Europe.[67] As a result, the Sabah family, ruling the region in a loose alliance with the Ottomans for decades, was especially impacted by the larger geostrategic and demographic context of this European race to Baghdad. Caught in the middle, the family would find itself eventually torn apart. In this manner, conflict in Kuwait throughout the 1892 to 1899 period may offer future scholars yet another example of how local dynamics created by migrations, settlement arrangements, and opportunistic solicitations to outside patrons, contributes to our reinterpreting the political economy of modern imperialism.

At the heart of the growing strategic importance of Kuwait was the lucrative trade already being conducted through the free port. Of particular interest is the fact that large amounts of products from the major Indian Ocean ports eventually docked in Kuwait.[68] Such trade both supplied the larger hinterland with much coveted food, gold/silver, labor, and weapons, and permitted regional producers of pearls, baskets, and camel products to access the larger commercial world.[69] As a consequence, many initial surveys into possible destination/access points for proposed railroad projects calculated that Kuwait was the preferred end point.

By the 1890s, Kuwait and its immediate hinterland became a particularly complicated arena, posing new challenges to Ottoman authorities based in Hasa, Basra, and beyond. At the center of Ottoman concerns was that Russian and British provocateurs, commercial agents, and government representatives were animating local Kuwaiti and regional politics. In particular, it was the flow of weapons through Kuwait that often ended up in the hands of occasionally rebellious locals and/or migrants that became a particularly unwelcome development.[70] One of the consequences of this was a rapid shift in local power, ultimately pitting established commercial interests with links to Bombay (but not necessarily Britain) against a newly ascendant political elite that would divide the Sabah family and permanently place them in the middle of Great Power calculations.[71]

The turning point took place when power transferred to Shaykh Muhammad al-Sabah in 1892. As a result of this, a perceptible tension animated the internal affairs of the commercial and political elite of Kuwait.[72] In the course of the transition, the youngest of the promoted members of the ascendant family, Mubarak al-Sabah, suddenly thrust himself into the daily affairs of not only his family's operations, but those of crucial merchant allies as well. It seems that as a result, Mubarak succeeded in the initiation of new trade lines with hitherto excluded merchant interests, including British agents based in Bushire in Persia.[73] This new commercial arrangement created an increased flow of imported goods from a wide range of European-protected merchants, a development that challenged previous commercial monopolies in Kuwait.

All of this, in turn, created a perceptible transfer of economic power in the port city. The misuse of privileges accrued to the new "prince" immediately compromised well-established networks of trade and political patronage that also had links to Bombay commercial interests. As rivals to Mubarak's power maneuvered to use their connections in Bombay in order to squash him, the new escalation led to direct British involvement in Kuwait.

It is important to stress again at this point that such political calculations were all based on integrating refugees into the larger administrative, commercial, and political story. The entire Kuwaiti dynamic was predicated on controlling migrations that had intensified due to the on-going commercial transformations caused by Ottoman administrative advances in Baghdad and Basra, new access to land along the Euphrates, and paid labor opportunities. Peoples struggling to survive in drought-ridden Eastern Arabia—as well as fleeing political violence that in part manifested itself in the form of Wahhabi-driven persecutions of indigenous Shiite communities—sought Ottoman sanctuary.[74] The end result for these polities having to accommodate such flows of human migration was an internal power struggle that opened a window of opportunity for both outside powers and a number of local actors to become agents for change as they facilitated, or challenged, the ambitions of men like those around Mubarak.[75]

In the Balkans, this whole process was only exacerbated by the arrival in 1881 of European-backed debt commissions charged to operate as customs agents at the empire's major ports and border posts in order to harvest Ottoman trade revenues for the repayment of debt to European banks. The often frantic efforts by the Ottoman administration to cater to the demands of its outside creditors and the heavy-handed attempt by debt-collection operations invited far more instability as formal trade patterns were disrupted. In response to increased formal oversight of trade, as per the banks' demands, people attempted to circumvent regulatory mechanisms, expanding parallel trade networks as a result. Ironically, such local adaptations to heavy-handed regulations further frustrated the attempt by private finance to "penetrate" these regional economies.[76]

Indeed, it seems the conditions that had wrought so much violent opposition to Ottoman government in 1878 during the first phase of refugee settlement did not fully subside in the subsequent decades. The same district of Gjakova/Yakova that, as noted earlier, had led to the spectacular murder of an imperial delegation (and patriarch of a leading local family) in 1878 continued to crack at the edges due to lingering issues with refugees. One example of this upsurge in violence in Gjakova was an otherwise generic family feud that quickly devolved into a larger community rivalry that took on the dynamics of Catholic on Muslim violence. As the local *mutassarif* of Gjakova, Şakir Pasha tried to pacify members of the warring families by using both coercion and money, the combination of bribes and threats backfired. The attempt to essentially bribe a select group of local Catholic Albanians (who were actually refugees from mountainous lands ceded to Montenegro in 1878) not only hoped to address a lingering "sectarian" tinderbox, but also to reintegrate these refugees into the state's graces. The problem was the inducements included giving these refugee families more land, which rubbed indigenous families the wrong way.

For two Albanian Muslims, Süleyman Batushi and Luca Babi, representing a newly created committee of aggrieved locals, the transfer of their community's land to these Catholic refugees duplicated the mistakes of the state 20 years earlier. These Catholic refugee families had been apparently already compensated in the 1870s with portions of this host community's forests and pasture. Such lingering issues (and pent-up resentments) over land highlights the dangers of simply interpreting the violence as either a clash between Christians and Muslims, or a local "nationalist" hostility toward the Ottoman Empire. In fact, considering what has been discussed throughout this chapter regarding the impact of refugees, the confrontation with the Ottoman official Şakir Pasha speaks to lingering frustrations over earlier dispossession and reallocation of communal land.[77]

In the end, the state's ability to distribute land to certain targeted allies, local or foreign, offers the historian an important angle of analysis generally missed by the story heavily focused on Ottoman economic marginalization and systemic collapse. Another problem for the Balkans was that by 1896, even as a global economic depression had ended, suddenly changing weather patterns created new sources of instability.[78] After the Berlin Congress, for instance, shepherds were restricted to surviving within artificially designated spaces that were occasionally impacted by drought. In the past, the impact of drought could be mediated by taking flocks to other pasture areas; but since Berlin, these areas had been awarded to Austria-Hungary, Serbia, or Montenegro.[79] This made common winter pasture harder to find.[80] Soon the overuse of grazing lands put greater pressure on shepherds to push the limits of state boundaries. Meanwhile, crop production also dropped dramatically in the drought of 1895–8. With greater economic hardship, "traditional" practices, such as raiding, increased to compensate for depleted flocks and lost revenue. As a result, the Albanian (and increasingly Slavic Herzegovinian) populations living on either side of the post-1878 militarized boundaries began to accuse each other of stealing herds of sheep, provoking armed clashes that drew in both the Montenegrin and Ottoman forces.[81]

The subsequent tensions between dispersed communities developed a new urgency in the larger world. In their war with a Koumoudouros-led Greece in 1897, for example, the Ottomans had to deal with growing efforts by outside powers to directly encourage Ottoman subjects living along the contested border zones to disrupt life behind "enemy lines."[82] These calculated upheavals were only intensified by the new pressures put on owners and operators of the highly productive lands in what is now considered Macedonia/Kosovo. As in Mesopotamia, while rail lines plotted and construction initiated new value to these lands, the politics of provisioning the "tinderbox" that was "always" the Balkans animated a kind of refugee agency that continued to shape local relations for decades after "settlement." The crucial factor, however, was not sectarianism. It was the investment in new uses for violence among seemingly endless supplies of local proxies that reflect a Euro-American bankers' gambit to expropriate valuable lands from Ottoman sovereignty.[83]

As already seen in the previous chapter, one of the most important consequences of the sporadic outbreaks of violence was the growing latitude of the British, Austro-Hungarians, Italians, Russian, and French foreign ministries vis-à-vis direct intervention into the affairs of the Ottoman state. The Russians in particular played a destructive role by stressing the sectarian nature of violence in the Balkans, the solution to which—they and a large number of nationalist ideologues claimed—lay in the wholesale separation of "endemically" hostile communities. As a result, many locals recognized the potential for lucrative outside patronage and developed strategies to secure the latter by claiming persecution along ethno-national lines.[84]

In face of territorial redefinition and shifting opportunities for patronage, the inhabitants of these now openly contested districts recognized and then exploited the mechanisms of state seeking to establish order apparently driving imperial policies (policies that consistently tried to balance individual state interests against the fear of rampant violence). The range of possibilities presented to the local actor in face of the modern empire's attempts at reform was in many ways expanded as the state system manifested in the Berlin Treaty transformed how the Ottomans and their rivals organized the world. The period after 1878 is therefore particularly useful to thinking how boundaries, as applied in geographical as well as sociological terms, became key instruments of change for not only the state's centralization strategies, but locals as well.

The state, in other words, developed institutionally as a response to local instability. This dramatically changes how we study "reform" in the Ottoman case specifically; and I would suggest it also challenges the popular trends to link these new laws to a "will to improve" as suggested first by Michel Foucault and later developed by James C. Scott.[85] This means that the state was often compelled to use one community's resources to placate another's rebellion, a policy that created the conditions after 1900 for an endless spiral of violence, disgruntlement, and instability. Today, scholars fixated on finding the roots of the post-Ottoman nation in the violence revealed here often assert this all was a result of ethno-national tensions, simply mirroring the logic imposed at the time by various interests that something "natural" was behind violence between irreconcilably "different" peoples. We should resist the temptation to reduce complicated, diverse, and ever-shifting conflicts between many different stakeholders to be a product of primordial ethnic ambitions. This is especially important because an entire revolution in 1908, one that originated from the actions, of at most, several hundred men quickly proved very popular across all sectarian, regional, and class lines.

What was crucial to the peoples of the Ottoman Empire facing some apparent signs of fragmentation was the promises that the CUP could make to the citizens of the empire for a new form of government that advocated "freedom," "progress," and more importantly, "union."[86] In light of such popularity, the mantra of "Freedom, Unity and Progress" must be appreciated as values embraced by many Ottoman citizens prior to the 1908 revolution, a collective sensibility that may require revisiting events in the entire 1878–1908 period.[87] And yet, the apparent euphoria over the toppling of the Hamidian regime was coupled with the declaration of Bulgaria's formal independence (along with attempts to grab large parts of Eastern Rumeli, and the formal annexation of Bosnia and Herzegovina by the Habsburgs).

Amid these rapidly changing events were subsequent bursts of panic within the newly minted government. The new leaders of the empire also faced resistance from many entrenched members of the Ottoman regional elite, including those controlling areas discussed at length in this chapter. As suggested, the influx of *Niš muhacir* in the immediate aftermath of the Russo-Ottoman war of 1877–8 divided Kosovar society, pitting regime loyalists against politically active refugees. These landed elite, who had long resented the concessions the state was compelled to grant refugees, nevertheless recognized the Hamidian regime as their protector, if for no other reason than that it had helped deal with the challenges refugee constituencies posed to their long-term survival. The arrival of the CUP at the turn-of-the-century, bursting with ideological ambiguity, gave new impetus to those advocating the break-up of big land holdings belonging to the "conservative elite." The result was a divided political class for years to come.

Albanian/Bosnian/Chechen/Muhacir Ottomans were heavily represented on both sides of this struggle for power within Istanbul's inner circles. Indeed, the face-off between Bosnian and Chechen refugees on one side, and *Niš muhacir* on the other, is perhaps most emblematic of the schizophrenic condition of the political elite by 1909. While prominent local gangsters like Isa Boletini and General Şemsi Pasha, the Albanian commander of the Mitrovica garrison, with their Gheg Albanian volunteers tried to come to the rescue of their Sultan during the early days of the revolution, the fateful confrontation at the Ferizaj (Firzovik) railhead with upwards of 20,000 Kosovar Albanian "unionists" forever transformed the Balkans.[88]

The conservative elements of Ottoman Kosovo who were caught by surprise by the CUP coup of 1908, along with Isa Boletini, would soon have their revenge. Those intermittent rebellions in the areas under the control of conservative forces throughout Kosovo and Işkodra tried to resist in the hope of regaining power. This would be a struggle between "Albanians" long misappropriated in the post-Ottoman scholarship as nationalists, and those who continued to support the CUP, including many *Niš muhacir* community leaders. Not surprisingly, within months of the ascension of the new regime, Boletini found himself leading a politically complicated rebellion against this new Young Turk government. Unfortunately for him, the local revolts that he directed translated into massive countermeasures that broadened into state repression, violence, and, ultimately, political confusion for all the inhabitants of the western Balkans.

One of the ways this Balkan tension manifested in Istanbul was the attempt by largely Albanian troops in March 1909 to retake the halls of power on behalf of the Sultan's regime. The resulting counter-coups and garrison revolts in Istanbul constantly threatened the CUP government. While the broken Ottoman army was a problem, it was the defections from within by liberal "unionists" that marked the end of the "revolution."[89] As the regime took a more authoritarian turn making matters even worse for the increasingly shrinking "inner circle" of leaders, the ability of the state to provision the needy subjects were compromised.[90]

Part of the problem was Istanbul's elite could no longer trust Balkan intermediaries, once the chief ideologues of Ottomanism. Speculations circulated the empire that Bulgaria and Serbia were scheming to form a union to maximize their common interests in arresting Austrian expansion in the southern Balkans, dividing up Kosovo/Macedonia in the process.[91] This made the CUP government and its regional allies less capable of finding a "middle ground" to recreate a non-sectarian, ecumenical political space in parts of the Ottoman Balkans where fears of foreign-induced violence continued to shape local politics. The problem thus became something like a vicious circle. The more the CUP grew paranoid of lingering "pro-Hamidian" forces among the landowning classes in Kosovo, the more their distrust manifested in harsh police actions, actions that only assured more local rebellion.

By early 1910, the active encouragement, if not outright arming, of these dedicated and borderline opponents of the CUP government by neighboring states made the situation intractable. Ironically, the very identity politics the CUP and its supporters hoped to eradicate became the only recourse for opponents of the regime as it faced new forms of foreign interference. By 1910, the CUP, having survived several coups and numerous defections, became a violent, repressive regime, with an entirely different ideological centering, one that now invested in the state to forcefully transform a generic "society" as an object of scientific policy, rather than accommodation earlier promoted on the morning after the revolution in 1908.

Conclusion

The heavy-handed approach often taken to resolve local disputes over land use as refugees flooded the empire resulted in a new era of political consciousness in the Balkans. Such transformations in group interests helped set the tone for the "Young Turk" revolution of 1908, and what have retroactively been called the "nationalist" uprisings that followed.[92] One of the more glaring examples of how European-imposed reforms helped reconstitute local power in violent ways was the creation of "security" units, often linked to gendarmerie under the command of appointed European "advisors." While intended to have these units serve the "races" from which the troops came, these now armed men quickly became politically independent from the communities they were recruited to serve. This marked a dramatic change from how the Ottomans maintained security in the past.

Perhaps by design, the formation of gendarmeries instituted a competitive dynamic by actively taking away the responsibility of key landowning partners—both Christian and Muslim—to maintain order. As a result, the new local heads of the gendarmerie, given wide responsibilities by outside powers to keep "order," now had the incentive to extend into the former privileges of the landed elite to institute a new power dynamic. From this perspective, many community leaders from 1903 onward saw themselves at odds with what the Ottoman state was expected to do to reform the empire.[93]

The Young Turks found allies among these many disgruntled, often brutalized, communities. Such alliances between a "Westernized" segment of Ottoman elite society and locals outraged by the chaos European intervention brought to their homeland transformed the struggle over the way in which a new constitution could service the state by promoting an idealized "Ottoman" esprit. Equal citizenship in the empire for Muslims and non-Muslims alike meant that many claimants to leadership would have to address the demand for a stern hand as the Ottoman state wanted to assure that future interventions by Europeans would not be possible.

As these future allies of the CUP proved among the most hostile to Austrian and Russian reform programs discussed at length in the introduction of this book, a crucial decision by the Germans in particular to push for partition along these lines came to reflect a strategic turn vis-à-vis the Balkans.[94] What finalized the process of permanent alienation that upset refugee polities in the Balkans was the emergence of new kinds of constituencies. For all those invested in a process of political rent-seeking, as much as they had to demonstrate some identifiable loyalty to a cause, they also proved to be ideologically agile. As revealed in subsequent chapters, men historically vital to the Albanian, Armenian, Bulgarian, and various Arab national stories, often embraced opportunities that would be considered sacrilegious to future nationalist narratives.[95] In as much as these "ethnic entrepreneurs" acted in "contradictory" ways, the fact they also weaved in and out of playing formal governmental roles within the Ottoman context, meant the trajectory of continued state centralization (read modernization or Westernization) itself was inconsistent, multifarious, and internally contradictory. To refugees of different colorations, this constituted an instability bordering on collapse. As Zürcher explains most clearly in his numerous studies of the future ruling elite of a post-Ottoman, Young-Turk regime, the fact that so many of the key players in World War I and beyond were themselves of refugee origin may have contributed to the way in which they committed to certain brutal actions toward those threatening the security of the state during the war.[96]

Considering the enclaves of dislocation discussed in this chapter, and their strategic value to both imperial states and various constituent groups living through the last 40 years of empire, the intensity of the trauma of being a refugee exponentially grew with each new wave of intrigue. In time, state policies often stimulated the barometer of human suffering as policies of patronage translated into manipulative calculations linking individual and group pain to power. However, these sudden deviations in ethical governance debilitated neither Ottoman subjects nor outsiders. Often, enterprising groups exploited the value state authorities put into controlling violence, thus positioning their ability to start or stop violence as something outside interests can "rent" just like other services necessarily at work in refugee-infested environments, including supplying food and shelter. The kind of patronage networks that often resulted allowed many refugees inside the Ottoman world to survive the horrors of the era.

Without patronage, some aspiring refugee leaders could not produce the desired results for their constituents, resulting in their historical obsolescence. The fact that they failed does not mean, however, we should not consider the challenges facing them. Clearly the reforms introduced during this period created the conditions on the ground for a new series of local power struggles. Those who failed had just as much an impact on the effectiveness of Ottoman officials and their local counterparts as the new leaders who emerged; this fact created a dramatic and painful period of intra-communal strife. The often-overshadowed local battles for ascendancy, no matter how marginal to the larger scope of Ottoman bureaucratic gaze, ultimately reflected the full range of new possibilities of power present at this time of transformation. They also created conditions that ultimately broke down old or recently established social hierarchies and created new ones.

This was especially evident in the eastern and southern Macedonian zones of conflict, this time pitting Bulgarian, Albanian, Muslim, and Greek claimants against each other.[97] The subsequent interactions opened new calculations for aspiring irredentist politicians. The same applied to interest groups who identified an opportunity to conduct lucrative land grabs of much of what remained the Ottoman Balkans after Bulgaria's formal independence of 1909 and Austria's annexation of Bosnia and Herzegovina in 1908.

The plunder would only continue after the 1912–13 Balkan wars. The short-interim period before the larger European powers were dragged into the fray over a disintegrating Ottoman Empire. The signs were already there when Ottoman armies were able to roll back in 1913, to an extent, early Bulgarian and Greek victories in 1912, recapturing Edirne which nevertheless produced a new wave of refugees from the Balkans to Anatolia. The empire's entire Anatolian infrastructure was mobilized to move peoples back and forth, strategically agreeing with Greece to begin the "repatriation" of "ethnic groups" left on the other side of agreed-upon borders. The manner in which so many tens of thousands of Albanians, Pomaks, and Bosnians were shipped off into the strategic borderlands of Eastern Anatolia would leave many facing hostile local Armenian and Kurdish communities, whose own traumas of war included so many of their men conscripted (and perhaps dead or maimed). Added to the tensions was the immediate efforts by the Balkan refugees to self-organize, feeling entirely alienated in an utterly foreign land. The stage was set for numerous desperate acts of self-preservation and opportunism.

But before the horrors of World War I began the working model for all social engineering plans going forward had been negotiated in the 1913 Treaty of Bucharest that basically expelled the Ottoman Empire from the Balkans and put Balkan Muslims (and Catholics) in a precarious situation as neighboring states began to adopt new forms of population politics. All the states involved shifted policies dealing with Muslim "minorities" often starting to physically remove them on the basis of predetermined expendable demographic categories. While both Italy and Austria had their strategic reasons to demand that Albania (save Kosovo and Macedonia, consisting of more than half of Albanian-speakers in the Balkans and by 1912, entirely occupied by Serbia and Bulgaria) be granted independence, the primary strategy for Serbia, Greece, and Montenegro was to institute harsh measures to assure Albanian Muslim flight toward Anatolia. In the Aegean, the policies were based on the same operating principle that "minorities" were better off leaving. The massive scale of these calculations did not permit these projects to fully implement the stated goals in time prior to World War I.

Such unstable (but productive) situations help us better appreciate the kind of considerations at play for both state officers, who could easily see the limits of their influence, and local parties constantly repositioning themselves to maximize their security vis-à-vis local rivals and accentuate their leverage over the state. When these precarious balances of power, often negotiated after considerable violence, fell apart, as clearly happened in the last years of Ottoman rule throughout the Eastern Mediterranean/Arabian Peninsula, no single formula of social engineering patchwork, coercion, or economic corruption could suffice. In the next chapter we will turn to understanding the implications of this destabilization and the desperate efforts to re-establish order in the larger Eastern Mediterranean world.

Traveling the Contours of an Ottoman Proximate World

Introduction

The situation was such in the post-1878 Ottoman Empire that for a significant number of its citizens, the best way to initiate new kinds of exchange was from the dynamic settings outside the immediate reach of the state. In this chapter, instead of considering the unstable spaces within the confines of the Ottoman Empire, the focus will be on refugee zones of "exile" in bordering territories. As argued below, these fringe spaces consisting of recently formed independent states—the principalities/kingdoms of Serbia, Montenegro, Romania, and Greece—were populated by intermediaries who thrived (out of necessity) by being *first* Ottomans, and then members of the assortment of other sociopolitical associations made possible in the era. As developed below, all these borderline Ottomans operated as intermediaries in processes of epochal transformation that favored those who adapted to a constant flow of human, ideological, and material capital. More still, it was those who could mediate the emerging politics of "identity" as they constantly changed that succeeded in securing a place in the often violent, always dynamic transitional imperial world.

While I have already suggested in Chapter 2 that we cannot think of the rebellious guerrilla units—*çete/hajduks/komitadji*—who traversed these territorial boundaries of Ottoman/post-Ottoman societies in absolute terms, we must also guard against thinking of them or their periodic enemy "Young Turks" as having monopolized the political horizons of everyone living in the period. Perceived as such, the Ottoman refugee experience in the immediate, still highly contentious confines of domestic Ottoman politics, can offer a new set of issues to discuss within, what I will term a *proximate* context, how various levels of power are transformed.

What I mean by this rather inelegant phrase *Ottoman proximate* is that many refugees sat far enough away from the reach of the immediate effects of events in the homeland to have enjoyed different opportunities than their counterparts compelled to adjust to transformations within the empire. Sitting along the territorial peripheries of the Ottoman Empire, therefore, did not mean isolation. On many occasions, they constituted spaces of conjuncture that ultimately shaped the very dynamics of the modern world by the fact they directly influenced events inside the empire.

What is crucial to recognize about these spaces is that they were *near* enough that they presented expanded opportunities to straddle otherwise sharp divides shaping the lives of Ottoman refugees. As demonstrated below, many in neighboring Romania, Bulgaria, Serbia, Greece, Egypt, and other *proximate* Ottoman spaces played both domestic Ottoman roles and/or became major actors in their new post-Ottoman contexts. In this way, an analysis from an *Ottoman proximate* perspective challenges some of the prevailing notions of "diasporic" experiences that, in the larger scholarship, rarely consider Ottoman cases. In addition, refugee experiences in an *Ottoman proximate* constituted a geographic space that cannot be limited to retrospective geopolitical orientations.

The refugees discussed in this chapter thus integrate "Europe" with the "East," combining events in Geneva and Paris (where the future ascendant political elite of the post-1908 Ottoman Empire hashed out their scheme to wrestle power from loyalists surrounding the Sultan) with those refugees in Cairo, Sofia, and Bucharest, creating interconnected centers of refugee (diaspora) action. Indeed many of the prominent members of the CUP opposition in exile, as much as the proto-nationalist Armenian, Kurdish, Arab, Albanian, and Macedonian groups found throughout these areas (see Figure 3.1), prove to be paradigmatic examples of the itinerate Ottoman subject/actor weaving through various tiers of sociopolitical opportunities otherwise closed off by conventional studies of the refugee/exile and diaspora. Out of necessity, the domestic organization of anti-regime parties during the 1878–1912 period had important international links and vice-versa.[1] As observed below, for the historian, studying the activities of such agents of diasporic flux—that is people living in an unfixed geographic, ideological, and political orientation—necessarily (and productively) blurs the lines of distinction enforcing a European/Ottoman divide in the scholarship. To challenge this Euro-centric divide and then frame it as a historical dynamic, however, one must first deconstruct and reassemble the analytic value of the diasporic experience in a hitherto neglected *Ottoman proximate* context.[2]

Retaining the Ottoman in exile outside the diaspora

This first section will introduce a new set of parameters to think about Ottoman exile. These parameters will complicate the way we can position the experience of the Ottoman refugee in the larger scholarship on diasporas. In this respect, we aim to undermine the impression left by previous scholarship that the experiences of exile are adequately defined by the way we retrospectively identify/compartmentalize Ottoman exiles of multiple ethno-national, sectarian, and ideological associations. This place of exile is, in other words, far from being the stable space often logically attached to a "diaspora" with links to future nation-states.[3]

Considering the "fluid" environments in the *proximate* Ottoman refugee space, the best studies to date have reported frequently on ideological fissures that often confused the ethno-national orientations of diasporic communities. However, even

Kujtim nga Shqypënija   Mirash Luca me Shokë — Kastrat

Figure 3.1 Group of roaming guerrillas/occasional state ally.

the better studies of Ottoman exile experiences stubbornly resort to interpreting social conditions as if they were neatly excised from the "host" environment. Approached like this, the story of the Ottoman exile is told only in terms of its significance to the (post-) Ottoman context—a context that is itself external to the domestic politics of host societies. As a corrective, we must more purposefully consider integrating the Ottoman diaspora(s) in its host context(s), as well as remember that neither refugee nor host communities in the late-Ottoman world existed merely as precursors to post-Ottoman nation-states. Put in terms perhaps most useful to historians of the first half of the twentieth century, links maintained by refugee communities to their homeland—or even tertiary geographies yet to be discovered, such as in the Americas or Southeast Asia—coupled with their efforts to assimilate into host communities, represent the persistence of something akin to Ottoman identity just as much as transition to a post-Ottoman world.

Recall that for those leaving the Ottoman Empire who wished still to engage in domestic politics, it was crucial to remain close by, preferably in neighboring countries. This was especially true for politically active, often well-connected Ottoman subjects who viewed the periodic break-downs in domestic political order as opportunities to reload lingering, perhaps temporarily suppressed/persecuted operating models for long-term Ottoman survival. In this manner, members of the opposition to the Hamidian regime often lived an existence in which, neither ideological sympathy nor popular notoriety offered them a chance to realize their ambitions to change the Ottoman Empire for the better. Their ventures to change needed, rather, the space of exile in adjacent polities, not as a point from which to attack the Ottoman order, but to reform it.[4]

By focusing on politically active émigrés/refugees we can reinforce the underlying assertions made throughout this book that possibilities in the era of transition were mediated by a number of contradictory forces. This multiplicity of social, political, and economic factors contributing to the experience of exile thus logically makes it hard to argue that Ottoman refugees constitute a verifiable "community" with neatly defined interests. In this respect, my assertions run contrary to a literature that assumes that populations living as refugees, especially in the exile/diaspora space, possess a consciousness that heightens, if not "invents," modern notions of "homeland" that approximate those of the post-Ottoman world that many of us live in today.[5]

It is not clear, for example, how a self-identified Albanian-Ottoman activist in Bucharest, who may publish proto-nationalist newspapers and books, could ever claim to speak for probably more than 50,000 other Albanian migrants in Romania.[6] Unhelpfully, it is simply accepted in much of the scholarship that the newspapers published by organizations throughout the Balkans and larger Europe and the Middle East reflect the dynamism of the *Rum* Orthodox, Vlach, Armenian, Turkish, Kurdish, Albanian, Arab, and/or Ladino Jewish communities. On the contrary, most peripatetic Ottomans were simply not interested in participating in such politically active groups. Indeed, in Romania, Bulgaria, Egypt, or larger Europe, such organizations never enjoyed a membership of more than a few hundred people.[7]

The actual distinctions within these "diaspora" groups thus require closer analysis as dispersed, often openly hostile, rival communities. For example, a majority of Albanian-Ottoman activists residing in Romania, Bulgaria, and Egypt actually came from the Korçë region in what is today south-eastern Albania. This constitutes a (sub) regional orientation among members of the most active proto-nationalist groups that helps explain why those exile/refugee communities created in such *Ottoman proximate* contexts should never be treated as monoliths.[8] In other words, Albanian Ottomans living in exile simply did not coalesce around "Albanian" associations. As such, we must rethink how we study Ottoman refugee communities, choosing to focus more on smaller units that link members along criteria such as home region, village, economic trade, or at times religious association (especially among members of different Sufi orders/*tekke*). It was these decidedly sub-national loyalties that determined toward whom newly arrived Albanian-speaking Ottoman refugees gravitated in places like Romania, Bulgaria, Greece, and Egypt.[9] Therefore, more than simply undermining the fiction of refugees seeking to liberate their uncomplicated, socially uniform, ethnically pure homeland, we need to contextualize the migrants in their new social, political, and economic surroundings. One way we accomplish this contextualization is by moving beyond the translation of "ethnic minority" texts published in newspapers to the realization that the very space in which refugees operated was also far from settled, be it ideologically or demographically.

Another angle is the manner in which refugees and migrants more generally interacted with their hosts. Peoples who later in the twentieth century were more narrowly defined as Albanians, Greeks, Armenians, Yemeni, or Jews in exile, could and did become active agents in their Romanian, Egyptian, or Bulgarian host societies. In fact, the refugees' involvement in these countries' affairs may have shaped the hosts' state-building trajectories as much as those of their presumed homelands. In other words, there is a far more complicated, diverse, and consciously assimilationist process taking place that ultimately blurs the lines of distinction between natives (of what later became independent countries subsumed by the nationalist meta-narrative) and émigrés from the Ottoman Empire.[10]

The Balkan crisis in a refugee/diasporic context: Romania and Bulgaria

Romania

Much as within the Ottoman Empire, how refugees socialize in places like Bucharest, Sofia, or Cairo without police harassment—or to benefit from host government support—could mean the difference between playing on the margins of newly forming political life and establishing an organization with the potential for exerting influence. Most useful for this contrarian analysis of diasporic agency is the study of those efforts that were intended to expand individual or group civic participation in the immediate host context. In other words, many Tosk Albanian, Vlach (Aromanian), Anatolian Greek, North African, Armenian, and Yemeni refugees actually strived to assimilate into, and then actively engage with, the immediate communities within which they settled in Egypt, Romania, Serbia, and Bulgaria. Often, these host societies were far less hostile to integrating the dynamic Ottoman world that still existed around them than later assumed.

Of course, these were processes mediated by the changing domestic politics in these host countries. As such, there was simply no uniform experience in exile. In Romania, for instance, the situation was highly charged by the fact that the new state had to juggle the disparate groups left from the receding Ottoman administration. Romania's still ill-defined national spaces (at once challenged by Ottoman loyalists, an ever-aggressive Russian Empire to the northeast, and irredentist claims from Bulgaria and Serbia) challenged the process of "imagining" a Romanian sociopolitical identity and the role Vlach and Tosk Albanian refugees would play.

Seeing an opportunity to both assimilate large numbers of culturally marginal members of a now sizable "Ottoman" diaspora and extend influence deep into still contested Ottoman Balkan territories, the political and cultural elite in Bucharest invested resources on the Vlach, Tosk Albanian, and Tatar populations settled throughout Romania.[11] Through these Ottoman migrants, the Romanian nation-builders could, at the same time, strenuously oppose the Istanbul-based *Rum* Orthodox Church's hegemonic ambitions.[12] In this respect, the mostly Orthodox Christian Vlachs and Tosk Albanians residing in Romania simultaneously contributed to a struggle against the authoritarian *Rum* Patriarchate, as well as the threats to Romanian sovereignty coming from irredentist Hellenism and Pan-Slavism.[13]

Such cooperative activities extended to anti-Hamidian groups emerging in Romania (and Bulgaria) since the 1880s. Perhaps the most important case was the operations of the anti-regime CUP, directed from various cities in Romania, an *Ottoman proximate* locale for one of the party's founders, Ohrid-born Ibrahim Temo.[14] And yet, while Romania hosted competing political organizations whose primary orientations were geared toward influencing events within the Ottoman Empire, many also had a role to play in the government's efforts to unify disparate exile groups residing within certain Romanian contexts.

As a result of their long tradition of social and intellectual activism in such environments, many different Ottoman exile communities emerged throughout independent Romania.[15] As Bucharest was already a cosmopolitan city in which southern Albanians (Tosks) played an important role, social clubs and later schools increasingly opened with the financial support provided by the Romanian government and new refugees just beginning to settle there. In such settings, even exiles from entirely different parts of the larger Muslim world in Eurasia discovered opportunities for alliance in Romania. Research reveals, for example, that there was close collaboration between the Tosk Albanian leader of the CUP in Romania and the various Vlachs, Tatars, and Turks who settled there as exiles.[16]

These "colonies" in Romania (and to a lesser extent in Bulgaria) were for the most part derivations of older and considerably larger, richer and thus much better organized communities already established in cities like Bucharest, Constanţa, Brăila, Craiova, Călărşi, and Focşani when still under Ottoman rule. In fact, these foundations gave Ibrahim Temo and his early cohorts in the CUP an advantage over others.[17] Consequently, from the tumultuous 1875–8 period of war in the Balkans onwards, Bucharest, Dobruja, Constanţa in Romania, and later Sofia, Ruse, Vidin, and Plovdiv in Bulgaria, would be the destinations of choice for itinerate, self-consciously Ottoman exiles in search of a haven to pursue their oppositional political agendas.[18]

At the same time, however, every major language-group enjoyed considerable leeway to pursue the development of their distinctive cultural heritage. The numerous social clubs and newspapers that would soon emerge confirmed for many that Romania in particular was the center of, among others, Tosk Albanian cultural formation.[19] It would be a mistake, however, to interpret the operations of social clubs like *Drita*, as political monoliths.

Traditionally, the assumed "nationalist" activism associated with these clubs—newspapers, textbook publication, and schools—has been taken to imply that the "community" shared an agenda to develop a specifically Albanian nationalist consciousness as well as to advocate for an "Albanian" nation-state separate from the Ottoman Empire. On the contrary, the evidence suggests that in the pre-1908 Ottoman context these social clubs were supporting Ottoman unionist parties first. That is, they advocated for regional autonomy within a strengthened (and reformed, post-Hamidian) Ottoman state. In the particular case of the famous social club *Drita*, based in Bucharest, its leaders often communicated to the larger Ottoman diaspora via *Osmanli*, the publication of the CUP based in Geneva, to highlight their commitment to Ottoman union. To them, without a unified Balkans under Ottoman rule (or some other mega state), battles between rival interests would continuously tear at the seams of society, leaving the otherwise productive (and wealthy) homeland in a state of constant violence and social chaos.[20]

Crucially, at the same time as these emerging Tosk Albanian social clubs (and their Armenian, Arab, and Kurdish equivalents) aimed to overthrow a corrupt, reactionary regime in Istanbul, they appeared just as concerned with integrating with their host societies. In fact, their experiences as active participants in the cultural and economic life of newly independent Romania highlight the contested nature of life for exiles that often made it impossible for them to operate in the terms that modern historians believe are ubiquitous among nationalist separatists.[21] More often than not, the immediacy of host political considerations left these Albanian-Ottoman groups highly fragmented. Patronage from diverse constituencies both inside and outside of the Balkans, from foreign powers and, at times, the Ottoman state, served to increase factionalism within these diasporic groups.

This all resulted in confusion, and ultimately failure, with regard to attempts to unify disparate groups to pursue a common cause in the homeland. Paradoxically, the very fact that "Albanian" Ottoman refugees were so fragmented may suggest that the clubs emerging in this context actually were successfully representing a core constituency. In other words, while not a transcendent monolith, they did represent the interests of factions whose actions, rather than entire diasporas, prove the engines for change in such transitional periods. Indeed, these clubs actually reflected the idiosyncrasies of rival Tosk Albanian and *Rum* Orthodox clans which struggled over the considerable rewards available from free-spending outside patrons.[22]

The stakes grew as more money became available through fundraising in the Ottoman provinces, money that could be sent as transfers from branch offices of banks that had spread throughout the region. In other words, the changing role of "homeland" was in part reflected in the kind of money generated by clubs publishing newsletters that were then smuggled into the empire.[23] Conveying the right combination of things to the right audience could win big donations. Moreover, the greater the presence of a social club and its publications, the more likely a foreign official would send a report back to the foreign ministry of the Austrian-Hungarian or Italian states advocating support for what appeared an influential regional player.[24] In other words, a club gaining a reputation among European "intelligence" agencies for its influence over large numbers of Ottoman refugees could prove financially lucrative for its organizers.

Returning the focus to a diversity of communities in Romania and Bulgaria (as opposed to a monolithic "Albanian" or "Vlach" diaspora expected to reinforce the national teleology) helps strengthen this point. Prolific publishers of school textbooks and scientific material, for instance, seemingly fit the stereotype of Benedict Anderson's now ubiquitous thesis on a nationalism that is consolidated by attempts at standardizing language.[25] *Drita's* story, however, reflects a far more complicated set of issues that requires us to look beneath the veneer of its institutional order. Initially founded in 1884 by Anastas Avramidhin-Lakçen (someone who was as much Vlach and Romanian as Albanian) this social club actually functioned within a social and intellectual context that was far from organized along ethno-linguistic lines alone. In fact, every *Drita* publication appears to have been partially inspired by challenges from rival groups based both in Bucharest and beyond. Far from being "Albanian" therefore, *Drita* should be put into a larger Ottoman context that fused a multiplicity of Albanian identity politics with aims at strengthening the Ottoman Empire by way of reform.[26]

This argument is strengthened by the fact that *Drita's* opponents, each in their own way, pursued different agendas and found it necessary to challenge publically *Drita* because of its own success at raising funds.[27] In the final analysis then, it was *Drita's* "market share" that made it the target of enmity, and not necessarily its stake in some crucible of ethno-national consciousness.[28] The spoils of patronage also proved irresistible within *Drita,* and many of the same push-pull factors that created rival outside groups accounted for its internal divisions.[29]

In the end, Bucharest, Constanța, and Brăila proved to be refugee arenas infiltrated with the kind of class, cultural, and socioeconomic hierarchies found in any major European city at the time. Such socioeconomic divisions played a role in the way not only southern Albanians, but also many other Ottoman refugees ultimately organized politically outside their home regions. Recognizing that class, professional, and at times, cultural differences played a role in the way clubs like *Drita* recruited members and the form and content of the textbooks, newspapers, and novels they published, may prove the most important exercise in challenging academic conventions on Balkan nationalisms.[30]

The challenge for historians, therefore, is not to immediately ascribe "nationalist" motivations to groups like *Drita* in Romania or other *Ottoman proximate* contexts. Such groups' various agendas for the home regions, and for their Romania-based patronage, were not shared by every individual associated in some way to Albania. In eschewing this approach that only reads nationalism in the efforts of Ottoman diaspora groups, we allow for other possible concerns affecting refugee lives in Romania. Perhaps, as already suggested, various Ottoman diasporic materials were produced strictly to cater to local market demands.

There certainly was a large enough émigré population in Romania to justify publishing books that entertained as well as serviced a putative nationalistic need. In fact, it is clear from reading the content of many Albanian language books that the target audience was the local resident rather than Albanians residing back in the "homeland." Discussions about local cultural events, gossip about prominent Romanian politicians, and reports on seasonal trends in Romania's major cities hardly reflect a diaspora fixated on the homeland. Furthermore, considering these Albanian clubs were also populated by Vlachs means that, if they wanted to continue to enjoy the perks of living in their host countries, certain agendas that promoted ethnic and linguistic separatism were out of the question.[31]

It is revealing that luminaries of what retroactively would be called early Albanian nationalism rarely joined forces with other activists now long forgotten, many starting to move into Romania after the 1880s. In fact, they were often enemies. The nature of the animosity between leading Tosks and the latecomers quickly translated into such a clash of opinions that even a split within *Drita* emerged in May 1886. This split inside *Drita*, however, was not based on how members wanted to deal with regional differences alone. In Bucharest (and Sofia), the divisive issue would prove to be as much socioeconomic as political. The problem seems to have been that *Drita* had become a magnet for poorer laborers and artisans who flooded Romania after 1880, many of them seeking to establish themselves in their new host society for the long term. This influx of refugees upset many among the already established refugee communities in Romania.[32]

One possible explanation for such disruptions is that these refugees came from parts of the western Balkans that had hitherto no connection to Romania. As virtual strangers to the Tosk-dominated Bucharest scene, the refugees of rural background represented cultural differences too objectionable for many city-dwellers having to accommodate them. Not only were they seen as "backward" by many of the already established Francophile Tosk Albanians and Vlachs in Romania, but these refugees, already poor farmers back home, flooded well-established environments with a poverty that many felt unbecoming for educated members of these emerging communities.[33] More important to the larger Romanian context, the influx of skilled but desperate refugees inevitably put downward pressures on wages in Romania, a serious problem that threatened the balance maintained in the region. With the exception of an important faction within *Drita*, namely that gravitating around Nikolla Naço, who would be elected chairman of *Drita* as more and more refugees joined the party, most established members of the Bucharest-based diaspora shunned the newly arrived, mostly poor, and uneducated refugees.[34] As a result of the growing schism between the "new" migrants and the older, more established ones, the party split.

The defecting faction, which would later call itself *Dituria*, had much stronger links to wealthy Tosks, many of whom, like Ismail Qemali (Ismail Kemal), had also demonstrated strong political ties to Greece and Serbia, the very countries expelling those potential "Albanians" who were settling in Romania (and Bulgaria) by the tens of thousands.[35] The conflict of interest between more conservative elements of the traditional Ottoman Tosk Albanian diaspora in Romania and those wishing to accommodate the new arrivals did not stop at the organizational level. Even Sami Frashëri, the quintessential post-Ottoman era national hero, openly supported *Dituria* when it was initially formed.[36] This cost the populist (and perhaps a "nationalist" in our current sense of the term) Nikolla Naço political leverage in Romania and thereby significantly weakened *Drita*'s long-term credibility.[37] While in the end there may be any number of explanations for this split, it is important to note that Naço stood up on behalf of the new refugees while those who are celebrated today as Albanian nationalists years later did not.[38]

Bulgaria

The struggle for influence in Bucharest spilled over into neighboring Balkan states. In the wake of the turmoil in Bucharest, for example, Bulgaria became the next battleground for the rivals in Romania. In 1901 immigrants based in Sofia formed a society called *Dëshira* (the wish) in direct collaboration with the now thriving *Dituria* faction from Bucharest. The emergence of *Dëshira* of course should not be read as the sole source for understanding the overall sentiments of Albanians in Bulgaria. Indeed, the presence of any organization should not be read as universally accepted. This is especially important to point out regarding Macedonian activists based in Bulgaria during this period. While these competing groups' role in the increasing violence in the region has long attracted the attention of scholars as the quintessential nationalist struggle during the late Ottoman era, as with the Albanian cases discussed above, a great deal more was going on than attempting to overthrow the Ottoman state.

The Macedonian-diaspora in Bulgaria in fact consisted of a host of different "ethnicities" and political agendas. This complex demographic reality conditioned the emergence of various organized opposition movements—at times explicitly violent in their strategy—such as the Internal Macedonian Revolutionary Organization (IMRO), in and around Sofia. Additionally—making the network of political, ideological, and "ethnic" affiliations even more complex—members of the IMRO found common ground with Armenians, Albanians, and Turks within the emerging CUP, who, fleeing violence in Macedonia and Anatolia, also became "internal" refugees in the tributary principality of Bulgaria. These groups—often with the aid of competing Bulgarian political parties—interacted in a number of Bulgarian cities, each forming autonomous, and to some extent opposing, "revolutionary" cadres.[39] The nature of their competition reflected the fact that each struggled to find patronage essential to maintain operations, preserve positive relations with local police forces, and preserve the ability to pass on funds to clients in the "occupied" homeland.

The conscious effort to create a relatively safe arena for a variety of potentially valuable allies opposed to the Ottoman state offered many refugees the opportunity to interact. Perhaps most spectacularly, such interactions led to IMRO units actually collaborating at times with elements of Armenian Revolutionaries fleeing to Bulgaria after the 1890s.[40] In this regard, individuals representing, for example, the *Dashnaktsutiun* or Armenian Revolutionary Federation (ARF) and IMRO identified mutually useful interests with their native Balkan counterparts, at least insofar as they all opposed the Hamidian regime at the time.[41] The key here was the setting in which these groups interacted, one of an ideological underworld that until 1908, also saw the development of actively violent factions within the future CUP.[42]

That the CUP was itself multiethnic may help us reconsider the actual points of emphasis in regard to the collaborative attempts between refugee groups that appeared to strive on behalf of conflicting agendas. In Istanbul, Ottoman authorities often identified clandestine meetings between individuals who had no apparent common interests. As a result, the center of both the paranoid Ottoman government and outside interests' focus was the newly created associations, often still misunderstood in the Balkans as being nationalist. Many of these disparate groups relied on direct or indirect patronage from the outside powers, the Bulgarian government, or those influence-seeking operations based in Sofia.[43] The fact that these different groups were able to cooperate on occasion indicates that political objectives which often surpassed "national" or "ethnocentric" concerns did exist.[44]

On another level, such collaborations in Bulgaria between different groups may help explain the emergence of especially successful armed units who successfully smuggled an array of contraband into Ottoman territories. These goods included much needed weapons, anti-Hamidian printed materials, and even politically sensitive individuals the Ottoman state had deemed "criminals."[45] While it was always a dangerous activity, the fact these diverse Bulgarian and Macedonian groups were successful, especially with smuggling weapons, made them influential in a number of circles. For their part, it became obvious to both Ottoman officials and outside European observers that it was the growing IMRO *çete/komitaj* units whose notorious raids into Ottoman Macedonia using these weapons could, by targeting non-Bulgarian communities, instigate violent responses from their victims. Such destabilizing effects thus created tensions within previously harmonious/tolerant associations to the point that the "Macedonia Question" preoccupied European policy makers for years.

Of course the targeting of specific groups was a revolutionary tactic, akin to anarchists' use of bombs at the time. The consequences, on the surface, at least, did indeed instigate conflict. What is not always acknowledged, however, is the extent to which the resistance was predicated on collaboration across so-called ethno-national lines. Such alliances between exiled or internally displaced Albanians, Greeks, Armenians, Serbs, and Bulgarians prove crucial to understanding how such methods using violence eventually filter into many Ottoman, anti-regime groups like IMRO and CUP, both eager to hedge bets on across-the-board support against a common enemy.[46]

Again, perhaps the most intriguing developments in Bulgaria that helps flesh out this Ottoman refugee theme is the CUP (and Bulgarian nationalist) collaboration with Armenians. The presence in the Balkans of Armenians of various social classes most likely has a long history. As the Rumeli provinces required a particular quality of administrators, territories like Bulgaria, Thrace, and Macedonia long served as magnets for certain Ottoman-Armenian bureaucrats, bankers, and merchants who migrated from Western Anatolian hubs like Izmir/Smyrna and Istanbul. This may have been evident prior to the political tumult of the 1870s, with Ottoman default transforming the strategic importance of the Balkans to external powers and interests. But while there was an established Western Armenian presence in Bulgaria well before the 1870s, it was a series of revolts in Eastern Anatolia—the last of which ended in 1909—that led to perhaps thousands of Eastern Armenians seeking sanctuary in Bulgaria.

With this in mind, the question throughout is this: Just how much does the proven collaboration across different "ethno-national" lines change the way we understand the refugee space in these *Ottoman proximate* contexts? Drawing from the available scholarship it is safe to say that just as with Albanians and Macedonians, Ottoman Armenian refugees residing throughout Bulgarian towns struggled to find a place in these very different, but equally complex, sociocultural spaces.[47] What grabs our attention, however, was that part of the dynamism of the experience was, in fact, the sudden influx of radicalized Armenians fleeing the violence in Anatolia in the 1890s.[48]

Politically active Armenians based in Bulgaria quickly transformed with the influx of Eastern Armenians with experience organizing and fighting Ottoman forces. For example, it appears that Stepan Zorian (known by his *nom de guerre* Rosdom), one of the founders of the ARF in Bulgaria, quickly teamed up with the likes of Andranik Ozanian, a notorious guerrilla with a past in Eastern Anatolia.[49] This alliance was able to convince men of influence in Sofia to help finance joint operations with the likes of IMRO, a potential collaboration that immediately transformed how activists envisioned future strategies.[50] Crucially, this radicalization alienated many among the CUP hierarchy, especially those with axes to grind with an increasingly generic "Armenian" adversary in the larger "Great Power" struggle over access to the Persian Gulf by way of Persia and Transcaucasia.[51]

The growing ranks of well-trained (often by way of Russia) anti-regime activists also transformed the imagination of some Bulgarian politicians. The tandem of radicalized Armenian groups led by Andranik and Rosdom, for example, opened up new channels for Bulgarian state investment in violence in the Ottoman realm. Those promoting the use of new tactics in Ottoman Macedonia secured Bulgarian assistance to create training camps in which guerrilla units based in Bulgaria could receive the necessary skills to infiltrate Ottoman lands.[52] The collaboration expanded to also integrate these forces with the Bulgarian army after 1901. Crucial here, perhaps, was the deepening role, especially in the form of funds, of outside Armenian groups. This is especially the case with the Armenian Revolutionary Foundation, whose United States Central Committee in Boston contributed the lion's share of money to these entrepreneurial enterprises in the period leading up to the "Young Turk" revolution of 1908.[53]

Things got complicated, however. As we already learned in Chapters 1 and 2, violence in the Balkans became a very lucrative business. The transforming nature of conflict between some Armenian factions and the Ottoman Empire became a particularly attractive money-making opportunity for especially Eastern Armenians who could capitalize on the trust of locally based, Ottoman-Bulgarian-Armenian merchants. These relations fluctuated, however, depending on the larger situation in the Balkans. After the failed *Ilinden* uprising in 1903, for instance, the mood in Bulgaria was both energized and frustrated.[54] In this milieu the ARF organized a congress in Sofia, where delegates reached a formal decision to collaborate with IMRO, thus offering the erstwhile failed rebellion new blood. The central focus of this collaboration, at least for some entrepreneurs, was raising funds from those wealthy Armenian merchants long established in Bulgaria. Recall that Ottoman Armenians had for decades prior to the 1878 crisis lived in these regions of the Balkans, becoming quite wealthy (and thus largely resented by the local inhabitants). The manner in which money was raised from these Armenians produced new domestic political issues.

Due to the size of the Armenian merchant community in Bulgaria, especially in Sofia after 1885, the ugly turn of events in Anatolia, when the first of a series of massacres took place, proved a lucrative fundraising opportunity for a host of emerging activists. It seems that the heavy-handed, almost criminal methods used to shake down these wealthy merchants left many unhappy with the direction of the coalition forming just after the upsurge of violence in Anatolia. While the ARF seems to have expanded its operations largely on these extortionist methods of fundraising, they also infiltrated domestic Bulgarian politics. Far from gaining sympathy from Bulgarian officials after complaints about such threats from these fundraisers, the long-held resentments toward the old Ottoman Armenian merchant elite left them vulnerable to blackmail from all sides.[55]

It is not clear if such a relationship in the context of fighting the Abdülhamid II regime created new opportunities for CUP activists to bring some wealthy Armenians back into the Ottoman fold. What is clear is that these fissures within various Ottoman Armenian refugee communities make it difficult to generalize about their resistance to Istanbul over the next two decades. That being said, the destruction of the *Ottoman proximate* dynamic in Bulgaria did take place, reflecting the growing collaboration between Armenian radicals and the Bulgarian military. Such collaboration must not, however, be either assumed inevitable or immune to contradictions.

If Ottoman sources are right, by 1907, factions within the Bulgarian political elite were actively training dozens of Armenians to make, plant, and then detonate bombs inside Ottoman territories.[56] These training operations seemed to successfully link the talents of various newcomers from Russia sent specifically to teach the techniques of bomb use with those eager to mobilize young Armenians refugees residing in Bulgaria. Their combined efforts were, according to most accounts, ultimately geared to organizing military units that would engage the Ottoman regime throughout the Macedonia uprisings. Eventually, however, there were efforts to use these Armenians as distinctive units to fight alongside Bulgarian troops when needed. Indeed, in the Balkan War of 1912, some 230 actually did.[57]

Considering the connections between known bomb-making specialists who infiltrated Bulgaria and Ottoman Macedonia and the growth in the use of bombs in Macedonia after 1900, the fusion of different skillsets permitted a new kind of violence to emerge. This fusion also ultimately transformed the campaign that initially hoped to induce political change in a unified Ottoman society. This split would have had violent consequences once the CUP came to power in 1908.

Once violence employed against Muslims in Macedonia by Armenian/Bulgarian groups took place, it would serve as a motivating factor behind new forms of "population management" during World War I in Eastern Anatolia.[58] But focusing on these processes prior to 1908 as inevitable causal events leading to the violence of World War I skips a great deal still at work in the Ottoman refugee experience within the *proximate* space still revolving around a dynamic world in which the empire played a prominent role. Perhaps it is better to assume Ottoman émigrés, even in Bulgaria from 1878 onwards, first wanted to assimilate into their host societies.

Rather than privileging those "ethnic entrepreneurs" who purported to be representative of a larger, coherent "ethno-national" diaspora-led organizational dynamic, the operating assumption should be that it is not necessarily the case that individuals orient their lives in reference to idealized fictions of their former homes at the expense of fully integrating into their new social contexts. The diverse communities of migrants who moved beyond the immediate areas of conflict prove, just like their fellow refugees who continued to live in the Ottoman Empire, to be as much a part of their larger host society as being members of isolated, "exilic" enclaves. Indeed, these heterogeneous spaces were very much what Sami Zubaida termed "cognitive structures" that predated the mythologized, but still not consolidated, "location" of the ethno-national state in Bulgaria, Serbia, Greece, and Romania.[59]

The larger dynamic of a "politics of location" around issues like "Macedonia" in Serbian, Bulgarian, Ottoman, and Greek post-1878 settings reflects more the discursive chaos of transitional societies (without a teleological endpoint) that can really only be effectively analyzed by adopting a "cartography of the politics of intersectionality." Such an orientation can be laid out in productive ways by continuing with this theme of the *Ottoman proximate*. Moreover, this perspective may help us highlight further people's observed commonality as by-products of temporary exchanges within migrant/politically transitional spaces like Romania, Bulgaria, and, as we shall see below, Egypt in the 1870–1912 period, rather than merely assuming this commonality a priori.[60]

The multiplicity of refugee stories in the *Ottoman proximate* thus produces a broad range of constituent agents, often developing political and economic associations that completely undermine past attempts at fixing their activism in anachronistic nationalist terms. Here Stuart Hall's contributions to the understanding of these dynamics reveal a double vision that captures the complexities of any identity articulation within the context of exile.[61] This is all fleshed out in our case by historicizing various manifestations of individual/group association in transitional political environments like Bulgaria, while taking on entirely different significance in zones of exile like Egypt and Romania where the intrigues of patronage operated in a variety of geostrategic, socioeconomic, and ideological contexts.

Foreign government investment in Ottoman émigrés

Amid all of the politics within Bulgaria, Egypt, and Romania was a heavy investment in influencing the activism of Ottoman immigrant groups by foreign powers. The medium through which much of that activism took place was direct involvement by consular offices seeking out willing "representatives" to help mobilize their constituents. As such, any number of groups lurked in the shadows of of the Ottoman proximate, waiting to secure for themselves a role in extending an outside power's influence over events in the region.

In Romania, paradoxically, these interventions by foreign representatives were structured around the expectation that their clients represented cohesive diasporic communities—communities that supposedly took as an organizing principle some idealized version of national origin. But in reality, these locally based partners ended up exploiting rifts within communities to develop new, temporary cynergies of power and influence that often did little to help build a national polity. Italian politicians were especially successful with navigating these local political nuances. With large numbers of *Arbëresh* (Italian-Albanians) entering into the Italian government, they cultivated communal links without needing to rely solely on association with particular institutions, such as the Catholic Church. Unlike the Habsburg agents whose only point of contact was Catholicism, these Albanian-Italians could spread their influence through the culturally diverse western Balkans, making it possible for Italian interests to negotiate with Orthodox Christian and Muslim Albanians as well.[62] Aware of this thanks to the growing advisory role of *Arbëresh* inside the halls of Italian state power, the Italian Foreign Ministry supported prominent Tosk Albanians living in Rome in return for serving Rome as intermediaries in the Ottoman Balkans. Among the more active players in the period was Dervish Hima who became frustrated by the unrealized potential of the Bucharest communities. Learning from his Bucharest experiences, Hima would use his newly established base in Rome to initiate a particularly important period for both his small group of allies in the Ottoman diaspora and the Italian state.[63]

Using money supplied by the Italian Foreign Ministry, Hima began to mobilize different interests in Italy so as to bring order to an otherwise chaotic Balkan-Tosk Diaspora scattered throughout Europe. Hima appears to have been successful to an extent, convincing members of the Italian government to direct some resources to help his cadre of subordinates infiltrate and influence rival groups in Sofia and Bucharest.[64]

This desire to harness Tosk Albanians' potential was not lost on key regional activists, some who exploited the rival ambitions of outsiders to empower—enrich— themselves. Such opportunism did not always translate into productive collaboration, however, as noted in an open letter sent by the Vienna-based activist Mati Logoreci, to Dervish Hima's Rome newspaper, *Albania*.[65] Logoreci seemed sincere when he complained that prominent Tosks with strong connections throughout the non-Ottoman Balkans had done too little to include Northern Albanian (Geg) activists in their mobilization drives to influence domestic Ottoman affairs. It was as if most Tosks did not see Gegs living in the Kosovo and Shkodër provinces as close enough kin to warrant collaboration.

Such public displays of frustration from a man so closely linked to the Austro-Hungarian government paid off for Hima. Identifying a new angle for influence, Hima began to work openly with Logoreci with monies first provided exclusively by the Italians, and then soon after, by Vienna-based authorities as well. This alliance broke down a barrier that had long existed in the Balkans, uniting for the first time refugee activists aligned with the Austro-Hungarian Empire and those tied to Italy, with those *who would become "Albanians."*

Although it is often misunderstood, the political divisions within various groups of active reformers both residing in the Ottoman Empire and among the émigrés took on the contours of the Great Power rivalries spreading throughout the world. For their part, most Tosk activists simply had little connection with Vienna, the rival Catholic power in the region. Instead, they often forged strong relations with patrons based in Greece, Istanbul, or Romania. Hima's subsequent collaboration with Logoreci is thus especially informative because Hima's public engagement with Austro-Hungarian agents served any number of purposes. The least obvious was that it helped give Hima some leverage vis-à-vis his Italian hosts, who were especially concerned that their Habsburg rivals did not gain a foothold in southern Albania at their own strategic expense. Simply put, letters sent by Vienna-backed activists translated into political clout for Hima in the factional diaspora based in Italy, and ultimately in Bucharest as well.[66]

Hima used the possibility of Austro-Hungarian patronage to mobilize Italian funds, a windfall for him and for the allied groups he would soon be supporting in the Balkans and Egypt.[67] Such political capital earned from delivering the Italians to cash-strapped Tosk exiles in the Balkans and Egypt reflects the interactive dynamic that blurs the distinctions we often make between local and external, state, and society.[68] Ultimately, seeing a possible lucrative source of funds, the leadership at *Drita* invested the group's political influence in Romania to support Hima's activism in Rome; an alliance that led to continued interaction between Italy and Tosk exiles in the greater Balkans for years to come.[69]

This complex network of affiliations in the Ottoman refugee/émigré context also calls into question entrenched assumptions about, for example, "Albanian" unity in face of their putative "primordial" enemies. The fact is that many Tosk Orthodox Christian Albanian refugees spread throughout the Mediterranean openly lobbied for closer ties with Greece. Hence the presumption that every Albanian at home and abroad collectively feared Greek expansionism and united behind a common categorical "other" proves unwarranted.[70]

In Egypt specifically, we find an even more complicated interactive dynamic at work. Not only were competing Italian and Austrian-Hungarian agents influencing Ottoman exiles, but so too were the Ottoman state, Greece, and the British administration of Egypt (the *de facto* rulers since the invasion of 1882). More still, the increasingly isolated Egyptian sovereign of Balkan heritage, the Khedive himself, also invested heavily in Ottoman migrant politics. As such, Cairo and the larger Nile Delta region of Egypt were crucial centers of exile that underscored not only the inner workings of emerging Albanian, *Rum* Orthodox, Yemeni, Armenian, Bulgarian, and Syrian-Ottoman communities, but also Italian, British, Austrian, and French intrigue. For those non-Ottoman actors, the larger context of securing spheres of influence over lucrative trade networks, and with them, strategically vital political linkages, would center Egypt in a larger process for decades to come.

As recent scholarship has amply demonstrated, the entire 1878–1939 period in the Eastern Mediterranean was shaped by the constant flow of human beings.[71] These same factors pushing landless Maltese, Sicilians, and French peasants to North Africa also contributed to native North Africans to seek sanctuary in the Ottoman cities of Beirut, Izmir, and Istanbul. The at times unmanageable flux of people moving in and out of already tense situations meant the empire's peoples were in constant upheaval and socioeconomic disruption. As a result, many Ottoman subjects, uprooted by changing property relations in the Ottoman realm sought out regions where demand for unskilled or semi-skilled labor could assure gainful wage-earning employment. In this way, many flocked to Egypt, which was a major agricultural producer needing this kind of cheap labor. Similarly, the Egyptian government invested in massive labor-intensive projects like the Suez Canal and the irrigation of the Nile Delta. With a resulting booming labor market instigating large numbers of Ottomans to move beyond its borders, indigenous "Egyptian" political entrepreneurs, including the landed oligarchies linked with the family of Mehmed Ali, gained new leverage over trans-Mediterranean affairs.

The student of the region's history will recall that since the eighteenth century, Egypt drew immigrants from throughout the Mediterranean. In time, especially with the rise of the Mehmed Ali dynasty (1805–41), the state and landowning classes recruited laborers from the homelands from which most Egytian elite originated, including, and most relevant to the present discussion, Albanian-speaking Ottomans. This practice was significantly modified under the largely British dominated enterprise after 1882. After this inauspicious turn of events, the new regime steered the financially crippled Egyptian state toward investing heavily in supporting the creation of "nationalist cells" as a means to help destabilize otherwise entrenched Ottoman constituencies throughout the region. Crucially, many of these cells would find the resources—thanks again to British "patronage" by way of surrogate (Khedival) funds—to create branches throughout Europe and clandestine operations throughout the Ottoman Empire. Such a context proved especially lucrative for the many talented Ottoman writers and artists settled in Egypt. Their presence helped cultivate the panoply of modern-looking ethno-national, or sectarian orientated communities, a nurturing of communalism that would serve British imperial interests during and after World War I.[72]

It should not be too surprising, therefore, to learn that in time, almost all politically active Tosk Albanian members of the anti-Hamidian movement passed through Egypt. Many dissidents, including Ismail Qemali (who had become especially vocal in his support of British intervention into domestic Ottoman affairs), helped organize social clubs and raised money to support schools and textbook publications, which were later smuggled into Ottoman-Albanian territories.[73] This type of émigré "subversion" enjoyed the full logistical and financial support of the British via the Egyptian state. Indeed, the journals that various southern Albanian factions produced over time in Egypt—containing anti-Hamidian and, later, anti-CUP rhetoric—thrived in large part because of Egyptian (thus British) state patronage.[74]

The Khedive's active support of various Albanian interest groups in this context speaks to a broader set of forces at work that intimately linked events in the Ottoman territories with the larger world. As much as the raw materials flowing out of Ottoman ports and the persistence of the "Eastern Question" in diplomatic circles animated events, the often murky world of exile networks played prominently in the archived consular reports of all the major powers.[75]

In contrast with the well-connected Muslim Tosks described above, Orthodox Christian Tosk Albanian refugees/migrants took advantage of the identity politics being played out in the larger region. The Greek state in particular attempted to lay claim to every Orthodox non-Slav Christian living in the Balkans and the Middle East. For Orthodox Christian Tosks, the opportunity to exploit this was clear. For example, there is evidence that many seeking to obtain travel documents claimed Greek citizenship by equating their faith as Orthodox Christians to being ethnically Greek. The Austrian Consul Velić based in Cairo reported that the Egyptian government actually grew concerned that by liberally granting Greek nationality to Tosks willing to accept the label, Greece was trying to undermine the Egyptian economy and even its political stability by infiltrating local markets (and labor unions) and then diverting regional trade (and political loyalties) into "Greek" hands.[76]

The way previous studies on migrant communities in Egypt have understood the dynamics of, for instance, diaspora politics, labor union organization, and economic networks has missed much of this complexity. The failure to recognize that many categorical "Greeks" may have used the privileges of such an association to enjoy travel rights, while socializing as Albanians, Vlach, Bulgarians, or Serbs, has resulted in overemphasizing a number of links between proto-nationalist Greek or Italian identity claims and historical events in Egypt. In the case of increasingly self-identified Albanians, the Cairo-based newspaper *Toska* published an entire issue on the subject of Tosk Albanians claiming Greek citizenship in 1902.[77]

Such a willingness to reach out to interested foreign parties goes a long way toward presenting the varied and often conflicting interests of Egypt's Tosk migrant communities in a more nuanced manner. The Ottoman state monitored these activities and was frequently surprised by the profile of those who participated in the unity meetings held in Athens. For example, the Ottoman embassy in Athens reported that Ismail Qemali held negotiations with an organization called "Hellenismos" funded by wealthy Tosks and the Greek state.[78] This prominent ex-Ottoman governor apparently was prepared to forge a union with the enemy.

These developments suggest that personal identities in another *proximate* context were malleable and that a certain flexibility of sectarian identity was important with respect to community politics in the Eastern Mediterranean. Paradoxically, well-established institutions like the Orthodox Church and the Pan-Hellenic strategy of claiming virtually all the southern Balkans as culturally Greek provided an opportunity for a broad range of constituent groups. Tosk Albanians in particular actively exploited this loophole in order to benefit from Greek citizenship and its protection from Ottoman control when they traveled back and forth between Egypt and the Ottoman Balkans. Such protections gave many Tosks an advantage in Ottoman territories, where they established lucrative trading partnerships all along the Adriatic coast. It appears that this community also had strong connections with some elements of the Orthodox Christian Tosk community in Alexandria and Cairo.[79]

As seen throughout this chapter, there is a rich history behind this collaboration between Ottoman Albanian refugees/migrants and outside actors seeking both political influence and commercial opportunities. Some of these overtures to Ottoman Albanians in Egypt even reached the small communities in the Delta region like Beni Souef (Bini Suif), where considerable money was being made in the production of cash crops like cotton. Milo Duçi, son of a powerful cotton merchant from Korçë, established in Beni Souef a branch of the "Albanian Brotherhood" with direct assistance from the Khedive's office. Such assistance suggests a British role. Indeed, in addition to the political links between Beni Souef and Cairo, Duçi's family emerged as an important player in the general economic development of Egypt's delta region directed by Lord Cromer's office. By 1901, Milo Duçi started working with his well-connected uncle, Loni Logori, on projects that explicitly tied the commercial interests of members within the British administration and local landowners. Crucially, Logori, who had built much of the canal network in the Minah district several years earlier, was known to have maintained contacts with members of émigré organizations in Bucharest, Istanbul, Italy, and Brussels.[80] These interlinking channels of political, cultural, and economic exchange deserves greater scholarly attention in the future.

Indeed, reflective of the manipulative range of such actors, as already seen in Ismail Qemali's multiple partnerships, the same Duçi openly solicited Austro-Hungarian support. This partnership took place despite the distrust of many Southern Albanians in Egypt toward Vienna's ambitions in the Balkans. Regarding such counterintuitive alliances, documents produced by consuls based in Cairo during the period of 1880–1912 offer a rich picture of the way in which the Ottoman-Albanian migrants and the Habsburg Empire operated in Egypt.[81] The reports from the Austrian embassy from 1900 to 1902, in particular, reveal that alliances were formed around sectarian affiliations and then reconstituted around groups who maintained good relations with representatives from Italy, or, if they were Muslims, the Egyptian state.[82] Based mostly in Cairo, these government patriarchs had apparently also forged strong links with the well-established Ottoman-Albanian elite in Istanbul and with groups based in Napoli and Calabria. These latter ties could have constituted an *Arbëresh* block that cornered certain commercial and political niches in the greater Eastern Mediterranean world.[83] As noted in Chapter 4, these niches extended to the other side of the Atlantic with greater numbers of Albanians from Italy, Greece, or the Ottoman Empire itself, beginning to settle, along with so many other Ottoman refugees, in the Americas.[84]

While natives of the Balkans have a historical link to Egypt that partially explains their active involvement in the country's affairs since at least the late eighteenth century, Egypt's strategic place with respect to the Red Sea meant many Yemenis also migrated and traded there. Added to this dynamic is the presence since 1882 of the British administration in Egypt, an operation that by the 1890s nurtured opposition groups to the Hamidian regime. Among the most well-funded were the Arabic-speaking exiles who became known activist for regime change in Istanbul while based in Egypt.[85] By the 1890s, therefore, Cairo served as a crossroads of regional politics, a point of exchange in which the Khedive of Egypt, still nominally a subject of the Ottoman Sultan, facilitated British domination over a geostrategic epicenter of importance to French, Italian, Habsburg, Greek, and indeed Ottoman interests.

Clearly, all these powers sought to cultivate the many Ottoman refugee/migrant activists who passed through the region. As such, Egypt became a springboard for affecting life in many parts of the Ottoman homeland, including Northern Yemen, which had just recently been formally incorporated into the state centralization schemes of the Ottoman Empire. Especially interesting for our purposes here were the partisans of the recently anointed Zaydi Imam (Imam Yahya), whose domestic political struggles for legitimacy, as either an ally of the Ottoman state or rival claimant to authority over the highlands of North Yemen, spilled over into the Egyptian space.[86]

Very little is known about the nature of the clusters of migrants from Yemen living in Egypt, although there is little doubt that many did call various Egyptian ports their home. As with the previous examples of Albanian activists, with the growth of a largely British administration, Cairo was a point of intrigue for Ottoman Yemenis who sought to enforce some order in their spheres of influence in the larger Red Sea. Here the story of Sayyid Ahmed Yahya al-Kibsi from Hawlan province proves invaluable. His cultivation of a recently established relationship between his patron Imam Yahya, one of the claimants to power in Northern Yemen, and the Italian government is especially important considering Italy became active in the Red Sea by way of protecting Italian company interests in Eritrea.

It is not entirely clear how the dialogue began, but it appears that Kibsi actually solicited assistance from the Italians for personal reasons as much as on the Imam's behalf.[87] What stands out from Kibsi's interaction with the Italian consulate is his hope that the Italian state could assist him in dealing with his nominal sovereign, the Ottoman state. Kibsi lobbied Italian authorities in Cairo to put pressure on the Ottoman regime to free his father and uncle from prison on the Mediterranean island of Rhodes, a common destination for high-profile dissidents believed dangerous by the Ottoman administration.[88] In the hope of winning his loyalty—a loyalty deemed crucial to authorities in Rome to assure workable relations with a possible valuable asset in the on-going struggle for ascendency in the Red Sea—the Italian government did invest heavily in lobbying Istanbul to free Kibsi's relatives from exile on Rhodes.[89] One of the rewards for such collaboration was that Kibsi also secured a stipend from the Italians. Moreover, the consul in Cairo also paid the fees for the transport of Kibsi's liberated family members to settle in Egypt. Other than Kibsi, the Italians also seem to have been supporting other Yemenis closely associated with Kibsi, who clearly became during this time some kind of community leader within this pro-Imam faction living in Cairo.[90] This heavy investment in one man and his immediate network reflects both the assumed importance of Kibsi's family in influencing Yemeni affairs, and the linked desire of the Italian government to gain access to such affairs.

What is not so clear from these exchanges is what the Italians ultimately got in return. By the time Kibsi's family was freed from imprisonment, Imam Yahya was in direct negotiation with Istanbul to reconcile with the regime. Revealingly, Kibsi was one of the three delegates sent to Istanbul to negotiate on the Imam's behalf.[91] It is here that a new level of interstate power politics emerged. Serving as an additional layer of communication (and as it turns out, intrigue) between the Imam, the Sublime Porte, and the Italian government, was the legation's dragoman, Muhammad Arif Bey. Through his active role as intermediary and translator, Muhammad Arif Bey became an integral part of the politics behind these Italian/imam relations in Egypt. That being said, beginning in 1906 there was some indication that Muhammad Arif Bey was not entirely trusted by the Italian consul in Cairo. The consul himself suspected Muhammad Arif Bey of having ulterior motives concerning the affairs with Kibsi. The first signs of this occurred when reports reached the Italians that Muhammad Arif Bey was an agent of the secret service of the Egyptian royal family. Moreover, he was frequently seen meeting with the head of the Ottoman government representative office in Cairo, Muhktar Pasha.[92]

Loyalties in the Egyptian-based émigré community were without question manifold and volatile, which meant that unqualified reliance on a particular intermediary could prove dangerous. An individual who wished to could, for his own purposes, simultaneously serve and manipulate conflicting agendas of the Hamidian regime, the Khedive, the British, and/or the Italians. At one point, it is suggested that Ahmad Effendi Adib, himself once a loyal representative of the previous Zaydi imam in Cairo, was actively working for the Hamidian regime against the interests of the current Imam. In this respect, even Istanbul was prepared to work with willing members of the disgruntled Zaydi community, both in Yemen and among migrants.[93] That there were anti-Imam forces among the Zaydi in Egypt hints at a complex web of interchanging parts that linked events in highland Yemen—the intra-Zaydi struggle for power and the political struggles between Imam Yahya, some of his allies and enemies, and the Ottoman administration—with the machinations of imperial intrigue in the Red Sea.

This story line also suggests that a young man whose entire world was turned upside down by the arrest and exile of his father and uncle could adjust and ultimately make himself an essential component in this interplay of forces in Cairo. In a matter of a few months, Kibsi was able to convince the Italian foreign ministry and perhaps even Imam Yahya that he could serve as the essential intermediary. Eventually, he did become the Imam's main emissary during direct negotiations with the Hamidian regime. In the process, Kibsi also secured the release of his family members from Rhodes. It is clear from Kibsi's story that not all highland, "tribal" Yemenis were naïve, isolated people, but active players in a complex system of international, regional, and local Egyptian politics. Moreover, their leverage in this system enabled them to manipulate the interests of others and successfully negotiate for the betterment of their own constituencies.[94]

Paradoxically, such an eclectic environment hampered attempts to unify the dispersed émigré communities and ultimately diminished the ability of various groups to service outside patrons seeking to influence events in Yemen. What Egypt's contested political environment did help cultivate instead, much as in Romania mentioned earlier, was a broken and often hostile set of factions whose rivalries may have sabotaged as much as cooperated with their fellow "countrymen's" efforts to bring stability to their assumed shared homeland.[95] These conditions of factional competition and the resulting diminishment of individual communities' abilities to influence events would continue well after the collapse of the Ottoman Empire, a fact that ultimately explains why Euro-American finance capitalism so thoroughly dominates the world today.

Conclusion

All the cases noted above speak of the counterintuitive dynamics at work among the displaced inhabitants of the Ottoman realm. The case of Albanians and Yemenis in Egypt especially highlights the traumas of the so-called diasporic experience. These migrants' ambitions pitted contradictory interests against each other, leaving in the end refugees and migrants with a full range of possibilities (and limitations) otherwise unknown to native Egyptians or those still living within Ottoman-administered territories. Cairo as a center of exile thus underscores not only the inner workings of emerging trans-Mediterranean Egyptian communities, but also imperialist intrigues. Among the more important reflections of such agendas was European support of smugglers based on either side of the Red Sea.[96] The end result was a failed Ottoman state.

Undermining the power of the Ottoman administration in Yemen was clearly a long-term strategy that meant that the Italian authorities in Eritrea and the French in Djibouti went beyond protecting the "pirates" who threatened Ottoman economic stability. Indeed, they actively built "loyal" constituencies in these regions, a process that had long-term rewards for French and Italian commercial interests throughout the Red Sea. As seen above, Italian officials openly secured a place for Ottoman Yemeni political refugees in Cairo, cultivating intimate commercial and political associations that anticipated Italy's attempts to affect Yemen's affairs well after the Ottomans left. That the Yemenis themselves understood and manoeuvred in this space of operation is clear with the case of Ahmed al-Kibsi, who actively lobbied Italian authorities in Cairo to intervene on both his family's behalf and that of Imam Yahya. In the end, these efforts speak to a complicated interplay of agendas and ideas of what was possible in the world of refugees/migrants.

At the same time, Tosk Albanian refugees and migrants, hailing from all over the Eastern Mediterranean, called Egypt as much as Romania or Bulgaria, home. Beyond the economic interests that clearly were substantial (but beyond the scope of this study) were the political interests of the various parties engaging a plethora of groups. The heterogeneity of the community itself speaks to the complex conditions back in the Balkans, and cautions against the premature associations other scholars have made with late-Ottoman refugee activism and unified, self-identified nations. What must be explored in the future are the integrative functions of the trans-regional factors at work in *Ottoman proximate* contexts like those found in Cairo, Bucharest, and Sofia.

Among other interested parties, Greece, Italy, and Austria appear to have operated within a context of multiple loyalties and political alliances. What such conditions and varied resources did for those Ottoman refugees living in Egypt was just as much a question of personal ambition and growing opportunity as it was one of new collective identities for Albanians, Greeks, or Arabs/Yemenis. In this respect, one other aspect discussed here takes on special significance—namely the experience of the ontological outsider. There is no doubt that the refugees who resettled in the countries neighboring the Kosovo, Yanya, Manastır, and Yemen provinces experienced a certain associational trauma that shaped their political horizons for the rest of the Ottoman period. Like the Ottoman Empire, the ruling classes of the Ottoman state's imperial neighbors sought to structure societies that enacted unitary cultural and socioeconomic identities. The consequences for those identified as outsiders have been devastating over the course of the twentieth century.

All this must be read in the larger context of diasporic theory that has emerged in the past few years. It can be argued that the entire project of the modern state identified in these locales of exile employed technology and the self-aware institutions of state power to control diversity, develop uniformity, and, in the process, criminalize or anathematize the strangers within. In no time, European "reforms" in the Balkans imposed institutional structures and rhetorical tools that grounded local politics to reflect exclusively a secure triangulation of territory linked to identity. This would be an identity based on the ethno-national marker (often with a sectarian foundation) and the state. This rigidification of political possibilities took place inspite of the same agents of imperial policy in Arabia and the Balkans who understood that people were eminently mobile, and that the boundaries within which they operated had always been in flux.[97]

I suggest that, to the contrary of most assumptions about this modernization process, even as the structure of the "modern" person was being built and imposed along an axis of enforced inclusion/exclusion. But this would necessarily be a violent process. The experience of the outcast, noted here in its many forms, could not be so neatly contained. It is apparent with the cases of the resettled Ottoman refugees in Romania, Bulgaria, and Egypt explored above that locals had their own shifting notions of these markings of "modern" communal identity. The more that local turmoil directly affected the ability of local stakeholders to endure, new channels of survival, including trade and exclusionary rhetoric, were sought.[98] Their creation ultimately shifted power in new directions and thereby enabling international finance capital to secure a foothold in the Ottoman Empire.

As seen in the next chapter, such swings in political patronage and commerce ultimately compel us to reconsider the political economy of the refugee in the larger world. At once engaged in the larger world while resolutely adapting to contingencies, peoples from all these regions absorbed the initial impact of capitalism and forced a reorientation of modern life in ways more complicated than traditionally assumed. In the next chapter this variability of place, affiliation, and sense of community finds another expression in an entirely different kind of exile—that of overseas constituencies that no longer retain the *Ottoman proximate* dynamic but come to represent the Ottoman sensibility in arenas completely out of direct state influence.

Transitional Migrants: The Global Ottoman Refugee and Colonial Terror

...Give me your tired, your poor,
Your huddled masses yearning to breathe free,
The wretched refuse of your teeming shore.
Send these, the homeless, tempest-tost to me...[1]

Emma Lazarus, "The New Colossus" (1883)

Introduction

Although the majority of Ottoman refugees in the 1878–1912 period either remained internally displaced or settled in those *proximate* locales along the empire's porous frontiers, significant numbers actually found their way to new continents. Starting from the first steamships landing in the Americas via Marseille, Alexandria, or Trieste, eventually hundreds of thousands of Syrians, Palestinians, Armenians, Albanians, Greeks, and Slavs constituted the vital first wave of migrants to the Americas.[2] Through the toil of building communities from scratch, at times in face of unbearable institutional hostility and outright racism from their host state and neighbors, these pioneers deserve their decedents' praise.[3] Indeed, what is especially impressive from the now vast scholarship on both global migratory patterns in general and specifically Eastern Mediterranean variations is just how these nomads were able to preserve so much of their heritage.[4] At some point, however, there must begin some soul-searching that puts these heroic struggles into the larger context of modern exploitation economies under which many Ottomans were also suffering.

To do so requires that we remember that the concomitant factors inducing mass migrations across vast areas of the planet were not only the "dreams of greener pastures" offered by the much celebrated technological innovations like the steam engine, the telegraph, and new printing techniques (the commoditized fruits of a so-called Gilded Age). What accompanied such "wonders" of the modern age were also alienation from one's ancestral lands, community break-down, and brutal exploitation.[5] Fortunately, reading the literature on global migration does not disguise these "push/pull" factors that expunged so many hundreds of thousands from their homelands for the purposes of exploiting their desperation.[6] From recent studies we learn that the demand for cheap labor came from both the expanding plantation and mining operations. These labor intensive operations became the investment of choice for those eyeing profits "overseas." Similarly, industrialization in the metropole created its own demands for and on people forced to sell their labor just to survive.[7]

The products these exploitative relations released onto the world satiated the highly integrated "market's" increasing demands created by cash-based economies. As profit margins grew with each new concession in distant, recently "discovered" corners of the planet, this demand for various types of wage workers transformed the relationship between capital, company, state, and society. As elsewhere, the inhabitants of the Ottoman Empire became a major source for this kind of "satanic mill" that ultimately destroyed both supplier and recipient societies.[8] As discussed below, just as in the Americas, Africa, and Asia, one of the most important factors behind the massive Ottoman emigration was the "market" demand for cheap labor, a reflection of the changing focus of finance capital.[9]

While this story, in parts, has already been explored by scholars, I identify here a very different, much smaller group of Ottoman refugees that may darken an already depressing story. Far from being tragic personal stories, the cases presented here suggest that some Ottomans actually served this new financial order, some even becoming among the wealthiest trading families in the world as a result. Far less spectacular, but equally vital to the gradual imposition of a Euro-American financial and then political order, was the Ottoman petty merchant, small shop owner, and "jack-of-all-trades" peddler increasingly identified in the scholarship.[10]

As a combination, these two very different kinds of Ottoman refugees intersected with the world at a time when the Euro-American juggernaut was just beginning to gain traction.[11] Such an intersection within a larger "circulation" of goods, practices, and peoples, was crucial to the financial engine that built the modern capitalist world; ascendant Euro-American trading corporations needed accomplices at crucial junctures.[12] In other words, Euro-American imperialism took its "destined" genocidal turn by often calling on various Ottoman subjects (in addition to a wide range of other indigenous actors throughout Africa and Asia) to make themselves useful in ways contradictory to their normative place in world history.[13]

For a small, but significant minority of Ottoman refugees, destinations as diverse as Southeast Asia, Eastern Africa, and the jungles of the Americas offered sets of opportunities—as well as challenges and frustrations—for at times unsavory collaboration with global capitalism. Succinctly put, the untold hundreds of thousands of Ottomans traversing the major oceans of the world between 1878 and 1939 did leave an imprint on the host societies within which they settled.[14] In order for the theoretical aims of this chapter to work, however, readers must appreciate that what permitted Ottoman refugee complicity in the horrors of Euro-American Empire was the expedient suspension of strict, hierarchical divisions rigidly enforced in some colonial contexts. This means that in Southeast Asia, East and West Africa, and many parts of the Americas, being Arab, Turk, Albanian, Armenian, Muslim, or Ottoman

Christian did not carry the same advantages and/or disadvantages as in a late-nineteenth-century Ottoman imperial setting. In short, there was something about many exilic settings in which Ottomans found themselves that made the "normative" racist categories of Euro-American civilizational politics suddenly inappropriate, if not totally counterproductive, to the agents of capitalist expansionism. Studying transitional migrants, in other words, requires exploring how some Ottoman peoples, as much as some Cantonese, Gujarati, Bengali, Gulf Persian/Arab, and Hadhrami, became the "middlemen" for different kinds of trans-regional networks crucial to making global capitalist power work.[15]

The Ottoman refugee and the world of plunder

As argued throughout, there is more than one possible way to approach the category of migrant/refugee agency. Here we explore how, despite all the opportunities to do otherwise, many individual Ottoman refugees did not so much confront Euro-American imperial violence as deflect its rhetorical violence. In this respect, as the emerging "science" of imperialism ripped apart Ottoman society, in other colonial contexts some of the very refugee victims fleeing such violence actually became useful intermediaries for this same Euro-American financial empire. In one of the greatest tragic ironies of this era, the foundational borders of Western imperialism, that is the "biological boundaries dividing Anglo-Saxons or Teutons and the inferior races . . .," were strategically blurred when it served capitalist interests.[16] That is to say, the various taxonomies of global imperialism that brought new weight to racial and ethnic difference—modern objectifications that proved destructive inside the Ottoman Empire—did not appear entirely applicable to many Ottoman refugees settling in other imperial contexts.

Accepting this paradox means writing about juxtapositions rather than providing comparisons of types of settlement, colonization, or modernization. The examples provided below, therefore, are not meant to elucidate similarities with patterns other scholars have identified in Irish, Tamil, or Cantonese "equivalents." Ottoman voyagers to new worlds proved distinct, both from other migrant groups, and from each other. In many ways, the only approach for us today to tell such different, un-generalizable, individual migration and integration stories is to abandon entirely the lexicon in active use to study events inside the Ottoman Empire, and perhaps even migration history more generally. In its place must be the acceptance that there were a multiplicity of different roles, for different peoples in different settings, that require case-specific explanations. Here the cases revolve around the relative power afforded to "settlers" vis-à-vis the indigenous "lesser races." In such a calculus, Ottoman refugees often became one of the ugly tools of empire rather than one of its victims.

The power quotient

As seen earlier, from roughly the period of 1830 to World War I, global finance capitalism rapidly transformed previous mercantilist socioeconomic orders. Connected to these changes was the imposition of new institutional, ideological, and military agendas suited to accommodate a dramatic shift in what I call the balance-of-violence in the world. Well until the 1850s, for example, there remained a limit to the scale and intensity of violence that colonial/imperial enterprises could use.[17] Indeed, certain material constraints on Euro-American powers left the regions between the "colonist" and the "colonized" much closer to parity (especially if the "colony" was found on the other side of the world). In this respect, the notion of "Gunboat diplomacy" and a superior Euro-American technological violence risks mischaracterizing the political niceties of empire prior to 1850.

In Southeast Asia, before this suggested shift in power through violence, Euro-American companies traded with local intermediaries whose own political skills assured that the desired products for global markets made it to port.[18] The same held true for Eastern Africa, and the Persian Gulf, where trade agreements were signed between Omani Sultans, sovereigns of Ras al-Khaymah, and foreign companies well into the 1850s on terms that were equally beneficial.[19] In both cases, Euro-American trading companies just did not have the resources to monopolize the economic productivity of these highly valued sources of spices, minerals, and high-end finished products. In other words, without the "monopoly on violence" linked to the crucial shift in state/society relations transforming Europe only in the first part of the nineteenth century, the great European trading companies were compelled to engage commercial partners, not subordinate subjects.[20]

Things began to change, however, with the rise of modern finance capitalism developed by a small cartel of family-run banks. By the early 1840s, with heavy backing from these major European banks, trading companies like the British East India Company (EIC), the *Vereenigde Oost-Indische Compagnie* (VOC) or Dutch East India Company (or their Saxon, Genovese, and American rivals) had become major conglomerates.[21] Being able to generate huge sums of money by way of new kinds of financial instruments—bond issues and shares on London, Paris, and Amsterdam stock markets—gave these companies considerable advantages over their hitherto equal trading partners in Asia, the Ottoman Empire, and Africa.[22] Not only could these companies invest in better ships and more talented accountants, but they also cornered regional economies by way of controlling supply chains.[23] In time, they began to invest in political intrigues in their most coveted regions. In many cases, the aim was to create even greater advantages over rivals by leveraging others' political stability with improved trade conditions for a select group of local partners.[24]

There was, however, a ceiling on how high these financial "innovations" could raise profits. New cartels in the Euro-American world still had to deal with independent sovereigns who remained their suppliers of the most coveted raw materials and cash crops feeding "market" demand.[25] It is at this point that these companies' investments in capturing the parliamentary regimes back in Europe and the Americas began to pay dividends. Through corruption and growing state/company synergies requisite for a new stage of financial imperialism, these companies started to co-opt the vast revenues of Euro-American states by way of buying the legislative and executive wings of their host governments. Crucially, it became a part of normal political life that the men who would allocate state funds to do the bloody task of violently subjugating indigenous peoples on behalf of these cartels were also to become share-holders of the companies involved.[26] This crucial web of "conflicted" interests completely transformed the balance of power in the world as company and bank interests began to serve the state and vice-versa.

Subsequent state-funded military expeditions—for crown and country the landless Welsh and Scottish troops purportedly screamed—did much of the dirty work for those powerful "stakeholders" concerned with their investments in far off Punjab and Southern Africa.[27] It is at this critical intersection of the state and financial capital that the kind of imaginary "world" dominated by "civilization" could become a reality as well.[28] What had formerly been just hyperbole about the "White Man's Burden" and the evangelical quest to give native "savages" their gift of Christianity (and small pox) became the blueprints for domination over the next century.[29]

While the lurid stories of how modern capitalist imperialism mobilized financial, technological, and human resources to conquer the world are well documented, the task of this present overview is to situate this capitalist violence with the arrival of Ottoman refugees in many of these zones of exploitation. Where much of this exploitation took place, one could often find one of two kinds of Ottoman refugee. What characteristics they share—such as their likely involuntary need to leave their homelands—were crucially mediated by the very different roles they would play in the larger world, which included mutually profitable relationships with the forces of capital. To support my suggestion that these small groups of Ottomans actually helped the utter destruction of all resistance to Euro-American capitalism, I proceed to look at distinctive parts of the world in which these two types of Ottoman operative serviced capitalism's not entirely inevitable march to global domination.

Using the South China Sea region as our primary area of focus, it is important to stress how rapidly relations between peoples once cooperating in mutually beneficial trade agreements broke down by the 1850s. This vast region (see Map 4.1) linking Southeast China with the Philippine islands, Borneo, Celebes, and further afield the Malay Peninsula, was culturally heterogeneous, consisting of a multiplicity of competing Muslim mini-states. The manner in which all these sovereignties presided over a precarious, and constantly challenged wealth-extraction economy, necessitated the use of alliances between not only "rulers" but laborers as well.[30]

Michael Adas has described these pre-European South China Sea polities as "contest states" in which the temporary ruler was restricted by rival elite powers that were in turn constrained by forms of peasant resistance.[31] The power dynamics of Southeast Asia, in other words, was a highly mediated arena where peasants could "take to the hills" if relations with coastal-based trading interests did not properly address their ever-changing needs.[32] In these pre-European years (and not much changed with the arrival of finance capitalism's first wave of agents in the 1850s) the retention of manpower was crucial for any regional ruler. Correspondingly, peasants retained considerable leverage by way of their ability to threaten these lucrative trade relations. Put differently, without the coercive power to enforce an exploitative order, these pre-European patron-client relationships moderated the exactions of the ruling class, forcing ruler and ruled, employer and employee, to constantly renegotiate their terms of exchange.

Map 4.1 South China Sea 1899.

Criminalizing indigenous trade

James Warren has usefully termed the crucial channels that linked the disparate trading polities found on Mindanao, Borneo, Celebes, and Basilan the "Sulu Zone." It was in this polyglot, pluralistic space where Taosug, Iranun, and Samal communities constantly adapted to the changing contours of regional events. Much as noted with the so-called "Swahili" zones in East Africa,[33] these Sulu Muslim polities adapted to the new dynamics introduced with the arrival of competing European capitalist interests. Recall that European expansion in these areas enjoying a balance of violence focused first on getting "a foot in the door" of regional economies by signing trade agreements with indigenous Sultans on the major islands. Part of the attraction of these mercantile emirates of course was the fact they were relatively wealthy.[34] As they controlled successful trading hubs, the European companies eagerly competed against each other for the privilege to share the wealth with those willing indigenous rulers.[35]

In time, however, new opportunities would present themselves for some agents of Euro-American finance capital to actually undermine the negotiating power of these indigenous polities. Throughout South Asia, the Arabian Peninsula, and Eastern Africa, a coalition of Euro-American interests began a process—in retrospect suspiciously coordinated—that undermined the very structures of commerce upon which these wealthy societies functioned.[36] Apparently Euro-American forces targeted first and foremost the ability of these polities to continue to deliver the necessary manpower to meet a growing "market" demand for their harvested products.

In the South China Sea, labor-intensive plantation operations existed throughout the larger islands.[37] Beyond the plantations, interconnecting communities serviced by highly mobile and politically organized peasants provided more than just the tobacco, coconuts, and rice in high demand in the wider, regional markets. Forest products such as rattan and birds' nests, highly valued in China, were harvested in ways that successfully fused commercial hubs and their Muslim leaders with indigenous labor partners. Problems arose, however, when demand for these highly valued products outstripped labor supply.

Periodic shifts in labor demand created a new market niche for the "Sulu Zone" which indigenous entrepreneurs began to address. By accelerating and expanding "traditional" practices of "raiding" coastal communities in Spanish-held territories in present-day Philippines, a possible solution to the manpower shortages in the larger South China Sea world was at hand.[38] The problem was that a number of Euro-American companies also had access to a large pool of human beings—primarily from Burma, China, Bengal, and southern India—to send to these regions as laborers.[39] As such, rising Euro-American interests saw such indigenous sources of labor a threat to their long-term aims of monopolizing all aspects of regional trade.[40] In order to assure full-spectrum domination, the coastal raids by Taosug Muslim communities to capture new slave laborers would have to be suppressed.

Along with suppressing, or rechanneling, supply chains for both goods and labor, over the middle decades of the nineteenth century a coordinated effort was also put into suppressing the transportation capacities of powerful indigenous communities. As with labor in particular, dominating the distribution of goods was crucial to long-term Euro-American hegemonic goals. The armada of local vessels in operation in the South China Sea region, providing transport and thus revenue for their owners—some being both very wealthy *and* direct rivals to the Euro-American shipping companies seeking to enter into the local market—constituted a well-oiled regional economy that wove together tightly indigenous trading partnerships. These alliances, forged through marriage and, as in the case of Arab Hadhrami families, extending throughout the Indian Ocean, proved the most difficult challenge to the ambitions of European capitalists. Moreover, the autonomous nature of these operations meant most of these communities could still, independent of Euro-American partnerships, function and produce profits. Again, this system needed breaking apart.

In both cases—the monopolizing of labor supplies and dominating the distribution of goods—European agents of capitalism began to impose standards of exchange and eventually dictate what were permissible forms of commercial practice. Those not fitting these criteria were criminalized. By way of first insisting "laws" of trade be standardized, and then enforcing them in their own port courts—by the 1860s courts would be set up in Aden, Batavia, Bombay, Hong Kong, and later Singapore—European "gunboat" tactics imposed, through want of any possible military challenge, an order of commerce that would quickly give their ships (and companies) a virtual stranglehold on regional economies. Coupled with the eventual monopoly on money supply, by the 1880s the peoples of the South China Sea would witness the full-spectrum domination of their worlds by a cartel of Euro-American companies.

Crucially, it is with the formal "criminalization" of indigenous patterns of first labor recruitment/supply (strategically labeled "slavery" in Euro-American quarters) and second, local forms of transportation (called "piracy" or smuggling) that the initial steps toward this hegemony were taken.[41] The campaign in East Africa against "slavery" is now well-documented and enough healthy cynicism about the real objectives of the abolitionist movement surrounding it has penetrated the scholarship to not have to deal with the larger ideological context here.[42] What is useful is to quickly link this better-known campaign in the western Indian Ocean with the events taking place around the same time in the Sulu zone.[43]

The parallels cannot be ignored. The way mainly British justifications for confiscating indigenous ("Arab") owned dhows sailing traditional routes along the western Indian Ocean mirrors those efforts in Southeast Asia to undermine Sulu and Chinese transport is suggestive of a global push for this full-spectrum economic domination.[44] By linking, in particular, antislavery operations in Southeast Asia and the western Indian Ocean with the clear efforts at controlling the production, harvesting, and supply networks of both regions' most valued products, including human labor, we can begin to see the larger context in which some Ottoman refugees found their unique place as collaborators in this plunder.[45] Therefore, we first lay out the classic story of the oft-cited "antislavery" campaign in the western Indian Ocean region with the possible role of Ottoman migrants in its elaboration.

Plundering Swahili's future

In East Africa at the time, profiting from trade in gold, cheap labor, or ivory was dependent on being able to accommodate the Euro-American agenda. European and American ships would soon monopolize the open seas by way of its imposition of a regime of antislavery that systematically targeted the transport assets of these hitherto dominant trading operations.[46] Ultimately the networks that linked the outside world to the Omani Sultan based in Zanzibar, and to many Muslim hinterland polities like Bagamoyo, Tabora, Ujiji on Lake Tanganyika, and into the Manyema to the West, at least up to the Lualaba River (see Map 4.2), would be captured by European companies.[47] To accomplish this, European ships targeted locally owned dhows, and more specifically the profitability of their use for regional traders, thus disrupting the entire circuit of trade, leading ultimately to the subordination of the still independent polities of the "Swahili" coast to the political needs of European financial powers.[48]

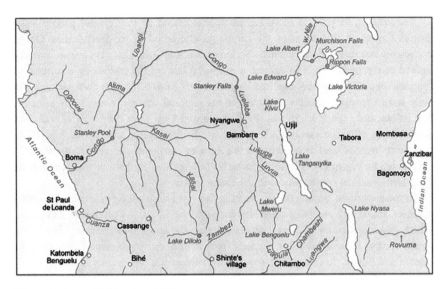

Map 4.2 Central Africa circa 1880.

The Euro-American financial order ultimately succeeded in dominating the region by declaring that indigenous forms of labor were akin to "slavery" and thus warranted, on "moral" and "civilization" grounds, suppression.[49] On the back of the subsequent antislavery campaigns, British ships in particular claimed the right to police the coasts of East Africa.[50] The first of these slave-trade suppression campaigns began in the late 1860s and were conducted exclusively by the Royal Navy. Soon, however, these operations were outsourced to individual captain and crews who profited handsomely. The further incentivizing of those joining "the fight against slavery" by paying rewards for capture turned the "duty" of slavery suppression into a profitable industry of its own.

This virtual industry quickly became known among those reporting on events from Zanzibar as a "racket," corrupted by the "rewards" offered by institutions raising money from worried white Christians back in Europe to ships that produced "freed" slaves.[51] While there were cash inducements for crews, the real allure to ships/crews-for-hire was the considerable financial rewards linked to the plundering and burning of local boats.

This form of legitimized piracy speaks of an enduring criminal rationale embedded in the practices of some Euro-American capitalists. The details of such a campaign merits discussion as there were mechanisms put in place that would prove to be the working model for similar operations to destroy local businesses throughout the world for much of the next century. More pertinent to the topic of this book, these aggressive attempts to monopolize all trade in the region directly affected the way Ottoman subjects and those who traded directly with Ottoman communities throughout the Red Sea and Persian Gulf would continue with their livelihoods moving forward.

Remarkably, in yet one more economic concession to the "greater power"—the British Crown at this point of the campaign attempted to suppress Indian Ocean commerce not under the direct jurisdiction of Bombay—the Ottoman Sultan, actually agreed in December 1889 to enforce a proposed ban on the trafficking of arms and "negros" in all its territories that had long benefited from trade with East Africa.[52] Not only were Ottoman subjects and indigenous regional traders immediately affected, but Italian and French traders in the Red Sea and Gulf were duly hurt as well. Not surprisingly, all those directly affected by the British decree that it was "illegal" to transport "negros" and arms between the African continent and the Ottoman realm responded by beginning even more lucrative "smuggling" operations that would have long-term political consequences in the entire region.[53]

In the meantime, among those watching the rapid destruction of local commercial families, there was plenty of open disgust with the British—Protestant—campaign, which possessed an air of hypocrisy considering the amount of "prison" labor being introduced to these same labor markets from British-company-owned operations in Assam and Burma. In this regard, those in the diplomatic community in Zanzibar not profiting from the plunder of East Africa's once great trading communities joined the indigenous outcry and condemned the "sham" that was the antislavery campaign. And yet, the end result was still the destruction of local traders.[54]

In the wake of such disruption of regional trade, arbitration courts were set up, to an extent as a response to complaints coming from well-connected traders throughout the Indian Ocean who saw their products looted during these raids.[55] These courts did not protect indigenous property, however. The practical utility of these courts was not to address the concerns of indigenous merchants but to give the whole process a necessary veneer of legitimacy and legality.[56] Again, the façade of procedure fooled no one. We know from reports written by uncomfortable diplomats that they disproved of the spectacle of so many sailors helping themselves to whatever they could find on "native" crafts while in the open seas.[57]

The crucial lesson to draw from this episode was the neat fusing of "universal" values being selectively applied with the commodification of the actual enforcement of cynical laws that assured British (and later, collective European) plunder of other peoples' wealth.[58] As an incentive for Euro-American ships to upset local trade, for instance, the cargoes of Arab dhows deemed to be smuggling "slaves" could be confiscated by any vessel flying the colors of a signatory to the Brussels Convention Act of 1890.[59] This formalization of European-sanctioned piracy—one that would assure the "spoils" were better distributed among signatory interests—practically destroyed local shipping from Mozambique to Sudan to Baluchistan.[60]

The consequence of this reduction of indigenous companies to modest, local fishing operations and passenger ferries was that European steamers gained exclusive reach of the high seas. As a result they could monopolize a key component of the ivory trade that opened the doors for establishing trading outposts in the hinterland. This quickly challenged those Arab trading centers until then still dominating the trade with Central Africa. In turn, with a growing claim to lands along the coast and immediate hinterland, European companies introduced a new labor regime that reordered peoples into "tribal" enclaves and introduced "coolie" laborers drawn from prisons in India and Burma.[61]

Again, the consequences for local communities were severe. Without the foundations of a wealth-producing mechanism, the Omani political classes long ruling over these areas were subordinated to being mere window dressing, posing as Oriental "chiefs" willing to sign treaties put before them in order to legitimize the *de facto* annexation of "Africa" by the signatory powers at the Berlin Congress of 1885.[62] Half a world away, at about the same time, Southeast Asia also would succumb to these same kinds of tactics.

The sun never sets on plunder: South China Sea

The long existing links in the larger South China Sea between the Muslim Emirates of Borneo, Mindanao, and Sulu became by the 1820s a thriving trade network. As more and more profits were drawn from the network, and trickling further and further afield, growing market demands put pressures on local suppliers to accelerate the harvesting of bird's nests and other forest products. This created an unprecedented demand for labor. Unable to tap any further into local sources, coastal Sultanates reached out to the Taosug or Balangingi "slave raiders" to fill the supply gap.[63] While not entirely new, the subsequent rise in prominence of these "boat peoples" role in supplying labor at this juncture is crucial.[64] The exploding regional economy made the Balangingi Sulu mariners vital suppliers of labor; and in this role they would eventually clash directly with the growing number of European ships drawn to the region by the very same economic opportunity.[65]

It may be worth noting that sea cucumbers, shark fins, pearls, and bird's nests were not highly valued in European or American markets. What drove their "value" to such an extent that regional rulers needed more laborers was that such "exotic" products could be exchanged for Chinese tea. The "strategic" value of cornering the supply of these indigenous products in Southeast Asia (and East Africa) could be equated to controlling the traffic of uranium, or "rare earths" today. The demand for a steady supply of certain local commodities in return for Chinese tea thus, more than anything else, affected the allocation and control of labor and the demand for fresh captives throughout the Sulu Zone.[66]

Tea was more than simply the crucial commodity in the development of trade between China and the tea-consuming world. As we learned from the Opium Wars and the "industrial spying" of Robert Fortune in the 1840s, the very heart of power politics coalesced around tea.[67] Reminiscent of the political economy of oil in the twentieth century, the intrigues between formal sovereigns and intermediaries over access to marketable supplies of tea contributed to a transformation of how the entire region's commercial, political, and social infrastructure developed over the next century. Even when attempts at capturing these lucrative trade networks failed, as when the Spanish first attempted to forcefully suppress the raiding that was largely taking place in their administered coastal areas of Mindanao, such efforts nevertheless set off chain reactions that had far-reaching implications for global trade and the eventual rise of Euro-American hegemony.

Over time, the Spanish, Dutch, French, and British operatives shifted from "stick" to "carrot" in these areas. The different coercive tactics used depended on the extent to which the Sultanates who could have been clients increasingly got in the way of larger ambitions. It is at this crucial set of intersecting forces that Ottoman subjects would be dragged into the fray.[68]

As in East Africa, the competition eventually took the strategic turn by which liberal morality became one of many tactics used to undercut indigenous networks. Indeed, dozens of missionary operations began to intensively work in just these contested areas of commerce and power. What proved more difficult in the Sulu Zone was actually gaining any rhetorical hold on the so-called slaver Arabs. Trading in the South China Sea was not fixed geographically and was highly determined by seasonal shifts in weather patterns and the relative stability of the ruler's relationship with his hired workers. Because of these factors, it was impossible to categorically pin down the targeted enemy. The indigenous Taosug peoples were as much a product of the seasons as was the availability of birds' nests and fish. They were highly mobile and continued to travel far and wide to find new captives for the region's demand in seasonal labor. In this context, European interests found it virtually impossible to prosecute a campaign of suppression—be it by sequestering ships and cargo or via the missionary—as witnessed in East Africa.

This realization not only changed the policies of Spanish officials in Manila, but crystallized the political relevance of Jolo, the capital of the Sulu Sultanate. For one, it became a new trading entrepôt, a focal point for the marketing of slaves that attracted a veritable navy of freelance "pirates" who actually expanded their operations to include the western coast of Celebes, North Borneo, and all of western and southern Mindanao.[69] These routes of both raiding and escape from the slow Spanish steamers patrolling the area led to trade patterns integrating in different ways, at different times. Driving this were the flexible raiding strategies and the relative value of captured labor. In other words, new social forces generated within the Sulu Sultanate by the booming trade with China and the rise of a multitude of possible partnerships with the flood of Euro-American ships coming through, actually created a new kind of "native" of the seas.

Long-distance slave raiding became a growth industry at the very time the Spanish, Dutch, and British were coordinating to eradicate it. However, the more the Spanish in particular invested in burning down coastal villages and besieging Jolo as punishment, the more raiding politics became the only way of life for tens of thousands of very capable, adaptive peoples.[70] The irony then is that the more Western civilization attacked "savage" peoples the results were not eradication or subordination of their "uncivilized" practices, but rather the self-initiated modification and often reinforcement of these practices. In time, the Spanish themselves realized that war with the indomitable Sulu only brought greater costs and disruption of trade. Their solution after ten years of initially trying to brutally destroy the peoples of the region was to turn them into their close trading partners.[71]

For their part, British authorities, often via allies such as the Sultans of Brunei and Sabah in North Borneo, also fluctuated between open hostility with the Sulu and playing factions off one another. As there was not much of a "central" state constituting the Sultanate of Sulu, but rather a dispersed collection of permanently mobile groups themselves comprised of autonomous communities, the politics of coercing or appointing "chiefs" practiced elsewhere proved impossible.[72]

The only means of pressuring such indigenous power brokers was to transform the labor supply chain in the region. As in Eastern Africa, most of the captive labor being rented out to plantations, work companies, or individual families were the victims of debt. It has been documented that Jolo inhabitants in particular were compelled to surrender for periods of time their individual freedoms to pay off political or commercial debts.[73] In many ways this was no different from the forces that led to millions of Cantonese becoming part of the tsunami of bonded (contract/indentured) laborers flooding the world labor markets in the nineteenth century.[74] In order for agents of Euro-American finance to dominate this geographically dispersed arena, it was clear that company management of the region's economic assets would have to be even less intrusive than would prove to be the case in East and South Africa, where a colonial government emerged. In the Sulu Zone and the larger region, empowered but dependent local intermediaries would be needed. These interminglings would include Ottoman refugees.

Trade, power, and the Ottoman opium dynasties

British East Asia

As a result of the First Opium War between Britain and China, lasting between 1839–42, compliant foreign traders started opening offices in Hong Kong. By 1841, the covalent British imperial/commercial operation occupied the island and not only continued to sell opium to China (usually through surrogates from either the Mughal, Persian, or Ottoman worlds) but also obtained extra-territorial rights in ports like Canton, Amoy, Foochow, Ningpo, and Shanghai.[75] In a shrewd move that secured its domination over those in face of demands from the liberal commercial elite in Europe to withdraw its monopoly license, the EIC imported Muslim Indians to monopolize the most lucrative markets that linked China's vast consumer base with Bengal and Bombay.[76]

Such linkages made the Malay Peninsula, by extension, strategically vital to the larger agenda in East Asia. As much as the Suez Canal would become the focus of rival empires after 1869, so too would Malay and the recently expanded trading posts of Singapore and North Borneo (Sabah state and Brunei).[77] Both outposts—gained by way of commercial treaties signed with marginal local "princes"—would begin to bear the weight of expanding capitalist imperialism for the next 50 years. As with Hong Kong and Canton, EIC (and later the North Borneo Chartered Company) strategies exploited local conditions, upsetting indigenous political relations by way of favoring one family over rivals with advantageous trading conditions. In time, what became known by 1867 as British Malaya was composed of three political entities under the direction of the British governor of the Straits Settlements.

Initially, these territories consisted of three EIC outposts—Singapore, Penang, and Malacca. By the turn-of-the-century, with tactics previously used in South Asia, Southern Arabia, and the Persian Gulf, the joint company and British crown representatives were able to coerce the once independent Malay emirates of Perak, Negri Sembilan, Selangor, and Pahang to accept British "protection," ultimately resulting in the 1895 Federation. Crucially, the British operatives and their Dutch corporate counterparts may have used a set of constructed social hierarchies in Malay and the Indonesia islands to help reconstitute the region's ruling classes in such a way that their power and wealth relied entirely on the good will of the EIC and later British administrators.[78]

In "native" policies replicated throughout the world, local "Arab" allies were deemed the most useful assets to help legitimize—give local cover to—these emerging exploitative relations. While a whole scholarly sub-field has emerged exploring how certain families came to be so prominent in Southeast Asia, it is often sidestepped that these families' prominence was at the very least buttressed by a Euro-American endorsed version of indigenous social hierarchy. In this matrix, certain "Arab Shaykhs" of sada/sayyid (decedents of the Prophet Muhammad) heritage were conveniently elevated above their "native" subordinates to justify political partnerships that benefited European companies at local expense.[79]

Such policies of creating "tribal" or "princely" hierarchies are now well known with respect to imperial strategies to co-opt certain local surrogates. Indeed, this policy of "indirect rule" was practiced throughout Africa, the Middle East, and Southeast Asia.[80] Part of its operating logic, as least in Southeast Asia, was one that permitted only those with proven genealogical links to Arabia, and specifically the Southern Arabian region of Hadhramawt, to secure a position within a "natural" political authority legitimized by treaty with British companies and crown.[81] What is important for our purposes here is that these select few would then be allowed to flourish, translating a genealogical (thus ideological) legitimacy into the accumulation of property and wealth by allies to the British. When Singapore, for instance, grew into a major trading port, it was the ad hoc manner in which the colonial government applied its authority that assured certain groups of "locals" would gain the upper hand over other, perhaps less cooperative natives.[82]

What allowed this process of selective empowerment of "native" collaborators to function was the nature of "thin" imperial power, based entirely on the arbitrariness of the application of law. Corporate, and later British state ordinances, acts, and precedents were never routinely enforced, but were rather used when necessary to help prop up and empower the right allies. As a result, members of an Indian Ocean trading network, consisting of some Yemeni Hadhramis, Ottoman Jews, Armenians, and Syrian Christians, often benefited from being the preferred surrogates for a sparsely populated "British" contingency in these Southeast Asian territories.

The work of Michael Gilsenan has proven especially illuminating in that the British use of the power to issue laws, often *ex post-facto*, and then to electively enforce them, gave their surrogates considerable leverage over "natives" whose lands were deemed especially valuable.[83] In this respect, there were frequent examples of British courts allowing rather egregious land grabs by in particular Chinese and Hadhrami merchant families via the administration's "right" to alienate property deemed either under misuse, or were "uninhabited" prior to their acquisition by the EIC.[84] This opened up minimally regulated spaces for the growth of "real property," which Hadhrami, Indian, Ottoman Jewish, Armenian, Syrian, and Chinese elite began to monopolize. In time, these holdings had the snowball effect of making the first favored families even wealthier, and thus more powerful. Such a system presided over much of British-administered Malay, Singapore, Borneo, and along the Chinese port-cities, including Hong Kong.

While it is Cantonese "pariah middlemen" who are best known to have opened access to certain trade possibilities, some Ottomans from Mesopotamia and Eastern Anatolia were also taking part. Especially valued for their links to lucrative markets on the fringes of the Ottoman Empire, Ottoman Jews and Armenians may have been the first native-born subjects to become directly involved, commercially at least, with the Indian Ocean region in this transitional period.[85] No doubt individual Ottoman Muslim subjects conducted trade throughout the centuries but it is a particularly visible group of Baghdadi Jews who make this story of the itinerate Ottoman most useful to my larger argument.[86]

The Treaty of Nanking signed by representatives of British capital and Qing China created coastal self-governing enclaves whose "Grey zones" were designed to allow various commercial interests to thrive under protection of the treaty. Some of the wealthiest entrepreneurs in this period ended up being Arabic-speakers, often referred to as Baghdadi Jews. The trajectory of these Baghdadi Jews is crucial to appreciating the importance European traders attributed to their networks. It was, after all, these Ottoman intermediaries' who assured links were created and then maintained between their Middle Eastern homeland and India.[87] These families, seemingly in partnership with London-based capitalist interests intermittently set up extensions of these networks to cover Singapore, Surabaya, Java, and Rangoon.[88] By the 1840s, this small group of Baghdadi Jews became deeply entrenched in the treaty-port system and created a major center of operations in Shanghai as well.[89]

It is from this hub that one David Sassoon, a refugee from Ottoman-ruled Baghdad, began to compete with the Parsi and British-native opium suppliers. After being chased out of Baghdad in 1833 by the newly appointed governor—the Sassoon family was the banker of the previous top administrator recently deposed by reformers in Istanbul—Sassoon continued to use his connections with the Gulf and found refuge in neighboring India.[90] With some members of the family maintaining large farmlands back home, he was able, out of his Bombay hub, to corner the cotton market in Basra, where most of the new lands were being transferred into cotton fields, and Gujarat.

The wealth accumulated from this early period allowed for the family's company—David Sassoon & Sons—to initiate an expansionist period whereby a veritable Baghdadi Jewish commercial network spread throughout Eastern and Southeast Asia.[91] In time, with this Ottoman Jewish network helping the family company expand trade links from Basra, through Persia to Gujarat and then to China—first by exporting Iraqi cotton increasingly being grown in reclaimed marsh lands, then opium—David Sassoon & Sons became the biggest "native" company in the region, with branches in East Asia and London.[92]

These were very much Ottoman trade networks whose Mesopotamian territories remained the "homelands" of these increasingly powerful families. Partially accounting for their long-term success was the strategy to constantly draw new recruits from within these Ottoman communities in exile. In this way, families like the Sassoons could spread their trade beyond the British commercial empire to Dutch and later Italian circles as well.[93] Crucially, it was long noted that these were Arab-Jews who almost "never employed Ashkenazi Jews."[94] That these families in Hong Kong and Shanghai insisted on conducting their business in their native Arabic well into the twentieth century may account for the fact family-run commercial empires at the time necessarily fused tight patron-client relationships by keeping everything "within the community."[95]

These Ottoman-based kinship relations created economies of scale by the end of the 1860s that allowed the Sassoons to control 70 percent of the opium trade between India and China.[96] In time, the family firm helped establish a cartel to maintain prices of Persian and Indian opium in Shanghai markets (The Shanghai Opium Merchants' Combine) helping other members of the Baghdadi Jewish community, especially Aaron Hardoon, to continue to sell the drug even after prohibition was declared in 1917.[97] Indeed, the scholarship places Hardoon at the head of these Ottoman-origin families, purportedly the wealthiest person east of Suez on account of cornering Shanghai's property market.[98]

Ottoman Jewish families, along with Armenians with connections to the Sassoons, flourished in other parts of Southeast Asia as well. In Singapore a small group of Ottoman Jews and Armenians cornered both the opium business and the labor market. Impoverished laborers like coolies and pullers—often originally prisoners in Assam and Burma—were particularly valuable commodities for these families as cash-crop plantations boomed on the neighboring islands. The Elias family, for one, exploited links to these supplies of cheap coolie labor to become the "copra" king of North Sulawesi.[99]

This wealth translated into growing influence within the major trading cities, especially Singapore. In contrast to the Dutch officials discussed below, British administrators figured they had a powerful tool in these families whose residence in Singapore could assure the maintenance of a growing commercial empire with minimal direct costs. The arrival of Ottoman-born Jewish families also helped British loyalists keep Muslim intermediaries on a tight leash.

The new, ever-present desire of local "princes" to be accepted by British administrators gave these company men considerable leverage when it came to negotiating political loyalties. It appears that part of the dynamic at work in Singapore that kept local Muslim (Arab) partners pliant was a so-called Anglo-Mania, in which all things British carried considerable weight in local elite circles. The desire to assimilate into upscale white European circles in Malaysia and Singapore was such that any amount of money would be spent to secure entry into otherwise inaccessible racial enclaves. Perhaps the most notorious parvenu of his time in Singapore was Sayyid Muhammad bin Sayyid 'Umar al-Saqqaf (1889–1931), for a short time, the owner of the famous Raffles Hotel.

Other families proved more cunning and less flamboyant. Accumulating wealth by way of large-scale land purchases, families like the Alkaf and the Alsagoff led a trend that resulted in a remarkable 25 percent of Singapore's real estate resting in a small group of Arab family hands.[100] This wealth allowed "Arab" families to mingle within white European circles otherwise reserved for regional sovereigns. Such patterns of assimilation, although reserved for the very wealthy, did indicate power in Southeast Asia was obtainable to non-Europeans as a critical political tool. Indeed, the way such wealth translated to greater political leverage is best reflected in how many of these allies of the British administration in Singapore translated their status to growing influence in Dutch territories, from Celebes, as already mentioned in the case of the Elias family, to the political heart of the Dutch East Indies, Java. This rise of British-linked Arab traders resulted in a growing Anglo-phobia in Dutch circles; as Dutch merchants were losing out to traders based in Hong Kong and Singapore, including Arabs, a reordering of the racial frontiers was needed.[101]

As more and more trade from Basra, Arabia, and Eastern Africa funneled to trade monopolies in Southeast Asia, the British envisioned supplanting all competing interests in the Middle East through the cultivation of this loyal band of local Hadhrami families. To this generation of British strategists, the fact an entire region was inhabited by Muslims played to their advantage, one which would be used to undermine Dutch (and Ottoman) authority with their respective Muslim subjects by way of presenting a commercial and, as we will see in the next chapter, spiritual alternative to these rival imperial regimes.[102]

Ironically, the early phase of this imperial rivalry plays itself out in neighboring Dutch Indonesia by way of Ottoman subjects who also thrived under Singapore's patronage. Several prominent Ottoman (and Julfan) Armenians had been able to expand their Singapore-based commercial operations to the islands east of Java, creating a monopoly in opium for the region.[103] Two Armenians of particular note were Agah Catchatoor Galstaun, a major trader in Penang and Singapore, whose wealth made its way throughout the Indian Ocean; and George Manook who was actually the Dutch government's financier of choice in Java.[104]

While they did very well as individuals, other Ottoman Armenians, who had early on invested in transport in the Dutch territories, lost out to a slew of new protectionist Dutch monopoly laws. These measures meant to protect Dutch companies led to the departure from the region of the once formidable Armenian Apcar family (Apear & Co.).[105] In this context, Dutch colonial policies at one point induced a shift in domestic relations between those deemed "foreign" and "indigenous" Muslims; the notion that there remained those *Vreemde Oosterlingen* or foreign Orientals living amidst the Javanese—in other words, Cantonese, Hadhramis, various peoples from India and perhaps, depending on context, from Celebes, Borneo or Malay—took hold. This shift resulted in the invention of different bureaucratic categories to reflect the changing political configurations. With an evolving policy, all Muslims with a claim to Arab heritage became the targets of public attacks. Revealingly, this free-for-all corresponded with extra-legal attempts by some of the most corrupted Dutch officials to force these wealthy "Arabs" to sell their properties for cheap under threat of deportation, or possible confiscation of their property.[106]

This agenda had a subsequent impact on relations between Muslims, one that began to sharply divide indigenous versus "Arab" Muslims. This factor also played into the Ottoman story, as the growing sense of fragmentation demanded a new statement of cohesion among all Muslims as "divide and rule" tactics were bringing hitherto stable communities to the brink of civil war. The recognition among many community leaders in parts of the world where Muslims were "ruled" by Euro-Americans that they needed a contemporary doctrine of solidarity to thwart any further deterioration, proved ready-made for the Pan-Islamic overtures supplied by state-sponsored clerics in the Ottoman domains. As we will explore in the next chapter, it appears that Istanbul would try to take advantage of precisely this tension.

In this regard, the next chapter explores a new generation of 'Alawi and Nakshabandi Sufi missionaries, mostly of Hadhrami origin, that were inserted into centuries-long networks of commerce and spirituality that linked the Indian Ocean with Southeast Asia. Crucially, however, this new generation was largely trained in a particularly Ottoman spiritual context, one which by the 1880s was infused in a rhetorical climate that was as aggressively "nationalistic" about a uniform Muslim cause under the umbrella of spiritual guidelines largely shaped by Ottoman state-funded centers of learning. It is suggested that these dozens of eventually very influential men with years of experience interacting in an Ottoman spiritual context, may have left an interesting imprint in Southeast Asia.

All this is to say that it was indeed a contentious space in which the Hadhrami increasingly were made to feel as outsiders. In part, others saw the more successful Hadhrami trading/political families as irresponsibly sacrificing the interests of the larger community, if not the larger "Muslim" world, by playing the role of the region's principal commercial intermediary with the Dutch and the larger Indian Ocean world.[107] The subsequent outburst of official Arabophobia concerned itself with the fear that Muslims could unite despite the racial, tribal, and legal differences highlighted in European ethnographies written in the period. Seeing an opportunity to more firmly dominate the commercial production of the Indonesia islands, the Dutch spent considerable resources implementing segregation policies devised by companies and their advisors.[108]

The "hybridity" noted in the larger Indian Ocean can service a reading of events in a way that complicates the "Hadhrami" experience.[109] The idea of a sustained, distinctive Hadhrami-Arab identity surviving this period of European ascendency using racism is not only counterintuitive considering the political and economic dynamics at work in these regions, but the very different historical phases when people defined themselves in different ways, demands that we question conventional wisdom. By sticking to the label "Hadrami," my concern is scholars may forget that colonial politics of the period required they operated under the myth of a finite ethnic association among "Hadrami." Unfortunately, this did not necessarily represent a working doctrine of association and disassociation among local people themselves.[110] We see this play out more clearly in the Philippines, first under Spanish and then American administration.

Philippines

Under very different circumstances, the Philippines also became a place for opportunistic colonization by people from the Ottoman Empire. The northern islands of what is today known as the Philippines had long undergone forms of exploitative farming by Spanish overlords. Often, the economic exploitation of the island peoples served as a pretext for equally violent campaigns by Catholic proselytizers. The traditionally Muslim areas in the southern region of the island chain, on the other hand, successfully resisted Spanish encroachments. However, as the entire South China Sea region became an arena for European (and merchant family) rivalries during the second half of the nineteenth century, the Spanish governors in Manila aimed to protect their valuable assets by strategically expanding deep into the Muslim Sultanates of Sulu and autonomous regions in western Mindanao, and especially Magindanao (the areas around Cotabato).[111]

As part of this last gasp of Spanish imperialism in distant East Asia, administrators starting in the late 1860s tried to infiltrate beyond the few heavily guarded coastal outposts to establish working fortress colonies in the mineral rich highlands of Mindanao. Documents suggest that the authorities in Manila adopted a combination of tactics that ultimately hoped to pit local Muslim communities against each other with lucrative offers of trade concessions and the use of foreign colonists. While the majority of these foreign colonists taking the Spanish up on their offer were to come from China, what interests us here are the numbers of Ottoman Arabs who appear in the records from this period onwards.

While it is still not clear who initiated the "open-door" policy, by 1881 there were hundreds of Ottoman subjects settled in Manila with an already established place in the local and larger regional economies. The "Ottomanos" or "Turcos" were seemingly coming from the Ottoman Empire itself, as well as other formerly refugee destinations.[112] By the end of the Spanish period in 1898 there were literally hundreds of Syrians, mostly Druze and Maronites, who resided throughout the Philippines. In the capital Manila, Syrians became well known both for their peddling businesses and trade in especially jewelry and watches.[113] By the time of the collapse of Spanish rule, these growing colonies in Manila had become major players in the wholesale sectors and import/export trade. This activity was large enough to attract the attention of French officials who were seeking partnerships to expand their modest commercial footprint in the region.[114]

It is still not clear how many links (if any at all) between these Syrians in the Philippines and French authorities were already established in the Levant. Recall that French merchants were actively interfering in the affairs of Ottoman Syria since the 1840s. French consuls throughout the world were encouraged to tap into the paternalistic feelings drawn from the "commitment" to especially Maronite well-being.[115] As in other corners of the world, the official French consul in Manila reported of an abundance of Syrian traders residing in the city, with considerable trans-regional contacts that should be used to improve French commercial interests.

While the French hoped to funnel Syrian business toward the modest French commercial community in Manila, there is evidence that the Spanish authorities offered considerable incentives for these same Ottoman Syrians to establish trading outposts in Muslim dominated Mindanao. These trading colonies eventually penetrated the entire island, even setting up supply stores along obscure river systems such as the Agusan.[116] It also appears that Spanish authorities looked toward Latin America to recruit "non-native" colonists to help subjugate the "Moros" of Mindanao. In the case of some Palestinian Ottomans like Gabriel Dabdub, who had initially migrated to México but then migrated again to Manila, the trip from Latin America was not so much an anomaly as a regular occurrence by 1881.[117] Other Ottoman Christians like Juan Awad also infiltrated Mindanao areas after being offered large land concessions. Awad, a native of western Syria took the land and invested in harvesting hemp and coconuts.

His particular enterprise was so successful that by 1885, this Maronite pioneer settler supposedly converted hundreds of locals to Christianity while becoming wealthy.[118]

Such entrepreneurialism expanded throughout the 1890s, and to most corners of the Philippines. Just prior to the Spanish-American war, for instance, we learn that the Syrian merchants with stores in Manila were doing their greatest business supplying fellow Syrians/Arabs spread throughout the provinces. These small cartels of Ottoman Syrians—many who held Ottoman passports issued in Singapore—began to monopolize the retail trade in parts of the Bicol and Visayas islands as well as the major towns of the Spanish territory.[119] They were also fixtures in the weekly markets of most major trading posts.[120]

This is a pattern of community building that is now well studied in the case of the Americas. In New York there were hundreds of Ottoman "immigrant" peddlers who attracted both scorn and admiration in early turn-of-the-century society.[121] More impressive still, in Buenos Aires, 53 percent of resident Ottomans were reportedly peddlers or small business owners.[122] Further north, Ottomans made up 90 percent of the *mascates* (peddlers) in São Paulo.[123] These small businesses became the seeds for a surge in entrepreneurialism and eventually domination of certain sectors of early twentieth-century Latin American economies.[124] What is now long forgotten is that part of the boom in these economies was the continued link to the homeland. Revisionist work on the Ottoman economy in the last half century demonstrates that in some sectors tied to the businesses the Ottoman diaspora operated in the Americas and East Asia, the imperial economy continuously outperforms its European rivals.[125] The major commercial operations of the world appreciated this success and wanted to coax members of these networks (or those who could eventually tap into them) to help develop their respective overseas investments.

In the Spanish Philippines, therefore, the authorities knew that these Ottoman migrants would not just be selling trinkets. Once established, many Ottoman immigrants/ refugees became involved in tobacco and copra (dried coconut) cultivation, a set of investments in plantation style economies that would eventually attract American capitalists after 1898.[126] Syrian manufacturers in the Philippines also cornered the regional embroidery market. Once the Americans occupied the Philippines, the Syrians gained direct access to US markets for its finished clothing. The ascendant Ottoman Syrian companies in Manila thus began to supply established Lebanese and Ottoman Jewish family-run businesses in the United States, an opportunity provided by Euro-American expansionism.[127]

Conclusion

As seen with the use of intermediaries throughout Southeast Asia by commercial interests and their colonial administrators, the organizing strategy of Euro-American Empire was at first to destabilize, and then co-opt indigenous stakeholders. Not only was it cost-efficient to appoint, in partnership, indigenous allies, but, increasingly these hierarchies produced new synergies for the larger imperial projects. The most striking example was the expanded trade networks someone like David Sassoon could offer the British investors profiting from the company's mastery of various lucrative markets. The Spanish too tapped into the flow of Ottoman refugees, some of whom actually first settled in México and the rest of the Americas. Using these mostly Syrian merchants, but also the occasional *Rum* Orthodox and even Albanian, to settle those areas ostensibly closed off to Spanish authorities, not only could Spain expand business between the islands within the Philippines, but it could also bring hope to the idea of eventually linking these southern regions to the rest of the archipelago.

And yet, despite all the efforts at introducing Chinese "coolie" labor into Mindanao, and the dramatic rise in the migration of Ottoman Syrians throughout the islands, Spanish authorities seemed to never gain an upper hand. One of the persistent problems for Spanish authorities was that all their overtures to create more trade opportunities between their areas of control and the Muslim polities ultimately had little impact on trade patterns. They had little influence over the population which led to even more violence.

One especially intriguing problem was the foreign Muslim missionary/traders reportedly migrating directly to Mindanao from foreign lands. As these "infiltrators" settled in strategic areas of the vast island, especially around Cotabato (Magindanao), an already autonomous Muslim polity simply seemed more impervious to subjugation. These "Arabs," as Spanish records identified them, married locals and thus become full-fledged members of their adopted communities. Crucially, the strengthening of these communities with intimate links to non-native Muslim traders suggests a foreign element may have been part of this steady stream of counter-colonialism of Mindanao since the middle of the nineteenth century.[128] Not able to stem the infiltration, the Spanish doubled their efforts to recruit Cantonese settlers to basically invade the Mindanao highlands in the hopes of changing the political dynamics of the region entirely. The subsequent outburst of violence actually signaled the introduction of an administrative "model" upon which the US Army, Mindanao, and the entire Sulu Zone's next colonial masters, would try to expand.

By the time the Americans drew the Philippines away from a defeated Spanish empire in 1898, the labor and political dynamics in the so-called southern islands demanded constant attention. Saddled by conflicting and contradictory stated agendas in the Philippines—a mandate for expanding empire *and* expanding civilization—the clashing constituencies, from missionaries, to industrialists and their managers, identified the Muslim regions as priority. These rough areas would require the kind of violent "white love" the native peoples of North America received over the course of the nineteenth century.[129] The parallels did not escape the invading Americans. In their early reports, the US Army, for instance, maintained that the Muslim peoples of the southern region, known as Moros since the Spanish era, were savages akin to Native Americans.

While America's arrival had accelerated the co-optation of some of the larger polities—the Sulu Sultanate, for example—the consequence was a free-for-all in much of Mindanao and adjoining areas. Faced with a multiplicity of organized armed groups constituted by independent polities scattered throughout "American" territories, the military men found themselves in a new frontier skirmish, this time on its far-eastern front. In 1901, the army commander of the southern islands submitted a report advocating a change in policy toward the Moros. In it, the racial shortcomings of the Moros were neatly fused to the peculiar historical role played by the Army in the construction of American Indians as "savages." Brigadier-General George Davis equated the "Mohammedan savages" he had to face in the mountains of Mindanao and throughout the Sulu Islands with "the Indian tribes on our western frontiers." This correspondence neatly evoked for his audience back home what became an institutional memory of "marauding braves led by indomitable chiefs."[130]

By 1903, the logical linkages translated into strategies of applying the same kind of violence proven to have worked with North America's "savages." Fearful of continued uprisings, the Commission charged with administering the Philippines created the Moro province and delegated its administration to Major General Leonard Wood. Having begun his military career chasing Geronimo of the Bedonkohe Apache, General Wood quickly adopted similar methods of suppression in respect to local Moro resistance that, according to him and his superiors at the time, were the only means to deal with so-called savages.[131] With the assistance of other noted native-hunters like John J. Pershing and the Colorado Volunteer Infantry, the violence against Mindanao's people took on a life of its own.[132] The military history of the subsequent campaigns in the highlands of Mindanao and throughout the islands of Basilan and Jolo have been well researched. This research has been especially helpful in appreciating how the particularly notorious massacre at the Battle of Bud Dajo in 1906 made it difficult for promoters of American Empire to market a war for "civilization" to a country in the throes of economic crisis.[133]

While this cannot be the place to pursue this aspect of the story too much further, what the Americans discovered was that their interactions with Muslims as subjects— and even more, as dangerous adversaries—left them at a loss as to how to deal with this new kind of difference. In what is beginning to emerge as an entire subfield in the study of American Empire, scholars like Robert Vitalis and Jonathan Schmitt are now revealing that a new form of social science—the rise of International Relations within the discipline of Political Science—would complement an already fertile industry of anthropology once used to "know" the peoples of North America.[134] What is striking about American policies in these early years in Mindanao is the kind of resources they elected to harvest to deal with the Moro (Muslim) resistance that at once duplicated certain policies toward Native Americans—for instance signing a "treaty" with the "chief" of Sulu in return for peace—but then moved well beyond.[135] The subsequent modification of previous methods entailed harnessing the "culture" of those resisting American civilization to pacify them. In some cases, this strategy of "Benevolent Assimilation" meant using Ottoman refugees as surrogates.[136]

For one, the Americans would resort to a logic which imputed a particular knowledge of the "ways of the native" to those who shared these peoples' faith, leading them to employ Ottoman refugees as intermediaries among the indigenous populations. This supposedly "natural" affinity between indigenous and Ottoman Muslims was even noted by US Army generals, in whose eyes, local "Mohammadians" were basically "Turks," or sometimes, "Arabs." In this regard, American officials resorted to tactics previously used by the Spanish.

As did their predecessors, American authorities engaged the Sultanate of Sulu (recognized by the Americans as "sovereign" as their mission at that stage was framed as a "mandate" to a still skeptical American public) through the use of external Ottoman surrogates. As the racial frontier between Anglo-Saxons and natives required careful management, an intermediary like the Ottoman Muslim could serve as the necessary filter. In other words, the ready-made tactic of the Spanish to encourage Ottoman "Turks" or "Arabs" to serve as the useful middleman seemed the most cost-efficient, and crucially for the next chapter, ethnographically "logical" solution to an otherwise intractable conflict.[137]

As much as there was a violent hatred for all things "Moro" in the largely racist American administration, those officials sent to study the natives revealed another aspect of the colonial divide: a condescending fascination with the Moro occasionally grew to become a begrudging admiration for an idealized object of scientific study.[138] The critical actor in the scientific campaign to fight Moro resistance was David P. Barrows, a trained anthropologist who was given the responsibility to both study the peoples of the south and then devise a way to best manage them. Sent to the region during the middle of the brutal military subjugation of the resistance, Barrows expressed some melancholy about what he saw. He believed the taming of the peoples of Mindanao and larger Sulu was a kind of sad passing of a by-gone era. To this future President of the University of California, the destroyed Moro "pirate states" were the only native Filipino "political achievements of any consequence." As such, these peoples, while in need of the "benevolence" of the American Mandate, nevertheless deserved some dignity.[139] One way to accomplish this was to invest some serious scholarly attention to their study, as if an archeological artifact.

What is crucial here for the Ottoman connection is that Barrows sought to find a "scientific" way to avoid what he thought was becoming genocide akin to the destruction of so many of North America's warrior peoples. His answer to this moral quandary was to study the Moros as Muslims and thus Orientals who did have claim to a once glorious civilization.[140] As such, these slightly more civilized people than the "pagans" Barrows had to deal with in the North of the Philippines, deserved a complimentary role to the larger American civilization project, one that would rely on future cooperative and productive partnership with the superior American rulers.[141]

To assure this process would take the right path, in 1901 Barrows appointed an Ottoman American of Lebanese/Syrian heritage, Najeeb Saleeby, to the position of vice-president of the Bureau of Non-Christian Tribes.[142] Saleeby's main task was to use his particular skillsets as an Arabic-speaking Arab (albeit Christian) to "study" these peoples. Expected to provide the kinds of insights presumably only a fellow "Oriental" could gain, Saleeby, a trained physician and not an ethnographer with local language skills, eagerly took up the project nevertheless. His resulting publications demonstrated an interest in the region's considerable history. He accumulated Muslim manuscripts and, just as the British were doing with their useful intermediaries among the Hadhrami throughout the Indian Ocean world, started to lay out a genealogical schemata that could help American administrators identify Mindanao's "royal" class. Moreover, having no knowledge of the local languages, Saleeby nevertheless claimed to have been able to translate the codes of laws used by the Magindanao and Sulu Sultanates from their family and community archives.[143]

This use of Moro manuscripts armed Saleeby (and thus the American project as a whole) with a documentary, textual framework to present the Moros as a distinct, historically rooted, and thus, (semi) civilized people with whom the Americans could do future business.[144] The utility of accessing (in every way mirroring the Orientalist experts servicing French, Italian, and British imperialism elsewhere) Moro laws through their own texts meant the Americans could find a starting point from which they could, if needed, begin to reconstitute "customary" authority in order to help pass over responsibilities of governance to these very peoples the American military Governor had just brutally suppressed.

Crucially, Saleeby was not the only Arab of Ottoman descent to have worked on behalf of the American government in their quest to pacify the Muslim populations of what became the Southern Philippines. David Barrows also solicited assistance from Shaykh Mustafa Ahmad to fine tune a text book the chief educator in the Philippines hoped would be used in schools set-up in the Sulu region.[145] It seems Ahmad had secured so much trust from Barrows and the American administration that he was charged with also finding a suitable Mufti, or supreme spiritual guide, to oversee the development of the Muslim community. To this end, Ahmad actually recruited Sayyid Muhammad b. Wajib al-Jilani from Istanbul, presumably under the advice of the Ottoman authorities at the time.[146]

This connection to Istanbul by way of religious institutions is remarkable considering just how "alien" this part of the world was to things Ottoman. And yet, that an Ottoman religious scholar is recruited to move to Mindanao on behalf of an American regime demonstrates an aspect of Ottoman foreign relations largely ignored in the now copious scholarship on "Pan-Islamism" and the "Politicization of Islam" in the Hamidian era. This one moment of collaboration between Istanbul, several Muslims and Christians of Ottoman origin, and the US Military Administration of the southern Philippines may warrant a new look at what were the actual issues facing the Ottoman state at this crucial period of transformation. As much as the scholarship posits that the Ottoman state was in the throes of "modernizing" its institutions, this process may have included more than expanding public education and road works. The Istanbul/ Ottoman migrant/US Military collaboration may suggest that the Ottoman state was seeking to harness the practice of faith to serve a foreign policy end.[147] Here then, we can begin to think, in the next chapter, how itinerate Muslim subjects could have contributed to a new conception of a possible utilitarian use of Islam as a weapon of the imperial state in its campaign to become a global power.

Missionaries at the Imperial Ideological Edge

Introduction

It is a methodological problem that scholarly convention remains hostile to the necessary deconstruction of "Western" assumptions about the way religion fits into Ottoman state policies towards the empire's diverse subjects.[1] The following lays out an at times counterintuitive polemic against those prevailing methods of writing Ottoman histories as an exclusively Muslim, Armenian, Albanian, *Rum*, or Slav Christian story. In the process, I hope to undermine the contradicting logics of how religion in general and Islam (and Muslims) more specifically is expected to perform as an historical causal "agent" during the tumultuous 1878–1939 period. To do this, I will try to complicate an already emotionally charged set of issues found in national historiographies while exploring events along the Indian Ocean fringe of the Ottoman Empire. In these Eastern African and Southern Arabian locales, it is possible to test how the categories conventional scholarship employs not only work to distinguish groups of people, but to deduce the groups' motivations and loyalties. In addition to ultimately proving theoretically inadequate, these categories will also prove to be historically misleading.

The main thrust of this chapter is to reaffirm that we do not gain anything from fixing human beings' associations to a faith, or by extension, a presumed larger religious community—Muslim "umma," Catholics, Jews—if such associations are assumed to explain relations towards one "minority" group or another. This corrective applies especially to the tendency to link peoples' faith to the violence recorded throughout the territories of the late Ottoman Empire. Unfortunately, violence between communities in the Balkans or Anatolia, for instance, is often framed in terms of each adversary's religious affiliation. In this respect, Ottoman history has always been framed in terms of its "Islamic" character.

To many historians of the period, the very erection of schools, madrasas, mosques, and "religious" regulatory bodies by the 1850s was emblematic of a pro-active Ottoman state trying to harness, among other things, "Islam" for the very "modern" goal of linking group spirituality to expanding "state" interests. This, it is argued, was the Ottoman administration's policy in times of violent turmoil when many peoples were uprooted and on the move. The idea was that with the establishment of state-funded institutions such as schools and reliable religious centers, these otherwise dispersed and often desperate peoples could find sustenance and begin to resettle.[2]

But it has been argued elsewhere that such costly enterprises were ultimately steered toward select groups and/or regions whose access to the decision-makers translated into the flow of state funds. In other words, regardless of actual need, what in the end determined where certain resources were allocated was the strength of regional representation within the halls of power.[3] The principle of course continues to apply today in modern "democratic" societies where state largess is often distributed to select constituencies due to their privileged access to decision-makers.

We should, therefore, reconsider the manner by which "Islam" performs the imperial state project, both for "Christian" interests who are regularly identified as working through "Muslim" proxies to use as an imperial weapon against rivals, and the Ottoman state itself.[4] Muslim attacks against Armenians or Greeks (as Christians), for example, may be read differently, with other possible social, political, or economic explanations for the violence thereby offering historians an alternative to the simplistic (often manipulative) explanation of events through a religious (or ethno-national) prism.

In these matters of figuring out how power (and violence) is used, and in whose interests, it seems we may be better served by narrowing (by way of expanding) our focus beyond any one assumed explanatory category. Some scholars writing about Middle Eastern societies have already argued for such a different approach. I have in mind those who have moved beyond drawing conclusions about the relative extent to which one's religious practices reflects a political orientation based solely on supposed "ethno-national" associations, doctrinal affiliation, or "tribal" linkages.[5] With this corrective scholarship serving as an inspiration, I make it my task here to render the linkage between religion and imperialism more complicated by inserting a new kind of refugee/migrant into the fray.

By looking in particular at a multi-year, transregional campaign to convert large numbers of "native" East Africans to Islam using the talents of Ottoman-trained missionaries, I will begin to close this preliminary study of the refugee/migrant with yet more complications that are meant to induce further research and debate, rather than assert any incontrovertible alternative truth. I will ultimately conclude that there is no identifiable pattern to how different Muslims interact with the world. Drawn from examples of Sufi missionaries' activities in East Africa, far from being a "policy," we learn that the linking force drawing the Ottoman refugee to events elsewhere may be entirely out of any single state or religious institutional control.[6]

Crucially, it is not challenged here that the factions within the Ottoman state at various times made formal gestures at streamlining the relationship between the bureaucratic elite and religious authorities in various Muslim (and Christian and Jewish) institutions. There were measures taken that aimed to address certain "imperial" concerns. In this regard, the "office" of the Shaykh ül-Islam and the *Rum* Patriarch, for instance, became increasingly important, at least at the formal level, as the greater influence of outside institutions began to cause communities to fray at the "sectarian" seam. Indeed, by the time of the Hamidian regime, these offices in particular took on the appearances of being propped up by the Ottoman state in the hope of influencing certain social practices and the organization of communal life to assure loyalty and stability.[7]

But as we will see with the peculiar case of how factions within the Ottoman state, already in the 1860s, sought to create an administrative bridge to some of its hitherto disparate Sufi orders, the function of this bureaucratic move cannot be so "obvious." Without a healthy distrust for what "Islam" as a category of analysis does for us, such "Muslim" institutions will almost "naturally" lead us to believe that the Ottoman state moved toward "state centralization" by the simple act of setting up, for instance, a Council of Sufi shaykhs.

But as with the more complex story behind building schools in the Balkans and setting up armed militias in Kurdistan,[8] the erection of "religious" advisory bodies may be less the product of a drive at enhancing government power, à la Foucault, and more a reflection of a complicated set of networks increasingly seeking a partnership with the empire for purposes entirely specific to the "client." These variables meant politics were at play, not edicts imposed from the Sultan *cum* Caliph. In other words, even the Hamidian regime, just like its diverse imperial rivals with their own supposed "Islam" policies, was as much negotiating with complex, ever-changing "Muslim" constituencies as dictating to subjects.

This assertion will carry more weight after first demonstrating how scholars have over-interpreted the significance of the creation of several administrative bodies and then expanding on the suggestion that imperial policies vis-à-vis subjects, peoples, and the faithful are constantly mediated by very different contexts. In other words, there can be neither a uniform Islamist policy nor a singular "Muslim" agent of history.

Meclis-i Meşayıh

Recent work on what is posited as Ottoman state attempts to centralize Sufi orders over the course of the *Tanzimat* and then Hamidian era has been welcome.[9] Brian Silverstein in particular, has rearticulated the large body of work in Turkish on the subject to consider a new measure of central state power that aims to institutionalize certain religious practices with the assistance of a select group of Sufi shaykhs.[10] Leaders of five Sufi orders operating in the Ottoman Empire appointed to form the Meclis-i Meşayıh (the Council of Shaykhs), were ostensibly asked to help harness the social networks attached to their orders so that the Empire could rule more effectively. As the objective was purportedly the expansion of state power over previously autonomous Sufi *tekkes* (lodges) with large followings, this move appears at first to parallel those processes at play in Europe at large. Thanks to a tendentious reading of Foucault, for example, we are encouraged even to link Ottoman state sponsorship of "reform" to the extension of state power. Of course, this mobilization seems, on the surface, perfectly logical considering the fact that there existed a vast universe of autonomous Sufi *tekkes*—upwards of 8,000 in the Ottoman Balkans prior to 1912—that were nominally under some form of Ottoman administration. These lodges could have, in theory, aided in strengthening state power over its population. For this observation to have any useful purpose, however, we must fully contextualize the various actors involved in this process.

By all accounts, like-minded reformers within some Sufi orders had, by the early *Tanzimat*, found common purpose with government reformers. Seeing a general need to both develop their respective communities into becoming active agents in the changing world, coupled with a related need to exert greater authority over their vast networks of loosely connected "brotherhood lodges," shaykhs found enough incentive to embrace the *Tanzimat* and Young Ottoman secularists. In this respect, it may be worth reminding those familiar with the scholarship on liberal reform throughout Europe that Ottoman reformers themselves were not so quick to decry the Ottoman spiritual heritage as some would suggest. It is true that the most prolific of this generation of reformers looked down on some Sufi "folk" practices in unregulated, rural areas. But considering the wide range of spiritual interests so many of the *Tanzimat*-era thinkers demonstrated in their writings, and indeed their own patronage of Sufi orders in their home districts, the story of Ottoman state reform and "secularism" prior to the Hamidan era cannot be considered equivalent with the range of personal motivations among individual reformers.

Charismatic Sufi shaykhs (who may have been entirely independent of any "central lodge" of any particular order) had a history of leading their often isolated rural communities into confrontation with neighbors and the state. The relative autonomy of these often mobile spiritual guides increasingly became the issue of political order rather than the religious orthodoxy of their messages. In this regard, community spiritual leaders often played independent roles in times of crisis, including those such as food shortages or the influx of refugees. Without a dominant state or an alternative source of legitimate leadership, it was often these spiritual guides who filled in the void. Often, the manner in which they did this was rallying local communities against the failing state or some other identifiable source of the community's collective pain.

To scholars the seemingly requisite move by the modernizing state to create a new hierarchy of scholarly training in order to ensure that the "message" conformed with contemporary, established mainstream interests necessarily reflected a move to harness religion as an extension of government.[11] We are told, for instance, that by 1836, ". . . the Ottoman state's policy toward the [Sufi] orders amounted . . . to so many efforts to bring them more fully under inspection and control as part of its [the Ottoman state's] broader project . . ."[12] Such attempts at incorporating Sufi orders thus reflected a greater project of Ottoman "governmentality," an "obvious" reference to forms of state centralization that historians have increasingly sought to apply to an Ottoman case as part of a larger "global phenomenon." The problem is this opportunistic fusion of observable institutional developments with useful interpretive models to understand the emergence of modern power misuses the affiliation of those participating in these projects while also ignoring the specific contexts discussed throughout this study.

Contrary to the global-mechanistic model integral to the meta-narrative of modernity, the attempt to incorporate by way of committees the many disparate circles of autonomous authority (Sufi and otherwise) in the Ottoman territories had its origins first at the provincial level, and second, at least a decade earlier than the creation of the *Meclis-i Meşayıh*. As was seen in the careers of the best of the Balkan-based *ayân* governors and then reformers like Midhat Pasha, the precursors to central state projects directed from Istanbul were often developed by innovative provincial administrations. Their task was to better maintain relations with disparate community leaders from areas that were known for their rebelliousness. For example, an outburst of resistance to a series of new taxes on landowners in Northern Albania in the mid-1850s compelled the governor Menemenli Mustafa Pasha to focus less on collecting the egregious taxes and more on simply finding a means to communicate with often disparate (and even rival) rebellious landowning families. The governor's solution was setting up a mutually useful cooperative council.[13]

Community leaders in the immediate area around the city of Shkodër who joined this committee, called the Committee of the Shkodër Mountains (CSHM), were given formal titles and salaries. In return, they were expected to reestablish and then preserve stability in areas previously only nominally under state control. Such overtures initiated a process of regional integration that would open the door for at least imagining a greater direct state role in the day-to-day operations of these previously isolated regions. This was not, however, a unilateral imposition of *state* power; but rather a locally negotiated détente through which very different interest groups could interact to respond to any number of contingent factors upsetting local stability. This "centralization" in other words was not a linear process leading to a greater state project, but a product of a multiplicity of interests informed by a changing local context in the 1850s. This is a crucial point to emphasize when we reconsider just what was at stake for an Ottoman state calling on various Sufi leaders to attend periodic meetings at some government building.[14]

In this light, it may be more useful to consider the underlying objective behind the creation of the *Meclis-i Meşayıh* in the terms of the CSHM. Rather than being an instrument of government as the state seeks to control religious leaders, the rationale for such a council may have been to encourage disparate religious leaders to begin a dialogue with the state. If nothing else, a new kind of relationship arises when stipends and even a quasi-bureaucratic title is offered a Sufi shaykh. At its formal level, the assembly of shaykhs was "expected" to produce reports that would then be delivered to the empire's Shaykh al-Islam.[15] Considering that upwards of 35 central *tekkes* were incorporated into this body at the initial phase, the assembly did have a broad geographic representation. And yet, the decision (or resignation) to incorporate only members of five Sufi orders—Sadiye, Kadiriye, Sunbuliye, Halvetiye, and Naqshibandiye—is suggestive of the autonomy many of the empire's religious leaders maintained.[16]

For those mostly Istanbul shaykhs participating in the Council, there were clearly divergent interests at stake. We learn that after its creation in 1866, the Council immediately exhibited a formal disaggregation by way of issuing greater weight to some members over others. It is never explained how the configurations were negotiated (for it surely was a negotiated process) but from among the 35 *tekkes* (individual Sufi lodges drawn from one of the five represented "universal" orders) there was a further distinction between "official *tekkes*" (*tekâya-yı resmiye*) and "private *tekkes*" (*tekâya-yı hususiye*). Having reached this division of authority, the Council then initiated the creation of a "central *tekke*" (*merkez tekke*) for each of these five orders, which were then expected to implement the Council orders and recommendations in the larger world. It is not clear how this actually worked considering those *tekkes* left out of this inner circle were thought of as independent of any "central" organization.

Crucial to a scholarship largely focused on tying Ottoman policies to a larger "Pan-Islamic" narrative, this recognized autonomy from the formally presumed "authority" of these "central *tekkes*" applied to, among others, those Nakshibendiye orders (sub-branches) that were linked to Central Asian or Indian lineages.[17] In other words, certain standards and doctrines, particular to each of these participating, individual lodges, (and not a centralized state-sanctioned, "official" theology) were the operative criteria for participation. There was no central operation to influence what was taught and what was said in the disparate Sufi *tekkes* in the larger world. In this respect, it is not clear how we should be talking about "Islam" and "Muslims," even individual Sufi orders, in aggregations that imply general commonality.

What was clearly not at play here was a global process of integration directed toward ideological or political control. Indeed, the Ottoman state and its small group of individual Sufi lodges did not even try to integrate Balkan, Central Asia, Indian, or Arab orders. Those participating in the Council were largely from Anatolia and Istanbul. In this regard, it is hard to see how such a Council actually would service a "regime" that was supposed to have "politicized" Islam in order to attain greater formal authority over first Ottoman society and then the global "umma" in general.

It gets even more complicated once we cut through the rigid superstructure of "Islam" as our categorical filter to interpret policies and events. There was actually a multiplicity of associations and councils of advisors that the Ottoman state and even the Sultan's office engaged at various times. While the Council of five Sufi *tekkes* mentioned above was in existence, there was also another tier of associations with which the palace at least interacted, granting an equal, if not greater, deferential weight to other religious/Muslim leaders associated with different scholarly and ideological traditions.

To this point, historians have argued that part of the Sultan's "reactionary" disposition was due to his close affiliation with conservative Sufi orders. In possible contradiction to the Council, therefore, Abdülhamid II surrounded himself with shaykhs from the Shadhiliyya, Sanussiyya, and Rufaiye branch *tekkes*. Crucially, these men came from mostly North Africa or the larger Indian Ocean region—this time from outside the Ottoman realm altogether. Again missing from this closed circle were natives of the Balkans and Arab world. What then, was the function of the *Meclis-i Meşayıh* in relation to the Sultan's inner-circle of advisees? To answer this, or rather to offer a working hypothesis, requires a layered understanding of individual loyalties and spiritual networks (and their links to lager family networks) and, most importantly, the abandonment of "Islam" as an organizing principle.[18]

The most provocative, intriguing intersections of Muslim activism at the time have only tenuous connections to anything formally attached to the Ottoman state. Rather, dispersed through many of the autonomously operating centers of learning within the Ottoman Empire's boundaries (and in Cairo, Morocco, Bukhara, Isfahan, and Delhi) there existed deeply entrenched ideological factions. Crucially, these factions' loyalties were not to the Ottoman state (or the other imperial patron states) but to particular ideological/spiritual trends, often associated with a small circle of allied scholars who, for our purposes here, emerged in a context where their disparate homelands around the world faced Euro-American violence.

Below, we look at what I chose to characterize as itinerate spiritual rebels, who adopted controversial methods akin to missionaries, and demonstrated a broad range of intellectual and administrative capabilities. These missionary rebels of the Indian Ocean were all products of processes taking place outside the Ottoman Empire. And yet, their doctrines were formulated within its boundaries. In other words, the Ottoman Empire was a sanctuary for refugees of capitalist expansionism. Amid such upheaval, these refugees' associations with particular Sufi orders in specific locales at certain times prove invaluable to our attempt to break free of the Orientalist epistemologies that still drive scholars to study "Islam" and "Muslims" as something objectively accessible. What is instead at work in the hushed halls of learning in Mecca or Istanbul and the steamy jungle enclaves of Sufi missions to convert "pagan" Africans, are distinct constituencies who, in many situations, act in reaction to specific processes in ways that only tangentially can take on the contours of normative (anti) imperialism. In other words, what is transpiring in the Indian Ocean's western fringes from the 1860s to 1900 is not a product of a state-run institutional network based on religion, but rather on a set of migratory contexts, in which events proceeded independently of any recognizable central body and category of analysis.

The personalities involved in this story were animated by discriminating ideals that derived from both their particular theological context and their own migratory history. In fact, we cannot separate the two as we study the larger Indian Ocean context which relates to these migrants underlying concerns and, tangentially, the Ottoman Empire. As none of the crucial spiritual leaders discussed below were born in the Ottoman realm—they had all, however, ended up migrating there, as refugees or as students— the particular interest they have in engaging the larger dynamics of the world reflect as much their trans-regional orientations as any Ottoman state effort to harness the plethora of talents coming to its shores. This multi-tiered associational context thereby justifies another detailed investigation into what is going on in the "liminal" spaces of being Ottoman in a transitional world. As can be seen from an Ottoman representation of the continent, "Africa" hardly constituted a target for exploitation (see Map 5.1). Its territorial configuration remained ambiguous, contingent, and malleable.

Forging trans-regional lines of resistance: Ottoman origin missionaries

One crucial element that leaves an Ottoman coloration on the lives of peoples living far beyond the direct influence of the state was the diversity of the empire's religious/spiritual/ideological associations. In particular, the nineteenth-century emergence of certain kinds of religious mobilization, in the form of long-established and recently reconstituted Sufi traditions—Qadiriyya and 'Alawiyya—reveal a constantly modifying set of spaces that reflected the changing social and economic conditions. From the Comoro Islands to Mindanao and especially along the East African coast and hinterland, men who effectively became Sufi missionaries combined their families'

Map 5.1 An Ottoman's Africa.

commercial interests with an ambition to expand very particular expressions of their faith. Again, these were not attempts at transmitting a universalist mission but direct responses to the specific conditions each faced in their transient worlds. Just what this all means to our larger discussion about the migratory experiences of a post-imperial world is best explained by situating these Sufi missionaries in a number of different contexts at once.

First, the men who became the proselytizing force of one last wave of resistance to expanding Euro-American power were all children of either other scholars, repackaging their father's already established mission to infiltrate new corners of the Indian Ocean worlds, or sons of wealth who had the material resources to migrate to the Ottoman Empire's great centers of learning and study under the era's greatest thinkers. Such children of merchant families who maintained bases of operation in Indian Ocean towns like Lamu, Stonetown (Zanzibar), Shibam (South Yemen), Surabayya (Java) and Penang (Malay), helped cultivate the generation of activist scholars whose underlying sense of purpose to protect both business and spiritual roots was in part a reaction to changes caused by the rise of Euro-American imperialism.[19] Proselytizing in direct competition with Euro-American expansionist projects in East Africa from the

1870s to World War I, their dual roles as merchants and purveyors of revolutionary messages to their adopted constituencies set a standard of engagement that had long-term consequences for both (Muslim) intellectuals and the way in which "Islam" was instrumentalized by various administrations. Put into this context are the intensive debates over procedure, practice, and moral authority in the various scholarly forums established in the larger Ottoman Empire during this period.

As we will see, the parameters of these debates were largely set in the context of engagements between various Sufi scholars and the personalities attached to the other dominant trend of "modernization" in the so-called Islamic world, the Salafists.[20] This "Salafist" reformism, part of the *nahda* ("awakening") movement emerging out of British-administered Cairo (this fact is crucial), has been the primary focus of scholars of "modern Islamic" thought. As a consequence, scholars have neglected to explore the iterations of dissent to this so-called paradigmatic shift.[21] More importantly, it is the Sufi missionaries emerging out of Mecca and Istanbul that represent this challenge to an emerging network of scholars closely linked to British administrations in not only Egypt, but throughout India, and eventually East Africa and Southeast Asia.[22] Ultimately, this constituted a doctrinal clash that itself may have complicated the application of such "reformations" deemed to be the essential transition phase in "modern Islam." Significantly, what we may succeed in doing here by highlighting these tensions is drawing the process away from being entirely a product of "Western" influences and returning our focus on various local and regional contexts.[23]

The events discussed below take place in a far richer ideological context than allowed in much of the literature fixed on neatly defined sectarian communities. As these Muslim missionaries often faced violent confrontations with Euro-American capitalism, their connections to the Ottoman world certainly expanded the terms of political debate at the empire's center. Moreover, the dynamism of the entire period gains that much more complexity with these missionaries returning "home." To help bring these local and regional dynamics into play, it may be helpful to tie all of this into how scholars of Jewish and Catholic transformations in the same period tried to make sense of the spiritual and political diversity.[24] Indeed, considering the manner in which some sources (and current historians) mobilize "Islam," there may be some useful lessons to gain from comparing how Catholicism and Judaism became constructs of particular sets of conditions unique to the late nineteenth century.[25]

The Sufi factions studied here may have constituted such an "international association" by way of being mentored by great men of the age, like Ahmed Dahlan or Fadl b. 'Alawi b. Shal (Fadl Pasha). But for us to make this argument work, other factors producing a global context is necessary. The larger setting that may work to mirror to an extent Abigail Green's "Jewish Internationalism" is located possibly in the manifestly commercial disruptions caused by the different kinds of productive exchanges between indigenous (Indian Ocean) communities and expansionist (but still not yet entirely dominant) Euro-American interests.[26] In other words, it is through the prevailing frustrations, fears, and anger instigated by otherwise disparate experiences of this confrontation with an increasingly generic "European devil," filtered through the teachings and speculations of two key scholars, that we see the contours of distinctive Sufi communities take form.

Again, it is the combination of very contextually specific intersections of scholarly networks, forged in the spirit of a response to the infringements on the dignity of the community from which each member comes—Penang, Comoros, Yemen, Oman, or Zanzibar—that makes their distinctive, momentary iteration of a missionary agenda worthy of studying. It is in specific responses to the larger dynamics of the world that we find the context for each (of many) "Muslim" constituencies taking shape. And it is this especially interesting set of different (sometimes, for important moments, intersecting) projects that actually contributed to the particular way in which global capitalism and its association with new forms of imperial states emerged.

By looking at the particularly fluid Ottoman migrant/refugee context in which large numbers of peoples in Eastern and Central Africa convert to forms of Islam brought to them by these Indian Ocean (nominally Ottoman) Sufi shaykhs, I believe we can open up a new terrain to study the broader sensibilities we now import to people who are part of a "Muslim," "Catholic," or "Jewish" community. Again, these associations in the documentation must be understood as references constantly mediated by new mediums of communication—by the newspaper for sure, but also by the forceful content of individuals' missionary message. This I would suggest warrants thinking about a distinctively new form of religious "internationalism" characterized by the emergence of a "sectarian politics" that the best scholars in the field have found within Ottoman Christian and Jewish "communities."[27]

Ottoman internationalism

To make these broader theoretical/methodological interventions I want to highlight the exploits of men who were involved in a quintessentially Indian Ocean story. As scholars with a deep training in several traditions, with the most prominent and common associations being the Qadiriyya and closely linked 'Alawi traditions, they were able to create new, temporary networks that left their imprint on the transformations of modern capitalist empires.[28] These were Sufis who believed that as much as Muslims engaged their faith in locales such as schools, mosques, and other institutions of state, the mechanical transmission of the wide range of uses of Islam diluted the spiritual, moral, and psychological importance of the message transmitted from guides to the larger public.

In the context of the period, a small group of scholars based interestingly enough in Istanbul and Mecca/Medina, actually stressed the need to return to the spiritual inspiration of "experience" as constituted in specific contexts. Their agenda directly contradicted the goal of the centralization reforms supposedly mobilizing Sufi orders for a larger imperial project. Instead, these missionary Sufis believed that their spiritual function only attained meaning in those communities that were experiencing certain forms of stress throughout Asia and Africa because of Euro-American expansion. This emergence, then, of a truly nineteenth-century "internationalism," in this instance of Qadiriyya and 'Alawiyya spiritualism, can only be measured when we realize it corresponds (and reacts) to the predation of British merchants from the 1830s onwards in locales throughout the Indian Ocean. In other words, we may best appreciate the depth of this Ottoman infused missionary spirit by considering the violence and oppression communities in the larger Indian Ocean experienced during Euro-American expansion. Put differently, the missionary activism monitored throughout emerged under a very specific context and cannot be considered part of a larger, global phenomenon.

At best, this was an "international" dynamic specific to a very distinct Ottoman constituency. These Qadiriyya and 'Alawiyya shaykhs interacted within the Ottoman Empire through the mediation of a set of institutions (and attached personalities) to whom they could gravitate. As a result, in the Ottoman context, these exiles from foreign Muslim lands could form a reconstituted community of refugees that responded to their plight by forging a kind of missionary project to challenge Euro-American ascendency. Crucially, this project, developed and even partially funded by the Ottoman state, did not necessarily resonate with other members of Ottoman society in the sense that it became part of domestic imperial debate. In this regard, for this particular set of constituencies (among so many others), it was neither a holy book, nor a myth of universal brotherhood, but a common dislocation that served as the crucible for forging a new kind of global Muslim community.

Again, far from being the work of imperial bureaucracies and scheming operatives of a "global" force that remains stuck within categories like "Muslim," "tribe," or "nation," the agents discussed below were individuals and the short-term communities they created by way of dialogue and missionary-style preaching intersected at crucial junctions of human migration, tragedy, and politicization to help create a new Muslim polity. I ultimately argue that this autonomous, independent intellectual class emerging out of a larger Ottoman context constitutes a vital force to resisting Euro-American imperialism and should be the starting point for reinvigorating our investigation into the range of spiritual possibilities available to people, even in seemingly desperate conditions leading indigenous peoples to convert to a "foreign" faith.[29]

Ottoman internationalism in East Africa

This then returns us to the issues of conversion and the ways in which we want the phenomenon to help us understand the transformations of the period. In Eastern Africa there took place a wave of conversions in the 1870s that completely transformed the political structure of the so-called "Swahili" society. While European Protestant missionaries usually receive the attention when this wave of conversion is studied, it was the numerically far more successful missionary projects led by a group of Sufis who had the greatest historical impact.[30] Recently trained in the Ottoman Empire, these Qadiriyya and 'Alawiyya shaykhs, most of Indian Ocean, Hadhrami origin, not only transformed the "demographics" of the hinterland of the largely Swahili coastal zones, but most likely also compelled the early European commercial operations to adopt very different strategies as they sought to expand their businesses beyond the ports.[31]

Behind this explosion of conversion "to Islam" was the rapid growth of Qadiriyya missionaries flocking to those regions extending beyond the coastal towns long established to service the larger Indian Ocean economy.[32] What these *Baarabu* ("Arabs") or *waungwana* ("Muslim lower class/non-Arab") ventured to do as they joined the caravan parties pushing deeper and deeper into the forests of the areas north and west of the "Lake Districts" was to accomplish what later Protestant missionaries sought in these same areas.[33] Among other things, they aimed to establish an infrastructure based on spiritual associations that could bridge hitherto debilitating political and cultural differences.[34] It is not that these chasms were only pitting indigenous, neighboring constituencies against each other, but the very "in-fighting" served as windows of opportunity for "Christian" Ethiopian and British/Egyptian/Turkish expansion. Each deeper schism within these hinterland societies offered another opportunity for foreign expansion as each external interest patronized rival communities to the point of open civil war.[35]

By extending into these besieged Bugunda principalities, the Ottoman origin Sufi missionaries created a trade network that linked once "isolated" East African coastal towns like Mogadishu, Lamu, and by extension, Zanzibar, to these areas on the borderlands of newly drawn imperial frontiers.[36] In this respect, the first wave of traders/proselytizing Sufis by way of the Indian Ocean transformed the contours of spiritual politics in these regions rich in gold, ivory, and human laborers.[37] Not unlike what would emerge in rival settlements later within the "Free Congo State" and various German and British missionary outposts, these Qadiriyya and 'Alawiyya settlements expanded as larger numbers of indigenous peoples of the areas north and west of Lake Tanganyika were drawn by the opportunities offered by conversion. As such, "Islam" itself transformed as hinterland communities increasingly converted. Such "popular" conversions complimented the politically important conversion of community leaders.[38]

Economically this "mass" conversion meant large numbers of hitherto "slave" laborers beholden to once powerful local oligarchs formed new constituencies that were no longer susceptible to pressures of the region's labor-extraction regime. Rather than having to pay back their "debts" in the form of labor, many of these now Muslim lower castes became themselves merchants in the trade with the larger Indian Ocean market. This transformation is crucial as many of these same "pagan" communities were beginning to face British/Egyptian expansion through Ethiopia as adversaries defending their own market niches. As the once lucrative trade routes to the Nile regions were cut, the incentives for new alliances with the once distant East African coast grew for these hinterland communities. It should be noted that similar calculations were at play throughout the regions further south and west, so that the Congo, for instance, by the 1880s was flooded with Belgian arms and thus witnessed the rise of competing "Arab" proto-states like Nyangwe that required the integration of these newly formed Muslim polities.

It also may be assumed that part of the missionary activity responsible for this transformation was motivated by the need to react firmly to the growing European pressure along the coastal regions. That being said, the growing European interest in the hinterland later on was itself linked to strategic concerns the earliest European companies had with establishing legally binding "spheres" of influence in advance of other trading companies, be they European or Arab. As such, it was thanks to these Qadiriyya and 'Alawiyya missionaries arriving from Ottoman Hijaz that locally based Omani landowners and wealthy Swahili merchants were given the opportunity to make a preemptive strike against European expansion into the regions. Such efforts to twart European financial capitalism's expansion was especially important in these hinterland regions as it is these parts of Central Africa from which all the valued commodities that made their regions so wealthy came.

This collaboration offers us new insights into the validity of framing events in the period in terms of a universal Islamic movement. The landed elite of Zanzibar funded what were basically expansion programs throughout this period. Ostensibly expeditions into the hinterland, the first fully funded Muslim "raids" reflected how local elite patronage resulted in the conversion of indigenous peoples in the interior of Central Africa, again, a crucial turning point in domestic politics that would likely inform how European expansion in the region would unfold. In all likelihood, the theory behind such campaigns was to assure long-term control over the ivory and gold the rest of the world coveted.[39] As these operations expanded in a number of directions, the most infamous being led by Hamid bin Muhammad (Tippu Tip), the major settlements of Tabora and Ujiji became of greater regional significance and by the mid-1880s, the focus of imperial rivalries.[40]

Despite the logic behind such investments in collaborating with Ottoman-based Sufi missionaries, there is still debate about why coastal "Arab" money went to such an extent into the business of conversion.[41] At a simply economic level, the creation of large trading hubs in the hinterland certainly made the "mass production" of valuable ivory and other "jungle" products possible; the benefits of capturing a greater portion of that market seems self-evident. But scholars remain puzzled as to how missionary work aided in the material gains of Omani and coastal landowning elites. By actively converting peoples west of the lakes (*Manyema*) who, as already noted, were the traditional sources for "labor" on the coastal clove plantations or for the pearling operations in the Persian Gulf, these campaigns into the hinterland actually depleted a lucrative "source" of profits.

While true, the reader must recall that aggressive measures to suppress this form of labor by Euro-American traders started already in the 1860s. In response, these landowning elite may have felt it no longer feasible to risk cargos in order to supply the growing demand for cheap labor in the larger world.[42] Reflective of these calculations, the regional economy had indeed transformed. As more and more of the maritime trade suppressed by aggressive European piracy was being justified by abolition campaigns mobilizing new forms of anti-Muslim sentiments during the Gladstone era, it may have been wise to shift tactics and actually create a unified Muslim constituency who collectively could resist European commercial expansion in Eastern and Central Africa.[43]

Again, the logic behind setting up secure trading outposts in the hinterland thus partially accounts for why local money would invest in the caravans increasingly accompanied by Ottoman-linked Sufi missionaries.[44] There is another, somewhat distracting debate, however, that is reflective of the larger methodological problem discussed throughout. Some scholars trying to offer a theological/spiritual explanation for the aggressive proselytizing suggest that local cultural elite—Arab landowners and their spiritual guides—wanted to penetrate the jungles of the Congo in order to bring in new blood to a regional "umma" the Arab community supposedly felt had abandoned proper Islamic "practice" for more "idiosyncratic" African/Swahili ways.[45] Ultimately, key segments of the scholarship insist that the real reason for such a wave of missionary work on the back of expanding commercial links between coast and hinterland was an attempt to standardize Muslim practices. The logic being that a new wave of properly trained Africans would overwhelm the "wild" habits of "folk" Islam.[46]

This fixture on practice seems misplaced however, considering among other things, the larger context affecting the political economy at the time, the kinds of debates emerging out of the Ottoman centers of learning, and finally those Sufi orders organizing the large-scale conversions. It was clear that the declining "waungwana," (local Muslim, non-Arab member of the merchant/landowning elite) eventually saw it in their own interest to support the new Sufi-led conversions. But far from being the conveyors of an orthodoxy or even aping the "reformism" of the era so many scholars have been trained to highlight, these Qadiri and 'Alawi Sufis had an agenda to make their message universally acceptable, a process perhaps better characterized as an attempt at popularizing their faith.[47]

Making Islam more colloquial, rather than formal and thus distant to the masses, addressed a larger concern among some firebrands working within Ottoman scholarly institutions at the time. To men like Ahmad Zayni Dahlan, Sayyid Fadl Pasha, Ahmad al-'Attas, Ahmed al-Idrisi, and Ibn Sumayt, the Euro-American encroachments in the Red Sea, Persian Gulf, and larger Indian Ocean were going to have long-term consequences, both for the practices of Muslims and the intricate patronage networks linking merchant families with the scholarly purveyors of the faith.[48] The best way to challenge this Euro-American expansion was increasing the practice of Islam, not restricting its utility to a small group of literate men.

As some scholars of the larger Indian Ocean have thankfully demonstrated, the most active missionaries were disciples of two key intellectuals of the era based in the Ottoman Empire. Crucially, they were also members of major trading families in the larger region. The Hadhrami/Swahili/Southeast Asia sada (sing. Sayyid) families experiencing full-frontal attacks from Euro-American expansionist capitalism were, in other words, the missionaries converting the hitherto ignored East and Central African masses. More crucially, this must all be placed in the context of a completely ineffectual (if not inimical) Ottoman Sultanate that consistently refused both to apply diplomatic pressure or even patronize efforts to confront expansionist Russian, British, Dutch, and American "Christian" empires. And yet, independent of the larger dynamics of Ottoman state policies vis-à-vis "Islam"—again a theme misappropriated by scholars fixated on generic categories rather than context—there were circles of resistance to European expansion fully operating from within the territories of the Ottoman Empire. We can call these circles the incubators of Ottoman spiritual refugees whose flight to and from the empire fed into the missionary work of Sufis against the Euro-American finance capitalist tsunami.

Refugee Ottoman missionaries

While largely forgotten today, the primary figure behind this new missionary spirit was one Ahmad Zayni Dahlan al-Makki (1817–86). Based in Mecca from 1871, Dahlan trained all the important reformers within the 'Alawi tekke who themselves became the major personalities in this expansive spiritual response to Euro-American imperialism. As many of Dahlan's students would come from South Yemeni families directly affected by the changing political economy of Indian Ocean trade, the significance of this transfer of knowledge and ideological spirit taking place within the Ottoman Empire is all the more meaningful once we link Dahlan to the itinerate personalities frequenting his Mecca office.

Dahlan was by training a Shafi'i scholar whose reputation was such that by 1871, he was appointed the Mufti of the Shafi'i *madhab* in Mecca by his peers. It is from this position that he gained a significant following and was especially influential on these previously mentioned Hadhramai young men who would eventually become the 'Alawi (and Qadiriyya) scholar vanguard seeking to expand "Islam" into Eastern Africa. Dahlan's prominence in an Ottoman imperial context can only be fully appreciated, however, by identifying his role as directing an entire generation of 'Alawi scholars toward not only a confrontation with "the West"—by extension the ultra-orthodox Wahhabis who became key allies of Western interests—but most importantly, with the much celebrated reformist Salafis based in Cairo.[49]

What is so often missing in the discussions on this "*nahda*" (awakening or renaissance) that informs much of the literature on the "Modern" Middle East, is some introspection into the larger trope of "awakening" in the nationalist historiographies focusing on a de-Ottomanification period after World War I.[50] What often translates into a generic reference to a Cairo-based reformism (modernization) and its polar opposite "literalist" orthodoxy (Wahhabism) is actually in need of greater attention.[51] Not only were there distinct ideological currents challenging the ascendency of Euro-American capitalism on its very distinct, Indian Ocean-referential terms, 'Alawi and Qadiri Sufis simultaneously opposed both of the Abduh/Rida and Wahhabi currents. The only way we can appreciate this outside the confines of a "Pan-Islamist" trope, however, is to invest further into contextualizing the goals of these mostly Hadhrami missionaries converting large numbers of Eastern Africans in the 1870s and 1880s.

This leads us to the doctrinal stratification which must be incorporated into the context of these movements. Dahlan's two-volume *al-Futhat al-Islamiyya* (1884) openly embraces the Ottoman Sultan as the preferred hinge on which all Muslims operate. As he wrote, the need for an operating, united sociopolitical order was predicated on the support of the Ottoman Empire, his benefactor in Mecca. This public confrontation with the lingering intolerance of Hanafi and Wahhabi doctrines afflicting Ottoman society still resonates today.[52]

Despite what at first glance appears open polemic with Europeans, especially the British, those Wahhabis and separatists advocating challenges to the Ottoman role in the larger world actually serviced the interests of European imperialists. In this context, the idea of introducing Islam to the Swahili world appealed to Dahlan and his Ottoman loyalist disciples. The motivation to introduce Islam in previously "ignorant" corners of Africa was predicated on the belief that these Ottoman-based Sufis' variation of Islam could bring harmony to humanity if this era of reform truly took hold. In turn, these Ottomans envisioned their form of Pan-Islamism breaking the stranglehold of those proponents of a strict, textual-based focus on doctrine (*taqlid*). The concern here was many of the victims of finance capitalism's empire had no use for such inaccessible polemic. The world they faced was entirely beyond the means of spiritual text to engage.

These Ottoman-based Sufis actually sought to liberate humanity, Muslims or not, by way of an activist introduction of Islam as a praxis, crucial to those needing a spiritual counter-weight to the political dissolution of their communities, economies, and institutions. What is vital here is their emphasis on delivering a message of "salvation" against the European menace in a "popular" language accessible to each people. Islam offered in the "vernacular," rather than strictly in Arabic meant the otherwise obscure claims of the missionary were immediately accessible to those targeted for conversion.[53] It also meant Islam practiced in these areas would be necessarily reflective of immediate conditions; faith in other words would be a living and not universalist apparatus serving external interests.

Just as Protestant missionaries had translated the Bible in various vernaculars to facilitate their evangelism, 'Alawali proselytizers in East Africa sought to make Islam accessible to local populations. This strategy, however, was controversial, as debates about the proper dissemination of the Quran (extending even to the potential heresy presented by the printing press) were still being waged. What is important to remember here—and, again, why context is crucial—is that Sufi (and Shadiliya) leaders made the decision to allow local exigencies to temper orthodoxy. More important still, these activists believed that the *message* of liberation was not compromised if delivered in Swahili, Malay, Javanese, or Bengali.

The larger doctrinal and practical debates pitting Hanbali and Hanafi scholars against those like the Shadhiliyya and even Salafists of Cairo, were around the legitimacy of *ijtihad*, a principle based on the need to argue about the relevance of scripture in contemporary terms. The nature of the struggle between Dahlan and the British protected reformists in Cairo, therefore, does have importance beyond identifying a general ideological embrace of the principle of *ijtihad*. I bring this aspect to the study because it is not enough to keep our analysis at a legal level of abstraction. Because while it seems the overarching "reform" movement can apply to all these groups on account of their use of *ijtihad*, it misses the crucial context of their more specific debates about how one actually uses the intellectual products of these practices. For the Sufis around Dahlan and Fadl Pasha, it was confronting Euro-American power in all its manifestations, one that was not entirely the case with Abduh, Afghani, Rida, or even members in the Hamidian regime.[54]

The fascinating doctrinal debates emerging from the rise of this community of "scholars of the sea" should remain a center of our attention not only because of the ideological issues at play but because these debates also reflect changes in the regional economies. Recall that these Sufi missionary *cum* scholars made up part of larger family-first merchants networks. The context, therefore, of their life-changing experiences was an often dual mission of expanding the family's commercial networks by way of gaining political influence in communities of settlement all along the vital trading towns of the larger Indian Ocean and, for some, gaining an education fitting a member of such families. The result was this crucial "friction" between indigenous responses to rising Euro-American interference and the dual evils of paganism and expanding Christianity propagated by British, Belgian, and Germany missionaries *cum* merchants. It is at such a confrontational level that we can situate a second scholar to help us break apart essentialist readings of "Islam" in modern world history.

Fadl b. 'Alawi b. Sahl, later known as Fadl Pasha, was notorious among the British for most of this career as an Istanbul/Mecca-based scholar.[55] His was a fascinating itinerary whose impact on larger affairs of the 'Alawi suggests an Ottoman refugee dynamic is at play at the intellectual and cultural level that ultimately complicates the stories we tell of "Islam" during this period.[56] Hailing from Malabar (known as Kerala today), Fadl Pasha's homeland was known as a major pepper-producing region. As such it was highly coveted by European trading companies beginning to challenge Guajarati and Malabar traders long dominating trade in the region.[57]

Cursed by the wealth produced by such trade, Fadl Pasha's homeland fell into political chaos as British trading companies started to patronize select members of the Hindu aristocracy as a means to instigate disruptive violence. The result was continuous upheavals in the 1830s and 1840s as competing "sects" fought against each other to gain access to British business.[58] In response, leading figures, like Fadl's father, directly confronted the foreign intruders.[59]

When coming of age, Fadl Pasha joined his father's cause, ultimately leaving him at odds with a newly installed local regime that favored granting British businesses privileges reminiscent of those granted by the Ottoman Empire.[60] Being more fortunate than most rebellious locals on account of his standing in the community, Fadl was simply exiled from his homeland. The fateful decision to move to Mecca, recently reintegrated into the Ottoman fold after a ruinous period of Wahhabi tyranny, would prove vital to one last period of indigenous Muslims' struggle against the forces of liberal capitalism. Sayyid Fadl arrived in Mecca in 1853, meeting Ahmad al-'Attas, a future Sufi luminary in his own right.

His exile in Mecca turned into assimilation. By the middle of Fadl's career he became a leading Ottoman intellectual who would have a profound impact on Ottoman internationalism and the way many global Muslims began to see the world vis-à-vis expanding Euro-American capitalism.[61] Be it through spiritual meanderings that tried to make sense of the shifting power dynamics in the world or the practicality of leading a violent resistance against the British imperialist project, Fadl Pasha would leave an imprint on the world around him.

Several scholars have linked Fadl Pasha to the violent resistance to British expansions throughout the Indian Ocean.[62] This leadership may have also included the Jeddah riots against European traders in 1858.[63] It is in this context of agitation and activism that Fadl Pasha's theological links expanded. Future Sufi masters like Ahmad b. Hasan al-'Attas and Ibn Sumayt first became associated with their own ideas of the "Sufi way" or path in the form of missionary work during these highly volatile, but equally intellectually productive times.[64]

It is a curious set of diversions in his life that probably made Fadl Pasha a magnet to like-minded men of the larger Indian Ocean. As a result of his popularity, Istanbul rewarded him with a permanent place in the intellectual core of the empire. Armed with Ottoman patronage, and a title of Pasha, Fadl Pasha immediately used his new influence to directly confront British expansion in Arabia. Such efforts may have included a series of intrigues that led to his emerging as a key ally for new Ottoman reformists like Ali Pasha, who oversaw the *Tanzimat* as Grand Vizier in the 1860s.

While still engaging in domestic political machinations, Fadl Pasha's struggle against British expansion in South Arabia began to take shape. Though not entirely certain, evidence suggests that by 1870, Fadl Pasha was in Mecca. This would have allowed him to engage Ahmad Zayni Dahlan and also become a major proponent of Ottoman expansion into the Yemeni highlands in 1872.[65] It is at this junction as a well-established intellectual that it seems he solicited a meeting between his son and the commander of the Yemeni operations Ahmad Pasha for the purposes of egging on the Ottoman army to actually push onwards from newly captured San'a' deep into Eastern Arabia. The push would have most likely led to Dhofar, where Fadl Pasha would in fact momentarily rule with local consent between 1877 and 1878.

A firm advocate of Ottoman expansion at the crucial period when British commercial operations were being transferred to Bombay-backed administrations, Fadl Pasha aimed to tear Arabia away from the growing British influence by way of his actions in the southern Arabian region of Dhofar, in present day Oman. Based in Salalah, Fadl Pasha initiated various diplomatic campaigns to extend Ottoman influence in the area. The Hadhrami/'Alawi, who had been marginalized by British supported sultans of Hadhramawt, were his primary base of support in Southern Arabia.[66] With almost a year based in the region and raising local alliances in neighboring Hadhramawt, Fadl Pasha made quick enemies with British authorities stationed in the area. In time, the British officials translated their fears into diplomatic pressure on Istanbul to expel the upstart.

Locals allied with Sayyid Turki, ruler in Muscat and ally of the British, were eventually rallied to force Fadl Pasha to return to the safety of Ottoman Hijaz. Forced to leave Southern Arabia, Fadl Pasha spent the rest of his life in Istanbul, where he became a member of the previously mentioned small circle of advisors to the Sultan. This appointment is crucial as it corresponded with the period when Abdülhamid II actively engaged in "Pan-Islamism."[67]

Some scholars who bothered to study this giant of the era were not impressed with his commitment to the larger cause of Pan-Islam. Anne Bang, for one, characterizes his Pan-Islamism as purely political.[68] Perhaps this is true. At the same time, however, it actually helps reinforce the earlier point made about the realistic place Ottoman state-funded institutions could hope to occupy in the shaping of local, regional, and global affairs. As a member of one of the various councils established by the reforming, centralizing Ottoman state, Fadl Pasha may have seen such membership necessary to extend his influence in the affairs of the Ottoman state, which otherwise neglected the Indian Ocean. While his earlier attempts at coaxing the Ottoman Empire to expand into Dhofar failed, his recognition of the limits of his "patron's" influence in the larger world vis-à-vis his hated British enemy most likely tempered his ambitions. His goal, like those of the 'Alawiyya discussed throughout, was not to hope for an Ottoman rescue, but to independently expand influence by way of missionary work.

Considering these acknowledged limitations, Fadl Pasha nevertheless is able to patronize individuals in this Indian Ocean uprising against the British. In this sense, Fadl Pasha used his proximity to the Sultan to engage with the large numbers of scholars likely to pass through the Istanbul. Indeed, in 1886, when prominent scholar Ibn Sumayt passed through Istanbul on his way from Java to Zanzibar, Fadl Pasha used his position to grant Sumayt access to some powerful factions within the empire's working elite. The Grand Vizier, Khayr al-Din Pasha, himself a Tunisian refugee, for instance, was convinced that Ibn Sumayt, along with the still reigning Sultan Barghash of Zanzibar, could create a meaningful barrier to Euro-American encroachment. Both the Grand Vizier and Fadl Pasha worked together to recruit the young Hadhrami to return to Zanzibar and continue to push back Britain from East Africa.[69]

This serves as a crucial junction because the association with doctrinal debates that play such a heavy role in the way scholars of the time (and our generation of experts then use to identify trends, factions, and processes) tends to obscure the larger contours of the Sufi orders' activities. Many of these *tekkes* would vacillate between open resistance to outsider influence and openly embracing them, depending not solely on doctrinal grounds, but on their constituencies. As stressed here, members of the 'Alawiyya and Qadiriyya orders were actively embracing the conditions in which they were expected to live, conditions that did not warrant diplomacy with the British (as would be the stress in the Ottoman Empire) but open confrontation. This missionary message of resistance, disseminated flexible doctrines meant to fit with conditions on the ground, thus giving more meaning to the conversion of many *Manyema* (or natives of the regions west of Lake Tanganyika). Their context was crucial. It also led to a re-socialization of "Arab" or sada/sayyid politics in Asia. These formal members of a landed elite class had begun to resent the empowering dissolution of hierarchies based on an increasingly familiar notion of racial borders being erected all over the world.[70]

It is important to note that, just as in the Balkans, this conflict and instability created opportunities for indigenous entrepreneurialism. However, while in the Balkans these opportunities were generated by the manufacture of local/global "ethnic" communities, in East Africa and Southeast Asia, Ottoman migrants/refugees were given the opportunity to self-segregate in more pronounced ways. In the last chapter it was the commercial opportunities available to many that led to collaboration with Euro-American capitalists. In the spiritual realm, the opening up of lands once neatly defined by linguistic and genealogical hierarchies by Sufi missionaries, using their "internationalist" method of preaching to "African" Muslim communities in Swahili, caused new traumas for those self-identified sada/sayyid elite. In this respect, resistance to Euro-American capitalism became more complicated as "Arabs" were now vulnerable minorities whose usefulness to German, Belgian, and British administrators only grew as distinctive anti-imperialist movements expanded along "populist," almost "fanatical" Muslim lines.

As in Southeast Asia, many of the dislocated Arabs, just a few years earlier perhaps embracing the rebellious missionary spirit flowing from Ottoman Mecca (independent of the state), began to see their long-term interests shift. The resulting successful expansion of "Islam" into the African hinterland set the social and political parameters of post-WWI possibilities. For those who could not countenance the transition from being rulers over Africans to ruling with Africans, many actually began to serve as surrogates of Euro-American empire.

The tensions that arise are crucial because reformists in British-controlled Cairo began to identify "Islam" as a useful tool to help reinforce "cultural" acceptance for the divide between the ruler and the ruled. This increasingly racialized setting—perfectly fitted for British, Dutch, German, and American administrative policies—would forever delineate between "folk" and "formal" Islam that scholars of empire eagerly reinforced. To fully appreciate the consequences of how these potentially tedious, textual debates played out, we must understand that the actual consequences of these growing doctrinal divides on social hierarchies increasingly translated into power politics. In this new scenario, political and cultural collaborators, like those "middlemen" in Southeast Asia and perhaps even some of the "Salafist" clerics in Egypt, were embraced as legitimate by way of their association with formal/orthodox practices, while those not fitting the role of ally of empire, were condemned for their "shirk" or idolatry.[71]

Here then we have a set of rationale for violence against many different kinds of usurpers of power that must be distinguished from any larger talk of "Islam." The events in the confines of East Africa during a period of large numbers of conversions to "Islam" also afflicted political dynamics impossible to replicate within the Ottoman Empire, along these same lines. But as much as it can be argued that these were "isolated" or "outside" something like an "Ottoman" experience, the very fact these events in East Africa and Southeast Asia, by way of migrating natives being trained and forging new communities in their temporary Ottoman homes, offer us the chance to appreciate events and processes that are distinctively "domestic" and thus must be treated as distinct from any global process. This then suggests we must understand the forces that compel people to form new group associations, invoking Islam no doubt, as specific cases taking place at particular points of time. Considering it in these terms helps us to argue for a new way to explore how the Ottoman Empire's many dissimilar regions experienced collapse in different ways. This must be done piecemeal, however, with the complex politics involving religious, ethnic, and socioeconomic difference in specific corners of say Central Anatolia, East Africa, or the Balkans, all treated distinctively from those politics of survival experienced elsewhere.

Importantly, even within the expansionist corporate state monstrosities surfacing in the form of "the Raj," the underlying "logic" of how such operations worked was not entirely reductionist. As discussed in the last part of this chapter, operatives for these imperial projects were discerning enough when dealing with the peoples of the world. In particular regards to the Ottoman Empire, there is ample evidence to point to British, German, Russian, and Austro-Hungarian policy-makers openly acknowledging the usefulness of exploiting the very diversity of "Muslims" and "Orientals." To them, in other words, the rigid binaries we are often encouraged to believe exist within "colonial" practices did not reflect any reality.

Instruments of abstraction

It should be seen as ironic that the same "Ottoman Empire," registered to play a role in the ontology of civilizational difference, had since the 1840s been in the hands of an "enlightened" and "modern" bureaucratic elite largely free of sectarian loyalties. This in face of an increasingly self-identified "European" state insisting on institutionally organizing its various imperial possessions along, as it turns out, constructed social hierarchies based on a narrow reading of what constituted religious (and or "tribal") communities. Indeed, this underlying logic of non-European peoples divided along sectarian (and racial) lines served as the foundation to a colonial organogram of humanity that shaped how competing imperial powers would agree to divide up the world.[72]

And yet, historians of the Ottoman period immediately following the *Tanzimat* era identify tell-tale signs of the same "colonial" "modernity" seeping into the retrograde Hamidian regime. Variations of a "colonial Ottomanism" started to pop up in the kinds of institutions the regime established, from "tribal schools" designed to educate "savage shaykhs" and thus "civilize" the "natives," to a reordering of the daily regimentation of social and bureaucratic time in far-off Mosul and Yemen. Those who have written of such new trajectories of the Ottoman Empire represent a new phase in the scholarship which unfortunately has embraced almost entirely the rhetorical "logic" of an apparently "Western" state-building project. In this section, I express my distress at an apparent rush by scholars of the Ottoman Empire to finding parallels or, at best, modifications of something adduced in nearly paradigmatic terms as modernity.[73]

The issue for me here is not the presence of the institutions that emerge in a formal sense, but the way historians today expect them to work for a larger scholarly, theoretical project while failing to place these periodic institutional innovations into a much more dynamic, non-deterministic context. While I have continued to express my frustrations with the way policies toward "tribes" and "backward ethnic" groups—in the context of Yemen and the western Balkans—I will focus here specifically on how "Islam" as a unit of analysis (and Muslims) are similarly mobilized to avoid doing the heavy-lifting of contextualizing policies and practices in vastly different settings, be it along the edges of the Ottoman realm, or deep within. More specifically, it is questioned here just how much more we can go to the religion/sectarian well to account for the kinds of policies the "modernizing" Hamidan state adopted.

As I see it, there is a curious disconnect between what seems to have been a prevailing oversimplification of how "Western" operatives believed the Ottoman world functioned and the subtleties of the actual strategies these operatives used when engaging the latter. Far from seeing the world in neatly segregated categories, the manner in which some external actors "manipulated" internal tensions suggested a more nuanced understanding of the Ottoman "world," an understanding that appreciated Ottoman "society" as dynamic with a human social, political, and ideological diversity vulnerable to outside manipulation. More importantly here, we are increasingly led to believe that the Hamidian state sought to engage in the "modern" state-building process by eliciting its own variations of "colonial knowledge." Additionally, we are told that this same ideologically rigid enterprise (at least when following the logic of the prevailing scholarship on the Hamidian regime) also sought to deflect outside threats by interfering in other empire's Muslim affairs based on a suspiciously similar essentialist construction of Islam and the way Muslims lived their faiths.[74]

In the context of the prevailing scholarship of late Ottoman imperialism, this Hamidian quest to "harvest" the faith and the faithful for purposes of competitive imperialism constitutes the "politicization" of Islam narrative that renders all of the spiritual diversity of these vastly different regions and people hostage to the very reductive reasoning of nineteenth-century Orientalists.[75] This reading of the dynamics at play beneath the surface of the formal documentation seems entirely out of place when situated in the larger scholarly context of how we actually understand the world.[76] Indeed, the very dynamic exchanges between various factions of the Ottoman state and the autonomously developing regional, trans-regional projects to address specific interests/concerns highlight that no single "Islamic" politics existed.

By 1878, all the powers were faced with the difficult problem of administering large Muslim populations, often in contentious settings whereby imperial and commercial expansion necessarily targeted Muslims' lands and property. Under such conditions, each occupying power was vulnerable to the rebellion of discontented "minority" subjects. In the context of this potential for rebellion against those *ruling*, any lingering tensions provided opportunities for external interference. Each empire, in this manner, framed "Islam" and "Muslims" as both the source of tensions, and if properly harnessed, the solution.[77]

As evident throughout this study, Ottoman territories as diverse as Albania, Yemen, and Diyarbakir exemplified these arenas of contention. The struggles between a variety of imperial and indigenous rivals within these vastly distinct territories both served global interests and diverse local constituencies.[78] In these contexts, all actors with the means invested in ways to harness specifically identified "Muslim" refugees. They did this as refugees were the potential source of violence while also, if properly steered, could be the resource needed to quell it.[79] As discussed in Chapter 2, we see this thinking applied to the influx of Muslim Circassian refugees from the 1850s onwards. The Ottoman state strategically settled hundreds of thousands of Muslim refugees into enclaves along areas deemed both volatile and vulnerable to external Christian influences.[80] As expected of these refugees, loyalty to the larger cause of the empire, no matter how that was articulated, was synonymous with these resettled communities' long-term interests.[81]

Oversimplifying the dynamics at play in these contexts has long proven to be a methodological roadblock. For example, something for decades known as "Pan-Islam" was purportedly a strategic opportunity for a variety of interests involved in the "Great Game." In these terms, the role of "Islam" in the context of this "Great Game" is entirely dependent on the assumed ethno-taxonomic and spiritual orientations of non-Western peoples. Such configurations prove highly suspect when seen through the filter of Ottoman refugees.[82]

To use one example, the literature on the refugees of Ottoman collapse often asserts qualitative differences between the experiences of "Armenian" internally displaced peoples and those of "Muslims" during the same period of tragic events throughout the last half century of Ottoman existence. As posited in the scholarship, the crucial factor here was the very fact one group of victims of war was "Christian" and the other "Muslim." The difficulty with breaking out of this neat, but ethically suspect binary compass is that the tools available to the historian often seem inadequate. Generic categories such as sectarian or ethno-national identity used to capture an "experience" as vast as famine do so to distinguish particular categories of people from others, not to explore the actual diversity of experiences and fluid contexts. Indeed, any binary construction of a disaster invariably serves certain ideological purposes while completely distracting us from understanding the immediate, local contexts that led to mass starvation, the plundering of plantations, violence against the landed elite, and subsequent state (global) responses.

While the tragedies of many Ottoman territories have become the foundations of post-Ottoman nationalist historiographies, some of the most striking features of these especially charged narratives are the uncritical assertions that sectarian difference and its correspondent "ethnic" and thus "national" affiliation accounts for who actually died and who did not. Armed with a certain set of categories, scholars have consistently claimed that they can identify the opposing "sides" in these volatile "mixed" regions by way of individual categories of people. But it is clear that, even among "European Christians" at the worst moments of genocide, the kind of influence Russian, British, American, German imperial agents, company representatives, and global revolutionaries alike hoped to acquire in the Balkans or Anatolia was not restricted to any one particular "group."[83] Instead, Russian, French, and British agents, for example, are known to have invested as much human and material resources into patronizing "Muslims" as "Christians" in Anatolia and throughout the Caucasus during and after World War I. And yet, far too many scholars are still unwilling to read beyond a selection of documents that only seem to reaffirm the generic categories of analysis still in use today.

One proposed alternative way of reading into the attempts by various "Christian" powers to find local "Muslim" clients in the context of a larger struggle for influence in the Transcaucasia, Eastern Anatolian region, for instance, is to abandon drawing conclusions by any strict use of "Islam," "Muslim," or some ethno-national reference alone.[84] There may be other ways to explain, for instance, the murder of "Armenian," "Kurdish," and "Turkish" villagers that need not refer to the criminals in terms of their "race," "creed," or sect.

At the same time, the manner we choose to inspect certain resulting associations formed over the course of such violent times may prove useful. In these same periods of horror, is there not a place for highlighting the acts of caring for those weak and destitute that led not to death, but survival? More still, what do we make of the religious conversion of a person, or an entire village for that matter, who faced deportation and likely death? In a related way, whose interests does it serve that these "Armenian Catholics" became "Muslim Turks" in the context of a famine, war, and imperial collapse?

Such questions are crucial in respect to reanimating how we understand collective action, especially if it registers as violence in the documentation. As it now stands, the animating factor behind any form or scale of resistance to institutional rule in the Ottoman, British, Habsburg, Romanov, or French Empires is framed either in sectarian, racial, and/or ethno-national terms.[85] If there is violence in the mountain villages outside of Bitlis, for example, it is assumed that there are tensions between Christians and Muslim inhabitants, Kurdish, Assyrian, and/or Armenian shepherds or clashes between Ottoman troops and a resistant proto-nationalist local "group."[86] It is a rare study indeed that dissolves the neat sectarian, tribal, and ethnic lines of distinction dominating the literature on Anatolia/Mesopotamia. It is even more rare to read studies that seek to break out of the "Western" ontologies that determine the manner in which we read resistance to Euro-American capitalism.

Much of the scholarship on Russian and other European imperial projects in contested "frontline" territories, such as in Central/South Asia and Africa, is framed in these terms of clashing civilizations and "modern" universalist projects.[87] As a counter to this reading, even the latest revisionist approaches to understanding "Pan-Islam" through the Ottoman filter prove disappointing. When contrasted with the very dynamic and sophisticated corrective studies within national historiographies, especially in the Balkans and Central/Eastern Europe, it is rather unsatisfactory that we are still fixed on such categories as Albanian, Muslim, Christian (Protestant, Orthodox, Catholic) and Armenian to try to decipher the violence and upheavals along the so-called borderlands.[88]

It is even more disappointing when the scholarship invokes sect, tribe, and ethnicity to try to explain what happens in these same territories when facing a constant flow of refugees, migrants, missionaries and "foreign" troops.[89] Again, while there have been challenges to the superstructure of "Ottoman Studies" and the epistemologies that confine the study of "Pan-Islam" to a "universal" struggle with "Christianity" or "the West," unless we disaggregate with specific cases the categories of analysis, in other words, complicate them to the point they no longer have any meaningful value as explanatory tools, we simply repeat the essentialist "crimes" of the past.

One way of breaking out of the logical confines of "Islam"-as-category that we may want to consider is how factions within the Ottoman Empire's bureaucratic elite reacted to Russia's expansion into Ottoman territories after 1878. Recent work has provided new insights into how, at this stage of crisis, strategists imagined a functional value to extending links with peoples in Russian-Occupied Caucasia and Central Asia.[90] As already seen in Chapter 2, Chechnya indeed becomes of primary strategic interest for these reasons. My concern is that we too quickly identify the animating factor being an "imperial" one rather than perhaps considering the role of informal, small-scale and unofficial agents in encouraging a strategic shift.

In this respect, it was because of the sudden flood of refugees from the 1850s onwards that events in Caucasia became of such immediate concern to various actors inside the Ottoman Empire. In the same way, large numbers of Central Asian and North African refugees also streaming into the empire, may have all contributed to a new kind of Ottoman politics by the very fact of their often very visible refuge in the empire. Concerns over the "unsightly" masses of destitute refugees languishing in public spaces throughout Ottoman cities, or the periodic violence over food and land, may have been the key element to putting the interests of these peoples onto the agenda of Ottoman elites. Considering this possibility means these were domestic political issues, not necessarily a "Pan-Islamic" one that remained abstract and conceptual, rather than immediate and personal.

The crucial work of Lâle Can has revealed a far more restrained Ottoman response to the constant solicitation from Central Asian community leaders to assist their polities under the siege of Russian expansionism in the 1860s and 1870s.[91] This failure to embrace the increasingly violent confrontations with expanding European empires in Asia, the Arabian Peninsula, and eventually Eastern Africa suggest not only a state incapacitated, however. There are crucial synergies of interests that seem requisite for any wide scale investment in any overseas confrontation; as such the questions we also need to ask is whose interests would be served if (and when) empires clashed over what were basically revenue producing lands.

This hesitance to indulge in expensive military campaigns either by proxy or directly was not only a characteristic of the Ottomans, of course. Almost all the confrontations today lumped under the rubric of the "Great Game" could be more usefully studied as first sources of debate within the inner circles of imperial power. In respect to British, Italian, French, or German state investment in defending the individual commercial expansionist agendas of companies, be it in Southeast Asia, South Africa, or East Africa, the crucial dynamic was the relative influence companies had within the inner-circles of political power. We know, for instance, that certain banks and trading companies had the ear of key decision-making individuals. Indeed, many policy-makers were themselves shareholders in these commercial enterprises. This marriage of interests applies also to the Ottoman Empire by the middle of the nineteenth century.[92]

The problem for those peoples facing the possible onslaught of predatory capitalism is that they often had no direct access to either the bureaucratic elite or the Sultan's inner core of advisors. For the most part, by the middle of the 1850s, these crucial positions of influence were inhabited by Istanbul-based Europeans, Ottoman subjects corrupted by the patronage of European interests, or bureaucratic elites whose strategic and ideological orientation was predicated on maintaining better relations with Europe, rather than confrontation.

In this sense, far from perceiving it as a "natural" reaction to try to mobilize distant "fellow Muslims" or even "fellow Turks" against Russian or British expansionism, we should consider the dynamics arising from the flooding of the empire's borders with refugees. To this we should also add that evidence of the eventual ascendency of some crucial members of the new military and political elite from among this *muhacır* hoard suggests some of the policies adopted toward Eurasia may have been driven by those with a personal interest, rather than an automatic proclivity to "Pan-Islam."[93]

In this way, the "politicization" of Islam needs contextualization and, more crucially, diversification as a theme of study. Ottoman policies, just as their foreign "Christian" counterparts within domestic Ottoman affairs, did not treat uniformly all "Muslims" or "Christians."[94] They did not treat all refugees equally either.[95]

What may be the transformative dynamic ultimately at play in the transitional order that leads to Ottoman collapse was the political tensions emerging in other Muslim regions of the world. These tensions were most likely the product of implementing an increasingly rigid divide separating the "social scientists" set of ontological truths and the immediate need for maintaining stability. As cultivated in the Americas in the form of administrative practice among "native" peoples (creating the conditions for which indigenous peoples can only organize around "tribal chiefs"), and then extended to

European universities to be studied by a new discipline of anthropology/sociology, new configurations of humanity distinguishing "different" races and civilizations took on a new administrative reality. This is another way of saying that the issue of categories of analysis, linked to the science of demography that had already left its mark on how Ottoman frontiers were drawn in 1878, became not only a tool of convenience, but increasingly the operating logic of self-serving bureaucrats and their finance capitalist masters. Objectifying and then disaggregating "mixed" polities like the Ottoman Empire not only produced new exploitative opportunities by way of the violence of separation, but, as we will next see in the conclusion, also in the subsequent "efforts" to resolve and settle the conflicts. The resulting exodus of millions upon millions of peoples, the untold hundreds of thousands of deaths along the way, all proved incredibly lucrative for certain operatives of the Euro-American financial Empire.

Conclusion: Perversion as conversion

In an attempt to first alert the reader to, and then address, these methodological issues, I wished to use this last section of the book to challenge how *Religion* works as a normative concept in many different kinds of human-induced disasters. More specifically still, the manner in which *Religion* is thus used by very different sets of actors, in relentlessly changing contexts, leaves open a much wider theoretical and narrative terrain than usually permitted in the charged national histories of a post-Ottoman era. As such, I wanted to take the risk of asking what goes on in times of horrific human suffering and what kinds of dignity can we draw out of those ultimate gestures of being alive in such conditions: compassion.

While it may seem at first tangential to this discussion on conversion and the liminal (or no-man's land) spaces of Ottoman/itinerate Sufi subjects confronting Euro-American expansionism in East Africa, Southeast Asia, or Eurasia, there is an important institutional/procedural context that needs exploring as we try to reach a conclusion to this story about the refugee. Considering how all imperial/colonial administrations emerging at the end of the nineteenth century actually faced the problem of ruling over "Muslims," it would seem the entire era was fraught with potential violence. The problem, however, is that the violence was not always a product of sectarian tensions.

As evidenced by studying those occupation regimes charged with the responsibility of governing over former Ottoman Muslim populations (as seen in Chapter 2 in respect to Serbia after 1878), occupation strategies considered more than just the most efficient ways to pillage the resources of newly "conquered" peoples. At least until 1912 in the Balkans and Eastern Anatolia (where expansionist Russia occupied all the territories east of Kars and Ardahan after the war of 1877–8),[96] non-Muslim administrations managing newly incorporated Muslim majority populations adopted a combination of strategies that rarely fixated on sectarian binaries alone. These agendas necessarily included finding local intermediaries who could assure that along the immediate frontiers of the Ottoman Empire, stability would prevail.[97] The issue is how shall we interpret the dynamic exchange that took place in such settings that were not all about colonial violence directed at "Muslims" per se, but also a product of attempts to bring some workable agreement on how to usefully integrate incorporated peoples and lands into a larger administrative, state power fold.[98]

Where policies differed was in how they attempted to secure an occupied people's acquiescence to the new political order. As these distinctive experiences, often within the "same" imperial scheme, took on different colorations depending on time and place, a general concern was achieving the subservience of "Muslims" (and other Christian/Jewish "minorities") through an assumed spiritual or "cultural" equivalent of the economic and political "middlemen" discussed in the last chapter. In this respect, the cooperation of community leaders, including local imams, priests, and shaykhs, *could be* deemed vital for the new occupation administration to work.[99]

Crucial to this chapter was the extent to which we wanted to focus on what animated the kinds of decisions taken to realize the effective management of diverse newcomers (as refugees) or newly incorporated subjects. At some point, occupation administrative strategies evident in so many documents, at the rhetorical level, clearly adopted reductive logic to characterize the "nature" of these subject communities. Abstractions as imprecise as Muslim and Christian, along with "native," "tribesmen," and "savage" are also evident in a broad range of inter-imperial exchanges—treaties, trade agreements, boundary management protocols, commissioned "fact-finding" reports—emerging in the period now dominated by financial oligarchs. From the diplomatic agreements settling conflicts between nations of "peoples" to the creation of internationally accepted rules of engagement for occupation regimes, the guardians of liberal capitalism were often the first to associate a community's identity with its religious affiliation. Accordingly, added to the textual evidence of an apparent "colonial" knowledge about religious, sociological, and economic constituencies, was the assumed linkage between community and leaders. The way we read this documentation suggests entire communities were loyal to institutional hierarchies manned by influential men who represented their confession. For the imperial agent seeking the collective acquiescence of the community in question, the operating logic was, again all at the theoretical level, to capture the services of these communal leaders. If properly harnessed, these shaykhs, imams, and priests could *ipso facto* command the loyalty of the "flock."

On the surface, it is hoped many readers can see why such assumptions are problematic. And yet, this is how European Orientalist scholars of the period, mostly linguists who maybe traveled once in their lives to the "region" of their expertise, explained the power dynamics of the "Islamic" world to an increasingly interested commercial and political ruling class just about to venture into the "East."[100] These are the same resources many are still committed to harvesting in the hope of explaining the dynamics of Ottoman, post-Ottoman life—in particular certain forms of violence. The concern here is taking a new look at just what "religion" meant to an assortment of actors engaging in the far more complicated administrative universe of Ottoman and rival imperial states; polities which in their own ways, faced dynamic periods of transition characterized in part by people moving in and out of their ability to control.[101]

Conclusion

Cocktail a la Turco: The end

What's the recipe for a Turk? Take the 25 de Março [downtown São Paulo market district] street cocktail shaker and put in a Syrian, an Arab, an Armenian, a Persian, and Egyptian, a Kurd. Shake it up really well and—boom—out comes a Turk. [Guilherme de Almedia][1]

Turco de mierda . . . Turco bruto[2]

To claim that one has understood ("with Western eyes") the entirety of these many Ottoman migrant, often refugee lives (or *any* variant of Ottoman experience, for that matter), and to then reduce them to an expedient record of mass-murder and anti-Christian pogroms is to do grave injustice to a *human* history that will never be fully contained by categorical particulars, whether they be Muslim, Albanian, Armenian, Arab, or Turk. Unfortunately, the particularly egregious and ahistorical stigma of "Turkish" barbarism has lingered for decades in the literature. Either as a useful, self-explanatory trope or as a necessary counterpart with which to juxtapose one's own, more sophisticated scholarship, the entrenchment of generalizations about the entire period covered in this book has left little room for nuance. Worse still, these lingering pathologies infesting the scholarship, most evident in the vast literature—mostly framed in condemning or defensive terms—on the horrifying events in Eastern and Western Anatolia from 1912 to 1925, have shaped much of how we read into the post-Ottoman world. More daunting still is the geographic scope of the Turkish boogeyman as it crossed continents and survived, in sociocultural incubators as diverse as popular literature in Serbia, newspaper editorials in Beirut, and the musings of the São Paulo/Rio de Janeiro intelligentsia well into the 1930s.

The most obvious place to look for the entrenched stereotypes about the paradigmatic Turkish "other" is the Balkans. As evidenced by a large body of sophisticated, crucial revisionist scholarship, associations with Islam and the invading "Turk" find their way into the national political discourse of all the countries of the region.[3] Indeed, "even in Muslim Albania" the reference to history under the Ottoman flag is mobilized to emphasize ontological difference between Europe and the Orient.[4] The on-going debate in Albanian societies in Kosovo and Albania (not so much in Macedonia) is the relative need to liberate Albanians' "European" heritage from 600 years of Turkish (read Muslim, Oriental) domination.[5]

The same holds true for Latin America, where tens of thousands of Ottoman Arabs (Jews, Christians, and Muslims) and natives of the Balkans settled.[6] Despite periods of the nostalgic repackaging of Latin America's "Oriental" heritage—most often in commoditized forms—the Ottoman experience in Latin America has been stamped out through generational asymmetries.[7] While there have been some brave attempts to temper the racism linked to anti-Arab/anti-Semitism prevalent in popular culture for decades in Arabo-American identity politics, the contributions to these discourses across the Americas nevertheless have been dominated by a tenacious self-hatred among those with clear Eastern Mediterranean (and Muslim) heritage.[8]

A few scholars have partially explained why such hostility toward their Ottoman heritage in the Americas manifested so early on.[9] The most crucial issue appears to be quite straight-forward: the host societies in which so many Ottomans settled were plagued by race politics.[10] Moreover, there was the violence of the international labor regime, rapid industrialization, and growing disparities in wealth between landowners, global financial interests, and workers. These tensions, often fused with the new ("social scientific") racist discourses infiltrating the literate world, had a profound impact on the way peoples of many different (often "mixed") heritages interacted within their mosaic migrant settings.[11]

It is indeed telling that for the most part, xenophobia directed toward Ottoman subjects paralleled other momentary outbursts of anti-foreigner discourse throughout the Americas. In Veracruz State México, for instance, the anti-African and anti-"Indian" politics experienced throughout the late nineteenth and early twentieth centuries also dragged the growing numbers of Ottoman Syrians migrating to the region into the nativist mix.[12] At the same time, however, the "Orientalist" label may not be entirely useful here when considering the larger context of class and race politics in the Americas. Therefore, as much as recent retrospectives want to highlight that Syrians were victims of the visceral nativism that spread throughout Latin America and manifested in the United States in the form of anti-non-"European" immigration laws, there are more nuanced approaches to appreciating the Ottoman migrant experience.[13]

The race/blood politics of México in particular actually offered Syrians the ability to straddle the divides that became functional under the brief French period in the mid-nineteenth century.[14] Drawing from recent work on the subject, it seems that in locales increasingly informed by racial differentiation, the very nature of the self-employment Syrians pursued allowed them to serve as a bridge across, rather than a part of, the ontology.[15] For example, many almost proto-typical "Arab" peddlers provided the services of supplying isolated communities the kinds of goods otherwise unavailable. This necessarily cut across racially segregated zones in Latin American and Euro-American cities and rural communities.[16] The Ottoman-Syrian merchants, in other words, could peddle their wares at the fringes of many different temporary but still violent social divides.[17]

The idea that Syrian merchants (often identified in the generic "Turco" frame) were highly adaptable and were not caught up in race politics afflicting Mexicans is a helpful supplement to the larger argument made here about the utter lack of structure to the migrant/refugee experiences.[18] As well known in the literature by now, because Ottoman Syrians/Palestinians did not neatly fit any of these entrenched, New World categories, they did business everywhere and with whomever they saw fit. They treated native peoples as customers as "fairly" as they did *mestizos* and pure blood "white" Europeans.[19]

Such a service proved vital not only to individual profit-making operations, which did grow in many cases to become great commercial successes.[20] These global "hybrids" for many years also served the unarticulated—but eventually identifiable—patterns for expanding state authority in hitherto isolated, "unconquered" territories inhabited by indigenous "savages" and "half-breeds." Recall that many of the destinations of these Ottoman refugees were so-called "frontier" societies. Countries throughout Central America and South America, and even the United States, all struggled at the turn-of-the-century to assert authority over vast lands that still were at the early stages of integration into the national, thus global economy. In this context of emergent territorial consolidation, the "itinerate Turkish/Ottoman" peddler often initiated "contact" with indigenous and mixed-blood populations; and as much as the grandee families that worked in partnership with British, Dutch, Spanish, and American commercial interests to secure profitable relations in Southeast Asia, these Syrian/Lebanese/Palestinian hybrids performed similar "middlemen" roles in the Americas.[21]

Far from being the voluntary proselytizers venturing off to Africa and to a lesser extent the eager merchants helping to plunder Southeast Asia, the very manner in which these true outcastes ultimately settled in the New World serves as a testament of these remarkable peoples' ability to survive. By taking their different stories into account, we can also complicate the highly segregated and racialized national historiographies of all these American societies. The stereotypical itinerate Ottoman "Turco" merchant provided the service of barter trade in otherwise cash-poor communities on the fringes of "civilization."[22] In doing business in these chaotic, often violent zones of capitalist expansion, these roaming Ottoman-Arab merchants exposed these jungle and desert outposts to potential further "development."[23]

Crucially, as these were equally zones of genocide in which indigenous peoples faced the expansion of planation scale industrial agricultural development, these Ottoman subjects were playing the "pioneer" role of establishing a foothold in these coveted, contested regions.[24] They, in essence, became the colonists needed to start providing the basic services like the dry foods shops, hotels, and ferry services throughout the frontiers of the Americas.[25]

Those with a bit of knowledge of the history of this period in the Middle East will probably see this as more than an odd coincidence. Indeed, the sad irony is that many of these same Palestinians/Syrians helping to destroy native peoples' societies in Amazonia and Central America would soon realize that their homelands were undergoing very similar types of predatory, colonist capitalism.[26] During the late Ottoman period and then well into the British/French Mandate era, these itinerate Ottomans' ancestors' farmlands had equally been "bought," leveraged, and transferred in the form of concessions to European settlers whose exclusivist doctrines immediately pitted them against "native savages."[27] As Ottoman Arabs served the role of helping settle "empty lands" in Central America to the detriment of the indigenous peoples of Costa Rica or Honduras, so too would foreign men/women establish Ashkenazi "kibbutz" and German Mennonite enclaves amid the traditional lands of Palestinians.[28] As front men for an expansionist capitalist project in the Middle East or the Americas, these peoples registered the extent of the crimes against humanity capitalist greed brought to the world only after their own confrontation with organized racism in the context of the post-Ottoman world.[29]

As large numbers of Ottoman subjects would soon learn, these acts of capitalist imperialism relied on a form of mental, physical, and material subordination. This book has argued that there are a number of inconsistencies in the purported—often patronizing—claims made by those engaging the refugees of a collapsed Ottoman Empire in "humane ways." For one, they underestimate refugee agency. What often resulted when victorious Europeans drew up new borders from the carcass of the Ottoman Empire was a destructive narrowing of rhetorical paths that former subjects of the Empire could take. Peoples directly affected by these new configurations, which often had terrifying consequences for those deemed "outside" the legal framework of the post-Ottoman state, were given little recourse for action. To the self-appointed managers of post-Ottoman societies, there even was no time for engaging in partnerships, let alone honoring the solicitations of desperate peoples.

Rather, there was a bureaucratic imperative to run Euro-American empires in, say, Iraq, on the cheap.[30] This attempt to streamline everything into manageable sociocultural units, often framed in entirely new social constructs based on "ethnic" or "sectarian" community identities, had adverse consequences to those expected to endure the human price.[31] Entire regions were created that would benefit certain "tribes" as long as they collaborated with the Mandate authorities.[32] Those outside these protected ahistorical spaces became the necessary victims. In short, "collateral" to the institutional transformations and the governing protocols of the British and French Mandates—both given formal cover by the League of Nations—was an indigenous amalgamation (and disaggregation) that was both coerced and violent.[33]

As part of this books' project, it is observed that indigenous peoples were not blind to the destructive tactics introduced by these exploitative regimes. Indeed, as much as the response was taking the form of violent resistance, often around a loose coalition that today is labeled in terms of "Arab" revolts, Bulgarian bandits, Swahili pirates, or "bedouin" uprisings, there were also attempts to lobby international bodies presumably neutral in these matters. The frequent attempts, for instance, to communicate directly to the League of Nations, through the use of petitions and sending delegations to make individual cases of disgruntled constituencies, suggest an interesting point in time in post-Ottoman history.

Unfortunately, there was a glaring disparity between what in theory *should* have been the role of the League of Nations or the International Red Cross Society and the reality. It is posited here that much of the subsequent violence may in part be blamed on the sheer arrogance of the "international community" and the manner it dealt with Ottoman refugees.[34] As documents drawn from the League of Nations' archives attest, former Ottoman subjects, many with no other representation than their petitions, had been time and again thwarted by the inner bureaucracy of this quintessential Euro-American institution.[35] As these self-appointed guardians of "progress" ignored

Lebanese, Albanian, Palestinian, Kurdish, Laz, Assyrians, and Turkish pleas for justice, the trajectories for these peoples to adopt other means seemed assured.[36]

After nearly 15 years of conflict that brought mass starvation, cholera, typhoid outbreaks, and genocide to their world, the refugees of the destroyed Ottoman Empire were faced with new indecencies and unwarranted harassment. The very lands upon which their wretched, broken bodies had been thrown as refugees once again became the focus of competing commercial and thus, imperial state interests. This "interwar" period introduced new forms of exploitation and violence throughout the post-Ottoman Balkans, Anatolia, and larger Middle East. The resulting travesties, including massive expropriations of individuals/communities' property, forced "population exchanges," new forms of social hierarchies ("divide and rule") and finally the full integration of these regions into a regime of "nation" building, all provided the fodder for the next Euro-American project.[37]

As historians, the best we can do to critically study the genocidal crimes of the period is move away from reading the Eurocentric colonial project on its terms (or categories). If done successfully, we may gauge shifts within spaces outside the reach of Euro-American power, or in other words, those beyond observation. This means acknowledging that much of this transitional period still escapes the modern projects of codifying and cataloging. As such, at some important level, Ottoman refugees remained impossible to use as an object of analysis and thus a component in the planning of the modern state. But it is also here at this void where a significant tension remains for the post-Ottoman regimes seeking to harness the powers awaiting them. This tension is our ethical wedge.

At this point our efforts help us measure just how aggressive "development" models and new ideas for organizing globally shaped the capacities of the state to control population movements. In order to fully harness, and thus exploit, the "untapped" human resources made available by the destructive forces of war in the Eastern Mediterranean world, imperialist powers, for instance, sought to regularize refugee life. I argue that it was the codification of the refugee experience by the 1920s, via new methods of demographic accounting, bureaucratized racial/ethnic/ confessional classifications, and the control of migration that became the emblem of the modern world. As much as sociologists and ethnographers were called to serve the larger agendas of population control and efficiently shifting the destitute (thus eager cheap laborers) to where cheap work was needed in the globalizing economies, the refugee's historic association with the homeland necessarily had to transform. This may be deemed the most important consequence of the Ottoman Empire's collapse.

Once serving as an anchor of sorts, be it a spiritual reference, or by the late nineteenth century, a government which could provide travel documents increasingly needed for individuals to move around the world, the Ottoman Empire fragmented into separate, in most cases until the 1930s, still violent, occupied territories. This process meant refugees had an almost complete dependency on the forces of capital in their attempt to sustain a meaningful existence.[38] For the men and women made refugees by the Ottoman collapse, the relationship with the ascendant financial system was dispossession, forced migration, and terrible working conditions.

Losing the imperial anchor

As a way to close this book while beginning a new discussion on the transitional era where the Ottoman world literally vanished with horrific consequences for so many of its inhabitants, I offer one last emblematic example of the new order of abstraction imposing new limitations. This case involving Palestinians wishing to return to their Middle Eastern homelands now under British administration sharpens our appreciation for the consequences of a collapsed apparatus of living that had sustained human diversity for centuries.

As discussed throughout, for most of the 40 years or so Ottoman Arabs traveled across the Atlantic to find their fortunes in the Americas, they demonstrated an ability to navigate the racially charged contexts of rapidly "developing" regional economies. What most likely transformed the Ottoman refugee over the years was the sudden fact that a new international order emerged without an Ottoman Empire in it. That meant the once multicultural life in the Ottoman homeland, more particularly Palestine/Syria, transformed with the imposition of a new racist order in the 1920s.

In a stunning set of documents preserved in the League of Nations' archives, the sheer racism of the operatives of a "New World Order" propagated by a self-identified "West" during the Mandate regime governing Palestine sabotages any attempts to characterize the era in purely economic or political terms. The prevailing racist taxonomies that began to transform how the Euro-American political and economic elite framed their operative interests around the world in the nineteenth century had a dramatic impact on Ottoman Arabs when they found themselves without formal state backing. In this case at hand, the Ottoman castaways were Palestinians seeking permission to return "home" in British-Occupied Nablus Palestine.[39] As the region had been strategically carved out of any number of different geographies (including a unified Arab or greater Syria) by the League of Nations and their partners, hundreds of Palestinians needed permission to return home—something akin to an entry visa from British authorities.

While large numbers of specific types of immigrants, especially from Europe, continued to flow into Palestine, another type of migrant was increasingly deemed dangerous. In the case of Members of the *Sociedad Fraternidad Palestina*, their request to return from their established home of Honduras, San Salvador, and the larger region to their homeland was denied on the grounds they carried Ottoman documentation. The logic here was that by their being Ottoman, they immediately became "Turks" and had right of return only to Anatolia (the Republic of Turkey).[40] Native Arab-Palestinians, armed with birth certificates written in Ottoman attesting to their homeland being Nablus, were no longer acceptable in a recently transformed categorical governmentality of targeted exclusion and inclusion. The hard facts of a post-Ottoman world order was Slav Jews continued to colonize targeted "frontiers" of Palestine to fulfill a newly invigorated Zionist project while members of the *Sociedad Fraternidad Palestina* were denied their right of return, already in the 1920s.

Taken from any angle, this constituted ethnic cleansing that predates the 1948 creation of Israel and the presumed beginning of the population politics of European colonialism. But it is clear here that this later campaign actually compliments the already aggressive population politics of the Mandate era.[41] What this case must do is inform how we think again about the interwar era in a context of refugee life in a post-Ottoman world. The horrors of World War I and a population politics directed at targeted "enemies" of the vulnerable Ottoman state did not dissipate with the formal partition of the empire. Rather, the context in which the genocide of Armenians, Balkan Muslims, and South Asian peoples of many affiliations remained and perhaps took a new, advanced level of organization with the collapse of the Ottoman Empire. This new strategy of exclusion forever cast out millions of human beings from their homes on the basis of ethno-national categories only relevant with the collapse of the Ottoman world.

The loss of the Ottoman anchor for those poor Palestinians in Central America and México has an equally tragic twist with the previously mentioned simplistic historiographical formulas that equated an Ottoman heritage to a "Turkish" one.[42] At present, accompanying the vacillating disgust and naïve curiosity with genocide is a set of new discussions about what *actually* happened during the transitional era. While it is the vibrant intellectual community in Turkey itself that does most of the heavy-lifting of reconsidering, and complicating, the late Ottoman past, scholars from countries long "liberated" from the "Turk" have also successfully broken taboos and now shed new light onto the era.

It all started with war. War was the means by which new political elites in neighboring, former Ottoman territories like Bulgaria, Greece, and Serbia identified an opportunity to rewrite the demographic landscape and in turn, claim a historical association with newly "ethnically cleansed" territories. As a consequence of the Balkan Wars of 1912 and 1913, in particular, entire city neighborhoods were razed, names of villages changed, their inhabitants expelled, or more dramatically still, collectively "converted."[43] To many, the problem was that the beginning of World War I left these states not enough time to complete the ugly task of erasing the Ottoman Empire from "Christendom."

As in the Americas, an Ottoman human "refuse" lingered in independent Balkan countries where some of these "left-over" communities survive until today. Despite a long period of imposed socialism and declarations of brotherhood, Balkan Muslims lived in constant fear that one more round of "ethnic cleansing" will come sweeping through their communities.[44] This is especially the case in Bulgaria and the former Yugoslavia, where a century now of living as "minorities" often led to opportunistic, "functional" blood-letting campaigns in the larger contexts of "national" politics.[45] In Yugoslavia, the non-Slav Albanian Muslim (and Catholic) evolved into a bureaucratic category especially susceptible to periodic state-led expulsion campaigns—throughout the 1920s, 1935–8, 1953–67, and then again in the 1990s—that passed through the region.[46]

Invariably castigated as "outsiders" and "fifth-column" threats to national security, the labeling of entire regions of Kosovo, Novipazaar, Montenegro, and Macedonia as inhabited by generic "Muslim Albanians" often meant the organized expulsion of those communities.[47] In order to justify such measures to an occasional outside traveler bearing witness to the violent process, or delegations sent by the newly created League of Nations at the request of Albania (a member state), the Serbian/

Yugoslav state often rolled out historians, demographers, and anthropologists.[48] In an often repeated exercise throughout the post-Ottoman Balkans, operatives of "ethnic cleansing" campaigns resurrected the "professional knowledge" of race sciences first developed in the United States at the turn-of-the-century.

In the 1920s, for instance, state authorities eager to continue a process of expulsion started in 1912—briefly disrupted by World War I—sent an army of European-trained ethnographers to "Southern Serbia" to identify those communities least likely to ever accept Serbian rule.[49] These ethnographers and human geographers adopted many of the same racist epistemologies identified in other Euro-American contexts to identify and catalogue the "sub-human" characteristics of hybrid "Turks" whose very "nature" made efforts to assimilate them into a modernizing Serbian/South Slav society "scientifically" impossible.[50]

While these stories now make up a core aspect of Albanian (and Turkish, Greek, Bulgarian) historical memory vis-à-vis Serbia's torment, it has usefully been forgotten that the dynamics around such systemic violence was informed by a set of ideological and disciplinary frameworks that, once instrumentalized, as by the CUP after 1910, transformed the way once heterogeneous societies interacted with each other.[51] These same ideological principles based on racial segregation and biological hierarchies influenced the intellectual elite of the early twentieth-century world. They ultimately mobilized a so-called fertility politics to justify why violent state-led colonialization/expulsion in Yugoslavia (and earlier in Greece and Bulgaria) was necessary in order to maintain the long-term demographic balance of society.[52] Forced expulsion, the signing of "population exchange" agreements—popularized as a diplomatic "solution" already in the immediate aftermath of the first Balkan War of 1912—and ultimately colonization were all tactics used in the Balkans, as well as throughout the Euro-American dominated world.

Crucially for our purposes, it was a newly consolidated Turkish Republic, administered since the late 1920s by, among others, refugees originally from Macedonia and Kosovo, which actually signed these population exchange treaties with Balkan countries. In their own need for "excess Turks" (Muslims) to colonize the vast territories of Eastern Anatolia, both depopulated and exposed to hostile neighbors, the paradigmatic "refugee" state adopted not so much the justifications for "expelling the Albanian/Turk" but the underlying logic that Muslims and Christians just should not live together any longer.[53] To the detriment of hundreds of thousands of Balkan Muslims who were not initially expelled in the immediate aftermath of World War I and Ottoman collapse, the cruelest irony is their fate was sealed by the complicit actions of officials who themselves were often victims of these very same reductive "positivist" rationales.[54]

Disappointingly, the irony of such "exchanges" has not registered in much of the scholarship. For most, the categories at work to flesh out such population-exchanges seem entirely acceptable, indeed, logical. While one of the most contentious themes in the literature on post imperial refugees has remained the origins of the undeniable violence surrounding the empire's last century of existence, it is only tangentially studied in connection to the massive movements of people caused by, for instance, the Balkan Wars of 1912 and 1913. As descendants of those expelled from various corners of the Ottoman Empire were forcefully settled in others, the crucial goal for those wishing to explain their own specific tales of suffering has been to provide basic details and perhaps individual stories. The theme, however, remained the generic *muhacir* tragedy in the larger scholarship.[55] The end result was that neither narrative embraced the dynamic environment in which different refugees from different parts of the empire were actually forced to settle into what became war zones. This was neither an individual tragedy nor one reducible to a generic narrative, but a constantly shifting friction of human beings trying to survive.[56]

More crucially, the "ethno-national" and confessional terms evoked to finalize the painful, frequently violent forced "population" exchanges from 1913 onwards make their way into the logic of the scholarship today. It is as if these organizing principles, more or less constituting an "imperial unconsciousness," have no resonance to readers today as relics from an era where racism, politics, and "science" intersected at violent junctions of modern history.[57] Despite that legacy, even the most careful scholars, at particularly opportune times, will abandon all circumspection and theoretical (let alone ethical) caution, and explain the horrors of the Ottoman collapse in the quintessentially racist terms of Turkish, Armenian, Ethnic, and Muslim "difference."[58]

As demonstrated throughout, perhaps with a greater care for contextualizing actions, reactions, and the growing presence of state-like institutions, the dynamics surrounding the refugee experience, ambiguous spirituality, and even genocide can become operational for something other than the ethno-nationalist agenda cloaked in primordialism. Indeed, through these five chapters we can observe ways in which the ebb and flow of human beings cross occasionally in anachronistically defined "ethno-national" spaces. Realizing this could help us monitor patterns otherwise lost when attempting to assign greater historic narrative weight to these stories.[59]

Consciously attempting to work around these hermeneutic quandaries, I acknowledge that this book does little to set a definitive story about a number of contradictions, dialectical contentions, and implicit institutional failings of late Ottoman and post-Ottoman periods. But this lack of definition is the point, in the end. The *muhacir* of the late Ottoman era is rather an amorphous energy that harbors the *potential* for action and the symbolic capital of an entire imperial operating logic. Indeed, rethinking these variable refugee/internally displaced migrant experiences may also lead us to consider how they reconfigured kinship and identity for the duration of the twentieth century, something I would hope an aspiring younger scholar would consider taking up.

But we must do so cautiously. How scholars want this phenomenon of human movement to work for them has often resulted in unjustified assumptions and misleading generalizations. Far too often, for instance, nationalist foundational claims about population movements in general, and the *muhacir* in particular, have been overstated. At best, the categories which may help explain a refugee experience in the 1878–1939 period transform within different settings, and are not entirely linked by a simple association to the Ottoman regime in power—be it Sultan Abdülhamid II, the various Unionist regimes, or the competing nationalist projects prior to 1923. In all these cases, the refugee experience warrants more nuance, even amid the horrors of Armenian genocide and the forced expulsions of Balkan Muslims and Anatolian *Rum* Orthodox Christians. The goal here is not so much to think outside the box, as to (not) recognize the box in the first place. In other words, disaggregating the Ottoman refugee from the post-Ottoman narratives that have all sought to confine the experiences to suit certain, often precarious and highly contested political orders, offers us a new opportunity to bring depth to narratives of a distinctly post-Ottoman origin.[60]

In the process, this book acknowledges that there are some serious ethical pitfalls awaiting those of us making this leap into studying (and perhaps manipulating for ideological purposes) the past; especially when we tune our story to such predetermined agendas that assert claims of association to primordial ethno-national identities. At the best of times these are spurious claims to an understanding of an historical agent's intent. At the worst of times this is used to collectively excoriate/implicate forever an entire community's ideological position. The task of this book was not to assemble the refugee's pain for the purpose of consumption, and thereby kill the dead, but instead to expose the aesthetic sadism too often put on display by the historian and her audience, both grimly desirous of historical objects in agony at the hands of the ontological evil, Oriental other.[61]

I addressed these ethical concerns by highlighting ways we can identify diverse, contextually driven manifestations of refugee order. Interspersed in several chapters, attention was paid to a particularly interesting aspect of Ottoman diasporic/ refugee agency. Petitions have long been sent by Ottoman subjects to government officials, foreign representatives and by the end of the empire, to League of Nations headquarters, a learned right of subjecthood that empowered local constituencies to lobby the Ottoman state directly, circumventing perhaps an abusive local governor or establishing a formal communication link when one did not previously exist. Such strategies were equally mobilized in times of sudden changes like the Berlin Congress of 1878. Telegrams of protest not only circulated to Istanbul but bombarded European capitals, demonstrating how affected locals attempted to influence "Great Power" thinking over how proposed boundaries dangerously complicated their lives.[62]

Considering the various stakeholders engaged in this late Ottoman story and the possible angles with which to study the refugee phenomenon, I argue that reading these petitions reveals how experiences of forcefully uprooted communities from 1878 to 1939 created new kinds of tensions between the migrants themselves *and* local populations often caught between the refugees and state officials. As new conditions demanded new methods of interaction, the confusion, tension, and ever-changing adaptations ultimately resulted in opportunities of empowerment for a potentially large range of previously obscure sets of actors inside both state bureaucracies and local communities. This calculus only grows more complex when Great Power diplomacy enters into the fray.

Ultimately, the purpose of juxtaposing in this book a multiplicity of different kinds of refugee experiences is to highlight the range of trajectories still experienced by indigenous peoples—despite (or perhaps because of) external interventions. At the same time, I wanted to demonstrate why the prism of the so-called modern state is not always the best medium through which historians can study these contingencies imposed by the dynamics of population movements. Put differently, by studying these experiences as a "relational" process that influenced how various modernist projects moved into new arenas—in the form of state centralization plans or direct occupation by foreign interests—we may begin to identify new local (and metropolitan) constituencies. These temporary polities force us to think differently about what transpired prior to the "Young Turk" revolt of 1908, or during and after World War I.[63]

At the heart of the long-term success of this set of transforming political orders was the fact that the Ottoman Empire's fortunes were shared by large numbers of peoples at any given time. As long as things went well for individual clusters of people who shared temporary interests, the empire served as an invaluable vehicle for local power, fortune, and protection. If things did not go well, people coalesced in ways that sometimes applied direct pressure on the larger state to do something about it. This was true from the very beginning of the Ottoman enterprise in the early fourteenth century and, as evidenced by the stories discussed in this book, remained a fact until, and even beyond, the empire's end. This dynamic give-and-take across existing communal lines is rarely acknowledged in the literature today.

As I expand on this notion of persistent Ottomanism, I again question the forces that are presumed to singularly animate the way human beings socialize in specific contexts. Exposing the underlying dynamics of the purported dislocation of so-called Ottoman refugees will prove equally subversive to the discourse of ethno-national identity formation as to its linkages to modernity. In these cases, understanding the forces that animated human movement and then (re)settlement requires a great deal of analytical flexibility. For as much as refugees failed to fit the normative descriptions of the helpless victims of fate, so too will the lives of the foreign, the outcast, or "other" living in exile prove laden with contradictions and thus provide the foundation for different possibilities erased in the meta-narrative of post-WWII Western hegemony.[64]

In this respect, one must also remain vigilant as to not oversell the specificity of the Ottoman history. We cannot assume that an all-encompassing, narrative of the empire that distinguishes the Ottoman Empire from an equally spurious aggregate "West," can account for the historical complexities of either. Though it might be productively linked to Ottoman history as commodity, the Ottoman Empire as freighted with the decadent, despotic exotica for which the "Western mind" portends inevitable collapse cannot be helpful. Even more than this, one must not approach the Ottoman Empire as uniform on the spatial or temporal register. The Ottoman Empire changed drastically over time; and at a given historical moment, no one locale under Ottoman suzerainty necessarily looked or functioned like another.

This book thus disaggregated the geographic focus, not to dislodge an enterprise that seeks to monitor on a large scale how to interpret change, but to serve as a reminder to younger scholars to not fear the logic of this "project." This applies to geographic abstractions and social organizational assumptions, especially those forcefully linking Muslims, Christians, Kurds, Arabs, Armenians, Albanians, Turks, and "tribes" to a universal Ottoman (as declining, "sick") imperial experience. It equally applies to the assumed limitations of refugees, who may more usefully be called intermittently in this book, *itinerate Ottomans*. This notion of itinerancy more productively captures the way Ottoman subjects thought about the changing world around them, how they associated with others (refugees or hosts) and even what kind of political and economic role they had in their often-temporary settlement surroundings.

Again, this point of emphasis does not identify an exact time and place for a process of decline or for a terminal disaster. The dynamics of imperial collapse were never uniform and constituted to different peoples and different times entirely distinct experiences. In this sense, what is ultimately at stake in this book is the attempt to capture the diversity of experiences which allowed for that lingering notion of an Ottoman sensibility to survive at times when subjects of the empire, as either refugees, former refugees, or future refugees, clung to their Ottoman qualities, even in the most destitute conditions. In the end, these itinerate Ottomans constitute an historical force whose diversity and surprising resilience requires a reader's patience, flexibility, and ultimately empathy. As such, this book initiates what shall be a series of studies on these remarkable human beings whose very journeys through, across, under, and beyond the historical conventions dominating the analysis of "transitional" periods make the study of the Middle East/Eastern Mediterranean/Third World all the more vital to my personal revisionist project.

!;

Notes

Introduction

1   Bishop Fan Noli's activism eventually saw this lowly priest in a small Massachusetts Albanian Orthodox Christian neighborhood become first foreign minister, then prime minister, and eventually president of a short-lived "democratic" Albania in the 1920s. For details consult Robert C. Austin, *Founding a Balkan State: Albania's Experiment With Democracy, 1920–1925* (Toronto: University of Toronto Press, 2012): 2–6, 54–74 and Nicola Guy, *The Birth of Albania: Ethnic Nationalism, the Great Powers of World War I and the Emergence of Albanian Independence* (London: I.B. Tauris, 2013): 221–42.

2   An impressive stand out for its interdisciplinary approach is Dawn Chatty, *Displacement and Dispossession in the Modern Middle East* (Cambridge: Cambridge University Press, 2010): 7–179.

3   Hayden White, *Metahistory: The Historical Imagination in Nineteenth-century Europe* (Baltimore: Johns Hopkins University Press, 1975) and Rifa'at 'Ali Abou-El-Haj, "Historiography in West Asian and North African Studies since Sa'id's Orientalism," in Arif Dirlik, Vinay Bahl, and Peter Gran (eds), *History after the Three Worlds: Post-Eurocentric Historiographies* (New York: Rowman & Littlefield Publishers, 2000). Recently, Cooper has warned those aiming to "give voice" to the once "voiceless" to guard against replicating some of the ethnocentric pitfalls of their ideological opponents writing the more "mainstream" narratives. Frederick Cooper, *Colonialism in Question: Theory, Knowledge, History* (Berkeley: University of California Press, 2005).

4   As often noted by careful observers, abandoned refugees frequently become key actors, be it in the context of a never-ending conflict within their own "diasporic" communities, their eternal enemies responsible for their plight, or within their "host" society. For insight into how violence in the context of a contentious existence in "host" societies produces new communities out of refugees see Liisa H. Malkki, *Purity and Exile: Violence, Memory, and National Cosmology among Hutu Refugees in Tanzania* (Chicago: University of Chicago Press, 1995). On how "refugees" are a necessary component in the rewriting of the narratives about their plight see Tania Murray Li, "Ethnic Cleansing, Recursive Knowledge, and the Dilemmas of Sedentarism," *International Social Science Journal* 173 (2002): 361–71.

5   The Ottoman Empire has been usefully studied as a product of human mobility, albeit in a sometimes cursory, overly social scientific abstract manner. See Reşat Kasaba, *A Moveable Empire: Ottoman Nomads, Migrants and Refugees* (Seattle: University of Washington Press, 2009). The especially crucial population movement from parts of the Balkans to Anatolia has increasingly attracted close, detailed studies. Starting with Alexandre Toumarkine, *Les Migrations des populations musulmanes balkaniques en Anatolie (1876–1913)* (Istanbul: Isis Press, 1995) up to Ismail Arslan, *Selanik'in Gölgesinde bir Sancak: Drama, 1864–1913* (Istanbul: Bilge Kültür Sanat, 2010).

6 Michael E. Meeker, *A Nation of Empire: The Ottoman Legacy of Turkish Modernity* (Berkeley: University of California Press, 2002) tells a far less violent story.

7 In this respect, there has been a long tradition, especially among Turkish scholars, to reference issues around the refugee as a metaphor for the larger tragedy of imperial collapse. At its best, the Ottoman refugee (*muhacir/göç* in Turkish) story serves to weave a larger set of explanations for how imperial collapse has tragic human consequences, see Donald Bloxham, *The Great Game of Genocide: Imperialism, Nationalism, and the Destruction of the Ottoman Armenians* (Oxford: Oxford University Press, 2005). For a useful survey of the nationalist historiography that mobilize the theme of *muhacir/göçmen* to assert unequivocally that Modern Turkey is a nation of Turks, see Erik J. Zürcher, *The Young Turk Legacy and Nation Building: From the Ottoman Empire to Atatürk's Turkey* (London: I.B. Tauris, 2010): 6–53.

8 Kemal Karpat, *Ottoman Population, 1830–1914, Demographic and Social Characteristics* (Madison: University of Wisconsin Press, 1985) and Justin McCarthy, *Death and Exile: The Ethnic Cleansing of Ottoman Muslims, 1821–1922* (Princeton: The Darwin Press, 1995).

9 Bilal N. Şimşir, *Rumeli'den Türk Göçleri*, 3 vols (Ankara: Türk Tarih Kurumuyu, 1989); Nedim Ipek, *Rumeli'den Anadolu'ya Türk Göçleri* (Ankara: Türk Tarih Kurumu Basımevi, 1994); Ahmet Halaçoğlu, *Balkan Harbi Sırasında Rumeli'den Türk Göçleri (1912–1913)* (Ankara: TTK, 1995) and Basil C. Gounaris, "Social Cleavages and National 'Awakening' in Ottoman Macedonia," *Eastern European Quarterly* 24.4 (January 1996): 409–26.

10 I draw on Fabian's depiction of the distancing of modern colonialism as a linear graph drawn along the two dimensions of time and space extending from the now and here of Western civilization to the then and there of "savage society." Johannes Fabian, *Time and the Other: How Anthropology Makes its Objects* (New York: Columbia University Press, 1983): 27. This frame of reference is evident in even how "non-Western" historians write about their respective societies' relationship with imperial collapse, a methodological shortcoming that obstructs our ability to consider deeper explanations for why certain processes take place in one location, but are entirely different elsewhere. For the full-range of scholarship on the "theme" consult Panikos Panayi and Pippa Virdee (eds), *Refugees and the End of Empire: Imperial Collapse and Forced Migration in the Twentieth Century* (New York: Palgrave Macmillan, 2011).

11 See Lene Hansen, "Past as Preface: Civilizational Politics and the 'Third' Balkan War," *Journal of Peace Research* 37.3 (May 2000): 345–62 and Keith Brown's careful analysis of the legacy of events in 1903 on how post-Yugoslav politics in Macedonia mobilize history to dilute otherwise dangerously ambiguous questions about the origins of modern Balkan identity: *The Past in Question: Modern Macedonia and the Uncertainties of Nation* (Princeton: Princeton University Press, 2003): 9–21.

12 Such heroic and equally tragic stories often take the form of the Romantic Modernity narrative initiated by German thinkers like Herder, Fichte, and Arndt, a narrative already embraced by mid-century intelligentsia throughout Europe and even the Ottoman Empire. See for instance, Hans S. Reiss (ed.), *The Political Thought of the German Romantics* (Oxford: Basil Blackwell, 1955) and Serhiy Bilenky, *Romantic Nationalism in Eastern Europe: Russian, Polish, and Ukrainian Political Imaginations* (Palo Alto: Stanford University Press, 2012).

13 For a thoughtful argument against the kind of abstract universalism that often characterizes the narrative approach in the study of refugees, see "Introduction," in Sophia Mappa (ed.), *Les deux sources de l'exclusion: Economisme et replies identitaires* (Paris: Karthala, 1981): 7–55.

14 Selim Deringil, *Conversion and Apostasy in the Late Ottoman Empire* (Cambridge: Cambridge University Press, 2012).

15 Barbara Jelavich, *Russia's Balkan Entanglements, 1806–1914* (Cambridge: Cambridge University Press, 1991) and Brad Dennis, "Patterns of Conflict and Violence in Eastern Anatolia Leading Up to the Russo-Turkish War and the Treaty of Berlin," in M. Hakan Yavuz (ed.), *War & Diplomacy: The Russo-Turkish War of 1877–1878 and the Treaty of Berlin* (Salt Lake City: University of Utah Press, 2012): 273–301.

16 For a discussion of the manipulation of the historical narrative of ethnicity in the Balkans in respect to Macedonia, an Ottoman area mutually claimed by historiographies of Greece, Macedonia, Albania, Kosovo, Serbia, and Bulgaria, see Thomas Cushman, "Anthropology and Genocide in the Balkans: An Analysis of Conceptual Practices of Power," *Anthropological Theory* 4.1 (2004): 5–28. Controversial at the time of publication, Karakasidou advocated presenting a historical ethnographic reconstruction of state formation and then nation-building in a (largely refugee) community in southern Macedonia that remained stubbornly "Ottoman" in its orientations toward the political and economic elite of Greece well into the twentieth century. Her study successfully undermined the sweeping assertions by Greek nationalist narratives that ignored such lingering Ottoman associations. Anastasia N. Karakasidou, *Fields of Wheat, Hills of Blood: Passages to Nationhood in Greek Macedonia, 1870–1990* (Chicago: University of Chicago Press, 1997).

17 Isa Blumi, *Reinstating the Ottomans: Alternative Balkan Modernities, 1800–1912* (New York: Palgrave Macmillan, 2011).

18 A new interest among "American" historians in the violent displacements caused by transforming capitalist practices has inspired this book's analytical focus on as much the cultural as technical consequences of transitional societies. See for instance, Ned Blackhawk, *Violence over the Land: Indians and Empires in the Early American West* (Cambridge: Harvard University Press, 2006) and among others in an excellent new volume of the cultural impacts on/for capitalism, Sean Patrick Adams, "Soulless Monsters and Iron Horses: The Civil War, Institutional Change, and American Capitalism," in Michael Zakim and Gary J. Kornblith (eds), *Capitalism Takes Command: The Social Transformation of Nineteenth-Century America* (Chicago: University of Chicago Press, 2012): 249–76.

19 Although discussed in some detail in Chapter 4, a few valuable contributions to our understanding of this process of Ottoman migration to the Americas warrant citing here: Steven Hyland, "'Arisen from Deep Slumber': Transnational Politics and Competing Nationalisms among Syrian Immigrants in Argentina, 1900–1922," *Journal of Latin American Studies* 43.3 (2011): 547–74 and Michael Goebel, "Von der hispanidad zum Panarabismus. Globale Verflechtungen in Argentiniens Nationalismen," *Geschichte und Gesellschaft* (2011): 523–58.

20 Marius Turda, "Whither Race? Physical Anthropology in Post-1945 Central and Southeastern Europe," *Focaal* 58 (2010): 3–15 and Abdul JanMohamed, "The Economy of Manichean Allegory: The Function of Racial Difference in Colonialist Literature," *Critical Inquiry* 12 (1985): 59–87.

21 Edward E. Baptist, "Toxic Debt, Liar Loans, Collateralized and Securitized Human Beings, and the Panic of 1837," in Zakim and Kornblith (eds), *Capitalism Takes Command*, 69–93. I thank Richard Gassan for attracting my attention to this remarkable study.

22 America's rape of the Philippines, the mining industry's pillage of Southern Africa, France's scorched policies in North Africa, Britain's starving India into submission,

the list is only more infuriating when considering how the violence in the Middle East is used to entirely differentiate a European form of modern systemic murder, serving modernity and progress, from the horrors visited upon the Ottoman Empire and its successor states, which are labelled as entirely primitive and criminal.

23 Theodora Dragostinova, *Between Two Motherlands: Nationality and Emigration among the Greeks of Bulgaria, 1900–1949* (New York: Cornell University Press, 2011): 265.

24 Keith D. Watenpaugh, *Being Modern in the Middle East: Revolution, Nationalism, Colonialism, and the Arab Middle Class* (Princeton: Princeton University Press, 2006): 134–84.

25 Initial attempts to encourage "voluntary" migrations to help bring demographic "balance" to much of the former Ottoman Balkans had quickly transformed in 1912–13 to becoming parts of "swaps" of "national" populations in Thrace, at this point only between Greece and Bulgaria, but then mutating into a project that became scientifically endorsed to assure "ethnological settlement" that reflected the various post-WWI treaties—Neuilly (1919); Sèvres (1920); Lausanne (1923)—which all made such exchanges compulsory. What changed was the very reluctance of targeted peoples to leave, despite their "minority" status as well as the less-than-cooperative "majority" nationals who did not entirely embrace the idea of expelling neighbors. The issue of what I call that lingering Ottoman sensibility has dogged twentieth-century Balkan and Middle Eastern states, with periodic outbreaks of state-led violence specifically trying to accomplish what treaties and economic and political marginalization could not do on their own. Mark Levene, *Genocide in the Age of the Nation State: Vol. 2: The Rise of the West and the Coming of Genocide* (London: I.B. Tauris, 2013). On the violence of occupation regimes sanctioned as "Mandates" to help Arabs transition into the modern world, see for instance, Michael Provence, *The Great Syrian Revolt and the Rise of Arab Nationalism* (Austin: University of Texas Press, 2005).

26 This point is made in greater detail in Isa Blumi, *Foundations of Modernity: Human Agency and the Imperial State* (New York: Routledge, 2012).

27 Roderic H. Davidson, *Reform in the Ottoman Empire, 1856–1876* (Princeton: Princeton University Press, 1963) and Carter V. Findley, "The Tanzimat," in Reşat Kasaba (ed.), *The Cambridge History of Turkey, vol. iv, Turkey in the Modern World* (Cambridge: Cambridge University Press, 2008): 11–37.

28 Nazan Çiçek, *The Young Ottomans: Turkish Critics of the Eastern Question in the Late Nineteenth Century* (London: I.B. Tauris, 2010).

29 Ebru Boyar, *Ottomans, Turks and the Balkans: Empire Lost, Relations Altered* (London: I.B. Tauris, 2007).

30 This control over food would prove the key weapon of the modern state to subordinate vast numbers of "native" peoples. Mike Davis, *Late Victorian Holocausts: El Niño Famines and the Making of the Third World* (London: Verso, 2002) and John Darwin, "Imperialism and the Victorians: The Dynamics of Territorial Expansion," *English Historical Review* 112 (1997): 614–42.

31 At one point during the build-up to World War I, a trans-continental struggle for ascendency over assets increasingly deemed essential for survival of industrial economies, such as oil, coal, and manpower took place. Germany, for one, had invested heavily in harnessing a relationship with the Ottoman Empire, and by extension, the "Islamic" world in order to undermine French and British power beyond Europe. As both rival powers, and the Russians for that matter, exploited the assets of Muslim peoples throughout Africa and Asia, the German strategic

thinking, informed in reductive terms familiar to those critical of British and French Orientalist thought, imagined it possible to use the Ottoman's local knowledge and legitimacy to dominate Africa. See political report found in PAAA, R21128, AZ A10334, Fritz Bronsart von Schellendorf's report: "Die Aufteilung Afrikas—Deutschland und der Islam," dated Berlin, 16 February 1915. For an extensive study on German efforts to incite revolt among British and French Muslims by way of propaganda, see Tilman Lüdke, *Jihad Made in Germany: Ottoman and German Propaganda and Intelligence Operations in the First World War* (Berlin: LIT, 2005).

32 Some scholars have used their access to the papers of a few men to make general statements about Ottoman society, often leading them to identify currents of racial hatred that would account for, in the subsequent decades, mass murder committed by thousands of accomplices who could have never accessed the personal diaries of say Nazim Pasha or MP Mehmed Hulusi. If Deringil, for example, really hopes to link these men's private notes to Armenian genocide or the rise of Pan-Islamic sentiments among millions, more than simply linking someone to "tell-tale" phrases or terms is needed. In other historical fields, such reductive reasoning would not pass as acceptable, but in a field where Orientalist universalism still prevails, it apparently does not take much more than a simple reference to Islam juxtaposed to Christians to lay the groundwork for genocide during a World War no one in the 1890s could predict. BBA Y.PRK.Ş 3/55, Esseyid Mehmed Hulusi memorandum, dated 22 December 1890, cf. Deringil, *Conversion and Apostasy*, 206.

33 Nader Sohrabi, *Revolution and Constitutionalism in the Ottoman Empire and Iran* (Cambridge: Cambridge University Press, 2011): 72–134, 224–86. For reflection on the counterrevolution and the way in which Ottoman conservatives perceived the threats of these changes, see CUP sympathizer Yunus Nadi, *Ihtilal ve Inkılab-ı Osmani* (Istanbul: Matbaa-ı Cihan, 1909): 33–41.

34 Relying on internal documents of the Grand Orient Ottoman lodge and linked orders, such as the Grand Orient of France, Eric Anduze has revealed the emergence of a powerful faction within the CUP that was directly linked to the French Masons. Preaching that a utopian revolutionary order would emerge from the 1908 regime change, such intersections of foreign influence had still unconsidered consequences on the direction of the Ottoman period of parliamentary dictatorship better known as the Unionist era. Eric Anduze, *La franc-maçonnerie de la Turquie Ottomane, 1908-1924* (Paris: L'Harmattan, 2005). See also M. Şükrü Hanioğlu, *The Young Turks in Opposition* (New York: Oxford University Press, 1995): 33–41.

35 Emel Akal, *Milli Mücadelenin Başlangıcında: Mustafa Kemal, Ittihat Terakki ve Bolşevizm* (Istanbul: Iletişim, 2012) and Ilham Khuri-Makdisi, *The Eastern Mediterranean and the Making of Global Radicalism, 1860-1914* (Berkeley: University of California Press, 2010).

36 Michael Laffan, *Islamic Nationhood and Colonial Indonesia: The Umma below the Winds* (London: RoutledgeCurzon, 2003).

37 Daniel Clayton, "Colonizing, Settling and the Origins of Academic Geography," *The Wiley-Blackwell Companion to Human Geography* (2011): 50–70.

38 Mary Edith Durham, "Some Montenegrin Manners and Customs," *The Journal of the Royal Anthropological Institute of Great Britain and Ireland* 39 (1909): 85–96; Mary Edith Durham, *Through the Lands of the Serb* (London: E. Arnold, 1904) and Franz Baron Nopcsa, "Ergänzungen zu Meinen Buche über die Bauten, Trachten und Geräte Nordalbaniens," *Zeitschrift für Ethnologie* 59.3/6 (1927): 279–81.

39   Andrea Pieroni, Maria Elena Giusti, and Cassandra L. Quave, "Cross-Cultural
     Ethnobiology in the Western Balkans: Medical Ethnobotany and Ethnozoology
     among Albanians and Serbs in the Pešter Plateau, Sandžak, South-Western Serbia,"
     Human Ecology 39.3 (2011): 333–49. Ethnographer Anton Blok has explored the
     dangerous reductionism found in so much of the literature focusing on "primitive"
     southern peoples, be they in Sicilia or the Balkans. In one important study, Blok
     revisits Freud's notion of the "narcissism" of minor differences as the source of
     conflict between neighbors, Anton Blok, "The Narcissism of Minor Differences,"
     European Journal of Social Theory 1.1 (1998): 33–56.

40   Peter Hertner, *The Balkan Railways, International Capital and Banking from the
     End of the 19th Century until the Outbreak of the First World War* (Sofia: Bulgarian
     National Bank, 2006) and Basil C. Gounaris, "Railway Construction and Labour
     Availability in Macedonia in the Late Nineteenth Century," *Byzantine and Modern
     Greek Studies* 13.1 (1989): 139–58.

41   Lyndon Moore and Jakub Kaluzny, "Regime Change and Debt Default: The Case
     of Russia, Austro-Hungary, and the Ottoman Empire Following World War One,"
     Explorations in Economic History 42.2 (2005): 237–58.

42   Şevket Pamuk, *The Ottoman Empire and European Capitalism, 1820–1913: Trade,
     Investment and Production* (Cambridge: Cambridge University Press, 1987). As
     explained more fully in Chapter 1, the Ottoman Empire's rash decision in 1875
     to stop all payments on its debts left the international banking interests and bond
     holders scrambling to negotiate directly with the Ottomans to refinance the debt,
     using various forms of collateral, including valuable Ottoman lands in the Balkans.
     If Russia's expansion stood unabated, these payment schemes (and all the initial
     investment in the rail roads) could easily be threatened.

43   Fujinami Nobuyoshi, "The Patriarchal Crisis of 1910 and Constitutional Logic:
     Ottoman Greeks' Dual Role in the Second Constitutional Politics," *Journal of Modern
     Greek Studies* 27.1 (2009): 1–30.

44   This is a crucial turning point for a number of once ubiquitous institutions in
     Ottoman society. It was not only the Sultan as the symbolic head of the empire who
     was losing control over large portions of the Balkans as "Christian" communities
     were gaining increasing autonomy, but it was the *Rum* (Greek) Orthodox Church as
     well. George Mavrogordatos, "Orthodoxy and Nationalism in the Greek Case," *West
     European Politics* 26.1 (2003): 117–36. Similar infringements starting in the 1840s on
     Eastern Churches such as the Maronites and the Armenian Catholics had been driven
     by powerful Anglo-Saxon Evangelical movements which actually secured protected
     status from the Sultan by way of gaining the Armenian Protestants "millet" status in
     1849. On the manner by which these traditional establishments violently reacted to
     especially Anglo-Saxon missionary infringements, see Joseph L. Grabill, *Protestant
     Diplomacy and the Near East: Missionary Influence on American Policy, 1810–1927*
     (Minneapolis: University of Minnesota Press, 1971); Harrison G. O. Dwight,
     *Christianity in Turkey: A Narrative of the Protestant Reformation in the Armenian
     Church* (London: J. Nisbet, 1854); Robert F. Zeidner, "Britain and the Launching
     of the Armenian Question," *IJMES* 7.4 (1976): 465–83; Jeremy Salt, *Imperialism,
     Evangelism and the Ottoman Armenians, 1878–1896* (London: Routledge, 1993) and
     Ussama Makdisi, "Reclaiming the Land of the Bible: Missionaries, Secularism, and
     Evangelical Modernity," *The American Historical Review* 102.3 (1997): 680–713.

45   Austria-Hungary and Russia actually signed a pact in 1876 agreeing to divide up
     the Balkans into their mutually beneficial "spheres of influence," Solomon Wank,

"Foreign Policy and the Nationality Problem in Austria-Hungary, 1867–1914," *Austrian History Yearbook* 3.3 (1967): 37–56.

46 Hanioğlu, *Young Turks in Opposition*, 200–95 and Sohrabi, *Revolution and Constitutionalism*, 53–62.

47 Hanioğlu, *Young Turks in Opposition*, 12–22, 31–2.

48 Daniel P. S. Goh, "States of Ethnography: Colonialism, Resistance, and Cultural Transcription in Malaya and the Philippines, 1890s-1930s," *CSSH* 49: 1 (2007): 109–42.

49 On how "victims" of violence in the Balkans translated their traumas to Eastern Anatolia after 1912, see the crucial work of Ümit Üngör, *The Making of Modern Turkey: Nation and State in Eastern Anatolia, 1913–1950* (Oxford: Oxford University Press, 2012): 42–50. While neglecting the role of Balkan and Chechen refugees, Michael Reynolds' crucial work nevertheless masterfully highlights the clashing external and domestic interests that lead to the horrors in Eastern Anatolia during World War I, *Shattering Empires: The Clash and Collapse of the Ottoman and Russian Empires, 1908–1918* (Cambridge: Cambridge University Press, 2011): 140–66.

50 Anton Blok, "The Enigma of Senseless Violence," in Goran Aijmer and Jon Abbink (eds), *Meanings of Violence: A Cross-Cultural Perspective* (Oxford: Berg, 2000): 23–38. As noted in the context of Algeria, there is a tendency when studying imperialism from within a discourse of imperial description, to associate violence to certain types of peoples exclusively and then claim it as a sign of native deviance and criminality corrected by European civilization. James McDougall, "Savage Wars? Codes of Violence in Algeria, 1830s-1990s," *Third World Quarterly* 26/1 (2005): 117–31.

51 Anton Blok, "The Enigma of Senseless Violence," 26.

52 Blumi, *Foundations of Modernity*, 11–32.

53 The same tropes were used to justify Austro-Hungary's occupation regime in Bosnia-Herzegovina. On how Kállay, the Austro-Hungarian chief administrator in occupied Bosnia-Herzegovina, understood and then applied these operational principles, see Robin Okey, *Taming Balkan Nationalism: The Habsburg "Civilizing Mission" in Bosnia, 1878-1914* (Oxford: Oxford University Press, 2007): 74–122.

54 On the particulars of this theme, see Üngör's impressive new contribution to the oft-repeated story of Ottoman destruction by way of "unionist" violence directed at potential rivals within a surviving empire, Üngör, *The Making of Modern Turkey*, 28–33.

55 This devolution was a process by which a certain faction of political actors—at the time led by Bahaeddin Şakir, Mehmed Talat Bey, Ziya Gökalp, Yusuf Akçura, and Mehmed Nazim—steered the state in a direction many within society did not necessarily approve. Üngör, *The Making of Modern Turkey*, 25–54. Framed in the language of "modern" state administration, the template for mass expropriation of properties, which had a dual function of enriching the perpetrators and destroying the Armenian (and *Rum* Orthodox) communities, actually came from Euro-American imperialism. In other words, the CUP thugs were latecomers to this horrible "Great Game of Genocide." See Hilmar Kaiser, "Armenian Property, Ottoman Law and Nationality Policies during the Armenian Genocide, 1915–1916," in Olaf Farschid, Manfred Kropp, and Stephan Dähne (eds), *The First World War as Remembered in the Countries of the Eastern Mediterranean* (Beirut: Orient-Institut, 2006): 49–71.

56 Richard C. Hall, *The Balkan Wars 1912-1913: Prelude to the First World War* (London: Routledge, 2000) and M. Hakan Yavuz and Isa Blumi (eds), *War &*

Nationalism: The Balkan Wars (1912–1913) and Socio-Political Implications (Salt Lake City: University of Utah Press, 2013).

57   This rush to apply "science" to population politics in Anatolia had been developed by non-Turkish Ottoman sociologists and ethnographers, including the German-trained, Albanian-born ethnographer Naci Ismail Pelister and Ziya Gökalp who adopted European schemes to "settle" refugees in Anatolia, Üngör, *The Making of Modern Turkey*, 33–42.

58   After reading the scholarship surrounding the Armenian Genocide, one cannot doubt that for a key group of men—from the lower end, the criminal, perhaps even deranged Mehmed Reşid, to the purely "modern" bureaucratic operative, Talat Pasha—coming into power at the right moment demanded an ideological turn akin to racism to take place. During war these men acted "logically" with horrifying effect. In this respect, I have no doubt about the resulting crimes. I just do not think it right to use the benefit of "hindsight" to implant intentions and "patterns" to otherwise dynamic processes that deserve a much closer look. The events of 1895, for instance, cannot be used to pre-sage later events, for it then also overshadows the triumphs, horrors, and mundane taking place in the meantime. Hilmer L. Kieser, "Dr. Mehmed Reshid (1873–1919): A Political Doctor," in H. L. Kieser and D. J. Schaller (eds), *The Armenian Genocide and the Shoah* (Zurich: Chronos, 2002): 245–80.

59   Taner Akçam, *From Empire to Republic: Turkish Nationalism and the Armenian Genocide* (London: Zed Books, 2004): 130–2.

Chapter 1

1   Be it forms of tax farming—often associated with violent exploitation by "Turks" or "Muslim" landowners over "Christian" peasant majorities—or inefficient methods of agricultural and industrial production, the linear trajectory of "Western" economic domination over the Ottoman lands necessarily links social and material backwardness to an assumed "modernity" that came by way of key "merchant" or European-educated bureaucrats. Murat Birdal, *The Political Economy of Ottoman Public Debt: Insolvency and European Financial Control in the Late Nineteenth Century* (London: I.B. Tauris, 2010): 10–11, 167–80; Şevket Pamuk, *The Ottoman Empire and European Capitalism, 1820–1913, Trade, Investment and Production* (Cambridge: Cambridge University Press, 1987); Michael R. Palairet, *The Balkan Economies, 1800–1914: Evolution without Development* (Cambridge: Cambridge University Press, 1997). For a good summary of these interpretations' weaknesses, see Keith Brown, *Loyal unto Death: Trust and Terror in Revolutionary Macedonia* (Bloomington: Indiana University Press, 2013): 41–69.

2   On the social side, as France, the United States, Germany, and later Italy were busy making citizens out of former African-slaves, Native Americans, Saxons and Sicilians, reform-minded Ottomans too adopted universalist ideologies. To men known as the "Young Ottomans," a strong liberal, constitutionally guided political system was the reform necessary to integrate the empire's impossible "mix" of peoples. Indeed, the political and cultural elite of the mid-century developed an all-encompassing program of "Ottomanism" that for decades steered the ideological thrust of the government to inculcate, through the growing print media, popular culture, and educational system, a sense of inter-sectarian union. It is possible to argue that this

formidable bureaucratic elite's efforts did indeed harness the capacities of the diverse population to orientate their aspirations away from perpetual communal violence. Such successes demand that we explore alternative explanations for the collapse of this distinctively "non-Western" enterprise. Şerif Mardin, *The Genesis of Young Ottoman Thought: A Study in the Modernization of Turkish Political Ideas* (Syracuse, NY: Syracuse University Press, 2000).

3   In the hands of more sophisticated historians of European state formation, such processes were never uniform and constantly shifted as a result of very different sets of conditions. This requires a multi-variant account of nineteenth-century state formation that still escapes the linear explanations of a singular event known as Ottoman collapse. For instance, I would prefer to not treat the events leading to the Balkan Wars of 1912 as part of a singular process of the "inevitable" Ottoman collapse but, as done in respect to French, German, and Spanish history, delineate parallel, often contradictory processes that may or may not ultimately account for anything we today insist to frame in terms of complete nation-states. As exemplary models for the study of the complexities of Ottoman stories, see Peter Sahlins, *Boundaries: The Making of France and Spain in the Pyrenees* (Berkeley: University of California Press, 1991) and David Blackburn, *The Peculiarities of German History: Bourgeois Society and Politics in Nineteenth Century Germany* (New York: Oxford University Press, 1985).

4   Blumi, *Foundations of Modernity*. For an excellent example of how such critical rethinking of nationalist discourse in the Habsbrug Slavic and Italian Adriatic territories can help challenge our conventions about conflict in multi-lingual societies and thus rewrite European early modern history, see Dominque K. Reill, *Nationalists Who Feared the Nation: Adriatic Multi-Nationalism in Habsburg Dalmatia, Trieste, and Venice* (Palo Alto: Stanford University Press, 2012). Crucial work exploring in greater detail the emerging patterns of governing "the local" in the Ottoman Balkans at the height of Midhat Pasha's influence in the late 1860s may also contribute to shedding light on the intricacies of productive interactions between the inhabitants of targeted regions for reform and those expected to both draw up policies and enforce them. See especially Safa M. Saracoğlu, *Letters from Vidin: A Study of Ottoman Governmentality and Politics of Local Administration, 1864–1877* (PhD Dissertation, The Ohio State University, 2007).

5   Considerable energy is invested by a new wave of Ottoman scholars—largely from Turkey—on aspects of this cultural subordination of indigenous life patterns to social and institutional modifications associated with Europe. Some, however, have usefully resisted jumping to assuming nothing of the changes in the nineteenth century was locally produced, Butrus Abu-Manneh, "The Islamic Roots of the Gülhane Rescript," *Die Welt des Islams* 34 (1994): 173–203.

6   For a benign review of the history of finance in the nineteenth-century European context, see Youssef Casssis (ed.), *Finance and Financiers in European History, 1880–1960* (Cambridge: Cambridge University Press, 1992). More helpful as explanations to what transpired since the nineteenth century as a consequence of strategic attacks on social and state structures by banking family cartels are Michael Hudson, *Trade, Development and Foreign Debt: How Trade and Development Concentrate Economic Power in the Hands of Dominant Nations* (New York: ISLET, 2009) and L. Randall Wray, *Modern Money Theory: A Primer on Macroeconomics for Sovereign Monetary Systems* (New York: Palgrave Macmillan, 2012).

7   The ideological diversity of these generations of Young Ottomans (later Young Turks) cannot be stressed enough. Not everyone in the movement embraced the secular liberalism and Social Darwinism that eventually ripped the empire apart in the ruinous attempt to transform Ottomans into "Western" style subjects of modernity. For an important comparative exercise in charting the progression of these factions, see in unison Zürcher, *The Young Turk Legacy*; and Hanioğlu, *The Young Turks in Opposition*, and M. Şükrü Hanioğlu, *Preparation for a Revolution: The Young Turks, 1902–1908* (Oxford: Oxford University Press, 2001).

8   See Mesrob K. Krikorian, *Armenians in the Service of the Ottoman Empire, 1860–1908* (London: Routledge, 1977). Other big *Rum* Christian families, or *paroikies*, included the Rodocanachis, Scaramangas, Petrococcinos, and Vaglians. See Ioanna P. Minoglou, "Ethnic Minority Groups in International Banking: Greek Diaspora Bankers of Constantinople and Ottoman State Finances, c. 1840–81," *Financial History Review* 9.02 (2002): 125–46. Whomever we ultimately identify as included in this compradore or "middlemen" group, the role of increasingly powerful indigenous allies in accelerating the foreign capture of local economies is indisputable. The key is not to single out "Greeks," "Jews," or "Armenians" but to identify the contingent processes by which individuals excelled in this role. Robert Vitalis, "On the Theory and Practice of Compradors: The Role of Abbud Pasha in the Egyptian Political Economy," *IJMES* 22.2 (1990): 291–315 and Gad G. Gilbar, "The Muslim Big Merchant-Entrepreneurs of the Middle East, 1860–1914," *Die Welt des Islams* 43.1 (2003): 1–36.

9   For a fine overview, see Robert Zens, "Provincial Powers: The Rise of Ottoman Local Notables (Ayan)," *History Studies: International Journal of History* 3.3 (2011): 433–47.

10 It is interesting that many of these men were not natives of the lands over which they were commissioned to rule. In Egypt, it was a group of Albanians, Turks, and Circassians who formed the inner core around Mehmed Ali. In Tunisia, Khayr al-Din Pasha al-Tunisi, who hailed from Chechnya, was also a vital political reformer in the 1830s. These were all men from refugee constituencies whose ascendency in the Ottoman military bureaucratic system required of them loyalty to the Sultan in addition to aggressive territorial expansion. Indeed, throughout the territories out of which the major reforms emerged were regional state governments staffed by itinerate Ottomans or political refugees from realms outside the empire. While such observations in themselves do not explain the nature of the relationships these regimes forged with Istanbul, they do reinforce the point that mobility, and the capacity to adapt and integrate (if not ultimately dominate) initially "foreign" sociopolitical spaces, may explain the kind of possibilities that existed for refugees seeking a safe-haven in the nineteenth-century Ottoman Empire.

11 Eventually, as in Egypt with Mehmed Ali Pasha, Derviş Pasha became part of the problem and went rogue on the empire as politics with Iran and local Kurds transformed the domestic political dynamic. For a report on Derviş Pasha's activities against rebellious Kurdish groups around the Iranian border, attacks that ultimately led the then Ottoman loyalist to recognize new opportunities, see BBA HAT 452 No. 22392, Erzurum governor, Celaleddin Pasha to Istanbul, dated 18 February 1817. On the rising (and then falling) fortunes of the autonomous Kurdish entrepreneurs involved in this process, see Sinan Hakan, *Osmanlı Arşiv Belgelerinde Kürtler ve Kürt Direnişleri (1817–1867)* (Istanbul: Doz, 2007): 27–44.

12 Scholars often stress that the Egyptian regime adopted a "French" model in its drive to expand state power as in Timothy Mitchell, *Colonising Egypt* (Berkeley: University

of California Press, 1988) and Khaled Fahmy, *All the Pashas Men: Mehmed Ali, His Army and the Making of Modern Egypt* (Cairo: American University of Cairo Press, 2002). It may, however, be more productive to think of the process as a hybrid that developed uniquely out of a local context, rather than a simple act of cutting and pasting from a "European" model that in the 1820s was hardly existent.

13 Fred H. Lawson, *The Social Origins of Egyptian Expansionism during the Muhammad 'Ali Period* (New York: Columbia University Press, 1991).

14 Asad J. Rustom, *The Royal Archives of Egypt and the Origins of the Egyptian Expedition to Syria, 1831–1841* (Beirut: American Press, 1936); Şinasi Altundağ, *Kavalalı Mehmet Ali Paşa Isyanı: Mısır Meselesi, 1831–1841* (Ankara: Türk Tarih Kurumu, 1988) and Muhammad H. Kutuloğlu, *The Egyptian Question (1831–1841): The Expansionist Policy of Mehmed Ali Paşa in Syria and Asia Minor and the Reaction of the Sublime Porte* (Istanbul: Eren, 1998).

15 Alan Mikhail, *Nature and Empire in Ottoman Egypt: An Environmental History* (Cambridge: Cambridge University Press, 2011): 161–7, 277–83.

16 Among other things, the region around Mersin/Adana (Cilicia) that Ibrahim Pasha developed (colonized) was perfect for cotton production, the quintessential cash crop of the era. See Meltem Toksöz, "Bir Coğrafya, Bir Ürun, Bir Bölge: Çukurova," *Kebikeç* 21 (2006): 97–110. For the timber, see Kutuloğlu, *The Egyptian Question*, 200–6. On how cotton production transforms newly acquired lands in Louisiana by the early 1830s, in a process that mirrors, if not parallels Mehmed Ali's investment in cotton production throughout the Eastern Mediterranean, see Walter Johnson, *Rivers of Dark Dreams: Slavery and Empire in the Cotton Kingdom* (Cambridge, MA: Harvard University Press, 2013).

17 In a search to increase revenues, the Ottoman Empire's reformers first emulated Egypt's considerable success with using state-held monopolies in opium, cotton, and silk, only to be forced to open the economy in 1838 as a concession to British, and later French, interests in return for their support against the state's internal rebellious governors. M. Şükrü Hanioğlu, *A Brief History of the Late Ottoman Empire* (Princeton, NJ: Princeton University Press, 2008): 70.

18 Blumi, *Reinstating the Ottomans*, 44–53. Similarly, Mehmed Ali and his sons were not the only stakeholders engaged in this enterprise that ultimately pitted an expansionist, quintessentially "modern" state against various other, often unnamed interests standing behind their imperial state surrogate (British, French, and/or Russian). The story still awaits to be told, for example, of just who helped finance the Egyptian state expansion, which required heavy borrowing in advance (presumably using future tax revenues as collateral) to actually pay for the vast public works and infrastructure development observed by so many admiring (and envious) Europeans.

19 I will explore this issue further in Chapter 4.

20 French intelligence agents posing as scientists were under no illusion that the Ottoman Empire, especially the Balkans, was a rich land awaiting exploitation. Ami Boué, *La Turquie d'Europe* (Paris: Arhur Bertrand, 1840): I, ix–x. A sentiment shared by British dignitaries who traveled to the region and lauded the revenue potential of numerous provinces. See a report by the Board of Trade after a visit in the early 1860s in Great Britain, Parliament, *Parliamentary Papers*, no. 2972, vol. 64 (1862): 475.

21 Neglected here, the innovative work of Christine Philliou on the often misrepresented role of the Ottoman Orthodox Christian elite of this era, the Phanariots, reveals what is deemed the "counterintuitive" integrationist role they played prior to the Tanzimat reforms. As such, they induced crucial structural adaptations in the Danubian

Principalities on account of the mutual dependencies emerging in face of the transformative pressures surfacing during the early modern era. Christine Philliou, "Communities on the Verge: Unraveling the Phanariot Ascendancy in Ottoman Governance," *CSSH* 51.01 (2009): 151–81. Similar insights were made in respect to the manner in which local elites in Diyarbakir (a mostly Kurdish and Armenian region) and Mosul (Kurdish, Turkmen, and Arab) were integrated into the larger governing enterprise of the early nineteenth century. See Ariel Salzmann, *Tocqueville in the Ottoman Empire: Rival Paths to the Modern State* (Leiden: E.J. Brill, 2004) and Dina Rizk Khoury, *State and Provincial Society in the Ottoman Empire: Mosul, 1540–1834* (Cambridge: Cambridge University Press, 1997).

22 Niall Ferguson, *The Ascent of Money: A Financial History of the World* (New York: Penguin, 2008): 278–83.

23 For an extensive report on Ottoman expenditures and its tax policies just when it began to float its first international loan, see Edmound Chertier, *Réformes en Turquie* (Paris: Dentu, Librairie-Editeur, 1858): 98–102.

24 To the editors of *La Semaine Financière*, Syria not only had a "great future," but promised those willing to "exploit" it "significant" returns in less than ten years, dated Paris, 8 November 1856, p. 1.

25 Already by 1825 the Levant Company, which once held a monopoly on trade with the Ottoman Empire, was forcefully closed down as a concession to European powers offering to help Istanbul defeat its rebellious regional governors. Indeed, within a decade, almost all Ottoman "trade barriers" were replaced by agreements that gave French, British, and Russian traders advantageous customs' rates that resulted in undercuting indigenous, especially Muslim traders. As argued throughout, these concessions in time produced the kind of socioeconomic dislocations that some link to outbursts of violence toward Christians throughout the region in the 1850s and beyond.

26 On the role local agents played in regional capitalization in Greater Syria and how provincial elites created the investment environment that would eventually lead to widespread French investment in Beirut, see Jens Hanssen, *Fin de Siècle Beirut: The Making of an Ottoman Provincial Capital* (Oxford: Oxford University Press, 2005): 84–104.

27 Indeed, it was a "Christian" revolt led by Tanyus Shahin against a besieged landowning class that induced various factions as far as Damascus and France to engage in the violence. These events are linked by scholars today by the rubric of "sectarian" war that became a trope to account for all violence in Lebanon and Greater Syria. See among others, Leila Fawaz, *An Occasion for War: Mount Lebanon and Damascus, 1860* (London: I.B. Tauris, 1994). More importantly, the manner in which those affected reacted, adjusted, and then engaged the various contingent forces to emerge from these new political economies contributed to the eventual forces of change that led to Ottoman collapse. The point throughout this book is to make sure we do not narrow the causal links to any one source or assumed predetermined process so often called "Westernization" or "modernization."

28 Ussama Makdisi, *The Culture of Sectarianism, Community, History and Violence in Nineteenth-Century Ottoman Lebanon* (Berkeley: University of California Press, 2000).

29 See Hanioğlu, *A Brief History*, 90–1.

30 In many ways, the concessions that ultimately exposed Ottoman societies to monopolistic financial interests, first and foremost by way of surrendering control

of money supply to a still unclear set of local and foreign interests, proved to be the perfect ruse for the same banking interests that faced intermittent resistance in North America. Euro-American colonialists/patriots like Jefferson and later Jackson rebelled against the privately owned Bank of England (which financed the already indebted British "royal" family) knowing perfectly well that the power to control money supply ultimately meant domination over the economy. "Give me control of a nation's money and I care not who makes its laws," goes the famous quote attributed to Mayer Amschel Bauer Rothschild, a contemporary of these epic struggles.

31 By 1838, the pro-British faction led by Mustafa Reşit Pasha gained access to power within a soon-to-be all-powerful bureaucracy autonomous from the palace. During the ceremony that promulgated the Hatt-ı Şerif of Gülhane, the newly appointed Foreign Minister acknowledged that he would always consult France in times of need: France . . . "insisted on our reforms and we wish to thank her for their successful completion." Victor Langlois, "Réchid Pacha et les réformes en Turquie," *Revue de l'Orient, de l'Algérie et des Colonies* 7 (1858): 15–16.

32 The most important feature of the "Beneficial Reforms" (*Tanzimat-i Hayriye*) was the transfer of power from the palace immediately after the death of Sultan Mahmut II in June 1839 to the bureaucracy of the empire, known as the Sublime Porte (henceforth Porte). This constituted a monumental transfer of effective power to an emerging bureaucratic elite whose fundamental agenda would be to draw from the experiences of streamlining government initiated by Mehmed Ali of Egypt and his sons. Carter V. Findley, *Bureaucratic Reform in the Ottoman Empire: The Sublime Porte, 1789–1922* (Princeton: Princeton University Press, 1980): 44–6, 167–71.

33 Donald Quataert, "The Age of Reforms," in Halil Inalcik and Donald Quataert (eds), *An Economic and Social History of the Ottoman Empire* (Cambridge: Cambridge University Press, 1994): 759–933. Of course this was mirroring processes occurring in China and elsewhere at the time, see Reşat Kasaba, "Open-Door Treaties: China and the Ottoman Empire Compared," *New Perspectives on Turkey* 7 (1992): 77–89 and Sedat Bingöl, *Tanzimat Devrinde Osmanlı'da Yargı Reformu: Nizamiyye Mahkemeleri'nin Kuruluşu ve İşleyişi, 1840–1876* (Eskişehir: Anadolu Üniversitesi Yayınları 2004): 113–45.

34 On conditions in areas north of Mosul in this period of rapid state expansion that resulted in violence and the government's retrenchment from efforts to rationalize the local economy see Hakan Özoğlu, *Kurdish Notables and the Ottoman State: Evolving Identities, Competing Loyalties, and Shifting Boundaries* (New York: State University of New York Press, 2004): 59–63. For similar events in the Balkans see Hasan Kaleshi and Hans-Jürgen Kornrumpf, "Das Wilajet Prizren. Beitrag zur Geschichte der türkischen Staatsreform auf dem Balkan im 19. Jahrhundert," *Südostforschungen. Internationale Zeitschrift für Geschichte, Kultur und Landeskunde Südosteuropas* (München), 26 (1967): 176–238.

35 Huri Islamoğlu, "Property as a Contested Domain: A Reevaluation of the Ottoman Land Code of 1858," in Roger Owen (ed.), *New Perspectives on Property and Land in the Middle East* (Cambridge, MA: Harvard University Press, 2001): 3–61.

36 In reporting back a conversation with the Grand Vizier, Sir Canning is said to have warned that if the empire would not address financial obligations it has with Britain and France, the state's very existence "may be compromised." NAUK, FO, 78/857, no. 262, Canning to Palmerston, dated Constantinople, 30 August 1851. The most astute of the Ottoman governing elite knew that they were dealing with genocidal thugs like Sir Canning who demonstrated time and again they could create events

through local surrogates that would devastate local communities and perhaps destabilize the empire altogether if they did not get their way. Faruk A. K. Yasamee, *Ottoman Diplomacy: Abdülhamid II and the Great Powers, 1878–1888* (Istanbul: The Isis Press, 1996): 43–71.

37 For detailed explanations of these reforms, one must read the Turkish scholarship, especially Abdüllatif Şener, *Tanzimat Dönemi Osmanlı Vergi Sistemi* (Istanbul: Işaret, 1990); Coşkun Çakır, *Tanzimat Dönemi Osmanlı Maliyesi* (Istanbul: Küre Yayınları, 2001); Musa Çadırcı, *Tanzimat Döneminde Anadolu Kentleri'nin Soysal ve Ekonomik Yapısı* (Ankara: Türk Tarih Kurumu, 1997) and Bingöl, *Tanzimat Devrinde Osmanlı'da*.

38 See Hanioğlu, *Preparation for a Revolution*, 289–311. Of course, this discourse on "civilization" very much mirrors the discourse in racist Euro-American circles facing their own indigenous savages throughout the period covered in this book. For a reminder of how "discourse" is understood here to reflect not a "definition" of a set of objects like the "savage" that is natural and ever-present, but rather the more dynamic process by which certain forms of power enable such objects to appear outside the contexts of subordination in which they actually are, see Michel Foucault, *The Archaeology of Knowledge and the Discourse on Language* (New York: Pantheon Books, 1972): 45. Again, many thanks go to Jon Schmitt for insisting on my clarifying my own terminological polemic.

39 New methods of instituting law would take immediate effect as "pre-Islamic" and extra-legal local traditions were deemed unacceptable barriers to the implementation of the legal and economic standards needed to modernize regions like Kosovo. See report from Prishtina branch officer of the Ziraat Bank, BBA TFR. 1.KV 22/2126, dated 27 June 1903.

40 Yusuf Akçuraoğlu, *Üç Tarz-ı Siyaset* (Istanbul: Matbaa-i Kadir, 1911).

41 Sohrabi, *Revolution and Constitutionalism*, 34–48. For those deemed irreversibly "savage," the qualifying use of state violence (or love, in the form of "education," in itself a modern form of violence) depended on context rather than a universal experience throughout the Ottoman Empire. For many, the opportunity to send children to Ottoman state schools was not missed, and any use of state violence required the right combination of local cooperation and logistical support. Nevertheless, by the 1870s, the results of attempts to apply state power to transform the still ontological "savage," were both horrific and transformative. As very different interests clashed at specific moments during decades of intermittent war, in Anatolia during the 1914–24 period, for example, it was the crucial ability of a state elite to unleash all the state's modern power to commit what amounts to genocide on their own (yes, rebellious) subjects that destroyed the Ottoman Empire. What proves crucial is understanding how foreign interests and the itinerate Ottoman played various roles in this quintessential "Westernization" process, all mediated by the constant pushback from local peoples.

42 Michelle Raccagni, "The French Economic Interests in the Ottoman Empire," *IJMES* 11.3 (1980): 339–76 and Jacque Thobie, *Intérêts Français dans l'Empire Ottoman (1895–1914)* (Paris: La Documentation Française, 1977): 43–54.

43 For a fine summary of who initiated the deepening financial relationship between European bankers and the Ottoman state prior to 1878, see André Autheman, *La Banque impérial ottomane* (Paris: Comité pour l'histoire économique et financière de la France, 1996): 17–47 and Christopher Clay, *Gold for the Sultan: Western Bankers and Ottoman Finance, 1856–1881* (London: I.B. Tauris, 2000): 142–228.

44 Edward Peter Fitzgerald, "France's Middle Eastern Ambitions, the Sykes-Picot Negotiations, and the Oil Fields of Mosul, 1915–1918," *The Journal of Modern History* 66.4 (1994): 697–725.

45 Philip E. Schoenberg, "The Evolution of Transport in Turkey (Eastern Thrace and Asia Minor) under Ottoman Rule, 1856–1918," *Middle Eastern Studies* 13.3 (1977): 359–72.

46 Andrew Lambert, *The Crimean War: British Grand Strategy Against Russia, 1853–56* (Oxford: Ashgate, 2011).

47 Vedat Eldem, *Osmanlı Imparatorluğunun Iktisadi Şartları Hakkinda bir Tetkik* (Istanbul: Iş Bankası Yayınları, 1970): 70; Ruth Kark and Seth J. Frantzman, "The Negev: Land, Settlement, the Bedouin and Ottoman and British Policy 1871–1948," *British Journal of Middle Eastern Studies* 39.1 (2012): 53–77; Ruth Kark and Seth J. Frantzman, "Bedouin, Abdül Hamid II, British Land Settlement, and Zionism: The Baysan Valley and Sub-district 1831–1948," *Israel Studies* 15.2 (2010): 49–79 and on Rothschild's investments throughout Syria/Palestine that permits land "development," see BBA BEO 204/15282, dated 21 June 1893.

48 André du Velay, *Essai sur l'histoire financière de la Turquie* (Paris: A. Rousseau, 1903): 412–14 and Autheman, *La banque impèriale ottoman*, 153–8, 168, 208–27.

49 Fitzgerald, "France's Middle Eastern Ambitions," 697–706; Edward Peter Fitzgerald, "Business Diplomacy: Walter Teagle, Jersey Standard, and the Anglo-French Pipeline Conflict in the Middle East, 1930–1931," *Business History Review* 67.02 (1993): 207–45; Volkan Ş Ediger, *Osmanlı'da Neft ve Petrol* (Istanbul: ODTü Yayıncılık, 2006).

50 Mehmet Hakan Sağlam, *Osmanlı Devleti'nde Moratoryum, 1875–1881: Rüstum-ı Sitte'den Dünyun-ı Umumiyye'ye* (Istanbul: Tarih Vakfı Yurt Yayınları, 2007): 11–27.

51 It got so bad by 1873 that Istanbul's liberals allowed the same financial advisors who pressured the ideologically like-minded reformers to open up Ottoman property markets to foreigners to create a stock exchange that would allow for the sale of Ottoman treasury bonds. This led to even greater foreign speculation as European markets at the time were sluggish, making the Ottoman Empire the only sure thing around. The reason for such confidence is crucial. As the East India Company proved over the years capable of coaxing the British state to pay for the coercive military operations to guarantee investments, so too were investors confident the Ottoman play was safe. Pamuk, *The Ottoman Empire and European Capitalism*, 62–8.

52 By the 1870s, the Ottoman state had more than £200 million in principal alone to pay back, meaning by defaulting, some very powerful interests were out to lose a great deal of money. Donald C. Blaisdell, *European Financial Control in the Ottoman Empire* (New York: Columbia University Press, 1929): 79–82.

53 The opening of the Suez Canal in 1869 transformed the Porte's reading of the situation in the Eastern Mediterranean. The increased importance of Britain's modest position in Aden and its subsequent occupation of Egypt in 1882 in particular lent new significance to overtures to the Ottomans by local leaders fearful of this European expansion. This was the case in the Arabian Peninsula. Ahmed Raşid and Ahmed Muhtar Pasha, ambitious Ottoman commanders who, in response to British challenges in the Red Sea, went beyond simply establishing a foothold in Yemen's commercial centers, but also aimed to rule all of the highlands at the expense of the still limited British presence in Aden. In this respect, requests for assistance in the usurping of British-supported families in the Arabian Peninsula played right into the hands of Ottoman bureaucrats advocating an aggressive response to European expansionism. Not only would new links to Yemen help thwart British expansion,

they could help secure agricultural lands that promised large increases in tax revenue for the central coffers as well as add upwards of 4 million people to the empire. See Blumi, *Foundations of Modernity*, 19–37.

54 For an understanding of how Yemen was seen in strategic terms by the 1872–3 campaign's principal administrative architect, see Ahmed Raşid, *Tarih-i Yemen ve San'a'*, 2 vols (Istanbul: Basiret Matbassı, 1291/1874): 2, 258–9, 351–5 and BBA, Irade-Meclis-i Mahsus 1922, Ahmed Muhtar Pasha's report to the Grand Vizier, dated 22 January 1873, documents 1–2.

55 Hanioğlu, *A Brief History*, 109–18.

56 A program spelled out by the sultan's office in BBA YEE 4/21 and BBA YEE 24/150/162/VIII, defter 8, f. 1–78.

57 By 1882, peasants paid an estimated 50 percent of the empire's taxes, contributing to a dramatic shift in rural life that would forever transform how people and their state institutions operated in the Red Sea and Balkan regions. On how peasants were especially hurt by heavy taxation in the Hamidian regime see Reşat Aktan, "The Burden of Taxation on the Peasants," in Charles Issawi (ed.), *The Economic History of Turkey, 1800–1914* (Chicago: University of Chicago Press, 1980): 109–13.

58 Scathing reports to the sultan on the state of the tax system in BBA YEE 13/26, Wüttendorf's report dated 13 February 1883 suggests a possible direct link to local instability and these new policies.

59 Reports were already coming from Niš that upwards of 210,000 Muslims were made temporarily refugees because of the violence in the region. PRO, FO, 195/1077, Reade to Elliot, dated Constantinople, 5 December 1876. They would all be accommodated in the economically strained borderland areas that would become the Kosovo province less than a year later. Since Kosovo as a province had less than 800,000 inhabitants at this time, the influx of so many migrants put immediate pressure on local communities. On the war itself, see James J. Reid, *Crisis of the Ottoman Empire: Prelude to Collapse, 1839–1878* (Stuttgart: Franz Steiner Verlag, 2000): 21–42.

60 Ali Hayder Midhat, *The Life of Midhat Pasha: A Record of His Services, Political Reforms, Banishment, and Judicial Murder, Derived from Private Documents and Reminiscences* (London: J. Murray, 1903).

61 To insure Ottoman integrity that protected British pretensions of economic (and linked cultural) hegemony, Britain used the subsequent diplomatic adjustments to plant garrisons on Ottoman Cyprus in order to enjoy ". . . imperial benefits equivalent to those which our strength and administrative skill can confer." Walter G. Wirthwein, *Britain and the Balkan Crises, 1875–1878* (New York: Columbia University Press, 1935): 399.

62 By 1868, British creditors formed the Corporation of Foreign Bondholders (CFB) which was influential enough to assure countries that were not regularly making their payments to their accounts that they would be shut out of the bond market. In other words, the bankers had leverage to shape British foreign relations. The CFB would be instrumental in shaping the Berlin Congress' financial scheme and stacked the Ottoman Debt Council that in 1881 co-opted the Ottoman State's revenue collection agencies in order to repay creditors. Edwin Borchard, *State Insolvency and Foreign Bondholders: General Principles* (New Haven: Yale University Press, 1951): 155–274, 391–528.

63 Clay, *Gold for the Sultan*, 503–59 and Birdal, *The Political Economy*, 104–6.

64 Smugglers like Isa Boletini evolved into such important players in regional economies that they soon became major political actors as well. Over time, Boletini's exploits as

a smuggler of wheat, weapons, and sugar gained him the reputation of ruthlessness, a commodity in high demand in various circles. Indeed, while now a "national hero" in Kosovo, Boletini was regularly associated with various foreign governments, including those of Serbia and Montenegro. Equally important however was his eventual association with Sultan Abdülhamid II, for whom Boletini served as the commander of the palace guard and then, when returned to his Kosovo base of operations, the Sultan's principal enforcer. Boletini served his master well for years and long opposed the revolution of 1908 that brought liberal CUP members to power. For elaboration, see Blumi, *Reinstating the Ottomans*, 67–81. On how gun trafficking offers a useful way to appreciate the "inversions" introduced by new revenues produced by such trade see Brown, *Loyal unto Death*, 144–69.

65 See Birdal, *The Political Economy*, 103–27 and a dated but still insightful study by Refii Ş. Suvla, "The Ottoman Debt, 1850–1939," in Charles Issawi (ed.), *The Economic History of the Middle East, 1800–1914* (Chicago: Chicago University Press, 1966): 94–106.

66 For a thorough contemporary reflection on Hamidian trade policies in these terms consult Celal Aybar, *Osmanlı İmparatorluğunun Ticaret Muvazensesi, 1878–1913* (Ankara: Devlet İstatistik Enstitüsü, 1939): 21–54. Details about the *Régie* are found in Birdal, *The Political Economy*, 129–65.

67 For an example of how officials intervened to assure more grain production, see BBA ŞD-Selanik 2008/41, dated 28 February 1879.

68 During the late Ottoman period tobacco exports grew in part thanks to the introduction of the American Tobacco Company, whose establishment of a factory in Salonica resulted in a 250 percent growth in exports between 1892 and 1909. In fact, by 1909, Kavalla joined Salonika as a major cigarette production center. Heinrich Stich, *Die welwirtschaftliche Entwicklung der Anatolischen Produktion seit Anfangs des 19 Jahrhunderts* (Kiel: 1929): 69–75.

69 *Dersaadet Ticaret Odası Gazetesi*, number 131, dated 3 July 1887, p. 184.

70 A modified version of the çiftlik system introduced at this time to reward local intermediaries willing to invest in labor management (and hopefully sop up some of the refugees still unsettled in the region) inaugurated major changes not only in landownership and taxation but also in agro-pastoral production. Many such estates were devoted mainly to wheat, cotton, or tobacco cultivation for export to foreign markets in European countries, ultimately pitting needs to keep food prices reasonable for so many millions of regional subjects against the fully accepted doctrine of maximizing profits. Somewhat as a compromise to this clear conflict of interests, the state was allowed (probably because foreign investors wanted to assure increased revenue to the state so it could continue to pay off its debts) to tax more heavily these commercial estates, Pamuk, *The Ottoman Empire and European Capitalism*, 9. The model for development became so successful, in fact, that by 1900 çiftliks had become the most common form of landholding in both Macedonia and Thrace; a total of 552 such estates were built in Macedonia alone, as much as 90 percent of which were located along major trade routes on the plains and in the valleys, Duncan M. Perry, *The Politics of Terror: The Macedonian Liberation Movements, 1893–1903* (Durham: Duke University Press, 1988): 25.

71 For a description of some of these profitable export-orientated farms in the Üsküp (Skopje) region, see Shukri Rahimi, *Lufta e Shqiptarëve për Autonomi, 1897–1912* (Prishtinë: Enti i Teksteve dhe i Mjeteve Mësimore i Krahines Socialiste Autonome të Kosovës, 1978): 51–8. The PDA helped introduce poppy cultivation into Kosovo,

which apparently became a vital regional tax earner from 1881 onwards. By 1888 up to 70 tons of opium was produced annually in Kosovo. See Kosova Vilâyet Salnamesi (1305/1888), 173. For its part, the Ottoman state invested in developing regional production by funneling money into the recently established agricultural bank, the Ziraat Bankası. The Kosovo branch office received the fourth highest amount of funding in the empire, behind three other provinces—Manastır, Hudavendigar, and Selanik (Salonika)—that also received large numbers of refugees. Tevfik Güran, *Osmanlı Devleti'nin Ilk Istatistik Yıllığı, 1897* (Ankara: T.C. Başbakanlık Devlet Istatistik Enstitüsü, 1997): 245–6, 419–20.

72   Engin Akarlı, "The Tangled Ends of an Empire: Ottoman Encounters with the West and Problems of Westernization—an Overview," *CSSAAME* 26.3 (2006): 353–66.

73   A large number of the landowning families of Vlora, Korçë, and Janina (Yanya), for instance, invested in educating their sons in the empire's elite technical schools and, even if Muslim, church schools like Zosimea in Janina. That said, many of the period's most known figures came from modest backgrounds, suggesting the Ottoman educational system allowed for talented children of the "lower" classes to work their way up the ranks within the professional schools. Perhaps the most famous student who did not come from a wealthy landowning family pedigree but still rose into prominence was Mustafa Kemal (Atatürk), who at one point was forced to quit school due to poverty. His greatest fortune was enrollment in military preparatory school. M. Şükrü Hanioğlu, *Atatürk: An Intellectual Biography* (Princeton: University of Princeton Press, 2011): 17–25.

74   Nathalie Clayer, "The Albanian Students of the Mekteb-i Mulkiye: Social Networks and Trends of Thought," in Elisabeth Ozdalga (ed.), *Late Ottoman Society: The Intellectual Legacy* (London: Routledge/Curzon Press, 2005): 289–339.

75   Ismail Kemal Bey, *The Memoirs of Ismail Kemal Bey* (London: Constable, 1920): 307–10.

76   Hanioğlu, *The Young Turks in Opposition*, 146–55.

77   It did not help that Qemali was charged with stealing monies given to him on behalf of the failed coup attempt in 1903. The plan had Receb Bey, a Gheg Albanian from Mat, leading a loyal band of troops to initiate an uprising in Salonica upon receiving the proper landing vessels to be provided by Qemali. Not only did Qemali fail to acquire the needed ships, but subsequent investigations into the matter convinced many that Qemali was a double, if not triple, agent working for a number of foreign interests including Greece, the Khedive of Egypt, and some British-based factions. Worse still, no one knows what happened with the £4000 given to Qemali. Hanioğlu, *Preparation for a Revolution*, 16–27, 331–2, 178ff.

78   Ismail Kemal Bey was not a loved man by his former associates. Many would report via the media and in conversations with foreign representatives that Qemali was nothing more than a "brigand" who could not be trusted with money. NAUK, F.O. 371/768, no. 7053 Lowther to Grey, dated Constantinople, 17 February 1909 (enclosed confidential letter no. 105).

79   Milen V. Petrov, "Everyday Forms of Compliance: Subaltern Commentaries on Ottoman Reform, 1864–1868," *CSSH* 46.4 (2004): 730–59.

80   Basil C. Gounaris, "Railway Construction and Labour Availability in Macedonia in the Late Nineteenth Century," *Byzantine and Modern Greek Studies* 13.1 (1989): 139–58.

81   Jason E. Strakes, "Between Two Masters: Khuzestan, Southern Iraq, and Dualities of State Making in the Arab/Persian Gulf," *The Arab World Geographer* 14.4 (2011):

336–61; Mahmoud Yazbak, "From Poverty to Revolt: Economic Factors in the Outbreak of the 1936 Rebellion in Palestine," *Middle Eastern Studies* 36.3 (2000): 93–113; Ellen Marie Lust-Okar, "Failure of Collaboration: Armenian Refugees in Syria," *Middle Eastern Studies* 32.1 (1996): 53–68; N. E. Bou-Nacklie, "Tumult in Syria's Hama in 1925: The Failure of a Revolt," *Journal of Contemporary History* 33.2 (1998): 273–89.

82 Donald Bloxham, "Terrorism and Imperial Decline: The Ottoman-Armenian Case," *European Review of History—Revue Européenne d'Histoire* 14.3 (2007): 301–24.

83 In the 1870s the agenda was to grant autonomy to neatly defined territories for Ottoman Christians under the pretext that they could not live securely under direct "Muslim" rule. This had its greatest impact in both Macedonia and Eastern Anatolia, where the Great Powers—largely under the British—declared the creation of six autonomous provinces—Van, Diyarbekir, Sivas, Erzurum, Bitlis, and Mamüretülaziz—from which Armenians (at least the Christians) would in theory live under a reformulated administration, Robert F. Zeidner, "Britain and the Launching of the Armenian Question," *IJMES* 7.4 (1976): 465–83.

84 For a valuable challenge to these vocabularies minted in contemporary studies by both journalists and diplomats, see Brown, *Loyal unto Death*, 14–40.

85 Jeremy W. Crampton, "The Cartographic Calculation of Space: Race Mapping and the Balkans at the Paris Peace Conference of 1919," *Social & Cultural Geography* 7.5 (2006): 731–52 and Ipek K. Yosmaoğlu, "Counting Bodies, Shaping Souls: The 1903 Census and National Identity in Ottoman Macedonia," *IJMES* 38.01 (2006): 55–77.

86 See reports on clashes that pitted the inhabitants of the Rugova valley with Slav-speaking settlers over ill-defined frontier pasture in various telegrams from Ipek (Peja) authorities to Istanbul. BBA TFR.1.KV 71/7092, telegram number 9106, dated 30 January 1903.

87 Such a spectacle worked like magic for the opposition, who used the frustrations of the majority of people living amid this morass, angry that outsider trouble-makers were constantly stealing property and often even murdering inhabitants. In the first few days after the 1908 summer revolt that brought the CUP into power and reinstated the 1876 Constitution (Kanûn-u Esâsî), heretofore suspended by the Sultan in 1878, the attempt to highlight the popularity of the revolution took many forms. Propaganda through the media included interviews with German military advisors, who, despite being loyal to the Sultan, nevertheless stressed that changes were needed as the CUP-led revolt (from within the same military units that von der Goltz advised) reflected the larger popular desire for stability. "Makedonya Meselesi Hakkında Goltz Paşa'nın Fikri," *Balkan*, dated 24 July 1908, 1–2.

88 See Perry, *The Politics of Terror*, 143.

89 Again, scholars eager to find "nationalist" activism in these very different events fail to put things in context. A classic example is the misreading of the mobilization of locals in western Kosovo during a critical period of breaking down law and order. Ismet Dërmaku, *Kuvendi i Lidhjes Shqiptare të Pejës "Besa Besë" 1899* (Prishtinë: NP, 1997); George Gawrych, *The Crescent and the Eagle: Ottoman Rule, Islam and the Albanians, 1874–1913* (London: I.B. Tauris, 2006): 125–6, and Kristaq Prifti, *Le Mouvement national albanais de 1896 à 1900: La Ligue de Pejë* (Tiranë: Akademia Historike, 1989).

90 Basil Gounaris, "Social Cleavages and National 'Awakening' in Ottoman Macedonia," *Eastern European Quarterly* 24.4 (January 1996): 409–26.

91   The events in question suggest transactions more akin to debates that grow in face of contingencies created by any number of issues—not primordial hatreds. Victor Roudometoff, *Nationalism, Globalization and Orthodoxy: The Social Origins of Ethnic Conflict in the Balkans* (New York: Greenwood, 2001) provides a nuanced explanation.

92   By 1897, although officially a staunch supporter of the territorial integrity of the Ottoman Empire, Prime Minister Gladstone (whose notorious fear mongering in 1876 regarding "Turkish slaughter of Bulgarians" brought racist taxonomies about the Balkans into domestic British politics) took secret diplomatic steps encouraging authorities in Greece to counteract Russian influence. Hoping to open another front against Russia, Gladstone's agents also encouraged Bulgarian-exclusive aspirations in Thrace, revealing a central concern of the economic forces behind British policy so that the Russians did not gain access to the Mediterranean. Jane K. Cowan and Kevin S. Brown "Introduction: Macedonian Inflections," in Jane K. Cowan (ed.), *Macedonia—The Politics of Identity and Difference* (London: Pluto Press, 2000): 1–4.

93   See AQSH F.19 D.32/4.f.62–70, f. 75–76, Ibrahim Temo to the sultan, dated Istanbul, 18 March 1901.

94   Said Paşa, *Said Paşa'nin Hatıratı*, 2 vols (Istanbul: Sabah Matbaası, 1328 [1910]), II: 220–6.

95   İlhan Tekeli, "Involuntary Displacement and the Problem of Resettlement in Turkey from the Ottoman Empire to the Present," *Center for Migration Studies* special issues 11.4 (2012): 202–26 and Sezgin Özden and Üstüner Birben, "Ottoman Forestry: Socio-economic Aspect and its Influence Today," *Ciência Rural* 42.3 (2012): 459–66.

96   It all degenerated into a form of baiting launched by 1876 by parties linked to outraged bond holders who faced Ottoman bankruptcy. After the Ottoman Empire decided to default on its loans, London-based surrogates of the banks began a campaign to demonize the Ottoman state with accusations of massacres in Bulgaria and later Macedonia, see for instance William E. Gladstone, *Bulgarian Horrors and the Question of the East* (London: John Murray, 1876) and Henry N. Brailsford, *Macedonia; Its Races and their Future* (London: Methuen, 1906). On the media coverage in Britain on Macedonia a few years later, a discourse aping the hysteria generated in the 1870s over Bulgaria, see Ryan Gingeras, "Last Rites for a 'Pure Bandit': Clandestine Service, Historiography and the Origins of the Turkish 'Deep State,'" *Past & Present* 206.1 (2010): 151–74, 11–13.

97   The Powers' irreconcilable aims made it impossible for them agree on a partition of the Empire which only exasperated international relations for years. Sevtap Demirci, *British Public Opinion towards the Ottoman Empire during the Two Crises: Bosnia-Herzegovina (1908–1909) and Balkan Wars (1912–1913)* (Istanbul: The ISIS Press, 2006): 11.

98   *Makedonya'daki Osmanlı Evraki*, no. 29 (Ankara: T.C. Başbakanlık Devlet Arşivleri Genel Müdürlüğü Yayınları, 1996): 13.

99   Fikret Adanır, *Die Makedonische Frage* (Wien: Franz Steiner Verlag, 1979): 141–59.

100 On measures to demonstrate the government's willingness to deal harshly with those "responsible" for the instability, see HHStA PA XII/319, Kral to Gołuchowski, dated Monastir, 2 August 1903.

101 Ibrahim Temo, a chief ideologue of the anti-government CUP initiated a series of conversations with other prominent residents on how to best funnel Ottoman state ambitions to reform the Balkans. AQSH F.19.D.12.f.1–2, Ibrahim Temo to Hamdi,

dated Ohrid, 21 April 1896. For later examples, see AQSH, F.19.D.18.f.2–3, Temo to Palace, dated 3 January 1901.

102   The "Vienna Scheme" eventually drawn up by the Russian Foreign Minister Count Lamsdorff and his Austrian counterpart, Count Gołuchowski, aspired to gain the approval of the other signatory powers of the Berlin Congress while maintaining their role as exclusive guarantors of regional security. It ultimately was scraped due to a new wave of "Bulgarian" inspired violence. Steven W. Sowards, *Austria's Policy of Macedonian Reform* (Boulder: East European Monographs, 1989): 26–7 and HHStA PA, XII/318, Calice to Gołuchowski, dated Constantinople, 25 March 1903.

103   See report on Bulgarian, Serb, and Greek activities in HHStA PA, XII/319, Calice to Gołuchowski, dated Yenikoj, 21 September 1903.

104   On the composition of these commissions and their stated goals, see AMAE Paris, CP Turquie no. 39, Bapst to Delcassé, dated Pera, 3 February 1904.

105   For contradictory reports from an Austrian and French Civil Agent about local Christian reactions to these reforms see HHStA XL/Agents Civils vol. 2, Müller to Gołuchowski, dated Salonique, 17 February 1904.

106   Austrian consul Kral, adopted an interventionist approach to the events, using the principles established already at the Berlin Congress in respect to the "inviolability" of sectarian communities to suggest Macedonia be reorganized in a manner that Lebanon had been in the 1860s. See HHStA PA, XII/319, "Memorandum," A. Kral to Gołuchowski, dated Monastir, 20 November 1903.

107   For a comprehensive report on the reform proposals and their translation into French and Ottoman that used these terms, see HHStA PA, XII/320, Calice to Gołuchowski, dated Constantinople, 13 January 1904.

108   HHStA PA XII/316, "Instructions aux Agents Civils," 27 December 1903.

109   Thomas Biolsi, "The Birth of the Reservation: Making the Modern Individual among the Lakota," *American Ethnologist* 22.1 (February 1995): 28–53.

110   See NAUK, FO 7/1341, "Memorandum by Gołuchowski," dated Vienna, 16 December 1903.

111   See report from Austrian consul Kral for the first iteration of such a plan in HHStA PA XXXVIII/392, no. 21, Kral to Gołuchowski, dated Monastir, 10 March 1903. Similar geographic configurations were imposed on Eastern Anatolia, with predictable results.

112   A total of 135 villages were designated to be outside Ottoman sovereignty. HHStA PA XII/329, Calice an Gołuchowski, dated Yenikoj, 20 June 1906.

113   Gustav Hubka, *Die Österreichisch-Ungarische Offiziermission in Makedonien: 1903–1909* (Wien: F. Tempsky, 1910): 71–3.

114   Gül Tokay, *Makedonya Sorunu: Jön Türk Ihtilalinin Kökenleri (1903–1908)* (Istanbul: AFA Yayınları, 1995): 56–86.

115   Gül Tokay, "Macedonian Reforms and Muslim Opposition during the Hamidian Era 1878–1908," *Islam and the Christian-Muslim Relations* 14.1 (2003): 51–65, 52.

116   Indeed, the secret headquarters of the CUP in the Ottoman Empire was based in Salonika, Macedonia's main port. More revealingly, it was in the very same forests where so much Greek, Bulgarian, Serbian, and Albanian "nationalist" activity took place during this volatile 1897–1908 period that the multi-confessional CUP-led revolt originated. The literature is vast on this period, but for interesting personal reflections on the violence that often broke out between rival armed political groups, see the memoirs of Enver Bey who would become so crucial to the post-Ottoman events in Anatolia as well. In Macedonia at the time of these reforms,

Enver Bey and others openly fought *Rum* Christian and Bulgarian "çeta," claiming
to have killed between 1906 and 1908 55 *Rum* and 173 Bulgarians. See Enver Pasha,
Enver Paşa'nın Anıları (1881–1908) H. E. Cengiz (ed.) (İstanbul: İletişim,1991):
52–6.

117   The privately funded Carnegie Foundation report offered some important (and
       revealing) conflict-resolution proposals that would for much of the twentieth
       century inform the thinking of Euro-Atlantic powers dealing with "racial difference"
       in other parts of the world. Carnegie Endowment, *Report of the International
       Commission to Inquire into the Causes and Conduct of the Balkan Wars* (Washington,
       DC: Carnegie Endowment for International Peace, 1914).

118   For a brilliant analysis of how the Carnegie Report's reference to the "traditional
       enmities" that divided Bulgarians from Greeks, Muslims from Christians (Carnegie
       Report, p. 96) and reinforced entrenched discourses of white European civilization
       vis-à-vis "primitive dark peoples," see Jonathan Schmitt, "Whose is the House of
       Greatest Disorder?: Civilization and Savagery on the Early 20th Century Eastern
       European and North American Frontiers," in Yavuz and Blumi, *Lasting Sociopolitical
       Impacts of the Balkan Wars*, 496–527.

119   The unfortunate phrase with all kinds of logical implications if not carefully
       qualified appears in the work of otherwise quite sophisticated readers of
       nationalism: Rogers Brubaker, "The Aftermath of Empire and the Unmixing of
       Peoples," in Karen Barkey and Mark von Hagen (eds), *After Empire: Multiethnic
       Societies and Nation-Building: The Soviet Union and the Russian, Ottoman, and
       Habsburg Empires* (Boulder: Westview Press, 1997): 155–80. As abstracted on
       maps used to help delineate the spacing of this "unmixing" process, competing
       cartographic claims by self-identified Serbian, Bulgarian, and Greek partisans all
       adopted language of racial criteria along lines used in Africa and North America at
       the time. See Henri R. Wilkinson, *Maps and Politics: A Review of the Ethnographic
       Cartography of Macedonia* (Manchester: Manchester University Press, 1951).

120   Within a few years, property and the use of "rights" proved the crucial wedges to
       help find a "solution" to the previous imperial mixing of peoples, a set of weapons
       that ultimately resulted in forcing population "transfers" by way of League of
       Nations' decrees, and later, in 1947, the "partition" of Palestine and India along
       sectarian lines. George Montandon, *Frontières nationales: Détermination objective
       de la condition primordial necéssaire à l'obtention d'une paix durable* (Lausanne: Self-
       Published, 1915).

121   Timothy Mitchell, "Everyday Metaphors of Power," *Theory and Society* 19.5 (1990):
       545–77.

122   William I. Shorrock, "The Origin of the French Mandate in Syria and Lebanon: The
       Railroad Question, 1901–1914," *IJMES* 1.2 (1970): 133–53; Ellsworth Huntington,
       "Railroads in Asia Minor," *Bulletin of the American Geographical Society* (1909):
       691–6; Philip W. Ireland, "The Baghdad Railway: Its New Rôle in the Middle East,"
       Journal of the Royal Central Asian Society 28.3 (1941): 329–39.

123   Meltem Toksöz, *Nomads, Migrants and Cotton in the Eastern Mediterranean*
       (Leiden: Brill, 2010): 43–56.

124   Refugees from the Balkans and Eastern Anatolia flooded Çukurova in Adana
       province forcing administrators to create new bureaucratic offices in an attempt to
       mobilize the newcomers to become productive residents. BBA I.DH, 1313/1311/
       Z-18, dated 11 June 1894. These regions flooded by refugees would soon become

sites of terrible violence, rarely considered in this larger context of demographic shifts and subsequent struggles over limited resources, including wage-earning jobs.

125　The entire Rumeli railway system entailed putting to work upwards of 11,000 employees by 1911. As we will see at the end of this chapter, this offered a number of entrepreneurs the chance to create new political circuits that directly affected the direction of the newly installed CUP government in 1908 and subsequent efforts to secure a productive order in the Balkans. Eldem, *Osmanlı Imparatarluğunda*, 208. The Oriental Railway, or *Beitriebsgesellschaft der Orientalischen Eisenbahnen*, a railroad company bought in 1890 by a consortium controlled by the Deutsche Bank and Wiener Banverein, serviced the famous Orient Express, linking Istanbul to Central Europe. Vahdettin Engin, *Rumeli Demiryolları* (Istanbul: Eren Yayincilik, 1993): 51–5 and Gounaris, *Steam Over Macedonia*, 42–8. These networks would fall victim to organized labor activism in 1908 as a result of the Young Turk revolt. Sami Özkara, *Türkische Arbeiterbewegung 1908 im Osmanischen Reich im Spiegel des Batschafisberichte, der volkswirtschaftlichen und politischen Entwicklungen* (Franfurt/Main: Verlag Peter Lang, 1985): 32–9. According to a British employee of the Sofia consulate, the organizers of the strike in Plovdiv were an Austrian named Georg Rump, an Armenian named Davidian, and two Bulgarians who "professed the socialistic doctrine." NAUK, FO 371/552, no. 35322 Vice Consul Shipley to Sofia Office, dated Plovdiv, 29 August 1908.

126　Aslı Emine Çomu, *The Exchange of Populations and Adana, 1830–1927* (Istanbul: Libra Kitap, 2011): 43–4.

127　Andrew G. Gould, "Lords or Bandits? The Derebeys of Cilicia," *IJMES* 7.04 (1976): 485–506 and Uğur Ümit Üngör, "Rethinking the Violence of Pacification: State Formation and Bandits in Turkey, 1914–1937," *CSSH* 54.04 (2012): 746–69.

128　Nadine Akhund, "Muslim Representation in the Three Ottoman Vilayets of Macedonia: Administration and Military Power (1878–1908)," *Journal of Muslim Minority Affairs* 29.4 (2009): 443–54.

129　Eric Hobsbawm has meticulously charted a progression of capital as it eviscerated older forms of social organization, arguing that the resulting modern state created a world order that ensured that the fragments of former empires remained financially subservient to it. Eric Hobsbawm, *The Age of Empire 1875–1914* (New York: Pantheon, 1987): 15–19.

130　Eric Hobsbawm, *The Age of Capital, 1848–1975* (New York: Mentor, 1979): 101–26.

Chapter 2

1　On the institutions erected to care for refugees after a series of modifications of the program that existed since 1860, see Faruk Kocacık, *Balkanlar'dan Anadolu'ya Yönelik Göçler* (PhD Dissertation, Hacettepe University, 1978): 105–6.

2　The troubles begin with the influx of upwards of 630,000 Crimean Muslims, Nogai Tatars, and Caucasians forced out by advancing Russian armies. Abdullah Saydam, *Kırım ve Kafkas Göçleri, 1856–1876* (Ankara: Türk Kurumu Basımevi, 1997): 86–8. See also Brian. G. Williams, "Hijra and Forced Migration from Nineteenth-Century Russia to the Ottoman Empire. A Critical Analysis of the Great Tatar Emigration of 1860–1861," *Cahiers du monde russe. Russie-Empire russe-Union soviétique et États indépendants* 41.1 (2000): 79–108.

3 In respect to regulated population movements, the role of the state not only monitored, and often hampered the flows of people to its sovereign domain, but also used powers that coerced people to remain in various locations, as well as expelled non-compliant groups. Phillippe Farques, "Migration et identité: Le paradoxe des influences réciproques," *Esprit*, no. 361 (2010): 6–16.

4 "Nationalist leaders" like Georgi Rakovski and Dimitar Berovski, often sought to forcefully assert their relevance to domestic Bulgarian politics by harnessing the early *hajduk* groups, steering their confused agendas of profit from pillage to serve their often extra-Macedonian agendas. Indeed, any faction of Bulgaria's dynamic political culture that held the reigns of state power used government resources to selectively support these various *komitadji* groups. As such, their acts should be read to suit the political purposes of their patron nations, as much as those of Macedonia. Such a dynamic meant the patronage that came from these sources did not entail formal control. These groups, often coming from very different socioeconomic roots, operated independently of each other and often in direct competition, leading many to gain the support of competing patrons. Among the most successful was the Internal Macedonia Revolutionary Organization (IMRO), established secretly in Salonika in 1893. Its primary goal was inciting a general rebellion against the Ottomans. This entailed forging alliances with all kinds of actors, including non-Bulgarians, such as Armenians, Serbs, and some *Rum* Orthodox Christians. In 1895, the Supreme Committee, or what alternatively became known as the External Macedonian Revolutionary Organization (EMRO) was established in Sofia. These pro-Bulgarian activists had split with the IMRO to proclaim that their ultimate goal was the annexation of Macedonia to Bulgaria. This would prove crucial as the EMRO opposed the formation of a Macedonian national consciousness, by extension of a goal of those behind the IMRO that aimed to create an independent Macedonian state. See Sowards, *Austria's Policy*, 14–27 and Perry, *The Politics of Terror*, 155.

5 That is to say, violence is not an exclusive state project, but one that was still used among political elites who could be identified as both extra-state and state actors at different times. See Charles King, "The Micropolitics of Social Violence," *World Politics* 56 (2004): 431–55.

6 These post-1878 regional offices appear to have had far more expansive powers than those of earlier bureaucracies established to care for migrants, a fact crucial to understanding the kinds of disputes that would arise among constituent groups in the Balkans and Eastern Anatolia. For example, the amount of resources pumped into settling refugees from two entirely different parts of the so-called Islamic world in a tiny corner of Syria almost seems overdone considering the resulting tensions between indigenous "host" communities and their new neighbors. Reports from the interior ministry suggest that upwards of a thousand refugees from North Africa and Bukhara were momentarily housed in Damascus awaiting transport to a newly created sub-district in the Hama Sanjak, with the costs being drawn from special funds just for such operations. These kinds of activities had an impact on how refugees reestablished communities in their new homes, often in a context of competition with local, indigenous "host" communities who viewed with frustration the amount of resources invested in these "foreigners" while the natives themselves remained vulnerable to periodic crisis. BBA I.DH 1365/1317/S-04, dated 16 June 1899.

7 Refugees from Bosnia often were provided a newly built village and a ready-made infrastructure as an inducement to fully assimilate into their new host environment, including on the outskirts of Ankara, which officials boasted had new medical

facilities, including a major hospital. BBA I.ML, 41/1318/Ş-35, dated Ankara 16 February 1901. To help these refugees settle in their new village in the middle of Ankara, farm animals, seed, and sacks of wheat flour were awaiting them upon arrival. BBA I.DH 1380/1318/Ş-21 dated Ankara, 15 February 1901. To get one particular batch of Bosnian refugees to their Ankara destination, a special set of trains was set aside for their transport from Istanbul. BBA I.HUS 85/1318/B-12, dated 11 November 1900.

8   Curiously, no matter how much the subject of violence toward Armenian or Assyrian Christians informs their research, few scholars ever explored the causal links between refugees and their own painful struggles in their new communities and the tensions with various indigenous Anatolian "Christian" groups whose persecution in subsequent decades became the requisite link between genocide and Western military defeat of the "Turks." There are a few notable exceptions, including Dennis, "Patterns of Conflict and Violence in Eastern Anatolia," in Yavuz (ed.), *War & Diplomacy*, 273–301 and Üngör, *The Making of Modern Turkey*, 42–50.

9   As it plays out in the scholarship regarding the Ottoman Empire and its vast array of regions and local economies, the fundamental weakness of the state to fully harness the productive capacities of the empire's economic potential left it susceptible to subordination to external interests. The economic domination as defined in this scholarship is comprehensive. The problem with these conclusions, however, is that so little is ever written of the micro-economic processes at play that may suggest the "decline" of the empire economically is far too broad an assertion, and requires greater circumspection. Socrates D. Petmezas, "Bridging the Gap: Rural Macedonia from Ottoman to Greek Rule (1900–1920)," in Lorans Tanatar Baruh and Vangelis Kechriotis (eds), *Economy and Society on Both Shores of the Aegean* (Athens: Alpha Bank Historical Archives, 2010): 355–95.

10 Individual communities forced to accommodate such large numbers of refugees after 1878, especially in the big cities of the immediate Balkan and Eastern Anatolian regions hardest hit—Salonika, Izmir, and Bursa—often developed innovative ways to raise the extra funds. In these three cities, as major host communities to Balkan refugees, local committees started with loans from the Ziraat Bank a lottery (*piyango*) with the proceeds helping to pay for the costs of hosting so many people. Interestingly, Protestant and Jewish community leaders in these cities forbade their members from playing, suggesting these fundraising measures were frequently at odds with how some communities hoped to retain their distinctive existence in face of such rapid changes. BBA I. HUS, 139/1324, doc. 110, dated 25 March 1906.

11 Özge Ertem, *Eating the Last Seed: Famine, Empire, Survival and Order in Ottoman Anatolia in the Late 19th Century* (PhD Dissertation, Florence: European University Institute, 2012): 143–78.

12 For reports on violence along the still contested boundaries separating the newly established principality of Montenegro and Kosovo province and measures taken to remove refugees from the area, see BBA, YA. HUS, 159/62, copies of telegraphs sent from Ipek and Cetinje to Interior Ministry, dated 14 September 1878.

13 The violent commandeering of stored food led to a number of clashes between locals and refugees, many who ended up roaming the Kosovo/Manastır countryside looking for sustenance. The situation at one point got so bad that the Manastır governor had to be replaced for failing to stop the violence. For details, see BBA, YA. HUS, 159/85, copies of telegraphs sent from Manastır and Prizren to Interior Ministry, dated 9 November 1878.

14 The politics of integrating captured and/or ceded lands in such periods of transition is a fascinating topic in desperate need of comparative analysis. See Constantin Iorachi, *Citizenship, Nation and State Building: The Integration of Northern Dobrogea into Romania, 1878–1913* (Pittsburgh: University of Pittsburgh Press, 2002).

15 A group of Bosnian refugees fleeing Serbian and Austro-Hungarian expansion, after a long period of enduring difficult relations with their host neighbors in Kosovo, finally secured state funds to create an entirely new district from lands skimmed off from the Osmaniye Kaza. See BBA I.DH, 1364/1317 doc. 1, dated 14 May 1899. The new district, called Çerkotice-i Bala, would accommodate upwards of 500 people. This policy of creating new communities would be repeated in all corners of the empire for the remaining 40 years.

16 This close oversight over potential areas of influence for the French consular offices in Beirut and Damascus on occasion produced seemingly "strange" bedfellows. For instance, Beirut had begun to see a surge in refugees from both Algeria (under French administration) and Chechnya (under Russian administration). In a series of disputes over residency rights, one Algerian named Shaykh Aziz used the eagerness of the French consulate in Beirut to help "protect" him in his dispute with a group of counterclaims made by Chechen refugees over the same lands. BBA BEO 316/23660, dated Beirut, 23 December 1893. These kinds of mutually beneficial relations between those previously persecuted by the French administration in their Algerian homeland and an entirely different bureaucratic operation from within the French Foreign Ministry also manifested in Algerian migrations elsewhere in the Ottoman realms. For example, the Adana region—Cilicia—would long play a central role in French interests in Anatolia, as the presence of large numbers of Algerian refugees settling in these areas offered the consul the opportunity to play the "good cop, bad cop" role and ingratiate some "Muslim" refugees when they faced local hostilities. BBA BEO 1113/83434, dated Adana, 21 May 1898.

17 Makdisi, *The Culture of Sectarianism*, chapter 1.

18 For a detailed report of the intersecting migrations due to the treaty, see HHStA, PA XVII, Montenegro Gusinje Frage, box 35, doc. 261, Sawas Pasha to Prime Ministry, dated Vienna, 16 December 1879.

19 On top of this group of refugees from Niš, it is suggested that the refugees settling from Bulgaria and Eastern Rumeli in Kosovo and Manastır numbered more than 140,000, McCarthy, *Death and Exile*, 90–1.

20 For the basic constitution of those Niš-Muslim Albanians who were forced to settle amid entirely different Albanian, Muslim, and Slav communities in Kosovo, Işkodra, and Manastır, see Nazmi Vishesella, *Vuajtjet e Kombit Shqiptarë-Muhaxhirëve me Shekuj* (Ferizaj: DinoGraf 2005): 123–45.

21 These natives of Niš's primary historian is Sabit Uka, *Dëbimi i Shqiptarëve nga Sanxhaku i Nishit dhe vendosja e tyre në Kosovë, 1878–1912*, 4 vols (Prishtine: Verana, 2004). Uka makes no distinction between the refugee and the host, leaving out a well-known dynamic to these Niš-refugee settlements. To this day the *Niš muhacir* are endogamous, retain their communal separation from neighboring Albanian communities by way of marriage.

22 Authorities identified Mehmed Hilmi as the primary leader of the *Niš muhacir* around central Drenica and the key go-to person in times when local cooperation was needed. That such a man could be deemed a potential ally of the state is crucial to understanding the variances at play in these refugee settings. See BBA BEO 893/66961, dated Prishtina, 10 January 1897.

23 These refugee groups were not only able to threaten violence to compel various host constituencies to address their needs, but also mobilize Ottoman legal codes to put pressure on the state. In correspondence it is evident that they demanded from local judges to act under the "guidance" of the laws of the state in order to ensure that direct state action was taken to stop both the annexation of Ottoman land and, more importantly, permit the return of refugees to their original homelands in neighboring Bosnia, Herzegovina, and Niš. Such forceful co-optation of local state institutions to advocate for an eventually failed cause of repatriation exhibits the range of political spaces in which refugees in Kosovo could fill. For the original statement written in Ottoman, see *Tercüman-ı Hakikat,* no. 21 (19 July 1878): 3–4.

24 One of the consequences over the land disputes facing host communities and *Niš muhacir* (mostly Albanian-speakers), were government efforts to administratively separate particularly ugly rivalries. In one Kosovo district, Vushtri, authorities attached the sub-district of Leşeniçe in order to secure some administrative distance between the two communities. BBA BEO 469/35163, dated 5 October 1894.

25 Added to the mix were the Circassian colonists the empire had sent to the frontiers of Herzegovina in mid-1877. The British Consul in Scutari (Shkodër) reported that Circassians found in northern Albania had just recently been the victims of forced expulsions conducted by Russian forces. NAUK, FO 78/2628, report no. 9, Consul Green to Foreign Office, dated Scutari, 10 February 1877. These former refugees who soon also joined others expelled from Herzegovina, thereby posed a threat to the internal stability of those host communities like Shkodër.

26 On the difficulties of settling these refugees see report from local administrator, BBA YEE 43/102, dated Prizren, 4 December 1879 and NAUK, FO 78/2988, Political Report no. 2.4, St. John to Salibury, dated Prizren, 7 October 1879.

27 For an extensive survey of the manner in which political communities emerged as a result of events caused by the resettlement of so many refugees in Kosovo after 1878, see Austro-Hungarian report HHStA, PA XII/312 Turkei Liasse XXXIII, documents 50–3, Consul Rappaport to Goluchowski, dated Prizren, 26 January 1899.

28 For greater details over land use all along the Montenegro/Kosovo border, see BBA Y.PRK.MYD 1/60, dated Ipek, 12 October 1880.

29 For details of these petitions that also made their way to European consulates, see AQSH, F. 24. D.5/1.f.1–2, dated 13 July 1878 and throughout the 1880s, see reports provided by Yusuf Ziya Pasha, BBA YEE, 7/23, documents 3, 5, and 6, dated 26 June 1886.

30 A crucial component to the *Rum* Orthodox Church remaining a loyal Ottoman institution was the constant attempts by Britain, France, and Russia to partition the flock into "national" autocephalous constituencies. This ultimately created significant breaks in authority and opened channels for political generations in Greece, for instance, to forge new spaces for action without the formal sanction of the Patriarchate based in Istanbul. See John A. Petropulos, *Politics and Statecraft in the Kingdom of Greece 1833–1843* (Princeton, NJ: Princeton University Press, 1968): 180–2. In this respect, the post-Ottoman state became the primary beneficiary of religious patronage and affiliation. In Greece this led to considerable confiscation of official Church lands, which were crucial in the process of settling landless peasants (a form of popular politics) and ultimately refugees. Massive files documenting the extent of the confiscation are available in LON, C 152, no. 62, Under Commission for Greco-Bulgarian Emigration in Greece, dated Salonika, 21 October 1926. The state of Greece was able to eventually force recognition of Greece's autocephaly in 1850. This

unilateralism would prove crucial in periods of rapid adjustment but would not save Greece, however, from becoming highly fractured. Charles A. Frazee, *The Orthodox Church and the Independent Greece 1821–1852* (Cambridge: Cambridge University Press, 1969): 171–93. For the process in Bulgaria, see Thomas E. Meininger, *Ignatiev and the Establishment of the Bulgarian Exarchate (1864–1872): A Study of Personal Diplomacy* (Madison: University of Wisconsin Press, 1970).

31   There is some evidence, however, that the Ottoman state initiated a campaign to confiscate communal lands and forests from the native inhabitants of frontier regions, such as Tuz along the new Montenegrin border, in order to accommodate refugees. In Tuz in particular, the practice caused great tension for at least a decade between indigenous communities, refugees, and state officials. BBA MV 32/24, dated 10 May 1888. These tensions got so bad that authorities started to move many refugees to Draç further south, a decision that would have long-term consequences for Albanian history. While not the place to develop my claims further, the struggle over land in Central Albania as a result of this influx of Bosnian Slav and Northern Albanian (Gheg) refugees led to the kind of land-regime dominated by the Toptani family (and its large private army drawing from these refugees) who would shape the direction of post-Ottoman Albanian politics for years to come. Out of this clan would arise, for instance, Ahmed Zogu, later ushered into power by Serbia in 1926 to help suppress a growing "democratic" regime with strong irredentist claims to Albanian populated lands under Greek and Serbian (Yugoslav) control. For more details, see for instance, Besnik Pula, *State, Law and Revolution: Agrarian Power and the National State in Albania, 1850–1945* (PhD Dissertation, University of Michigan, 2011) and Austin, *Founding a Balkan State*, 35–65.

32   It is important to point out that another reason for their fanatical support of the sultanate was the realization that these peoples had no home to return to. For Bosnians, with Austro-Hungarian annexation in 1908, the demise of the Ottoman Empire would constitute another disaster. For Chechens as well, with no other place to go, their relatively privileged role as the Sultan's enforcers gave them incentive to remain loyal to the end. Such calculations proved important when all these Balkan territories, and Eastern Anatolia, came under siege from 1912 to 1923 by separatist and irredentist "Christian" forces.

33   William N. Medlicott, *The Congress of Berlin and After: A Diplomatic History of the Near Eastern Settlement, 1878–1880* (London: Methuen & Co. Ltd, 1938): 162, 192, 221.

34   This also entailed disputes over pasturage in many western Kosovo districts. A number of reports suggest refugee families found it impossible to find proper land to feed their sheep due to local refusal to allow them access to their lands. Ultimately the matter reached Istanbul as local officials, fearful of a backlash, deferred to the Ministry of Interior. BBA BEO 2014/151002, dated 6 March 1903.

35   The consequences of this attack were months of reprisals against the perpetrators and then counterattacks, a spiral of vengeance that undermined stability in both the Yakova and Prizren districts. Eventually, members of the Prizren Committee were involved in the blood feud. See YA.HUS, 159/73, report number 62, signed Yakova Mutassarif Mehmed Seyyid, dated 21 September 1878.

36   Events summarized in a report composed a year later in BBA, YA.RES, 6/10, Report filed by Ahmed, dated 30 May 1879.

37   The British embassy in Istanbul reported in 1867 that the Pashalık of Niš and Novipazar, characterized as the "Albanian" frontier separating the then-autonomous

Serbian principality from the rest of the Ottoman Empire, was inhabited by at least 300,000 "Albanians." Presumably it was these people who were being targeted for expulsion in the 1870s. See enclosure in Political Report number 33, dated Belgrade, 19 October 1867, report written by J. A. Longworth sent to Lord Stanley found in NAUK, FO, 78/1974 no. 35, Longworth to Henry Elliott, dated Belgrade, 1 November 1867.

38 Maria Todorova, *Imagining the Balkans* (New York: Oxford University Press, 1997): 109.

39 In the Eastern provinces, the ripping apart of much of the Kars district by Russian occupation forces led to an influx of refugees. The arrival of so many refugees put the same kind of pressures on local capacities to accommodate them as already seen in Kosovo in the late 1870s. The resulting famines, disease, and devastation of long-term productivity may have some link to the eventual stress on communities that resulted in violence toward neighbors. It is also likely that as a result of such upheaval and human desperation, a new labor regime emerged as tens of thousands of desperate refugees were willing to work on large-scale farms found further west in Cilicia, for example. See Christopher Clay, "Labour Migration and Economic Conditions in Nineteenth-century Anatolia," *Middle Eastern Studies* 34.4 (1998): 1–32.

40 Marenglen Verli, *Reforma agrare kolonizuese në Kosovë, 1918–1941* (Bonn: Ilira, 1992): 23–41.

41 Worse still, Serbia fell into greater debt as it built up its military by buying weapons from abroad. Misha Glenny, *The Balkans: Nationalism, War and the Great Powers, 1804–1999* (New York: Viking, 2000): 220–1.

42 For insight into how these "new areas" (Novi Krajevi) were initially integrated into the newly created Kingdom of Serbia, Milan Milićević, *Kraljevina Srbija* (Belgrade: Drzavna stamparija, 1884) provides an eyewitness account.

43 Ružica Guzina, *Opština u Srbiji, 1839–1918: Pravno-politička i sociološka studija* (Belgrade: Rad, 1976): 237.

44 This was especially important in the "new areas" towns, where a majority non-Christian population lived before the war. According to Serbian historiography, disputed by a census conducted by Ottomans prior to the 1875–8 war, 41 percent of the population in "new areas" such as Leskovac was Muslim, see Vodosava Nikolić-Stojančević, *Leskovac i oslobodjeni predeli Srbije, 1877–1878 godine: Etnicke, demografske, socijalno-ekonomske i kulturne prilike* (Leskovac: Narodni muzej, 1975): 10–11. This presented considerable problems when large numbers either refused to leave or started to return from their temporary safe-havens in Austrian- or Ottoman-administered areas.

45 Ottoman officials report that Mehmed Nuri and his extended family were given funds to restart their community inside Serbian-administered Niš after having been earlier made a refugee by that same government. As much as this story suggests a policy of repatriation of the territories' Muslim farming communities, it also offers some indication of how difficult it was for some refugees to find a proper home in Ottoman territories. See BBA BEO 886/66436, dated 27 December 1896.

46 Guzina, *Opština u Srbiji*, 239.

47 Vladamir Stojančević, *Srbi i Bulgari, 1804–1878* (Novi Sad: Prometej, 1995): 199–203.

48 Miloš Jagodić, *Naseljavange Kneze vine Srbije 1860–1861* (Belgrade: Istorijski institute, 2004): 134.

49 Jagodić, *Naseljavange Kneze*, 134.

50 Guzina, *Opština u Srbiji*, 239–40.

51 Dobrosav Turović, *Gornja Jablanica. Kroz istoriju* (Belgrade: Beograd Zavičajno udruženje, 2002): 87–9.

52 Milan Spasić, "Podaci o agrarnim odnosima hrišćana u oslobodjenim krajevima, okruga Topličkog i Vranjskog za vreme turske vladavine," in Duško Kečkemet (ed.), *Vranjic kroz vjekove* (Split: Institut za historijn radničkog pokreta Dalmacije, 1984): 263–370.

53 There was considerable violence along the newly established borders between Bosnia and Serbia, where Ottoman officials reported that Albanian refugees constantly raided areas that had once been their homes but by 1878, had been transferred to Serbia. See BBA. HR. SYS. 128/22, Bosnia Governor report, dated Sarajevo, 31 May 1880.

54 Isa Blumi, "Contesting the Edges of the Ottoman Empire: Rethinking Ethnic and Sectarian Boundaries in the Malësore, 1878–1912," *IJMES* 35.2 (May 2003): 237–56.

55 BBA. HR. SYS. 305/131, Report from Manastır governor's office to Ministry of Interior, dated 24 November 1880.

56 İpek, *Rumeli'den Anadolu'ya*, 16.

57 One report reads that members from 31 communities resettled in still heavily populated Muslim areas. BBA. HR. SYS. 304/99, Interior Ministry report, dated 27 March 1880.

58 In March 1878, for instance, only a few days after the signing of the San Stefano Treaty, Pashko Vasa, a prominent Catholic Albanian, lobbied the British ambassador in Istanbul. In these meetings, Pashko Vasa called for an immediate reconsideration of what constituted "the true Bulgaria" in face of irrefutable demographic facts. NAUK, FO, 881/3673, No. 366, Layard to the Earl of Derby, dated Constantinople, 18 March 1878, enclosure signed by Wassa Effendi (the pen name of Pashko Vasa).

59 It is a remarkable thing to read in file after file of the League of Nation's (LON) reports how solicited European men dismissed the requests of indigenous peoples to help restrain the violent Mandate-era regimes in Syria and Iraq. In hand-written notes advising future readers consulting the reports, the author claimed the petitions were ". . . determined not serious" and thus could be ignored. From personal experience, such arrogance and selective "care" still persists today inside international "humanitarian" organizations. LON R 4106, Section 6a, folder 31771/1469, "Mandate Français sur la Syrie et le Liban: Petition de M.M. Abd el-Kaba et Fuad Ghandur," dated Beirut, 21 December 1933. These same people continued to write petitions seeking help from the LON in a land dispute with the French government, again the same suggestion that delegates simply ignore the letters, the last correspondence dating 1936.

60 For their part, Armenians were caught in the middle of an expansionist war that pitted Russia and the Ottomans against one another all throughout territories in which they made up a significant "minority" of the population. As a result, they feared that the crude calculations witnessed with Russian occupation regimes in areas further north would soon apply to them. One's religious affiliation played a big role in determining who could remain and who had to leave for the Ottoman Empire (or Iran, or even, in the case of many Armenians, Bulgaria, and Greece). The fears expressed by delegates present in Berlin were that the Ottoman Empire would also practice a "faith-based" policy of protecting border areas at the expense of Armenian stability. In the Treaty of Berlin, Armenian pleas for protection against the periodic attacks of Kurds and Circassians were heeded by outside powers. Unfortunately, the wording was flawed and as much of the Berlin Treaty (and an operational liberal logic predicated on

sectarian "difference") led to far more conflicts. Far from promising any improvement in the Armenians' condition, Article 61 of the treaty, for example, only looked good on paper: For as much as the "The Sublime Porte undertakes to carry out . . . reforms demanded by local . . . Armenians and to guarantee their security . . ." the lack of long-term changes in the Ottoman state's ability to provision such reforms would not bode well for the future. See Great Britain, Foreign Office, *British and Foreign State Papers, 1877–1878* (vol. 69), 1313–47 and (1880–1, vol. 72): 1196–207.

61 Tokay, *Makedonya Sorunu*, 32.

62 Michael Lascaris, "Greece and Serbia during the War of 1885," *The Slavonic and East European Review* 11.31 (1932): 88–99; Michael Palairet, "Fiscal Pressure and Peasant Impoverishment in Serbia before World War I," *The Journal of Economic History* 39.03 (1979): 719–40; Victor Roudometof, "The Social Origins of Balkan Politics: Nationalism, Underdevelopment, and the Nation-State in Greece, Serbia, and Bulgaria, 1880–1920," *Mediterranean Quarterly* 11.3 (2000): 144–63 and William N. Medlicott, "The Powers and the Unification of the Two Bulgarias, 1885: Part II (Continued)," *English Historical Review* (1939): 263–84.

63 Blumi, *Reinstating the Ottomans*, chapter 4.

64 In the now notorious scheme administered by Baron Rothschild who received a large concession of land from the Sultan in various parts of Palestine, a fund paid for the migration of Eastern European, Ashkenazi Jews to settle areas around Haifa where 22,000 units of land over time would be added periodically to the original concession. See BBA BEO 1449/108603, dated 1 March 1900. In Syria as well, the role of the Ottoman state to distribute land to refugees and for the purposes of "settling" so-called nomadic peoples had long-term consequences on larger society. A community of refugees from Bukhara, for instance, were dumped in the middle of the Syrian desert, in Zor (Deir ez-Zor today) with some hectares of land. As elsewhere, the underlying logic of distributing such groups in unpopulated areas was in large measure to help police the region suffering from banditry. BBA BEO 902/67589 dated 29 March 1897. See also Birgit Schaebler, "Practicing Musha: Common Lands and the Common Good in Southern Syria under the Ottomans and the French," *New Perspectives on Property and Land in the Middle East* (2001): 241–311.

65 BBA YA.HUS 327/43, dated 8 May 1895.

66 With the help of the community spiritual leader, Mustafa Nureddin Efendi, the Ottoman state began to settle a large group of Chechens south of Baghdad in these kinds of "empty lands" that, if cultivated, would bring new value (and revenue) to these otherwise unused parts of the Ottoman borderlands. See BBA BEO 1600/119976, dated 24 December 1900.

67 Sean McMeekin, *The Berlin-Baghdad Express: The Ottoman Empire and Germany's Bid for World Power* (Cambridge, MA: Belknap Press, 2010).

68 Among the more notorious "commodities" were humans for the growing labor market in the Middle East. See William G. Clarence-Smith, *The Economics of the Indian Ocean Slave Trade in the Nineteenth Century* (London: Routledge, 1989): 53–5.

69 An invaluable recent study of the complex links between Kuwait and the larger Indian Ocean helps broaden our appreciation for these factors, Fahad Ahmad Bishara, *A Sea of Debt: Histories of Commerce and Obligation in the Indian Ocean, c. 1850–1940* (PhD Dissertation, Duke University, 2012).

70 The local commander reported that a number of arms smugglers from Iranian ports had been caught trying to sneak weapons to the thriving weapons' market in Najd, a region that had been in the throes of a local power struggle for several years. BBA ŞD

2184/6, file no. 53, Palace to Basra chief administrator, dated, Istanbul, 28 December 1899.

71 It did not help that information about what was happening in other areas directly affected by the actions of local stakeholders was sparse. In often confused ways, bureaucrats on the ground would send periodically detailed fiscal reports that presented contradicting data, frequently making it impossible to ascertain what actually was going on in such a crucial territory as the Najd in central Arabia in 1882. BBA ŞD 2157/22, annual fiscal report sent by the treasurer of the Najd district, dated 25 December 1882.

72 On the death of 'Abdullah al-Sabah and the transfer of power to Muhammad al-Sabah, see BBA DH.MKT 2019/68, dated 12 November 1892.

73 The French were particularly concerned as it was their merchants based in Muscat, Oman who had the previous monopoly of the gun trade, which in many ways gave the French government authorities some influence in Kuwait and the hinterland. AMAE Nantes, Ambassade Constantinople D Baghdad 1890–1913, f. 13, Pognon to Minister, dated Constantinople, 4 January 1896.

74 Selim Deringil, "The Struggle against Shiism in Hamidian Iraq: A Study in Ottoman Counter-Propaganda," *Die Welt des Islams* 30.1/4 (1990): 45–62 and Juan R.Cole, "Shaikh al-Ra'is and Sultan Abdülhamid II: The Iranian Dimension of Pan-Islam," *Histories of the Modern Middle East: New Directions* (2002): 167–85.

75 Knowing there may be an Ottoman response to his disruptive behavior, Mubarak also staged a *coup* within his own family, murdering his older brother, and current sovereign of Kuwait, Muhammad, in May 1896. BBA Y.MTV 143/20, dated 22 June 1896. See also Frederick Anscombe, *The Ottoman Gulf: The Creation of Kuwait, Saudi Arabia, and Qatar* (New York: Columbia University Press, 1997): 96–9.

76 I cover this dynamic extensively in Blumi, *Reinstating the Ottomans*, chapters 2 and 3.

77 After several clashes and a great deal of money, the Italian consul reporting on the events suggested that numerous negotiations between Şakir Pasha, Batushi, and Babi, resulted in the transfer of some, but not all, of the land to neighboring Catholics. Although the problem had been solved as it concerned Batushi and Babi, whose personal lands were spared, others of the region, including the previously mentioned Ramazan Zakoki joined local Muslims to once again resist Şakir Pasha's plans. ASAME, Serie P Politica 1891–1916, Busta 666, no. 205/71, Consul to MAE, dated Üsküp, 8 September 1904.

78 BBA Irade i Dahiliye 2/N.1316, dated 13 January 1899.

79 Article 25 of the Treaty of Berlin (1878) granted Austria the right to "occupy and administer" Bosnia-Herzegovina. The pretext was to restore law and order: the actual intent was to obstruct Serbia and to curb the Russian influence in the region. In 1908 the occupation became permanent. See Yasamee, *Ottoman Diplomacy*, 56–72.

80 BBA MV 81/42, dated 6 October 1892.

81 BBA Irade i Dahiliye 2/N.1316, Report to Interior Ministry, dated 13 January 1899.

82 Douglas Dakin, *The Greek Struggle in Macedonia, 1897–1913* (Thessaloniki: Institute for Balkan Studies, 1993): 34–9 and Theodore G. Tatsios, *The Megali Idea and the Greek-Turkish War of 1897: The Impact of the Cretan Problem on Greek Irredentism, 1866–1897* (New York: Columbia University Press, 1984): 123–32.

83 This kind of baiting had been successful in 1876–7 when parties linked to outraged bond holders began a campaign to demonize the Ottoman state with accusations of massacres in Bulgaria, Gladstone, *Bulgarian Horrors*. On the media coverage in

Britain that mirrored the hysteria generated in the 1870s over Bulgaria, see Gingeras, "Between the Cracks," 1–18.

84 See Adanır, *Die Makedonische Frage*, 112 and Said Paşa, *Said Paşa'nın Hatıratı*, 2: 221.

85 James C. Scott, *Seeing Like a State: How Certain Schemes to Improve the Human Conditions have Failed* (New Haven: Yale University Press, 1999): 87–102.

86 For a first-hand account, see the memoirs of the Albanian commander of the troops who defected and thus began the revolt in Manastır in late July 1908, Adjutant-Major Niyazi, *Hatırat-ı Niyazi Yahud Tarihçe-yi Inkılab-ı Kebir-i Osmaniden bir Sahife* (Istanbul: Sabah Matbaası, 1910).

87 Despite the very clear message besieged communities sent to the world that disaggregating the Ottoman Empire along sectarian or ethno-national lines was not what they aspired to, advocates for the empire's fragmentation continued to beat the drums of ethnic "difference" as the "scientific" prognosis for the empire's ultimate collapse. In response to the declared agenda of the CUP to unite the peoples of the empire, the spin-doctors of global capitalism sarcastically retorted: "What nature has divided, man cannot unite." G. F. Abbot, "The Near Eastern Crisis," *The Quarterly Review* 210 (April 1909): 688.

88 For details see Blumi, *Reinstating the Ottomans*, 145–9. The Grand Vizier at the time was also an Albanian, Mehmed Said Pasha, as was Hasan Fehmi, the Mufti of Skopje and many others. For these men, the demise of the Sultan's regime could not be cause for celebration. Subsequent telegraphs to the Palace reflected the confused ambitions of those who feared any enduring fighting between factions in Kosovo would only expose the region to outside interference. It is crucial to point out that of those who communicated their support of the changes in a telegraph sent to Istanbul on 21 July 1908, the powerful *Niš muhacir* constituency were by far the most represented. Banu Işlet Sönmez, *II. Meşrutiyette Arnavut Muhalefeti* (Istanbul: YKY, 2007): 86–91.

89 Sohrabi, *Revolution and Constitutionalism*, 164–75.

90 BBA. HR. SYS. 345/2, Nizami to Rifaat, dated Berlin, 14 December 1909. Elite officers like Enver created the *Teşkilat-i Mahsusa* or Special organization that became the quintessential suppressive arm of ultra-liberal regimes that emerged in Bulgaria, Greece, and Serbia during the first half of the twentieth century. This secret police arm, increasingly servicing a small faction of the larger CUP party, often produced the intelligence that best serviced the demands of hardliners like Enver and Talat Pasha who would transform the state into a terror machine by 1915.

91 For a personnel account on the Serbo-Bulgarian alliance that was partially forged during this critical period leading up to the Balkan Wars of 1912, see Ivan E. Guesoff, *L'Alliance Balkaniques* (Paris: Hachette, 1915): 15–63.

92 Classic appropriations of the events in this period have long meant to suit post-Ottoman historiography trends. Beyond the previously mentioned material from the Balkans, in Turkey after World War II, it would be Ahmed Bedevi Kuran's *Inkılap Tarihimiz ve Ittihad ve Terakki* (Istanbul: Tan Matbaası, 1948).

93 BBA TFR. 1.KV 162/16108, Ipek Mutasarrif report n. 8 with enclosed supplemental report, dated 6 May 1907.

94 NAUK, PRO FO 800/43, "Memorandum by Lord Edmond Fitzmaurice, Situation in the Balkan Peninsula," dated Sofia, 16 December 1905.

95 The problem was these groups then became too powerful and even initiated campaigns to coerce "support" from local populations with the threat of death, a shift in local conditions increasingly reported throughout the region. Kidnapping, extortion, and expropriation of property became an effective enterprise for

terrorizing Ottoman subjects, a business so lucrative that members of the Bulgarian army co-opted these mixed local- and foreign-run operations. Vehmund Aabakke, *Ethnic Rivalry and the Quest for Macedonia, 1870–1913* (Boulder: East European Monographs, 2003): 100–2. This violence and the profits from it had a corrupting effect on Bulgarian political life, ultimately blurring strategic interests and simple profit-seeking, such as was the case in the selling of used weapons to anyone in Macedonia, a dynamic blurring of agendas found today in Turkey (2011–13) thanks to violence in Syria and Iraq. On how Bulgarian officials profited from selling weapons in Ottoman Balkan territories, even to "Greek" or "Albanian" groups rivaling officially supported "Bulgarian" bands, see Perry, *The Politics of Terror,* 166.

96   Zürcher, *The Young Turk Legacy,* 23–49.

97   For the Macedonian Question after 1908, see Mehmet Hacisalihoğlu, *Die Jung Türken und die Mazedonische Frage, 1890–1918* (Munich: Oldenburg, 2003): 123–45 and Sinan Kuneralp and Gül Tokay (eds), *Ottoman Documents on the Origins of World War One, The Macedonian Issue, 1879–1912, Part 2 1905–1912* (Istanbul: Isis, 2011): 362–475.

Chapter 3

1   As noted below, social and political "ethnic" clubs like *Bashkimi* (Albanian), *Cemiyet-i Ittihad-ı Çerakise* (Circassian), *Azm-i Kavi* (Kurdish), *Comité Turco-Syrien* (Arab/Syrian), *Hunchak* (Armenian), and *Ergatis* (Rum/Greek) all promoted a form of Ottomanism that embraced the idea of distinctive linguistic/ethnic associations but always firmly within an Ottoman state that protected these peoples from Great Power machinations. See for instance, Ileana Moroni, *O Ergatis, 1908–1909: Ottomanism, National Economy and Modernization in the Ottoman Empire* (Istanbul: Libra Kitap, 2010) and Hasan Taner Kerimoğlu, *Ittihat-Terakki ve Rumlar, 1908–1914* (Istanbul: Libra Kitap, 2009).

2   Although nationalism often has been identified as Europe's intellectual contribution to the changing world, there were other aspects of collective association available that challenge our reading of modern history solely in terms of the nation-state. Crucially, even there, communal foundations are laid by shared themes of dislocation, a kind of collective, formative trauma that replaces "diaspora" with a distinctly local approximation. Sumit Sarkar, *Beyond Nationalist Frames: Postmodernism, Hindu Fundamentalism, History* (Bloomington: Indiana University Press, 2002): 154–94.

3   Rogers Brubaker identifies the central problem with Diaspora as a factor of conceptual chaos that makes it logically impossible to analyse it as such. Rogers Brubaker, "The 'Diaspora' Diaspora," *Ethnic and Racial Studies* 28.1 (January 2005): 1–19.

4   Hanioğlu, *The Young Turks in Opposition,* 167–72.

5   James Clifford's challenge to such models stems from his understanding of how peoples in new homes are capable of pursuing "lateral connections" that are more important than a "teleology of origin/return." I base my own reproduction of the experiences of Ottoman migrants on this assumption that people are decentered and often seek to settle in their new homes rather than fight to return to the old. James Clifford, "Diasporas," *Cultural Anthropology* 9.3 (1994): 302–38, 305–6.

6   In English, the list is long of those who allow for a few men engaged in publishing to represent "Albanians" and their apparent ambition to remain exclusively "Albanian" despite their own distinctive heterogeneous cultural roots and their successes in

their "host" societies. For a number of critiques, Stephanie Schwandner-Sievers and Bernd J. Fischer (eds), *Albanian Identities: Myth and History* (Bloomington: Indiana University Press, 2002).

7 Ismet Dërmaku, *Nikolla N. Naço-Korça (1843–1913): Apostull i Shqiptarizmit* (Peja: Dukagjini, 2000): 95–101.

8 Nuçi Naçi, *Korça dhe fshatrat për çark* (Sofia: Mbrothësia, 1901): 14–41.

9 See Blumi, *Reinstating the Ottomans,* 112–22.

10 This approach is inspired by James Clifford's complaints that it is difficult to escape the simplistic linkage of Diaspora as a theoretical, abstract concept applicable to all cases, to various "discourses" or even historical "experiences" as retroactively claimed by the modern guardians of the national exile today. Clifford, "Diasporas," 307–8.

11 Max Peyfuss, *Die Aromunische Frage: Ihre Entwicklung von den Ursprüngen bis zum Bukarest (1913) une die Haltung Österreich-Ungarns* (Wien: Wiener Archiv für Geschichte des Slawentums und Osteuropas, 1972) and Ali Arslan, "The Vlach Issue during the Late Ottoman Period and the Emergence of the Vlach Community (Millet)," *Études Balkaniques* 4 (2004): 121–39.

12 Lucian N. Leustean, "The Political Control of Orthodoxy in the Construction of the Romanian State, 1859–1918," *European History Quarterly* 37.1 (January 2007): 61–80.

13 Gelcu Maksutoviçi, *Istoria Comunitatti Albaneze din Romania* (Bucharest: Kriterion, 1992): 10–16.

14 Ibrahim Temo, *Doktor Ibrahim Temo Ittihad ve Terakki Cemiyetinin Teşekkülü ve Hidemati Vataniye ve Inkılâbi Milliye Dair Hatıratım* (Mecidiye: NP, 1939): 197–8 and Hanioğlu, *The Young Turks in Opposition,* 77–8, 89–90.

15 For a rich study into Bucharest's nineteenth-century social and cultural history see, Harieta Mareci and Ştefah Purici, "Under Pressure for Change: Nation State Building and Identity Mutations in Modern Romania (1866–1890)," in Steven G. Ellis and Luďa Klusáková (eds), *Imagining Frontiers, Contesting Identities* (Rome: Edizioni Plus, 2007): 175–88.

16 Hanioğlu, *The Young Turks in Opposition,* 169.

17 As such, Temo became a de-facto founder of what would become the CUP. For details of how Temo articulated, by way of early polemical texts, the agenda of a still disparate (and small) opposition in Romania, primarily in Dobruja, see AQSH F.19.D.135.d.11, f.478, Talat to A. Zeki, dated Ruse, 27 April 1896. These early efforts became the foundation for a lager network of operations, noted in a series of correspondence between Temo and established "branches" throughout Europe, the Balkans, and Eastern Mediterranean. See list of branches established by Temo in both Romania and Bulgaria in Temo, *Ittihad ve Terakki,* 58–60 and AQSH F.19.D.106–3.d.270.f.1066, Temo to Ishak, dated Dobruja, 16 October 1898.

18 It is largely thanks to the assistance of Vasile M. Kogălniceanu, a representative of Constanţa in Romania's parliament, that Temo could first become a Romanian citizen in 1898 and then establish the widely accepted official CUP publication in the Balkans, *Voice of the Nation* (Sada-yı Millet). See "Sadayi Millet," *Osmanli Supplément Français* 5 (1898): 4.

19 For a detailed list of individuals and their contributions to this cultural development, see Maksutoviçi, *Istoria Comunitatti Albaneze din Romania,* 27–52.

20 In an open letter splashed across the front page of the leading opposition newspaper, the leadership reiterated their wish to forge an alliance with the estranged brother-in-law of the Sultan, Damad Mahmud Pasha, who had just become the most celebrated defector of the regime. *Osmanlı* 61 (1 June 1900). Having in late 1899 fled Istanbul,

the pro-British Damad Mahmud Pasha, along with his two sons Sabahaddin and Lutfullah, gave many in the opposition hope for a smooth transition from Abdülhamid II to another member of the family. The primary ally within the CUP at the time was the Tosk Albanian Ismail Kemal Bey (Qemali) of Vlora. Through Qemali's considerable diplomatic networks, the royal exiles' activities throughout Europe (and Egypt) in the winter of 1899 and throughout 1900 significantly changed the dynamics of Ottoman refugee organization. These movements were closely monitored by German officials, whose reports offer intriguing insights into Ismail Qemali's close links to Greek government officials. This evidence of close links to Greece is perhaps ironic considering his place in Albanian nationalist historiography. Qemali, the much celebrated "father" of the Albanian nation, was actively involved in this period with efforts to unite southern Albanian territories still administered by the Ottoman empire (Yanya and Manastır provinces), with independent Greece, often using CUP branch offices he opened throughout the Adriatic region as negotiation hubs. See PAAA, 732/2, Die Jungtürken 198, especially letter No. 115, dated Cairo, 8 June 1901, A. 9214. Ultimately, the intrigues involving Qemali and his close allies within the Damad Mahmud Pasha entourage led to the first of many splits within the leadership due in large part to Qemali's multiple role playing, Hanioğlu, *The Young Turks in Opposition*, 142–58.

21   On the media published during this period and how it fits the "national" teleology in Albania, see Ahmet Kondo, *Çështja Kombëtare në Faqe të Shtypit të Rilindjes* (Tiranë: 8 Nëntori, 1982).

22   Isa Blumi, "Capitulations in the Late Ottoman Empire: The Shifting Parameters of Russian and Austrian Interests in Ottoman Albania, 1878–1912," *Oriente Moderno* 83.3 (2003): 635–47.

23   School books published in Latin ("French") letters were reportedly being sent from their Bucharest publisher into Ottoman territories. BBA I.DH, 1102/86349, dated Bucharest, 15 September 1888. The same smuggling networks delivered weapons to mixed groups in Albania and Macedonia, BBA I.DH, 1005/79368, 10 October 1886.

24   Blumi, *Reinstating the Ottomans*, 121–3.

25   Benedict Anderson, *Imagined Communities: Reflections on the Origin and Spread of Nationalism* (New York: Verso, 1983): 33–6. Consolidation and standardization certainly played a part in the late Ottoman Balkans. For details of the alphabet debate among Albanians that actually led to the same issues for the Ottoman language, see Frances Trix, "The Stamboul Alphabet of Shemseddin Sami Bey: Precursor to Turkish Script Reform," *IJMES* 31.2 (1999): 255–72 and Frances Trix, "Alphabet Conflict in the Balkans: Albanian and the Congress of Monastir," *International Journal of the Sociology of Language* 128.1 (1997): 1–24. On the Albanian language written in Arabic script, see Ottmar Hegyi, "Minority and Restricted Uses of the Arabic Alphabet: The Aljamiado Phenomenon," *Journal of the American Oriental Society* 99.2 (1979): 262–9.

26   A point repeatedly made in this book is that far from being advocates for the creation of a single Albanian state, separate from the empire, Albanian members of groups in cities as diverse as Athens, Cairo, Bucharest, Rome, and even Istanbul focused on a number of issues concerning them in very different settings. The cultural club called "unity" (*Bashkimi*) in Istanbul, for example, was known for its advocacy for the creation of a single, universally accepted alphabet for Albanian, until then written in at least three different scripts. The tensions between regional groups, however, reflected their very different religious and political orientations. This made finding

a single working alphabet impossible. In particular, it was those factions seeking opportunities to reconstitute the Balkans under an Orthodox Christian umbrella who advocated using a combination of Greek and Latin letters for the Albanian script. In contrast, strict loyalists to the Ottoman Empire highlighted the value of retaining the current Arabic script, while Catholic Albanians and a number of leading intellectuals developed another alphabet using unique diacritical and Latin letters. Recognizing this was a contentious issue leading to a widening of the political chasm between factions, the editors of *Bashkimi*'s newspaper wrote that the meetings to find a common ground on an alphabet reflected the possibility that all the divisions in the Balkans—Christians and Muslims, rich and poor—could be reconciled through a common love for the new order provided by the Young Turk revolution. Such a message clearly suggests many Ottoman Albanians advocated strengthening ties to the empire, not its fragmentation. See *Bashkimi*, number 3, dated Istanbul (19 December 1908): 1.

27 It was later claimed that upwards of 300 Bucharest-based "patriots" who organized the committee to start-up *Drita* received funds from a variety of sources, which ultimately led to the purchase for 100,000 francs of a print machine in Vienna. Stjepan Antoljak, "Prilog historijatu borbe Albanaca za svoj alfabet," *Gjurmime Albanologjike* II.1 (1969): 23–57, 33.

28 The Albanian state archives are full of correspondence between activists who openly competed with other Tosk-run organizations in larger Romania and Bulgaria. One particularly important group—*Dëshire*—based in Sofia had provided the pretext for crucial alliances between Ibrahim Temo and Kosta J. Trebicka to form an alliance which ultimately secured a place within the region for the CUP as it pushed for leverage in the Ottoman émigré communities. See AQSH, F. 19. D. 30. d. 1–2, Temo to Trebicka, dated, 23 November 1901.

29 Dërmaku, *Nikolla N. Naço- Korça*, 80–131.

30 The most comprehensive study available on Albanian publishing before the creation of the truncated Albanian state in 1913 is Nathalie Clayer, *Aux origines du nationalisme albanais: La naissance d'une nation majoritairement musulmane en Europe* (Paris: Karthala, 2006): 411–538, 549–61.

31 For a comprehensive survey of the fundamental issues exercising Vlach communities and the possible role that Tosks were to play in shaping future claims by Romania on Vlach community interests in the southwest of the Balkans, see Nikolla N. Naço, *Viitorul Romanismului în Balcan: Scrisoare Deschisa* (Bucuresti: Tipografia G.A. Lazareanu, 1905): 12–43.

32 *Drita*, number 66, dated Sofia, 15 September 1905.

33 A report by the Albanian Protestant evangelical Gjergj Qiriazi on efforts to raise money in Bucharest for *southern Albanian*-language schools in Korçë, the quintessential Tosk city and the hometown of so many among the most prominent Tosk leaders in exile, demonstrates such a process of self-segregation. Concerns for events elsewhere in Ottoman Albania were rarely expressed in such campaigns. AQSH F.99.D.78.f.1, dated Bucharest, 23 October 1898. For a specific example of how efforts to raise funds for a school in Shkodër from the Bucharest community were thwarted by community leaders who resisted funding northern Albanian projects, see AQSH F.99.D.18.f.1–2, Filip Shiroka to *Drita*'s editors, dated Shkodër, 14 February 1892.

34 Clayer, *Aux origines du nationalisme albanais,* 302–3.

35 Again as advocate of Greek and Albanian unity, Qemali and his career are aggressively protected by Albanian nationalist historians. That being said, German

and Ottoman state condemnation of his "forbidden" overtures with Pan-Hellenists helps reiterate my larger arguments about the still precarious role exclusivist ethno-national identity claims played in the *proximate* context of the Ottoman refugee space. On official Ottoman condemnation of Ismail Kemal's operations in Corfu where he negotiated with Hellenist irredentists, see "Reyb-ul Menun," *Meşrutiyet* 6 (11 April 1901): 4. See also German intelligence reports in PAAA, 732/2, Die Jungtürken, 198, especially letter No. 44, consul to von Bülow, dated Athens, 16 August 1901, A. 12040.

36 Known in Ottoman contexts as Şemseddin Sami, see Blumi, *Reinstating the Ottomans*, 107–23.

37 Ahmet Kondo, "Kontributi i revistës 'Drita–Dituria' për përhapjen e ideve kombëtare dhe të njohurive shkencore (1884–1885)," *Studime historike* 3 (1970): 140–7.

38 A review of the events was made by someone using the pen-name Yodena in 1905 in *Drita*, number 58, dated Sofia, 4 March 1905. For his part, Naço, *Viitorul Romanismului*, 55–8, left his recollections on these events in an especially visceral fashion while the co-founder of *Dituria*. Visar Dodani also of Korçë, left his own memoirs that discussed these events Visar Dodani, *Memoret e Mija* (Constanţa, 1930): 27–54.

39 Indeed, it is clear from numerous CUP allied newspapers published out of Bulgaria— *Muvazene* in Plovdiv and *Ittifak* in Sofia—that there was some official Bulgarian support, despite the substantial pressure levied on the Sofia government by the Ottoman state, Hanioğlu, *The Young Turks in Opposition*, 123–4.

40 Ottoman officials reported that known rebels like Nahabetyan (Nahabedian) and Nalchjian, linked to the Eastern Armenian *Hunchak* (*Hincak* in Ottoman) movement, regularly entered Bulgaria through the port of Varna, gaining access to a "diaspora" in Bulgaria for the purposes of mobilizing small radicalized groups of Armenians. That said, it would be a mistake to forget that this organization often directly colluded with various non-Armenian players. The fact that the Russian government, for instance, funded these infiltrations—despite the Marxist origins of the movement—must influence how we interpret these engagements of a primarily Ottoman sociopolitical issue at the time. Ottoman officials also report that the movement adopted a multiple front approach to applying pressure on various possible audiences. Indeed, these *Hunchak* groups were reportedly formed in as diverse places as Iran as well as Varna and Sofia in Bulgaria and even Switzerland. BBA, YA.HUS, 507/143, dated 8 December 1906.

41 Stated as such by Simon Vratzian, a leader of the ARF, see Sarkis Atamian, *The Armenian Community: The Historical Development of a Social and Historical Conflict* (New York: Philosophical Library, 1955): 156–7 and Duncan M. Perry, "The Macedonian Revolutionary Organization's Armenian Connection," *Armenian Review* 42.5 (1989): 61–70, 63.

42 Hanioğlu, *Preparation for a Revolution*, 221–7.

43 Numerous intelligence reports from Sofia stated that activists from many parts of Albanian-speaking territories were occasionally meeting with their Macedonian, pro-Greek, and even Serb counterparts in Sofia. There were of course similar meeting points in Belgrade, Athens, Corfu, Geneva, and within Istanbul. BBA DH.MKT 2502/32, dated 23 July 1901.

44 Indeed, by 1907, albeit as a divided opposition, a faction under the leadership of Sabahaddin Bey called for a coalition of opposition parties, which included the now infamous "congress" to be held in Paris. The negotiations with both leaders of the

ARF and Hunchak parties exposed the depths of the divisions within the future CUP along first sectarian and second, according to one scholar, ethno-racial lines. Hanioğlu, *Preparation for a Revolution*, 191–200.

45 BBA, Y.PRK.MK, 12/66, dated 11 February 1903 in which Bulgar Committee actions are reported. In BBA, DH.MKT, 526/31, dated 18 July 1902, official's report of Petrov leader's operations in Kesriye district.

46 In regard to the on-again, off-again relations between CUP activists and the Macedonian Committee based in Ruse, Bulgaria, see the front page report "Makidonya Komitesi," *Osmanlı* number 29 (1 February 1899). These relations often soured when armed groups clashed in Macedonia itself, revealing opportunistic raids had as much economic as ideological value to the armed men. The failure to include the IMRO, some Greek and Serbian, as well as previously noted Armenian groups signaled to many in the press, including in the official CUP paper, that more needed to be done to secure an integrated Ottoman future. "Un bon débarras," *Mechveret Supplément Français* No. 4 (1 January 1908): 7–8, "Konferenz türkischer Revolutionäre im Ausland," *Neue Freie Presse*, 12 January 1908, and "Les Partis d'opposition de l'Empire ottoman," *Le Siècle*, 16 January 1908.

47 Mari Firkatian, *Retaining Ethnic Identity: The Armenians in Bulgaria* (New York: Routledge, 2008) and Milena Mahon, "The Macedonian Question in Bulgaria," *Nations and Nationalism* 4.3 (1998): 389–407.

48 And yet, the number of openly hostile, separatist Armenian "revolutionaries" in operation in Bulgaria were reportedly very small in comparison to the upwards of 35,000 Eastern Armenians who actually settled in Bulgaria over the 1890–1909 period, see Perry, "The Macedonian Revolutionary," 67.

49 Garabet Moumdjian, "Rebels with a Cause: Armenian-Macedonian Relations and their Bulgarian Connection, 1895–1913," in Yavuz and Blumi (eds), *War & Nationalism*, 132–75.

50 Dikran Mesrob Kaligian, *Armenian Organization and Ideology Under Ottoman Rule, 1908–1914* (Piscataway: Transaction Publication, 2011): 39 ff. 37, 243.

51 Some of the most outspoken, and increasingly visceral, anti-Armenians used the collaboration between small Armenian groups, often mobilized by anarchist ideologies, and Bulgarians, Greeks, and Russians. At these moments, the call for unity in a CUP context often pitted loyal Muslims, like Kurds and Albanians, against distinguishable Christian—Rum and Armenian—others. See "Arnavudlar ve Kürdler," *Osmanlı* 51 (1 January 1900).

52 Moumdjian, "Rebels with a Cause," 155–9.

53 Moumdjian, "Rebels with a Cause," 139–42.

54 This ill-conceived plan to force the hands of the major powers and eventually draw Bulgaria into an irredentist war with the Ottoman state in the Manastır governorate was concocted by a "secret" Macedonian-Adrianople Revolutionary Organization meant to initiate a joint rebellion in eastern Thrace and western Macedonia. With some support by local Vlachs, the Bulgarian rural populations in both the Adrianople and Manastır governorates declared independent republics after quickly taking over small towns in both regions. The internal divisions between various, often rival "revolutionary brotherhoods," however, proved decisive. As anarchists like the Gemidhzhi group and extreme right-wing nationalist groups under the leadership of Ivan Garvanov were embroiled in constant dispute, it left those who had taken up arms exposed. The result was they were crushed by local militias whose loyalty to the Ottoman state had not been anticipated. The subsequent oppression drove

a new wave of Ottoman Bulgarians to flee to Bulgaria, resulting in those Austrian and Russian initiatives discussed in the previous chapter. Barbara Jelavich and Charles Jelavich, *The Establishment of the Balkan National States, 1804–1920* (Seattle: University of Washington Press, 1977): 210–13. For Austrian officials' interpretation of the uprisings that instigated full European intervention in Macedonia, see HHStA PA, XXXVIII/392, Kral to Gołuchowski, dated Monastir, 19 July 1903.

55 The ARF program to collect money from rich Armenians was sanctioned by a special, secretive ARF body known as *Dashnaktsutyan Gamke Nergayatsnogh Marmin* (The Body Representing the Will of the Dashnak Party). See Moumdjian, "Rebels with a Cause," 147–52.

56 After complaints from Istanbul, Bulgarian officials reportedly investigated a secret school in Filipe where Armenians were allegedly learning to manufacture explosives. BBA, Y.PRK. MK, 22/36, dated 17 June 1907. These kinds of reports suggest little could be done by Ottoman officials to stop this dangerous escalation of violence. Three years earlier Ottoman reports suggested one Dimitri Kristov had applied these bomb-making techniques introduced by Armenian activists to training Bulgarians, see BBA, Y.PRK. ASK, 222/31, dated 2 October 1904. Soon after, reports reveal 8 Bulgarians were actually arrested by authorities for studying the use of dynamite, see BBA, Y.PRK. MK, 21/84, dated 29 December 1905, in which local authorities report that 8 Bulgarians are caught in Eastern Rumeli studying how to make dynamite.

57 Not an impressive number, in the end, when considering the fact that more than 8,000 conscripted Armenians provided the Ottoman army with "valiant service in the Balkans" during the same war. See Roderick Davidson, "The Armenian Crisis: 1912–1914," *American Historical Review* 53.3 (April 1948): 481–505, 491. See also Yıldırım, *Bulgaristan'daki Ermeni Komitelerinin*, 116–20.

58 There is little doubt that among some Armenian refugees, given an opportunity to attack the Ottoman state during the Balkan War of 1912, the goal was not just defeating an army but attacking Muslim civilians as an act of revenge for atrocities committed against Armenians in Eastern Anatolia years earlier. As reported by Leon Trotsky in Trotskii, L. *The Balkan Wars, 1912–1913: The War Correspondence of Leon Trotsky.* D. Williams and G. Weissman (eds) (London: Monad Press, 1980): 231, 284.

59 Sami Zubaida (ed.), *Race and Racialism* (London: Tavistock Publications, 1970): 4.

60 Avtar Brah, *Cartographies of Diaspora: Contesting Identities* (New York: Routledge, 1996): 20–5.

61 Stuart Hall, "Cultural Identity and Diaspora," in Padmini Mongia (ed.), *Contemporary Postcolonial Theory: A Reader* (London: Arnold, 1996): 110–21.

62 Blumi, *Reinstating the Ottomans*, 157–60.

63 Born Ibrahim Mehmet Naxhi in Struga in 1872, Hima became the chief liaison between fellow Tosk Albanians and Ibrahim Temo, the leader of the CUP in the Balkans. It was Temo who initially recruited Hima to the cause. Temo, *Ittihad ve Terakki*, 116–19. For a biography see Kristaq Prifti, *Dervish Hima (1872–1928)* (Tirana: 8 Nentori, 1987).

64 See ASMAE SAP Pacco 667, no. 1144/103, consul to MAE, dated Bucharest, 22 May 1902.

65 AQSH F.12.D.5.f.1. Copy of letter from Mati Logoreci to editors of *Albania*, dated Vienna, 1 July 1898.

66 Indeed, struggling to secure funds at this time for his besieged *Drita*, Nikolla Naço openly solicited funds from Austria using this triangle of action and counter-action. HHStA PA, XIV/13, Liasse VIII/I, Pallavicini to Gołuchowski, dated Bucharest, 8 January 1904.

67 In two letters sent by Devish Hima to Ibrahim Temo in 1903, it becomes clear how outside intervention had changed life in much of Kosovo. Hima describes how Italian and Austrian agents encouraged northern Albanian (Geg) Catholics to organize toward "liberating" occupied lands rather than collaborating with the CUP. AQSH F.19.D.32/2.f.278–280, Hima to Temo, dated Rome, 20 March 1903. There is evidence to suggest that Hima actively warned opponents of the regime that far too many Albanians remained loyal to the Sultan prior to 1908 to effectively lead an uprising from within Ottoman territories.

68 See also HHStA PA, XIV/24, Albanien Liasse XVI/4. Orhan Bey and Athanas Sina, "Aperçu über die albanesische Knabenschule in Kortscha und die Notwendigkeit ihrer Weiterentwicklung," (written in November 1899) enclosed in no. 2, Kral to Gołuchowski, dated Monastir, 4 January 1901.

69 Hima proudly claimed that he convinced the Italian state to invest in schools as a means to win over Albanian refugee/diaspora readers in Italy. Dervish Hima (Ibrahim Nagi), "Shkollat Shqipe," dated Rome, 22 October 1899 published in *La Nazione Albanese*, no. 20, dated Pellagorio, 30 October 1899. Apparently he was not just boasting, he actually did succeed in convincing the Italian government to fund those Bucharest and Sofia-based community organizations expressing a desire to open schools in the Ottoman administered Yanya province. ASMAE SAP Pacco 667, no. 1144/103, consul to MAE, dated Bucharest, 22 May 1902.

70 As late as 1907 Ismail Qemali advocated the creation of "*una liga Greco-Albanese*" in an effort to thwart Bulgarian domination in Macedonia. ASAME Serie P Politica 1891–1916, Busta 665, no. 365/108, Consul to Foreign Minister, dated Athens, 26 April 1907.

71 Julia Clancy-Smith, *Mediterraneans: North Africa and Europe in an Age of Migration, c. 1800–1900* (Berkeley, CA: University of California Press, 2010).

72 Such heavy investment in what were ostensibly anti-Ottoman groups cannot be taken outside the larger context of Egypt at the time. As Hanioğlu has argued, British support of these anti-Ottoman groups, including separatist nationalist movements, was intended to cause fragmentation as well as violent unrest, Hanioğlu, *Preparations of a Revolution*, 67–73.

73 One example where British interests and Qemali's still "unionist" predilections served a common cause was in the effort to keep Armenians firmly in the Ottoman camp. If not out of pure Ottomanist spirit, this interest in Armenians was at least hoping to assure Russia did not get the upper hand in Anatolia and the Balkans. See how still loyal Armenians linked Qemali with the British agenda, "Ismail Kemal Bey," *Pro Arménia* 12 (10 May 1901): 95. See also Blumi, *Reinstating the Ottomans*, 135–48.

74 Many of these journals, while short-lived, did articulate support for Albanian political rights in both Egypt and the Balkans, AQSH F.23.D.25.f.5–6, enclosure, 30 June 1900, copy of article, "Shqiperia dhe sundimi i saj i perkasin Shqiptarëve . . ." in the journal *Bashkimi i Shqiptarëve* published out of Cairo.

75 A prominent advocate for Albanian cultural rights and interloper with imperial agents, Faik Konitza, based in Brussels, once highlighted the close relationship the Khedive's family had with select groups of Ottoman Albanians living in Egypt. For instance, the uncle of the Khedive, Ahmed Fuad Pasha, supported the publishing of Albanian-language journals, both in Arabic and Greek script, throughout Egypt and the larger Mediterranean world. HHStA PA XIV/18 Liasse XII/2, Konitza à Zwiedinek, dated Bruxelles, 5 May 1899.

76 For details see HHStA PA XIV/16 Liasse XII/7, Velić to Gołuchowski, dated Cairo, 15 March 1901.

77   A copy of this paper, along with a commentary, may be found in HHStA PA XIV/16
     Liasse XII/7, Velić to Gołuchowski, dated Cairo, 15 March 1901.
78   BBA HR.SYS 128/18, 10070/157, Ottoman Legation to Sublime Porte, dated Athens,
     27 June 1902. See also Blumi, *Reinstating the Ottomans*, 118–24.
79   Stavro Skendi, *The Albanian National Awakening, 1878–1912* (Princeton: Princeton
     University Press, 1967): 175.
80   For more details see HHStA PA XIV/16 Liasse XII/7, Velics to Gołuchowski, dated
     Cairo, 18 December 1901.
81   HHStA PA XIV/16 Liasse XII/7, Velics to Gołuchowski, dated Cairo, 15 March 1901.
82   HHStA PA XIV/16 Liasse XII/7, Velics to Gołuchowski, dated Cairo, 15 March 1901,
     page 75.
83   This *arbëreshë* is a curious story in the late nineteenth-century context. Fully
     integrated into the newly unified Italian Republic, these largely "southern"
     communities actively participated in the Italian movement for national unification.
     And yet, their most active members—poet Girolamo De Rada and the lawyer
     Anselmo Lorecchio—both in government and out, took the spirit of the *Risorgimento*
     to invest in what many openly claimed was their Albanian homeland. As Lorecchio
     and his journal *La Nazione Albanese* forcefully stated, the Albanians should not
     aspire to complete independence, but rather to autonomy within the frame of the
     Ottoman Empire. Lorecchio argued that this approach would help to bridge regional
     and religious differences and would put in motion a process of cultural development
     and national consolidation, while at the same time resisting the expansionist aims
     put forward by Serbs, Montenegrins, Bulgarians, and Greeks. Francesco Caccamo,
     "L'Adriatico degli arbëreshë: il 'mare nostro' albanese e italiano," in Stefano Trinchese
     and Francesco Caccamo (eds), *Adriatico contemporaneo. Rotte e percezioni del mare
     comune tra Ottocento e Novecento* (Milano: FrancoAngeli, 2008): 133.
84   The Italian Foreign Ministry ordered its consuls in Buenos Aires and São Paolo to
     monitor Ottoman Albanian activists in those cities. Such concerns reveal a growing
     interest in harnessing the potential power of the Ottoman migrants in the Americas
     as much as in the larger Mediterranean. ASMAE Serie P Politica 1891–1916, Busta
     666, no. 4819/239, MAE internal message, dated Roma, 27 January 1905 and ASMAE
     Serie P Politica 1891–1916, Busta 666, no. 1388, Ministero dell'Interno to MAE, dated
     Roma, 21 January 1905. The Ottoman Empire also monitored such operations in
     the Americas, including those managed by Albanian activist Jasharik Drama, who,
     after holding crucial meetings with other Ottoman Balkan-natives about the rapidly
     changing situation in the region, reportedly left Trieste for South America. BBA MV
     163/74, dated Trieste, 18 March 1912.
85   Hanioğlu, *Preparation for a Revolution*, 67–73.
86   Isa Blumi, *Chaos in Yemen: Societal Collapse and the New Authoritarianism* (London:
     Routledge, 2010): 62–4.
87   The Italian foreign ministry was clearly intrigued by Kibsi's overtures and ordered
     background reports. In response, vice-consul Sola based in Hudaydah wrote an
     extensive report on Kibsi, essentially vouching for both his truthfulness and his
     family's influence in Yemen. ASMAI 91/9 f. 119, no. 133/39, Sola a Tittoni, dated
     Hudaydah, 22 April 1906.
88   The practice of exiling prominent Yemeni men to Rhodes is evident throughout the
     archives. By 1909, the new Young Turk government made efforts to improve relations
     with Yemen by freeing many of the most prominent exiles sent there during the reign
     of Abdülhamid. Among those repatriated were Muhammad ibn Mehmed al-Hirazi,

BBA DH.MUI 2–2/1 dated 3 September 1909 and Abdurrahman Effendi, BBA DH.MUI 97–1/6, dated 1 November 1909.

89 It would take another year and a half before Kibsi's wishes were granted and an entourage of more than 60 members of his family and close associates moved from Rhodes to Alexandria. ASMAI 91/9 f. 124, Report no. 771, dated Cairo, 22 June 1908.

90 The following men were listed as actively supporting Kibsi in Cairo: 'Ali Mansar Hasablan, Muhammad Hassan al Harasi, Hassan 'Ali, 'Ali Isma'il, and Salah Yahya Abd-al Rahman 'Ali al-Harasi. See ASMAI 91/9 F. 119, no. 530/168, Legation to MAE, dated Cairo, 25 May 1906.

91 ASMAI 91/9 f. 121, no. 73943/894, MAE to Istanbul, dated Roma, 6 December 1906, extract of letter written by a member of the Hawlan to Sayyid Ahmed Yahya al-Kibsi in Cairo, dated 2 October 1906.

92 ASMAI 91/9 f. 119, no. 586/200, Legation to MAE, dated Cairo, 19 June 1906. It is also noted that Muhammad Arif Bey is not the most accurate translator, raising the suspicions of some in the Cairo legation that he had conflicting interests. ASMAI 91/9 f. 121, no. 505/165, legation to MAE, dated Cairo, 21 April 1908.

93 ASMAI 91/9 f. 119, no. 586/200, Legation to MAE, dated Cairo, 19 June 1906, f.3.

94 Subsequent to the apparent fall from favor with Imam Yahya (as a result of Muhammad Arif Bey's letters?) it is suggested that the Italian office cut its funding for Kibsi off. In a desperate effort to regain his former assistance, Kibsi writes that he is in debt of 48 livres (pounds) and is urgently requesting funding. ASMAI 91/9 f. 125, no. 77590, Kibsi al-Yamani to Italian Legation, dated Cairo, 2 November 1908.

95 The levels of interaction between some groups in Romania and Egypt were key to understanding the development of new channels of communication that led to widespread use of Bucharest newspapers, such as *Drita* and *Albania*, in Egypt. HHStA PA XIV/16 Liasse XII/1, no. 51, Kral to Gołuchowski, 28 Juni 1904 reports on 460 copies of *Albania* and *Drita* distributed throughout Egypt.

96 Isa Blumi, "The Evolution of Red Sea Trade in the 19th Century Ottoman Yemen," *Journal of Turkish Studies Special Issue: In Memoriam Şinasi Tekin* 31.1 (2007): 157–75.

97 Rogers Brubraker, "Ethnicity without Groups," *Archives européenes de sociologie* XLIII.2 (2002): 163–89.

98 By 1901 in many parts of the *Ottoman proximate* space, radical elements within the opposition, especially the CUP, were cultivating a long-term strategy to concentrate energy toward unifying Muslims around common threats, increasingly deemed "Armenian" and "*Rum*" in "nature." See outbursts of anti-Christian sentiments among Ottoman Kurdish exiles in Cairo who were able to sneak their decidedly anti-unionist sentiment in official CUP newspapers. "Misir al-Kahire'den," *Osmanlı* 78 dated Geneva, 15 February (1901): 8.

Chapter 4

1 ... For I need them to colonize Alaska, the Philippines, Cuba, and Hawai'i.

2 Hyland, "Arisen from Deep Slumber," 548.

3 Kevin Johnson, *The Huddled Masses Myth: Immigration and Civil Rights* (Philadelphia: Temple University Press, 2003). Life for Caribbean migrants of African/Muslim origins to the United States in this period proved especially harrowing. Frank A. Guridy, *Forging Diaspora: Afro-Cubans and African*

Americans in a World of Empire and Jim Crow (New York: University of North Carolina Press, 2010).

4   Donna R. Gabaccia, "Is Everywhere Nowhere? Nomads, Nations, and the Immigrant Paradigm in United States History," *The Journal of American History* 86.3 (1999): 1115–34.

5   Richard White, "Information, Markets, and Corruption: Transcontinental Railroads in the Gilded Age," *The Journal of American History* 90.1 (2003): 19–43.

6   Adam McKeown, "Global Migration 1846–1940," *Journal of World History* 15.2 (2004): 155–89 and M. V. Elteren, "Workers' Control and the Struggles Against 'Wage Slavery' in the Gilded Age and After," *The Journal of American Culture* 26.3 (2003): 188–203. Marx's critique of this domination of labor by capital is still pertinent, *Capital: A Critique of Political Economy*, trans. Ben Fowkes, vol. 1 (New York: Penguin Classics, 1992): 876–99.

7   Jeremy R. Porter, "Plantation Economics, Violence, and Social Well-being: The Lingering Effects of Racialized Group Oppression on Contemporary Human Development in the American South," *Journal of Human Development and Capabilities* 12.3 (2011): 339–66 and Frans Buelens and Stefaan Marysse, "Returns on Investments during the Colonial Era: The Case of the Belgian Congo," *The Economic History Review* 62.1 (2009): 135–66.

8   To quote Polanyi: "To allow the market mechanism to be sole director of the fate of human beings . . . would result in the demolition of society. For the alleged commodity 'labor power' cannot be shoved about, used indiscriminately, or even left unused, without affecting also the human individual who happens to be the bearer of this peculiar commodity. In disposing of a man's labor power the system would, incidentally, dispose of the physical, psychological, and moral entity 'man' attached to that tag. Robbed of the protective covering of cultural institutions, human beings would perish from the effects of social exposure; they would die as the victims of acute social dislocation through vice, perversion, crime, and starvation . . . Undoubtedly, labor, land, and money markets are essential to a market economy. But no society could stand the effects of such a system of crude fictions . . . unless its human and natural substance, as well as its business organization, was protected against the ravages of this satanic mill." Karl Polanyi, *The Great Transformation: The Political and Economic Origins of Our Time* (Boston: Beacon Press, 2001): 76.

9   Sarah Gualtieri, "Gendering the Chain Migration Thesis: Women and Syrian Transatlantic Migration, 1878–1924," *CSSAAME* 24.1 (2004): 67–78.

10 While the primary focus in this chapter are the roles these Ottoman merchants would play for Spanish, American, British, and Dutch imperial administrations, French authorities throughout the world fully appreciated the value of harnessing the Ottoman Syrian/Maronite networks that connected the Caribbean, South America, France, and the Ottoman territories. Documents suggest the consul in Bogotá appreciated the role of the Arab middleman and was willing to sacrifice his energies to assure his office did not let the growing numbers of Ottoman migrants arriving in the city forget that France would be a useful patron who could facilitate their trade with the metropole. Ministère des Affaires Etrangères (MAE), Turquie/Syrie-Liban/Nouvelle Série 108, Boulard-Ponqueville to the Ministry of Foreign Affairs, dated Bogotá, 25 March 1902. For the linkage in the Caribbean see David Nicholls, "No Hawkers and Pedlars: Levantines in the Caribbean," *Ethnic and Racial Studies* 4.4 (1981): 415–31; David Nicholls, "Lebanese of the Antilles: Haiti, Dominican Republic, Jamaica, and Trinidad," *The Lebanese in the World. A Century of*

Emigration. The Centre for Lebanese Studies. London (1992); Brenda Gayle Plummer, "Race, Nationality, and Trade in the Caribbean: The Syrians in Haiti, 1903–1934," *The International History Review* 3.4 (1981): 517–39, and for West Africa, Andrew Kerim Arsan, "Failing to Stem the Tide: Lebanese Migration to French West Africa and the Competing Prerogatives of the Imperial State," *CSSH* 53.03 (2011): 450–78.

11 Put in these terms, perhaps it is worth reassessing some of the hagiographies of the "forefathers" produced by, in many ways, justifiably proud communities today. In México, such a task has proven especially difficult over the years as many first generation migrants changed their names to better assimilate in an at times xenophobic urban society. See Jacques Najm Sacre, *Directorio por familias de los descendientes libanese de México y Centroamérica* (Mexico City: Centro de Difusión Cultural de la Misión de México, 1981): 487–91.

12 Sebouh Aslanian, *From the Indian Ocean to the Mediterranean: The Global Trade Networks of Armenian Merchants from New Julfa* (Berkeley: University of California Press, 2011): 6–15.

13 Research has shown that prior to 1948—the year international forces installed the exclusivist, settler states of Rhodesia and Israel—migrant Ottoman Jews, Christians, and Muslims did not live differentiated lives in many parts of South America. In Argentina and Brazil in particular, a common Ottoman (geographic, linguistic, and cultural) origin helped peoples of all denominations still share complimentary socioeconomic interests. See Ignacio Klich, "Arab-Jewish Coexistence in the First Half of the 1900s' Argentina: Overcoming Self-Imposed Amnesia," in Ignacio Klich and Jeffrey Lesser (eds), *Arab and Jewish Immigrants in Latin America: Images and Realities* (London: Frank Cass, 1998): 1–37. According to the consistently excellent work of Jeffrey Lesser, Ottomans of distinctive faiths and ethno-linguistic affiliation lived in the same neighborhoods and retained a special place in Brazilian commercial and cultural life. Jeffrey Lesser, "'Jews are Turks Who Sell on Credit' Elite Images of Arabs and Jews in Brazil," in Klich and Lesser, *Arab and Jewish Immigrants,* 40.

14 There have been commissioned histories written about individual Ottoman-descendant families. Such hagiographies of the great families of Southeast Asia or México do what good commissioned histories do: they have effectively covered up the horrors many of these Ottoman migrants imposed on indigenous peoples throughout the tropical world on behalf of other empires.

15 Edna Bonacich, "A Theory of Middleman Minorities," *American Sociological Review* 38.5 (1973): 583–94 and Walter P. Zenner, "Arabic-speaking Immigrants in North America as Middleman Minorities," *Ethnic and Racial Studies* 5.4 (1982): 457–77. For a fascinating study of how regional merchants, financiers, *nakhoda*, and judges collaborated with Euro-American power by way of a changing debt and credit regime, see Bishara, *A Sea of Debt.*

16 Robert Vitalis, "The Noble American Science of Imperial Relations and Its Laws of Race Development," *CSSH* 52.4 (2010): 909–38, 911.

17 Christopher A. Bayly, *Rulers, Townsmen and Bazaars: North Indian Society in the Age of British Expansion, 1770–1870* (Cambridge: Cambridge University Press, 1988).

18 Constance Mary Turnbull, "British Colonialism and the Making of the Modern Johor 1 Monarchy," *Indonesia and the Malay World* 37.109 (2009): 227–48.

19 Blumi, *Foundations of Modernity,* 33–7 and Beatrice Nicolini, "The Myth of the Sultans in the Western Indian Ocean during the Nineteenth Century: A New Hypothesis," *African and Asian Studies* 8.3 (2009): 239–67.

20 Contrast the approaches two scholars of Bahrain take in respect to British capitalist relations with indigenous actors to appreciate the task of challenging anew the scholarship attempting to link these regions to a larger "global" context. Nelida Fuccaro, *Histories of City and State in the Persian Gulf: Manama since 1800* (Cambridge: Cambridge University Press, 2009) and James Onley, "The Raj Reconsidered: British India's Informal Empire and Spheres of Influence in Asia and Africa," *Asian Affairs* 40.1 (2009): 44–62.

21 Kerry Ward, *Networks of Empire: Forced Migration in the Dutch East India Company* (Cambridge: Cambridge University Press, 2008).

22 Huw V. Bowen, *The Business of Empire: The East India Company and Imperial Britain, 1756–1833* (Cambridge: Cambridge University Press, 2008): 84–117.

23 It has long been understood that controlling the distribution of food brought considerable leverage over otherwise autonomous peoples. For the EIC, a crucial turning point in their relative power over their Bengali clients, partners, and adversaries was large, periodic famines. During the famine of 1770, for instance, large areas of Bengal became dependent on food supplies largely controlled by the company. This constituted a golden opportunity to blackmail local rulers as individual company managers became incredibly wealthy from hoarding rice or grains. Nick Robins, *The Corporation that Changed the World: How the East India Company Shaped the Modern Multinational* (London: Pluto Press, 2006): 90–116. The links between starvation politics and European power is still largely overlooked in Western academia. One exception is the invaluable work on how the British used starvation to subjugate Persia during World War I. Mohammad Gholi Majd, *The Great Famine and Genocide in Persia, 1917–1919* (New York: University Press of America, 2003).

24 In the case of the EIC, it was able to collaborate with local rulers to actually create three separate mercenary armies in Bombay, Madras, and Bengal, with upwards of 257,000 Sepoys ("high caste Hindus") serving as the backbone of this corporate bludgeon. Donald Featherstone, "A Military Anomaly-the army of the East India Company 1757–1857," *The RUSI Journal* 138.1 (1993): 48–52.

25 Partnerships with British and Dutch companies helped some "Arab" Hadhrami traders gain the upper-hand and become in many parts of Java or Singapore the exclusive supplier to these European conglomerates. Such lucrative arrangements incentivized political tyranny. For Java see, Robert E. Elson, *Village Java under the Cultivation System, 1830–1870* (Sydney: Allen & Unwin, 1994), 255–8 and Singapore, Alfred R. Wallace, *The Malay Archipelago: The Land of the Orang-utan and the Bird of Paradise* (Singapore: Oxford University Press, 1986): 32.

26 Nicholas B. Dirks, *The Scandal of Empire: India and the Creation of Imperial Britain* (Cambridge, MA: Belknap/Harvard University Press, 2006).

27 Richard Price, *Making Empire: Colonial Encounters and the Creation of Imperial Rule in Nineteenth-Century Africa* (Cambridge: Cambridge University Press, 2008).

28 Andrew Sartori, "The British Empire and its Liberal Mission," *Journal of Modern History* 78.3 (September 2006): 623–42.

29 David Northrup, "A Church in Search of a State: Catholic Missions in Eastern Zaïre, 1879–1930," *Journal of Church and State* 30.2 (1988): 309–19. There must be room to think differently about how we study the settler experience, one that in parts of the Americas, as offered by Frederick Hoxie, was that by actually inhabiting the colonized land over a long period capitalist expansionism impacts the nature of that experience, especially in respect to relations with the indigenous population. Frederick E. Hoxie,

"Retrieving the Red Continent: Settler Colonialism and the History of American Indians in the US," *Ethnic and Racial Studies* 31.6 (2008): 1153–67. I thank Jon Schmitt for alerting me to this distinction and Hoxie's crucial interventions.

30 NAUK, FO 12/30, Admiralty of Under Secretary of State, dated Singapore, 14 July 1862. Much of this information was provided 15 years earlier in NAUK, FO 125/133 Information obtained by Charles Grey at Singapore from Wyndham relating to Sulu, dated 24 February 1847.

31 Michael Adas, "From Avoidance to Confrontation: Peasant Protest in Precolonial and Colonial Southeast Asia," *CSSH* 23.2 (1981): 217–47.

32 James C. Scott, *The Art of Not Being Governed: An Anarchist History of Upland Southeast Asia* (New Haven: Yale University Press, 2009).

33 Erik Gilbert, *Dhows and the Colonial Economic of Zanzibar, 1860–1970* (Athens: Ohio University Press, 2004). As Gilbert points out so well, by studying East Africa in this period we are always confronted by the debilitating cliché of an essential Arab whose very existence is predicated on competing with the undifferentiated European. Of course these interactions are much more complicated. The best way to approach this would be to see relations between, say Tippu Tip, the quintessential "Swahili-Arab" intermediary, and the European traders for whom he sometimes was willing to work, as constantly negotiated. We are not only dealing with sharp dichotomies, a dialectic between two essential historical forces—Arab and European—but a creole dynamic in which, in the case of East Africa, resists universal, static, and ahistorical characterizations. The biggest perpetrators of these sharp dichotomies have been Norman Bennet, *A History of the Arab State of Zanzibar* (London: Methuen, 1978); Norman Bennett, *Arab versus European* (New York: Africana Publishing Company, 1986) and M. Reda Bhacker, *Trade and Empire in Muscat and Zanzibar* (London: Routledge, 1992). Fortunately, there are nuanced approaches that have authoritatively challenged the neat definitions. Cooper, for instance, challenged conventional attempts to fix Swahili "identity" when its very usefulness as a category is due to its vagueness. Frederick Cooper, *Planation Slavery on the East Coast of Africa* (New Haven: Yale University Press, 1977): 159.

34 In the reports of British captains throughout the 1840s and 1850s, we learn of the growing trade with an even greater diversity of Atlantic interests. For a colorful description of life around the customs house in the early 1840s, where drunken American "Yankee" whalers upset local life, see ZNA, AA1/3, Hammerton to Aberdeen, dated Zanzibar, 2 January 1844. The amount of trade in 1859 was considerable with upwards of 960,000 Maria Theresa thalers exported to the Atlantic trade while a slightly less amount was annually sent to the larger Indian Ocean. See ZNA, AA2/4, Rigby to C. Wood, dated Zanzibar, 1 May 1860. On British companies' monopoly of dyed cloth (the commodity of choice for hinterland communities), and how this commodity figured into—for both Arabs and Europeans—the slave and ivory trade and the development of these periodic alliances, see ZNA AA2/4, Rigby to Russell, dated Zanzibar, 6 May 1860.

35 In contrast, the American ships were largely deemed interlopers in this part of the world until they were able to force their way in by way of the Spanish-American war of 1898, in which they sequestered all of Spain's Pacific Ocean territories including the Philippines and Guam. And yet, by the 1840s Boston-based whaling ships made frequent calls to the East Coast of Africa, establishing lucrative alliances with various Zanzibar trading families. It seems that the Omani Sultan strategized that his own ships could do just as well in bringing his spices to North America and attempted

to circumvent these American ships and trade directly with US ports. This gambit was apparently thwarted with the first of these ships being attacked at sea by the Americans the Sultan hoped to cut out of the business. Abdul Sheriff, *Slaves, Spices and Ivory in Zanzibar* (London: J. Currey, 1987): 99–100.

36 Resulting famine in parts of Eastern Africa both reflects the impact of predatorial capitalism and the window of opportunity to complete the task of full-spectrum domination of local peoples. Juhani Koponen, "War, Famine, and Pestilence in Late Precolonial Tanzania: A Case for a Heightened Mortality," *International Journal of African Historical Studies* 21.4 (1988): 637–76.

37 Anne Stoler, *Capitalism and Confrontation in Sumatra's Plantation Belt, 1870–1979* (New Haven: Yale University Press, 1986).

38 Detailed reports for the periods between 1848 and 1870 may be found in PNA, Zamboanga 1848–97, Bundle 11, SDS 15034.

39 Tania Murray Li, "Centering Labor in the Land Grab Debate," *The Journal of Peasant Studies* 38.2 (2011): 281–98.

40 Eric Tagliacozzo, "Trafficking Human Subjects in the Malay World, 1850–1910," in David Kyle and Rey Koslowski (eds), *Global Human Smuggling: Comparative Perspectives* (New York: The Johns Hopkins University Press, 2011): 87–107.

41 Called *Zeeroovers* in Dutch documents or *Illanun* in Spanish, the "pirate" of the vast region known as the Sulu Zone would become an engine for regional change for the first half of the nineteenth century.

42 Jennifer L. Gaynor, "Piracy in the Offing: The Law of Lands and the Limits of Sovereignty at Sea," *Anthropological Quarterly* 85.3 (2012): 817–57.

43 Nicholas Tarling, *Piracy and Politics in the Malay World* (Melbourne: F.W. Cheshire, 1963); Lennox A. Mills, *British Malaya, 1824–1867* (Kuala Lumpur: Oxford University Press, 1966): 323–29; and Leigh R. Wright, *The Origins of British Borneo* (Hong Kong: Hong Kong University Press, 1970): 39.

44 Gillen D'Arcy Wood, "The Volcano Lover: Climate, Colonialism, and the Slave Trade in Raffles's History of Java (1817)," *Journal for Early Modern Cultural Studies* 8.2 (2008): 33–55. For Dutch administrators, the campaign constituted a green light to apply for the necessary financial and material support to go and dispose the Muslim states of Palembang, Siak, Ache, and Johore in a drawn out period of bloody economic disruption. Some Dutch historians retrospectively have challenged the moralizing of the proponents of such colonial slaughters. Jacob C. Van Leur, *Indonesian Trade and Society* (Hague: Van Hoeve, 1967).

45 Michael Kempe, "'Even in the Remotest Corners of the World': Globalized Piracy and International Law, 1500–1900," *Journal of Global History* 5.03 (2010): 353–72.

46 François Renault, "The Structures of the Slave Trade in Central Africa in the 19th Century," *Slavery and Abolition* 9.3 (1988): 146–65.

47 The flourishing Swahili/Arab-ruled settlements at Nyangwe and Kassongo on the Congo constitute perfect examples of the complex political economy of resource extraction shaping the entire western Indian Ocean zone. Nyangwe, ruled by Hamid bin Muhammad al Murjibi (Tippu Tip) at certain points of time, was a major town that had rice, coconut, and tobacco plantations. It was producing large amounts of revenue from caravan taxes (*Hongo*) as trading expeditions seeking gold, labor, tobacco, and ivory connected the Muslim polities of Uganda, parts of Jimma, and Egyptian-administered Equatorial Province with the coast. These intermediary zones were often coveted by European capitalists. Melvin E. Page, "The Manyema Hordes of Tippu Tip: A Case Study in Social Stratification and the Slave Trade in Eastern

Africa," *The International Journal of African Historical Studies* 7.1 (1974): 69–84; Beverly Brown, "Muslim Influence on Trade and Politics in the Lake Tanganyika Region," *African Historical Studies* 4.3 (1971): 617–29; Ruth Rempel, "Trade and Transformation: Participation in the Ivory Trade in Late 19th-Century East and Central Africa," *Canadian Journal of Development Studies/Revue canadienne d'études du développement* 19.3 (1998): 529–52 and Reuben Loffman, "In the Shadow of the Tree Sultans: African Elites and the Shaping of Early Colonial Politics on the Katangan Frontier, 1906–17," *Journal of Eastern African Studies* 5.3 (2011): 535–52.

48   Gerald J. Pierson, "US Consuls in Zanzibar and the Slave Trade, 1870–1890," *Historian* 55.1 (1992): 53–68.

49   According to Rigby, upwards of 20,000 slaves were imported a year to Zanzibar, most who worked in the plantations for small salaries that were most likely parceled off, if not entirely, a large amount, to the "agent" who owned the individual for a certain period of time. Rigby also reported that large numbers of Spanish slavers were exploiting the region and shipping off their human cargoes to Cuba. ZNA AA2/4, Rigby to Wood, dated Zanzibar, 28 August 1860.

50   Gilbert, *Dhows and the Colonial Economic of Zanzibar,* 59.

51   The bounty for each "capture" was parceled out by each vessel's cargo capacity. For every 10 tons, the crew of the ship capturing the purported slave vessel received 5 pounds. Philip H. Colomb, *Slave Catching in the Indian Ocean* (London: Longmans, 1873): 77–8.

52   George Young, *Corps de Droit Ottoman* (Oxford: Clarendon Press, 1905): 192–206.

53   Blumi, *Foundations,* 65–9.

54   As reported by the American consul based in Zanzibar at the time, the system was entirely corrupted as captains would often exaggerate the length and size of captured boats in order to get the extra money awarded by tonnage. Indeed, Consul Ropes Jr said there was not much doubt in the mind of the British Council John Kirk (one of the directors of the Imperial British East Africa Company—thus profiting from empire) or American traders, that this was all a sham. Worse still for the Americans, it ruined their trade in the region. Realizing that Americans had just been successfully shut out of yet another lucrative market, Consul Ropes coldly noted that the entire Anti-Slavery propaganda campaign was simply cover for signatories to the Berlin Congress to colonize Africa. Norman Bennett, *The Zanzibar Letters of Edward D. Ropes Jr., 1882–1892* (Boston: Boston University, 1973): 100–21.

55   Pedro Machado, "A Forgotten Corner of the Indian Ocean: Gujarati Merchants, Portuguese India and the Mozambique Slave-Trade, c. 1730–1830," *Slavery and Abolition* 24.2 (2003): 17–32 and Clarence-Smith, *The Economics of the Indian Ocean,* 142–54.

56   Ports that had adjudication courts included Bombay, Aden, and Zanzibar. They were selectively used by various interests to shape the way in which captures took place, targeting key flows of "native" trade that followed monsoon cycles; as such, indigenous traders were forced to challenge captures in court on terms set by aggressive, predatorily capitalist interests, see Colomb, *Slave Catching,* 185–93.

57   ZNA AA3, Rigby to Bombay, dated Zanzibar, 14 May 1861.

58   Olivier Petre Grenouilleau (ed.), *From Slave Trade to Empire: European Colonisation of Black Africa, 1780s–1880s* (London: Routledge, 2004).

59   The Germans, with their own ambitions in Eastern Africa, initially opposed the campaign because it was tailored to secure British-allied companies a monopoly on trade in the region. But as the Berlin Congress of 1884–5 earlier had successfully

divided up "spheres of influence," the Brussels Conference Act of 1890 similarly functioned as an agreement between "gentlemen" to give legal cover for the plunder of indigenous wealth. While banning the distribution of arms to Arabs and "natives" (itself a clear indicator of the signatories' real intentions) the Brussels Act also formulized the pariah status of local transport vessels—dhows—pushing them even further from the mainstream economy. In one sense, then, the treaty attempted to legally define what a dhow was, thus making the habits of those using these vessels of slavery "legible" à la Foucault. Coupled with giving the legal power of any European ship to board and search all craft under 500 tons, this epistemological tyranny would have the desired effect. As no European ship in the Indian Ocean was under the 500 ton threshold, the specificity of the Act was geared exclusively to suppress "Arab" shipping. Again, it is crucial to point out that the jurisdiction of the treaty included Ottoman territories in the Red Sea and Persian Gulf, meaning any Ottoman vessel could be boarded and its cargo confiscated at the discretion of the European captain. Finally, with important implications for the how we understand the larger epistemological context of this emerging regime, anyone found on these ships who could be characterized as "negro" was automatically assumed to be a slave on the dhow. As the newly empowered joint-European apparatus registered thousands of dhows from Mozambique to Somalia, it instilled a "racial, legal and commercial borderland" in the region that completely subordinated it to the racial hierarchies becoming in vogue in the Euro-American world, see Gilbert, *Dhows and the Colonial Economic of Zanzibar*, 71–3.

60 Matthew S. Hopper, "East Africa and the End of the Indian Ocean Slave Trade," *Journal of African Development* 13.1 (Spring 2011): 39–65.

61 And yet, there were still considerable European, especially French, activities that brought coerced labor from Eastern Africa to various areas, especially Mauritius and Madagascar, to supply demands in these plantation economies. Richard B. Allen, "Satisfying the 'Want for Labouring People': European Slave Trading in the Indian Ocean, 1500–1850," *Journal of World History* 21.1 (2010): 45–73.

62 Suzanne Miers, "Slavery and the Slave Trade as International Issues 1890–1939," *Slavery and Abolition* 19.2 (1998): 16–37.

63 James Warren, "Who Were the Balangingi Samal? Slave Raiding and Ethnogenesis in Nineteenth-Century Sulu," *Journal of Asian Studies* 37.3 (1978): 477–90.

64 Between 4,000 and 6,000 Visayans, expert divers, were sequestered on an annual basis by the Iranun and Balangingi in 1845. Estimates of 302,575 of the "slaves" captured between 1770–1870 suggest a massive operation that required considerable military power, James F. Warren, *The Sulu Zone 1768–1898: The Dynamics of External Trade, Slavery, and Ethnicity in the Transformation of a Southeast Asian Maritime State* (Singapore: Singapore University Press, 1981).

65 James Warren, "The Balangingi Samal: The Global Economy, Maritime Raiding and Diasporic Identities in the Nineteenth-Century Philippines," *Asian Ethnicity* 4.1 (2003): 7–29.

66 James F. Warren, "Sino-Sulu Trade in the Late Eighteenth and Nineteenth Century," *Philippine Studies: Historical and Ethnographic Viewpoints* 25.1 (1977): 50–79.

67 Robert Fortune, *Three years' wanderings in the northern provinces of China: including a visit to the tea, silk, and cotton countries; with an account of the agriculture and horticulture of the Chinese, new plants, etc.* (London: J. Murray, 1847) and Tan Chung, "The Britain-China-India Trade Triangle (1771–1840)," *Indian Economic & Social History Review* 11.4 (1974): 411–31.

68   Katharine Bjork, "The Link That Kept the Philippines Spanish: Mexican Merchant Interests and the Manila Trade, 1571–1815," *Journal of World History* 9.1 (2005): 25–50. Eang Weng Cheong, "The Decline of Manila as the Spanish Entrepôt in the Far East, 1785–1826: Its Impact on the Pattern of Southeast Asian Trade," *Journal of Southeast Asian Studies* 2.02 (1971): 142–58.

69   PNA, Documentos de Insurgentes, *Mindanao y Sulu,* 1749.

70   Authorities in Manila pursued a brutal campaign of siege, forced relocation and the destruction of local vessels and villages, made possible for the first time due to steamers with heavy canon. José Montero y Vidal, *Historia de la Pirateria Malayo Mahometans en Mindanao, Jolo, y Borneo* (Madrid: Imprenta de M. Tello, 1888): 34–51.

71   See Warren, *Sulu Zone,* 299–315. Ship registers for the port of Manila and records of duties charged on each vessel departing Manila harbor (*almojarifazgo*) found in the Philippines' national archives tell of growing economic interdependence between Manila and Jolo in this period. PNA, *Mindanao/Sulu 1803–1890,* "Relación de los 45 cautivios venidos de Jolo," 1–72.

72   The inevitable influx of European gold/silver and arms created a new zone, a space that had cultural and social consequences and soon transformed imperial projects. Trade pacts between some of these itinerate Taosug datus (administrators) with communities of east Borneo reflect the growing complexity of new kinds of polities created by boom economies. New players came into the fray, opening up rivers to trading corporations/partnerships. Socially, new patterns of intermarriage as alliances between new constituencies arose, reflecting developing strategies to conjoin indigenous forces against a common outside threat. Kennedy G. Tregonning, *A History of Modern Sabah, 1881–1963* (Singapore: University of Malaya Press, 1966): 186.

73   A Spanish report in 1842 offers an especially interesting, detailed, ethnography of the labor regime in the Sulu Sultanate. References to *banyaga* (slaves) who nevertheless had families and were married to "free" spouses, and then debt slaves or *kiapangdilihan,* who were expected to pay off their personal debt through labor, which often entailed being transported to plantations or harvesting expeditions into the jungles looking for products, are revealing insights into these otherwise dehumanized narratives about the Sulu/Taosug. PNA, *Mindanao/Sulu 1838–1885,* "El Gobierno Politico y Militar del Zamboanga a El Governador Capitan General," dated Manila, 30 May 1842.

74   From California, Samoa, Philippines, Central America, to Singapore, millions of Cantonese were pure and simply enslaved for years of their lives to service the labor demands of Euro-American companies, by the 1890s effectively eliminating all the competition with their "humanitarianism." John A. Moses, "The Coolie Labour Question and German Colonial Policy in Samoa, 1900–1914," *The Journal of Pacific History* 8.1 (1973): 101–24; Bill Willmott, "Chinese Contract Labour in the Pacific Islands during the Nineteenth Century," *Journal of Pacific Islands Studies* 27.2 (2004): 161–76; Luz Mercedes Hincapie, "Pacific Transactions: Nicolás Tanco Armero and the Chinese Coolie Trade to Cuba," *Journal of Iberian and Latin American Research* 16.1 (2010): 27–41 and James F. Warren, *Rickshaw Coolie: A People's History of Singapore, 1880–1940* (Honolulu: University of Hawaii Press, 2003).

75   Frank Welsh, *A History of Hong Kong* (London: HarperCollins, 1977): 120–5.

76   At the heart of this business were Indian tea (just being planted), opium, and British-manufactured goods. Over time, many of these Muslims established their own trading companies. Cassumbhoy Nathabboy & Co., operating in Canton since

the 1830s, for instance, became one of the more conspicuous modules of British capitalism's network in East Asia. Solomon Bard, *Traders of Hong Kong: Some Foreign Merchant Houses, 1841–1899* (Hong Kong: Urban Council, 1993): 90–1.

77 North Borneo is a fascinating story involving the Americans, the Austro-Hungarian Empire and eventually Hong Kong-based financiers and bankers in London. Kevin G. Tregonning, "American Activity in North Borneo, 1865–1881," *Pacific Historical Review* 23.4 (1954): 357–72. The Habsburg consul in Hong Kong, Baron von Overbeck, along with American banker Alfred Dunt obtained a lease in 1878 for vast areas of North Borneo. Crucially, they signed treaties with both the Sultan of Brunei and the Sultan of Sulu, who in the interim ten years had become a dominant political player in the region. These investments went for naught, and eventually von Overbeck sold the lease to investors who received a "royal" charter and became ostensibly sovereign in the area under the name North Borneo Chartered Company. The company, by recruiting Cantonese settlers, became an expansionist company state taking many territories of the Sulu Sultanate, which until today, along with the Philippines, makes the claim that the entire region was never ceded by the Spanish, thus legally should be returned to Manila. British North Borneo Chartered Company, *Handbook of the State of British North Borneo: Compiled from Reports of the Governor and Staff of North Borneo, with an Appendix Showing the Progress and Development of the State to the End of 1920* (Hong Kong: British North Borneo (Chartered) Company, 1921); Leigh R. Wright, "Historical Notes on the North Borneo Dispute," *The Journal of Asian Studies* 25.03 (1966): 471–84; Ian Black, *A Gambling Style of Government: The Establishment of the Chartered Company's Rule in Sabah, 1878–1915* (Kuala Lumpur: Oxford University Press, 1983) and Marc C. Cleary, "Plantation Agriculture and the Formulation of Native Land Rights in British North Borneo," *The Geographical Journal* 158.2 (1992): 170–81.

78 Julia Adams, "Principals and Agents, Colonialists and Company Men: The Decay of Colonial Control in the Dutch East Indies," *American Sociological Review* 61.1 (1996): 12–28.

79 Martin Slama, "Paths of Institutionalization, Varying Divisions, and Contested Radicalisms: Comparing Hadrami Communities on Java and Sulawesi," *CSSAAAME* 31.2 (2011): 331–42.

80 Of the long list of studies on British practices, the most recent and perhaps most theoretically interesting for the purposes of this book is John M. Willis, *Unmaking North and South: Cartographies of the Yemeni Past* (London: C. Hurst & Co., 2012): 17–44.

81 There is plenty of scholarship on the growing interest in genealogies. In this regard it is not worth adding to this fine scholarship with much detailed analysis of the mechanisms of asserting such linkages to the Arabian Peninsula, but it may be useful to consider the kind of resources invested in perpetuating these associations at a time when the British merchant companies are just beginning to gain a stranglehold on the region.

82 Kazuhiro Arai, *Arabs who Traversed the Indian Ocean: The History of the al-'Attas Family in Hadramawt and Southeast Asia, c. 1600–c.1960* (PhD Dissertation, University of Michigan, 2004).

83 Michael Gilsenan, "Translating Colonial Fortunes: Dilemmas of Inheritance in Muslim and English Laws across a Nineteenth-Century Diaspora," *Comparative Studies of South Asia, Africa and the Middle East* 31.2 (2011): 355–71.

84 William Reno, "Order and Commerce in Turbulent Areas: 19th Century Lessons, 21st Century Practice," *Third World Quarterly* 25.4 (2004): 607–25.

85 Those "pariah" intermediaries benefited from special access to those with unique links to supply chains. Upon agreement with local emirs, sometimes under direct threats not yet fully explored in the scholarship, "Coolie" labor from the Cantonese provinces, Burma, and Bengal flooded Southeast Asia and Oceania with community-breaking replacement labor. Throw in a small army of "white trash" and other "pariah" settlers and within one generation, an entirely new racial pyramid emerged. Allen J. Chun, "Pariah Capitalism and the Overseas Chinese of Southeast Asia: Problems in the Definition of the Problem," *Ethnic and Racial Studies* 12.2 (1989): 233–56; Adapa Satyanarayana, "'Birds of Passage': Migration of South Indian Laborers to Southeast Asia," *Critical Asian Studies* 34.1 (2002): 89–115 and Anand A. Yang, "Indian Convict Workers in Southeast Asia in the Late Eighteenth and Early Nineteenth Centuries," *Journal of World History* 14.2 (2003): 179–208.

86 Jonathan Goldstein, "Singapore, Manila and Harbin as Reference Points for Asian 'Port Jewish' Identity," *Jewish Culture and History* 7.1–2 (2004): 271–90 and Jonathan Goldstein, "The Sorkin and Golab Theses and their Applicability to South, Southeast, and East Asian Port Jewry," *Jewish Culture and History* 4.2 (2001): 179–96.

87 Thomas A. Timberg, "Baghdadi Jews in Indian Port Cities," *Jews in India* (New Delhi: Vikas Publishing House Private, 1986): 273–81.

88 It is also known that large numbers of Syrian Christians and Muslims migrated to Indochina—Vietnam, Laos, and Cambodia—during this heightened period of migration to Malay, Singapore, and Philippines. Guy Lacam, *Un banquier au Yunnan dans les annees 1930* (Paris: L'Harmattan, 1994): 194 and Marcel Ner, "Les musulmans de l'Indochine française," *Bulletin de l'Ecole Française d'Eztreme Orient* 41.2 (1941): 151–202, 153.

89 Caroline Plüss, "Baghdadi Jews in Hong Kong: Converting Cultural, Social and Economic Capital among Three Transregional Networks," *Global Networks* 11.1 (2011): 82–96 and Chiara Betta, "From Orientals to Imagined Britons: Baghdadi Jews in Shanghai," *Modern Asian Studies* 37.4 (2003): 999–1023.

90 Cecil Roth, *The Sassoon Dynasty* (London: Robert Hale Limited, 1941): 31–6.

91 Joan G. Roland, "Baghdadi Jews in India and China in the Nineteenth Century: A Comparison of Economic Roles," in Jonathan Goldstein (ed.), *The Jews of China: Historical and Comparative Perspectives*, vol. 1 (Armonk: M.E. Sharpe, 1999): 141–53.

92 The Sassoons became known as the Rothschilds of the East. Stanley Jackson, *The Sassoons* (London: Heineman, 1968). On the Sassoons' business interests in Persia, in direct competition with the Rothschilds by the way, see Thomas P. Brockway, "Britain and the Persian Bubble, 1888–92," *The Journal of Modern History* 13.1 (1941): 36–47, 40–1 and Staal to Giers, dated 21 May 1889 in Baron A. Meyendorff, *Correspondence diplomatique de M. de Staal* (Paris, 1929): II, 31.

93 Claude Marcovits, *The Global World of Indian Merchants, 1750–1947: Traders of Sind from Bukhara to Panama* (Cambridge: University of Cambridge Press, 2000): 20–4.

94 Carl A. Trocki, *Opium Empire and the Global Political Economy: A Study of the Asian Opium Trade* (London: Routledge, 1999): 120.

95 Roth, *The Sassoon Dynasty*, 98.

96 Many were able to enter into the game by becoming the bankers "making advances to an already established groups of dealers [essentially] purchasing the crop before it was even planted." C. A. Trocki, *Opium Empire*, 112–15 and Chiara Betta, "The Baghdadi Jewish Diaspora in Shanghai: Community, Commerce and Identities," *Sino-Judaica* 4 (2003): 81–104.

97   British authorities based in Shanghai complained that Ottoman Silas Aaron Hardoon, sold in 1917 "1600 pounds of opium despite the change in international laws." NAUK, FO 671/452, nos 212–13, dated London, 12 July 1918.

98   Chiara Betta, *Silas Aaron Hardoon (1851?–1931): Marginality and Adaptation in Shanghai* (PhD Dissertation, University of London: School of Oriental Studies, 1997).

99   Eze Nathan, *The History of Jews in Singapore, 1830–1945* (Singapore: Herbilu, 1987): 27.

100   Another prominent Arab family in Singapore, the al-Kafs, ran the largest property group in Singapore between 1886 and 1907. National Archives Singapore (NAS), Alkaf transcript, 1–4. The family eventually expanded to philanthropic work in Hadhramawt, building roads, schools, and textile mills, diversifying into shipping by the 1920s. NAS B000523, Syed Mohsen Alsagoff transcript, dated 15 January 1983. This was mirrored by the Alsagoff family, which was involved in transporting Muslim pilgrims to Arabia and linking the Indonesia archipelago. Ulrike Freitag, *Indian Ocean Migrants and State Formation: I Hadhramawt* (Leiden: Brill, 2003): 46–61.

101   In 1885, Arab families had a formidable stranglehold on property markets in several Dutch commercial hubs, including 20 percent of all lands in Surabaya and 15 percent in Batavia (Jakarta). These families were by-and-large major partners with the British. Rajeswary Ampalavanar Brown, "The Decline of Arab Capitalism in Southeast Asia," in Ahmed I. Abushouk and Ahmed I. Hassan (eds), *The Hadhrami Diaspora in Southeast Asia: Identity Maintenance or Assimilation?* (Leiden: Brill, 2009): 109–33, 114–15.

102   In fact, an officer suggested investing funds to pay for a number of Muslims in the Dutch East Indies to study English in India, thereby inculcating the idea that the English were "liberal" and the Dutch "selfish" in comparison. The idea was that new loyalties could be forged with a minimal amount of charity toward Dutch Muslim subjects. IOR L/PS/10/629, Secret Document no. 275, W. R. D. Beckett, British Consul in Batavia to Foreign Office, dated Batavia, 6 September 1917.

103   Margaret Sarkissian, "Armenians in South-East Asia," *Crossroads: An Interdisciplinary Journal of Southeast Asian Studies* (1987): 1–33, 10–13 and Ulbe Bosma, "The Cultivation System (1830–1870) and its Private Entrepreneurs on Colonial Java," *Journal of Southeast Asian Studies* 38.02 (2007): 275–91.

104   Mesrovb J. Seth, *History of the Armenians in India* (Delhi: Gian, 1988): 131–4.

105   Seth, *History of the Armenians*, 126. The Haj business where the al Saqqaf and al-Habshi families dominated with their ships entailed having 5 to 6 thousand travelers paying large sums outside the Dutch system, which proved detrimental to the companies that had secured the monopoly that had earlier chased the Ottoman Armenians out of Indonesia. See McDonnell, *The Conduct of the Hajj*, 626–30.

106   Martin Slama, "Translocal Networks and Globalisation within Indonesia: Exploring the Hadhrami Diaspora from the Archipelagos North-East," *Asian Journal of Social Science* 39.2 (2011): 238–57.

107   There are two ways of looking at this: first, often highlighted in the explosion of scholarship on the Hadhrami of the region, the almost confrontational relations induced by Dutch segregation policies may have helped "strengthen the sense of Arabness" that emerged with the rise of a "sense of racial difference" separating "hosts" and Hadrami. Sumit Kumar Mandal, *Finding their Place: A History of Arabs in Java under Dutch Rule, 1800–1924* (PhD Dissertation, Columbia University, 1994): 101. But these sharpening divides may work in

the other direction; perhaps the frustrations expressed may have resulted at the time (retrospective insights gleaned from interviews decades after the events notwithstanding) in another response from some Hadrami. Indeed, many advocated the strengthening of spiritual ties that united the "umma." It is thus curious to read how much and how quickly the sophisticated studies about identity-politics reaffirm racial, sectarian, and class divides that, in theory at least, should be open to skepticism. I suspect here that the Ottoman angle may help us step away from accepting so quickly the disaggregation that colonial propagandists eagerly sought in the 1878–1939 period.

108 Nico J. G. Kaptein, "Arabophobia and Tarekat: How Sayyid 'Uthman Became Advisor to the Netherlands Colonial Administration," in Ahmed I. Abushouk and Hassan A. Ibrahim (eds), *The Hadhrami Diaspora in Southeast Asia: Identity Maintenance or Assimilation* (Leiden: Brill, 2009): 33–44.

109 R. Michael Fenner, "Hybridity and the 'Hadhrami Diaspora' in the Indian Ocean Muslim Networks," *Asian Journal of Social Science* 32.3 (2004): 353–72.

110 On the tensions within Java induced in part by Dutch policies to instigate distrust and xenophobic lashing out at Arabs, see Huub de Jonge, "Discord and Solidarity among the Arabs in the Netherlands East Indies, 1990–1942," *Indonesia* 55 (1993): 73–90.

111 Smelling an opportunity, the British in Malay signed treaties of protection with a number of regional Sultans, including the Sultan of Sulu, whose authority at the time constituted a vast chain of islands linking the Celebes and Borneo to Mindanao. Martin Meadows, "The Philippine Claim to North Borneo," *Political Science Quarterly* 77.3 (1962): 321–35. As with much of the region, periodic rivalries between the leaders of autonomous polities all along the coastal areas of these highly coveted areas left encouraged local potentates to sign with any outside bidder. We know that the French, Spanish, and British all made constant overtures to these long independent peoples. In contrast to the Berlin Congress of 1885 that "diplomatically" allocated "spheres of influence" to participating European states in Africa, there was no such agreement to share the spoils of Southeast Asia; and the consequences of this for indigenous communities were far from uniform. James F. Warren, *The Sulu Zone*, 126–45.

112 "Turcos" or "Ottomanos" appear throughout the Manila Gazette (Gaceta de Manila, 1881), which reported significant numbers of Ottoman refugees/migrants arriving in 1881.

113 Lewis E. Gleeck, *American Business and Philippine Economic Development* (Manila: Carmelo and Bauermann, 1975): 181 and Kunio Yoshihara, *Philippine Industrialization: Foreign and Domestic Capital* (Singapore: Oxford University Press, 1985): 117.

114 See *Le Moniteur Officiel du Commerce/Manille* where the French consul in Manila offers an elaborate description of the Syrian trader, dated Manila 11 January 1894. French authorities based in American-occupied Manila began to conduct an annual census of its Arab subjects by way of it Mandate over Syria. In 1921, 127 Syrians registered with the French consul, considering themselves subjects of the French Republic. Kohei Hasimoto, "Lebanese Population Movement, 1920–1939: Towards a Study," in Albert Hourani and Nadim Shehadi (eds), *The Lebanese in the World: A Century of Emigration* (London: I.B. Taurus, 1992): 65–107, 96.

115 Arsan, "Failing to Stem the Tide," 460–2.

116 Gleeck, *American Business and Philippine Economic Development*, 187.

117   Clarence-Smith, "Middle Eastern Migrants," 431. Ottoman Jews from Syria were
       also part of this contingency making a living out of trans-continental trade, with
       apparent links with the major Chinese port cities. These links are still not well
       established in the scholarship on Ottoman Jewish migration to the Americas. For
       general studies see Liz Hamui de Halabe, *Los judíos de Alepo en México* (Mexico
       City: Maguén David, 1989) and Corinne Azen Krause, *The Jews in Mexico: A
       History with Special Emphasis on the Period from 1850 to 1930* (PhD Dissertation,
       University of Pittsburgh, 1970).
118   William G. Clarence-Smith, "Middle Eastern Entrepreneurs in South East Asia, c.
       1750–c. 1940," in Ina Baghdiantz McCabe, Gelina Iarlaftis, and Ioanna P. Minoglou
       (eds), *Diaspora Entrepreneurial Networks: Four Centuries of History* (London: Berg,
       2005): 217–44.
119   For instance, Josef Abraham of Syria was granted the right of entry on 10 July 1891,
       PNA, Radicacion de Estrangeros, 1871–95, SDS 1755 for a complete list of Ottoman
       subjects arriving in Manila.
120   Clarence-Smith, "Middle Eastern Entrepreneurs in South East Asia," 234.
121   Sarah Gualtieri, "'Becoming White': Race, Religion and the Foundations of Syrian/
       Lebanese Ethnicity in the United States," *Journal of American Ethnic History* (2001):
       29–58 and Akram Khater, *Inventing Home: Emigration, Gender, and the Middle Class
       in Lebanon, 1870–1920* (Berkeley: University of California Press, 2001): 74.
122   Ignácio Klich, "Criollos and Arabic Speakers in Argentina: An Uneasy Pas de Deux,
       1888–1914," in Albert Hourani and Nadim Shehabi (eds), *The Lebanese in the
       World: A Century of Emigration* (London: I.B. Tauris, 1992): 243–83, 273.
123   Charles Knowlton, *Sírios e libaneses em São Paulo* (São Paulo: Editora Anhembi,
       1961): 23–49.
124   In 1907 Ottoman-owned businesses were listed, mostly focused on the sale of
       clothing and dry goods. By 1920, they owned at least 91 factories, which may have
       consisted of 4 or 5 workers in someone's home or a rented room, usually to make
       cloths. see Knowlton, *Sírios e libaneses em São Paulo*, 143. This would only expand
       to 468 of the 800 listed retail stores in the growing city.
125   Şevket Pamuk and Jeffrey G. Williamson, "Ottoman De-industrialization, 1800–
       1913: Assessing the Magnitude, Impact, and Response," *The Economic History
       Review* 64.1 (2011): 159–84.
126   Herbert H. Miller, *Economic Conditions in the Philippines* (Boston: Ginn & Co.,
       1920): 416–17.
127   Gleeck, *American Business and Philippine Economic*, 69–73. These operations got
       so big that by 1918, upwards of 60,000 women were working in these factories.
       By the interwar period the Ismailis from Lebanon were so influential as traders
       that they became the representatives of Winthrop-Stearns, the American
       pharmaceuticals company, Gleeck, *American Business and Philippine Economic*, 145.
       They also became major owners of real estate in Manila, see Yoshihara, *Philippine
       Industrialization*, 117. In a manner of years, through intermarriages with the Syrian
       Catholic families—Hashim and Hemadi—these new "Lebanese" conglomerates
       cornered the Manila property market, see Carlos Quirino, *Philippine Tycoon:
       The Biography of an Industrialist, Vincente Madrigal* (Manila: Madrigal Memorial
       Foundation, 1987): 53. As an interesting side note, the Hashim family owned
       the Manila Grand Opera House, see Gleeck, *American Business and Philippine
       Economic*, 96.

128 Some have argued that the Ottoman Sultan had the loyalty of the Sultan of Sulu and that first the Spanish and later the Americans observed that Arabs ". . . come [to Mindanao] under the guise of Koran expounders to feed on the people and whet their animosity towards Christians." Clarence-Smith, "Middle Eastern Migrants in the Philippines," 428.

129 Vicente L. Rafael, "White Love: Surveillance and Nationalist Resistance in the US Colonization of the Philippines," in Amy Kaplan and Donald E. Pease (eds), *Cultures of United States Imperialism* (Raleigh: Duke University Press, 1993): 185–218.

130 USNA RG 350/5/5075, Report of Brigadier-General George Davis, dated 24 October 1901, p. 2.

131 Charles Byler, "Pacifying the Moros: American Military Government in the Southern Philippines, 1899–1913," *Military Review* (May–June 2005): 41–5; Vic Hurley, *Jungle Patrol, the Story of the Philippine Constabulary (1901–1936)* (Dallas: Cerberus Books, 2011) and Michael C. Hawkins, "Managing a Massacre: Savagery, Civility, and Gender in Moro Province in the Wake of Bud Dajo," *Philippine Studies* 59.1 (2011): 83–105.

132 Frank E. Vandiver, *Black Jack: The Life and Times of John J. Pershing,* vol. 1 (College Station: TAMU Press, 1977); Geoffrey Hunt, *Colorado's Volunteer Infantry in the Philippine Wars, 1898–1899* (Albuquerque: University of New Mexico Press, 2006) and Donald Smythe, "Pershing and the Disarmament of the Moros," *Pacific Historical Review* 31.3 (1962): 241–56.

133 For official reports on the battle by the US Military, see USNA RG 94, Consolidated Rile no. 1108562, Report of Engagement, Wood to Secretary of War, dated 22 April 1905 [*sic*] and USNA RG 94, Bud Dajo Cons. File, NARA, "Deposition of Corp. James R. Miller, 6th Infantry, dated 3 June 1906. The battle proved an especially sensational event for the press, with a combination of glee in that 'six hundred outlaws killed to the last man . . .'" *Daily Review* (Decatur, Illinois) dated, 9 March 1906, and uneasiness of the ". . . terrible slaughter." *Trenton Times,* dated 9 March 1906, and then incrimination of the policy of President Taft and his appointed Governor of the Sulu Archipelago, Major Hugh Lenox Scott: "Battle on Mount Daajo [*sic*] was One of Extermination," *Washington Post,* dated 10 March 1906 and "Policy Caused the Needless Killing of Moro Women and Children," *New York Times,* dated 12 March 1906 and Moorfield Storey, *The Moro Massacre* (Boston, MA: The Anti-Imperialist League, 1906). For a study of the battle and the political scandal that followed, consult Robert. A. Fulton, *Honor for the Flag: The Battle of Bud Dajo-1906 and the Moro Massacre* (Bend, OR: Tumalo Creek Press, 2011): 12–52.

134 Robert Vitalis, "The Graceful and Generous Liberal Gesture: Making Racism Invisible in American International Relations," *Millennium-London School of Economics* 29.2 (2000): 331–56.

135 The Bates Agreement of 1899, barely a year into America's imperial stretch to the Philippines, would defer governance of the vast region of the Sulu islands to the Sultan in return for his acknowledgment that the Americans held sovereignty over the rest of the Philippines. A. J. Bacevich, "Disagreeable Work: Pacifying the Moros, 1903–1906," *Military Review* (June 1982): 50–1.

136 Peter G. Gowing, *Mandate in Moroland: The American Government of Muslim Filipinos, 1899–1920* (Quezon City: University of Philippines System, 1977): 47–57, 64–5.

137   Michael Hawkins, "Imperial Historicism and American Military Rule in the
      Philippines' Muslim South," *Journal of Southeast Asian Studies* 39.3 (2008): 411–29.
138   A reflection of the extent to which racist characterizations of the Taosug peoples
      resisting American forces in Sulu and Mindanao became an issue for propagandist
      in the States is Henry W. Savage's popular musical comedy entitled the "Sultan of
      Sulu," which made its rounds in American theaters in 1903. Paul Antonie Distler,
      "Exit the Racial Comics," *Educational Theatre Journal* 18.3 (1966): 247–54 and Jim
      McPherson, "The Savage Innocents: Part I, King of the Castle: Henry W. Savage and
      the Castle Square Opera Company," *The Opera Quarterly* 18.4 (2002): 503–33.
139   Appointed Secretary of Education in the Philippines from 1900, the future President
      of the University of California (1919 to 1923) wrote several useful monographs
      on the region. Most relevant here is his work as an Anthropologist, for which
      he received a PhD from the University of Chicago in 1897. See David Barrows,
      "History of the Population," *Census of the Philippine Islands, 1903. Volume I:
      Geography, History, and Population* (Washington, DC: United States Bureau of
      Census, 1905).
140   Similar conflicted sentiments—begrudging admiration for a worthy enemy—are
      evident in memoirs published years later, for instance, Vic Hurley, *Swish of the
      Kris: The Story of the Moros* (New York: E. P. Dutton & Co., Inc., 2011) and
      Daniel G. Miller, *American Military Strategy during the Moro Insurrection in the
      Philippines, 1903-1913* (KS: Army Command and General Staff College Fort
      Leavenworth, 2009).
141   Jeffrey Ayala Milligan, "Democratization or Neocolonialism? The Education of
      Muslims under US Military Occupation, 1903–20," *History of Education* 33.4 (2004):
      451–67.
142   Najeeb M. Saleeby, originally from the Beirut area, studied medicine after arriving
      in the United States, eventually becoming a US Army surgeon, a position that
      required his services in the Philippines. Gowing, *Mandate in Moroland*, 112,
      133–4.
143   Najeeb M. Saleeby, *Studies in Moro History, Law, and Religion* (Manila: Bureau of
      Public Printing, 1905).
144   Najeeb M. Saleeby, *The Moro Problem: An Academic Discussion of the History and
      Solution of the Problem of the Government of the Moros in the Philippine Islands*
      (Manila: P.I., 1913) and Najeeb M. Saleeby, *The History of Sulu* (Manila: Bureau of
      Printing, 1908).
145   Gowing, *Mandate in Moroland*, 218.
146   Gowing, *Mandate in Moroland*, 279–81.
147   Indeed, while the Americans recruited an Ottoman subject, apparently seconded
      by the Sultan's palace itself, there were other foreign (non-native) Muslims
      infiltrating to spur on locals to continue fighting the American invaders.
      One Habib Muhammad Masdali was deported in 1904 for proselytizing and
      encouraging peoples in the Sulu Islands to take up arms anew. The presence of
      such "Arabs" continued to be an issue for Americans. In 1913, for instance, Arab
      "teachers" used schools to spurn on resistance. See Gowing, *Mandate in Moroland*,
      154–9. Such "missionary" activities by foreign Arabs (presumably all from
      Ottoman territories) continued as reports of their arrest appear as late as 1920 in
      Zamboanga, Mindanao. See Gleeck, *American Business and Philippine Economic
      Development*, 76.

Chapter 5

1   John Ferris, "'The Internationalism of Islam': The British Perception of a Muslim Menace, 1840–1951," *Intelligence and National Security* 24.1 (2009): 57–77.

2   This was also most certainly related to the empire's investment in streamlining the way its subjects—again, of all denominations—were educated, both in respect to their faith and increasingly in more secular terms. Benjamin C. Fortna, *Imperial Classroom: Islam, the State, and Education in the Late Ottoman Empire* (New York: Oxford University Press, 2002); Cem Emrence, *Remapping the Ottoman Middle East: Modernity, Imperial Bureaucracy and the Islamic State* (London: I.B. Tauris, 2011); and Emine Evered, *Empire and Education under the Ottomans: Politics, Reform and Resistance from the Tanzimat to the Young Turks* (London: I.B. Tauris, 2012).

3   Blumi, *Reinstating the Ottomans*, 151–73.

4   Cemil Aydin, "The Politics of Conceptualizing Islam and the West," *Ethics & International Affairs* 18.3 (2004): 89–96.

5   Perhaps Ottoman historians who wish to explore links between collective action and any possible identification with religion can take time from their deciphering documents and read what anthropologists have been arguing about for decades now regarding the complex associations communities rely on when exploring even their spiritual orientations vis-à-vis a changing larger world. Talal Asad and Charles Hirschkind in particular come to mind.

6   As Michael Reynolds rightly concludes by observing the activities of Chechen rebels against Russian forces in the North Caucasus, "Contrary to the assumption that pan-Islam was an Ottoman product that inflamed local tensions between the Russian state and its Muslims, such tensions at times produced pan-Islamic sympathies that were *exported* to the Ottoman Empire" [emphasis mine]. Reynolds, *Shattering Empires*, 91.

7   Dimitris Stamatopoulos, "Ecumenical Ideology in the Orthodox Millet (19th-20th Century)," in Lorans T. Taruh and Vangelis Kechriotis (eds), *Economy and Society on Both Shores of the Aegean* (Athens: Alpha Bank, 2010): 201–47.

8   Janet Klein, *The Margins of Empire: Kurdish Militias in the Ottoman Tribal Zone* (Palo Alto: Stanford University Press, 2011): 15–18.

9   For an introduction to Sufism that is relevant to the larger intentions of this chapter, consult Alexander D. Knysh, *Islamic Mysticism: A Short History* (Leiden: Brill, 2000).

10 See Brian Silverstein, "Sufism and Governmentality in the Late Ottoman Empire," *CSSAAME* 29.2 (2009): 171–85 and Mustafa Kara, "İkinci meşrutiyet devrinde dervişlerin sosyal ve kültürel etkinlikleri," in Ahmed Yaşar Ocak (ed.), *Osmanlı toplumunda tasavvuf ve sufiler* (Ankara: Türk Tarih Kurumu, 2005): 533–8.

11 Silverstein, "Sufism and Governmentality," 194.

12 Silverstein, "Sufism and Governmentality," 196.

13 BBA, Irade Dahiliye 23192, Message to newly appointed administrator of Shkodër, Mustafa Pasha, dated 1856, folio 1.

14 Blumi, *Reinstating the Ottomans*, 76–8.

15 Thierry Zarcone, *Mystiques, philosophes et francs-maçons en Islam. Riza Tevfik penseur ottoman (1868–1949), du soufisme à la confrérie* (Paris: Jean Maisonneuve, 1993): 139–43. and Bilgin Aydın, "Osmanlı devlet'inde tekkeler reform ve Meclis-i Meşayıh'ın Şeyhülislamlık'a bağlı olarak kuruluşu, faaliyetleri ve arşivi," *Istanbul Araştırmaları* 7 (1998): 93–109, 98.

16 Silverstein, "Sufism and Governmentality," 197.

17   For more details see Aydın, "Osmanlı devlet'inde tekkeler reform," 93–109.

18   It is with the revolution of 1908, when many refugees from what became Russia
     rose to power within the CUP, that we really begin to see the Ottoman government
     making an effort to harness religion for a multiplicity of purposes. The CUP (or
     unionists) frequently intervened to assure pliant members sympathetic to their larger
     agenda dominated the Council's institutions across all the permitted Sufi orders. The
     Nakshibandi *tekke* of Mustafa İsmet Efendi in Istanbul, for instance, had one Shaykh
     Mustafa Hak imposed on it as its leader because he was a Unionist deputy from
     Bursa and a demonstrated apparatchik. See Ismail Kara, "Meclis-i Meşyaih, Ulema-
     Tarikat Münasebetleri ve İstanbul'da Şeyhlik Yapmış Beş Zatın Kendi Kaleminden
     Terceme-i Hali," *Kutadgubilig* (Istanbul) 1 (Ocak 2002): 185–214. This changed after
     the Balkan Wars where almost all of the disparate Sufi lodges in the Balkans were
     suddenly contributing to the refugee flood toward Anatolia. It is at this juncture that
     the state considered imposing new direct surveillance and ostensibly began applying
     centralization because of a sad, tragic set of events that completely uprooted hitherto
     autonomous religious practices (and practitioners). This speaks to another factor to
     being a destitute refugee; state institutions begin to grow more important for one's
     very survival, and, if harnessed quickly, lead to the expansion of power into the hands
     of bureaucrats. This situation quickly gained political importance as the CUP, upon
     taking power in 1908, used just such situations to expand state authority in areas
     where it never existed before.

19   Nurulwahidah Fauzi, Ali Mohammad, and Saim Kayadibi, "The Religious-intellectual
     Network: The Arrival of Islam in the Archipelago," *Ottoman Connections to the Malay
     World: Islam, Law and Society* (Kuala Lumpur: Islamic Book Trust, 2011): 1–31.

20   Henri Lauzière, "The Construction of Salafiyya: Reconsidering Salafism from the
     Perspective of Conceptual History," *IJMES* 42.3 (2010): 369–89.

21   In this regard, the British administration in Egypt played a role as they sought to
     manage anti-Hamidian forces. They did this by openly encouraging Arabic-speaking
     (as well as Balkan) exiles, especially religious scholars, to establish a presence in
     Egypt. See Hanioğlu, *Preparation for a Revolution*, 67–73 and Kamran I. Karimullah,
     "Rival Moral Traditions in the Late Ottoman Empire, 1839–1908," *Journal of Islamic
     Studies* 24.1 (2013): 37–66.

22   As such, the kind of exchanges taking place between ostensibly British subjects
     around the jurisdiction of a "Caliphate" is directly informed by that fact. Often this
     British imperial context is obscured by stories that aim to address the larger trends of
     scholarship fixated on how Muslims sought to adjust to changes within "Islam" or its
     presumed institutions rather than a critical interplay between disparate forces. John
     Willis, "Debating the Caliphate: Islam and Nation in the Work of Rashid Rida and
     Abdul Kalam Azad," *The International History Review* 32.4 (December 2010): 711–32.
     See also Ş. Tufan Buzpınar, "Opposition to the Ottoman Caliphate in the Early Years
     of Abdülhamid II: 1877–1882," *Die Welt des Islams* 36.1 (1996): 59–89.

23   Not only is the notion of an "Arab cultural awakening" problematic, but the heavy
     emphasis on a particularly "European" imprint on this necessary transformation
     again hints at larger ideological fixations with centering Europe in global history
     rather than exploring a diverse, often indigenous, set of contexts to help account for
     such dynamic periods of transformation. Daniel Newman, "The European Influence
     on Arabic during the Nahda: Lexical Borrowing from European Languages (ta'rib) in
     19th-century Literature," *Arabic Language and Literature* 5.2 (2002): 1–32 and Stefan
     Wild, "Islamic Enlightenment and the Paradox of Averroes," *Die Welt des Islams* 36.3
     (1996): 379–90.

24 Vincent Viaene, "International History, Religious History, Catholic History: Perspectives for Cross-Fertilization (1830–1914)," *European History Quarterly* 38.4 (2008): 578–607 and Abigail Green, "Nationalism and the 'Jewish International': Religious Internationalism in Europe and the Middle East c. 1840–c. 1880," *CSSH* 50.2 (2008): 535–58.

25 Christopher Bayly, *The Birth of the Modern World, 1780–1914* (Oxford: Blackwell, 2004), chapter 9.

26 Green has identified a certain dynamic of exchange that enabled for perhaps the first time, disparate, isolated Jewish communities to begin to think in global, unified terms. As a product of "Religious Internationalism" that may have helped transform the way people associated their faith with a larger community, the very emergence of "Jewish" identities becomes meaningful as an organizing principle in face of the ruptures soon to redraw the world's map. Green, "Nationalism and the 'Jewish International,'" 536–7.

27 Makdisi, *The Culture of Sectarianism*, chapter 1 and Green, "Nationalism and the 'Jewish International,'" 538–9.

28 In the Ottoman context, the Kâdirîhâne (Qadriyya) of Istanbul (mother-lodge of the Rûmiye sub-order of the Kâdiriye), was founded by Ismâ'il Rûmî in the seventeenth century. Again within the Ottoman Empire, in Istanbul and at times, in a wider geographic area, this lodge/order became a centralized institution over time. This central lodge appointed the Kâdirî shaykhs (Rûmî branch) who were supposed to cover the entire empire. In this regard, the disparate lodges situated in diverse locales as Hama (Syria) and Baghdad seem to have been adherents to organizational principles established in Istanbul. This does not, however, help argue that the Qadiriyya were in any way a "centralized" order with a hierarchy whose head, based in Istanbul, had any meaningful influence on how loosely affiliated member *tekkes* in East Africa or even Mecca, engaged their very specific constituent needs. For a useful summary, top-down history of the Qadriyya and other Sufi orders in the Ottoman Empire in the context of reforms in the last century of Ottoman rule, see Thierry Zarcone, "Shaykh Succession in Turkish Sufi Lineages (19th and 20th Centuries): Conflicts, Reforms and Transmission of Spiritual Enlightenment," *Asian and African Studies* 7.1 (2007): 18–35, 20–1.

29 The arena for debate about what constituted the Ottoman experience inevitably spilled into a growing awareness that the Muslim context reached far and wide. The Indian Ocean's well-established links for centuries with the Eastern Mediterranean meant regular contacts would invariably mean continued interest in the affairs of Muslim communities in Asia. The idea that a "globalizing Arabic media" in the late Ottoman and early post-Ottoman periods helped manufacture an Islamic space where information and opinions were circulated, debated and exchanged, may prove too eager to link "modern" forms of exchange to the changes. Yes, the newspaper contributed to how Ottoman readers secured information about Muslim inhabitants scattered throughout the world, but the ties were surely appreciated well before the newspaper. Michael Laffan, "'Another Andalusia': Images of Colonial Southeast Asia in Arabic Newspapers," *Journal of Asian Studies* 66 (2007): 689–722.

30 Robert W. Strayer, *The Making of Mission Communities in East Africa: Anglicans and Africans in Colonial Kenya, 1875–1935* (New York: Heinemann Educational Publishers, 1978): 25–64.

31 August Nimtz Jr, *Islam and Politics in East Africa: The Sufi Order in Tanzania* (Minneapolis: University of Minnesota Press, 1980) and Alessandra Vianello, "One

Hundred Years in Brava: The Migration of the 'Umar Bā 'Umar from Hadhramaut to East Africa and Back, c. 1890–1990," *Journal of Eastern African Studies* 6.4 (2012): 655–71. For an exploration of how genealogy may contribute to forging these transient groups, see Engseng Ho, *The Graves of Tarim: Genealogy and Mobility across the Indian Ocean* (Berkeley: University of California Press, 2006): 28, 37–41, 209.

32 Brad G. Martin, *Muslim Brotherhoods in 19th Century Africa* (Cambridge: Cambridge University Press, 1976). Brad G. Martin, "Muslim Politics and Resistance to Colonial Rule: Shaykh Uways B. Muhammad Al-Barawi and the Qadiriya Brotherhood in East Africa," *Journal of African History* 10.3 (1969): 471–86.

33 Deogratias K. Bimanyu, *The Waungwana of Eastern Zaire: 1880–1900* (PhD Dissertation, School of Oriental and African Studies, University of London, 1976): 124–74.

34 The resulting population known today as Ganda Muslims are largely excluded from the national narratives of twentieth-century states. Their significance in the day-to-day politics of these contested regions cannot, however, be ignored if we are to fully appreciate the linkages between migration flows, political, and economic alliances, and the kind of European imperialism that eventually established a foothold in these areas.

35 E. R. Turton (1970), "Kirk and the Egyptian Invasion of East Africa in 1875: A Reassessment," *The Journal of African History* 11.3 (1970): 355–70.

36 Marina Tolmacheva, "'They Came from Damascus in Syria': A Note on Traditional Lamu Historiography," *The International Journal of African Historical Studies* 12.2 (1979): 259–69.

37 The Swahili arrival to these hinterland regions of Buganda is dated to only 1840. Initial parities of missionaries were actually recruited by ruler Kabaka Suna (1830–56) who recognized the commercial opportunities for locals who could open links to the coastal Swahili/Omani regions. Kabaka Mutesa, succeeding his father in the late 1850s, extended this overture by formally incorporating Islamic practices, an attempt to symbolically reflect the commercial fusion with the hitherto inaccessible trade opportunities with the coast. See Arye Oded, *Islam in Uganda: Islamization through a Centralized State in Pre-Colonial Africa* (London: Wiley, 1974); Christopher Wrigley, *Kinship and State: The Buganda Dynasty* (Cambridge: Cambridge University Press, 1996); Benjamin Ray, *Myth, Ritual and Kingship in Buganda* (London: Oxford University Press, 1991).

38 Michael Twaddle, "The Muslim Revolution in Buganda," *African Affairs* 71.282 (1972): 54–72.

39 By the 1880s there were Indian bankers such as the "the Ivory King of Zanzibar," Ratu Bimji, and other banyans like Ladda Damji, who financed these expeditions on behalf of the Zanzibar sultan, Sayyid Majid. At the same time, however, they also managed Zanzibar's customs house, gaining considerable influence when British administrators in Bombay made their initial overtures for collaboration with willing local intermediaries. Richard W. Beachey, "The East African Ivory Trade in the Nineteenth Century," *Journal of African History* 8.2 (1967): 269–90. There were also local Muslim bankers, Nur Muhammad and Warsi Adwani in particular, whose place in the regional economy had been secured by profits from these earlier expeditions involving Qadiriyya missionaries into the hinterland. In fact, it was an Indian Muslim by the name of Jan Muhammad Hansraj who financed Tippu Tip's expedition in 1882, the same expedition that led to the creation of a vast ivory network linking the Congo Muslim/Arab enclaves of Kisinga and Katanga to

Tabora and Dar es-Salam. Leda Farrant, *Tippu Tip and the East African Slave Trade* (London: Hamilton, 1975): 78–86.

40 For a useful assessment of Qadiriyya in their larger institutional context, see Martin, *Muslim Brotherhoods*, 158–76. Such expansion was propagated further by scholars like 'Abd al-'Aziz b. al-Amawi and Muhammad al-Ma'ruf who introduced Shadhiliyya to Comoros Islands and Zanzibar, especially the Yashrutiyya branch. By 1894 Qadiriyya *tekkes* were established as the dominant order in Tabora, Ujiji, and beyond; it has remained this way since. John Iliffe, *A Modern History of Tanganyika* (Cambridge: Cambridge University Press, 1979): 212.

41 Jonathan Glassman, *Feasts and Riot: Revelry, Rebellion, and Popular Consciousness on the Swahili Coast, 1856–1888* (Portsmouth, NH: Heinemann, 1995).

42 Page, "The Manyema Hordes of Tippu Tip," 69–84.

43 Patrick Brantlinger, "Victorians and Africans: The Genealogy of the Myth of the Dark Continent," *Critical Inquiry* 12.1 (1985): 166–203.

44 Stephen J. Rockel, "Slavery and Freedom in Nineteenth Century East Africa: The Case of Waungwana Caravan Porters," *African Studies* 68.1 (2009): 87–109.

45 Janet McIntosh, *The Edge of Islam: Power, Personhood, and Ethnoreligious Boundaries on the Kenya Coast* (Raleigh: Duke University Press Books, 2009): 48–9, 138.

46 Anne Bang, *Sufis and Scholars of the Sea: Family Networks in East Africa, 1860–1925* (London: RoutledgeCurzon 2003): 133–6.

47 Scholars often jump to conclusions when they discover that locals in far-away places read regularly "influential" newspapers published by men like Rashid Rida, whose *al-Manar* (the beacon) serves as the quintessential emblem of "Islamic internationalism." It is not clear, however, how significant it is that someone reads one of many journals of the time. Should scholars today really trust that this offers a clue to the larger orientation of that society? One only need to look at the libraries of those kinds of people able to afford paying for a subscription of *al-Manar* to realize they were very broad readers indeed. Anne K. Bang, "Authority and Piety, Writing and Print: A Preliminary Study of the Circulation of Islamic Texts in Late Nineteenth- and Early Twentieth-Century Zanzibar," *Africa* 81.1 (2011): 89–107. Unfortunately, another methodological flaw that decontextualizes the reader's role is that articles in *Manar* are often treated as accurately reflecting the internal religious and social tensions existing in various different Muslim contexts simply because a few members of these communities read and write letters to the editors of the paper. Jutta Bluhm-Warn, "Al-Manar and Ahmad Soorkattie: Links in the Chain of Transmission on Muhammad 'Abudh's Ideas to the Malay-Speaking World," in Peter G. Riddell and Tony Street (eds), *Islam: Essays on Scripture, Thought and Society* (Leidin: Brill, 1997): 295–308, 298; Mona Abaza, "Southeast Asia and the Middle East: Al-Manar and Islamic Modernity," in Claude Guillot, Denys Lombard, and Roderich Ptak (eds), *From the Mediterranean to the China Sea: Miscellaneous Notes* (Wiesbaden: Harrassowitz Verlag, 1998): 93–111 and Jajat Burhanuddin, "Aspiring for Islamic Reform: Southeast Asian Requests for Fatwas in al-Manar," *Islamic Law and Society* 12.1 (2005): 9–26.

48 Much of this chapter's focus on these important scholars is reliant on the masterful work of Anne Bang, whose tireless pursuit of these crucial Sufi spaces in the Red Sea and larger Indian Ocean remains neglected by scholars working in these sub-fields.

49 See Bang, *Sufis and Scholars*, 134–5.

50 Natalie Mobini-Kesheh, *The Hadrami Awakening: Community and Identity in the Netherlands East Indies, 1900–1942* (Ithaca: Cornell University Press, 1999); M. C.

Ricklefs, "The Middle East Connection and Reform and Revival Movements among the Putihan in 19th Century Java," in Eric Tagliacozzo (ed.), *Southeast Asia and the Middle East: Islam, Movement, and the Longue Duree* (Paolo Alto: Stanford University Press, 2009): 111–34.

51 Not much has changed since the 1960s in this regard, with perhaps more emphasis on the apparent link of "Arab Nationalism" as a necessary by-product of "modernism." Compare Malcolm H. Kerr, *Islamic Reform: The Political and Legal Theories of Muhammad Abduh and Rashid Rida* (Berkeley: University of California Press, 1966) and Mansoor Moaddel, *Islamic Modernism, Nationalism, and Fundamentalism: Episode and Discourse* (Chicago: University of Chicago Press, 2005).

52 Having wrote and taught in an era when the first printing press came to Mecca, Dahlan was able to disseminate his challenges to Salafism through his devoted students. He wrote, for instance, a booklet outlining the suffering Wahhabis brought to Mecca during their rule in the first quarter of the nineteenth century, *Fitnat al-Wahhabiyyah*, and also a study refuting the entire Wahhabi doctrine and practices, *Al Durar al-Saniyyah fi al-Raddi 'alal-Wahhabiyyah*. He was a man who used history, most interestingly, to make his larger claims. This strategy was perhaps the model for his future students to begin their missionary work in Central Africa in the 1880s. In particular, it is suggested that his history of Islam's expansion into distant lands, *Al-Futuhat al-Islamiyyah* (1884), contributed to the subsequent wave of debate over the validity of Wahhabi-inspired doctrines in the larger world. On this particular text's reference to the Mahdi uprising against the British in 1881, see Heather J. Sharkey, "Ahmad Zayni Dahlan's al-Futuhat al-Islamiyya: A Contemporary View of the Sudanese Mahdi," *Sudanic Africa* 5 (1994): 67–75.

53 Bang, *Sufis and Scholars*, 75.

54 Indeed, there was a quietism with Javanese or Malay reformists who most modeled their activism after the salafists based in Cairo. So-called Islamic modernism and the linked *Irshad* movement in Java often tried to account for the collective expression of discord with events transpiring in the world by engaging with the spiritual polemics raised by Ottoman-based thinkers. It is crucial to remember that this is the social and intellectual environment from which the 'Alawiyya missionaries heading off to East Africa came. Indeed, it is likely that their families still based in Southeast Asia, out of clannish loyalty to the elite circles in which they operated, actually embraced the *nahda* sensibilities that Dahlan's disciples decried as being apologistic for British power. For some studies on these connections between British-dominated Cairo and Southeast Asian intellectual parvenus, see Mona Abaza, *Indonesian Students in Cairo: Islamic Education, Perceptions and Exchanges* (Paris: Cahier d'Archipel, 1994); Peter Riddel, *Islam and the Malay-Indonesian World: Transmission and Responses* (Honolulu: University of Hawai'I Press, 2001); Natalie Mobini-Kesheh, "Islamic Modernism in Colonial Java: The al-Irshad Movement," in U. Freitag and W. F. Clarence-Smith (eds), *Hadrami Traders, Scholars, and Statesmen in the Indian Ocean, 1750s–1960s* (Leiden: Brill, 1997): 185–98 and Muhammad Nur b. Muhammad Khayr al-Ansari, *Ta'rikh Harakat al-Irshad wa al-Islah wa-shaykh al-Irshadiyyin Ahmad Muhammad Surkitti fi Indunisiya* (Kuala Lumpur: International Islamic University, 2000). Articles found in *Manar* have long been treated as reflective of the internal religious and social tensions existing in various different Muslim contexts due to the changing consciousness of Muslims in the Malay-Indonesian archipelago. Bluhm-Warn, "Al-Manar and Ahmad Soorkattie," 298; Abaza, "Southeast Asia and the Middle East," 103–7 and Burhanuddin, "Aspiring for Islamic Reform," 9–16.

55 Seema Alavi, "'Fugitive Mullahs and Outlawed Fanatics': Indian Muslims in Nineteenth Century Trans-Asiatic Imperial Rivalries," *Modern Asian Studies* 45.6 (2011): 1337–82.

56 One recent attempt to place Fadl Pasha in a larger transitional context warrants exploring in conjunction with what is argued here, Wilson Chacko Jacob, "Of Angels and Men: Sayyid Fadl b. 'Alawi and Two Moments of Sovereignty," *Arab Studies Journal*, vol. XX, no. 1 (Spring 2012): 40–72.

57 Stephen F. Dale, *Islamic Society on the South Asian Frontier: The Mappilas of Malabar, 1498–1922* (Oxford: Clarendon, 1980): 43–54.

58 Christopher A. Bayly, *Indian Society and the Making of the British Empire* (Cambridge: Cambridge University Press, 1980): 88–146.

59 L. R. S. Lakshmi, *The Malabar Muslims: A Different Perspective* (Cambridge: Cambridge University Press, 2012).

60 Stephen F. Dale, "The Mappilla Outbreaks: Ideology and Social Conflict in Nineteenth-Century Kerala," *The Journal of Asian Studies* 35.1 (1975): 85–97.

61 Ş. Tufan Buzpinar, "Abdulhamid II and Sayyid Fadl Pasha of Hadramawt: An Arab Dignitary's Ambitions, 1876–1900," *Journal of Ottoman Studies* 13 (1993): 227–39.

62 John M. Landau, *The Politics of Pan-Islam: Ideology and Organization* (Oxford: Clarendon Press, 1990): 321–3 and Dale, *Islamic Society*, 119–52.

63 Bang, *Sufis and Scholars*, 68–9, 78.

64 Bang, *Sufis and Scholars*, 78–123. For a provocative reading of Fadl's work that tried to mediate between the role of the individual and changes in government taking place at the time, see Jacob, "Of Angels and Men," 49–60.

65 Blumi, *Chaos in Yemen*, chapter 2.

66 Abdallah S. Farsy and Randall L. Pouwels, *The Shafi'i Ulama of East Africa, c. 1830–1970: A Hagiographic Account* (Madison: University of Wisconsin Press, 1989): 159. It appears that the Sultan considered Fadl Pasha's plans for Dhofar and that this may have played a role in the uprisings against Sayyid Tukri of Muscat. Françoise Le Guennec-Coppens, "Changing Patterns of Hadhrami Migration and Social Integration in East Africa," in U. Freitag and W. G. Clarence-Smith (eds), *Hadhrami Traders*, 157–74 and Bernd Radtke, *The Exoteric Ahmad Ibn Idris: A Sufi's Critique of the Madhahib and the Wahhabis* (Leiden: Brill, 2000): 191.

67 Landau, *The Politics of Pan-Islam*, 71.

68 Bang, *Sufis and Scholars*, 88.

69 See also Kemal Karpat, *The Politicization of Islam: Reconstructing Identity, State, Faith, and Community in the Late Ottoman State* (New York: Oxford University Press, 2001): 272–4 and Bang, *Sufis and Scholars*, 91.

70 Howard M. Federspiel, *Sultans, Shamans, and Saints: Islam and Muslims in Southeast Asia* (Honolulu: University of Hawaii Press, 2007).

71 These lines are drawn more clearly today where Wahhabi "orthodoxy" neatly folds into Euro-American needs for a "native" medium to plunder Muslim lands with impunity while characterizing resistance as "illegal" in both international law and "religious" law. The emerging structure of this neat self-serving interaction of local entrepreneurs can be found in the Saud family with their religious allies or earlier, the "sada" "Arab" "Hadhrami" elite of the larger Indian Ocean world fully integrated into the Euro-American capitalist apparatus by the end of the nineteenth century.

72 It would also offer a working model for competing "liberal" politicians/businessmen in the Balkans and Middle East to aggressively advocate (nationalist) policies that would "modernize" (purify) their homelands by erasing the Ottoman past. Ioannis

N. Grigoriadis, "Redefining the Nation: Shifting Boundaries of the 'Other' in Greece and Turkey," *Middle Eastern Studies* 47.1 (2011): 167–82 and Slobodan Drakulić, "Anti-Turkish Obsession and the Exodus of Balkan Muslims," *Patterns of Prejudice* 43.3–4 (2009): 233–49. Specific to Bosnia, see Safet Bandžović, "Demografska deosmanizacija Balkana i kretanja bosanskohercegovačkih muhadžira (1878–1914)," *Bosna i Hercegovina u okviru Austro-Ugarske 1878–1918* (2011): 207–34.

73   For a helpful corrective to this limit, see Sabri Ateş, "The Margins of Empire: Kurdish Militias in the Ottoman Tribal Zone (review)," *CSSAAME* 32.2 (2012): 459–61.

74   Selim Deringil, "Legitimacy Structures in the Ottoman State: The Reign of Abdülhamid II (1876–1909)," *IJMES* 23.3 (1991): 345–59.

75   Kemal H. Karpat, *The Politicization of Islam*.

76   Cooper, *Colonialism in Question* and Robert Young, *White Mythologies: Writing History and the West* (New York: Routledge, 1990).

77   Usually studied in French, British, Russian, or Ottoman variations, each imperial project invested some resources into patronizing Pan-Islamist advocates, whose favored position within a certain empire was supposed to translate into greater influence for, say, Rome, in the larger "Islamic" world. The logic is so reductive that it almost does not need further analysis. And yet, its basic premise remains the dominating theme for a whole sub-field in "Islamic" studies and is thus still a question young historians may wish to explore as a viable objective. For literature on how various European interests imagined they could capture the "Muslim's" loyalty, studied by mostly skeptical historians not buying into the idea of "Pan-Islam", see for instance, Adriana P. De Carolis, "La Hamalliyya di Nioro del Sahel: politica coloniale e identità islamica," *Africa* 45.2 (1990): 236–60; Christopher Harrison, *France and Islam in West Africa, 1860–1960* (Cambridge: Cambridge University Press, 2003); M. Naeem Qureshi, *Pan-Islam in British Indian Politics: A Study of the Khilafat Movement, 1918–1924* (Leiden: Brill Academic Publication, 1999); Donald M. McKale, "'The Kaiser's Spy': Max von Oppenheim and the Anglo-German Rivalry Before and during the First World War," *European History Quarterly*, 27.2 (1997): 199–219; Merhdad Kia, "Pan-Islamism in Late Nineteenth-century Iran," *Middle Eastern Studies* 32.1 (1996): 30–52 and Tadeusz Swietochowski, *Russian Azerbaijan, 1905–1920: The Shaping of a National Identity in a Muslim Community* (Cambridge: Cambridge University Press, 2004).

78   The American missionaries who trail-blazed in much of Eastern Anatolia during the crucial pre-WWI period eventually became the source of new political orientations with "Christian" or "Minority" constituencies seeking independence from "Kurdish," "Arab" or "Turkish" neighbors by way of forging commercial, cultural, and ultimately political alliances with outsiders. Yvette Talhamy, "American Protestant Missionary Activity among the Nusayris (Alawis) in Syria in the Nineteenth Century," *Middle Eastern Studies* 47.2 (2011): 215–36 and Recep Boztemur, "Religion and Politics in the Making of American Near East Policy, 1918–1922," *Journal for the Study of Religions and Ideologies* 4.11 (2010): 45–59.

79   At times, refugees who were let loose in the country-side and turned into "bandits" (*eşkiya*) to maintain a living, could be "turned" around with the right coaxing. Once recruited, they could then be used to keep the peace. Sabri Yetkin, *Ege'de eşkıyalar* (Ankara: Türkiye Ekonomik ve Toplumsal Tarih Vakf, 1996): 160–8.

80   By the turn of the century, Kemal Karpat offered that the 2.5 million refugees from Russian-held territories actually outnumbered the number of Kurds in the Ottoman Empire. Karpat, *Ottoman Population 1830–1914*, 69.

81   Indeed, much of the concerns about how to fully integrate refugees left many in a bureaucratic black hole as policies toward refugees often changed. James J. Meyer, "Immigration, Return, and the Politics of Citizenship: Russian Muslims in the Ottoman Empire, 1860–1914," *IJMES* 39.1 (2007): 15–32. When properly conjoined, the fiercest loyalists to the Ottoman state (and later Turkey) were often those having just been victims of forced expulsion. Circassians were especially important to building the "National Movement" in 1918 that would begin the long and bloody war against neighboring states—Greece in particular—and the victorious powers to carve out a homeland for the empire's refugees. See Erik J. Zürcher, *The Unionist Factor: The Rôle of the Committee of Union and Progress in the Turkish National Movement, 1905–1926* (Leiden: Brill, 1984): 68–117. On what happened when a common cause was not yet clearly formulated in a "Turkish" republic and tens of thousands of Balkan Muslim and Circassian refugees lived under Greek occupation between 1920–2, a period in which Muslim killed Muslim, and Chechen community leaders sided with Greek occupation officials, see Ryan Gingeras, *Sorrowful Shores: Violence, Ethnicity, and the End of the Ottoman Empire, 1912–1923* (New York: Oxford University Press, 2009).

82   Caesar E. Farah, "Great Britain, Germany and the Ottoman Caliphate," *Der Islam* 66.2 (1989): 264–88 and Miron Rezun, "The Great Game Revisited," *International Journal* 41.2 (1986): 324–41. One excellent recent work that has raised the quality of the scholarship on these themes is M. Reynolds, *Shattering Empires*.

83   British authorities complained that French representatives seeking to secure an Armenian enclave linking with French mandated Syria were also soliciting the loyalties of Muslim Circassians to come and settle in the sparsely populated Cilicia. NAUK, FO 371/5048, Report number 5042, dated 20 May 1920. See also E. H. King, "A Journey through Armenian Cilicia," *Journal of the Royal Central Asian Society* 24.2 (1937): 234–46 and Sam Kaplan, "Documenting History, Historicizing Documentation: French Military Officials' Ethnological Reports on Cilicia," *Comparative Studies in Society and History* 44.2 (2002): 344–69. British occupation administrators in Batum, on the Black Sea, faced an equally puzzling, counterintuitive, alliance between the Atatürk Government and the Bolsheviks. These two rival groups actually worked together to suppress attempts by Ajari nationalists to forge a union with Turkish Nationalists, at the time attempting to fight off Soviet Russian advances in the Black Sea region. This in itself is an important indicator of how context, rather than deductions made from finite categories, explains the reversal of CUP policies during World War I to maintain sovereignty over the Batum region. See NAUK, FO 371/6269, report number 3304, dated Batum, 15 March 1921.

84   By fixating on associating rationales for policy and ultimately loyalties solely on an individual or "an empire" being "Muslim," not only are "grey areas" ignored (I would suggest for many it is a liminal rubicon that cannot be crossed if distinctions between "east" and "west" are to be maintained), but a now unacceptable essentialism remains operational. Frederick F. Anscombe, "Islam and the Age of Ottoman Reform," *Past and Present* 211 (2010): 160–89 and Deringil's welcome rebuke, Deringil, *Conversion*, 65.

85   As we have seen, violence in the Balkans and Eastern Anatolia becomes the paradigmatic expression of long subdued nationalist (and sectarian) aspirations of "suppressed" races, while outbreaks of disorder and acts of pillage are precursors to the inevitable expression of "Turkish" and/or "Kurdish" pathological, "racial" hatred of the Armenian "race." As argued throughout, however, these are all events

that must be treated in local, regional, and then trans-national contexts, not the other way around. That being said, contemporaries of these events clearly had other tools of analysis we no longer countenance as serious. F. D. Shepard, "Personal Experience in Turkish Massacres and Relief Work," *The Journal of Race Development* 1.3 (1911): 316–39; Bedross Der Matossian, "From Bloodless Revolution to Bloody Counterrevolution: The Adana Massacres of 1909," *Genocide Studies and Prevention* 6.2 (2011): 152–73 and Gaunt and Beṭ-Ṣawoce, *Massacres*, 5–34.

86   Zharmukhamed Zardykhan, "Ottoman Kurds of the First World War Era: Reflections in Russian Sources," *Middle Eastern Studies* 42.1 (2006): 67–85, 79–83.

87   For an excellent critique, see Andrew Sartori, "The Categorical Logic of a Colonial Nationalism: Swadeshi Bengal, 1904–1908," *CSSAAME* 23.1 and 2 (2003): 271–85.

88   As much as there have been attempts to fuse Homi Bhahba and Lacan into a more nuanced discussion about the self-evident "liminal" experiences of the late Ottoman Empire, the frame of reference still relies on units as rigid as "Muslim" and "Islam" to delineate where the threshold of "modern" hybridity begins and ends. Awad Halabi, "Liminal Loyalties: Ottomanism and Palestinian Responses to the Turkish War of Independence, 1919–22," *Journal of Palestine Studies* 41.3 (2012): 19–37.

89   In the Balkans, important corrective work has come out exposing the nuances to post-Ottoman state building in Bulgaria, Greece, and Yugoslavia, which all consisted of navigating very different early "national" projects in what were volatile and contested political, economic, and social spaces. Emblematic of the best kind of this work on transitional, still very Ottoman, societies, see Karakasidou, *Fields of Wheat, Hills of Blood*, 239 in respect to newly integrated territories in Macedonia and for the flexibility of Bosnian Muslim politicians during the early years of Yugoslavia, see Husnija Kamberović, *Mehemed Spaho (1883–1939): Politička Biografija* (Sarajevo: Vijeće Kongresa bošnjačkih intelektualaca, 2009).

90   Robert D. Crews, *For Prophet and Tsar: Islam and Empire in Russia and Central Asia* (Cambridge, MA: Harvard University Press, 2009): 24, 205, 300–2; Adeeb Khalid, *The Politics of Muslim Cultural Reform: Jadidism in Central Asia* (Berkeley: University of California Press, 1999): 195–8 and Alexander Morrison, "Sufism, Pan-Islamism and Information Panic: Nil Sergeevich Lykoshin and the Aftermath of the Andijan Uprising," *Past & Present* 214.1 (2012): 255–304.

91   Lâle Can, *Trans-Imperial Trajectories: Pilgrimage, Pan-Islam, and Ottoman-Central Asian Relations, 1865–1914* (PhD Dissertation, New York University, 2012). For a critique of prevailing literature, see pages 14–18 and for examples drawn from her cases covering as diverse regions as Bukhara and Kashgar, pages 169–289.

92   We learn from future Albanian "hero" Ismail Qemali in his memories how heavily invested he was personally in joint-venture mining operations with European-based companies throughout the Ottoman Empire, including in his home district of Vlora and the island of Imbros. As a self-declared liberal fully on board the march to "civilization," there was certainly important moments of conflicted interests when men like Qemali, from government posts, as members of Parliament after 1908, or influential oppositional leaders advocated for certain "reforms" that directly impacted the profitability of their investments. Ismail Kemal Bey, *The Memoirs of Ismail Kemal Bey* (London: Constable, 1920): 92.

93   For the particularly important role Chechens, Tatars, and other Russian Muslims play in the Ottoman military and then in the CUP, see Erik J. Zürcher, "The Young Turks—Children of the Borderlands?" *International Journal of Turkish Studies* 9 (2003): 275–86. See also Ryan Gingeras, "The Sons of Two Fatherlands: Turkey and

the North Caucasian Diaspora, 1914–1923," *European Journal of Turkish Studies. Social Sciences on Contemporary Turkey,* 2011. [Online] Online since 30 November 2011, URL: http://ejts.revues.org/index4424.html (accessed on 12 January 2013).

94   Or that matter "Turks" as a recent, most appreciated correction, attests. Michael A. Reynolds, "Buffers, not Brethren: Young Turk Military Policy in the First World War and the Myth of Panturanism," *Past & Present* 203.1 (2009): 137–79.

95   This point is made perfectly clear with the very different experiences certain kinds of refugees had with the host Ottoman society. In addition to revisiting Chapter 2 for further details on the Balkans and Arabia, a number of studies provide excellent examples of how miserable orphans and the truly forgotten Central Asian and Eastern Anatolian refugees were treated in Istanbul and elsewhere: Can, *Trans-Imperial Trajectories,* 169–93. See also Anthony Hyman, "Turkestan and Pan-Turkism Revisited," *Central Asian Survey* 16.3 (1997): 339–51.

96   George B. McClellan, "Capture of Kars, and Fall of Plevna," *The North American Review* (1878): 132–55.

97   George Gavrilis, "The Greek–Ottoman Boundary as Institution, Locality, and Process, 1832–1882," *American Behavioral Scientist* 51.10 (2008): 1516–37. Sabri Ateş, *Empires at the Margin: Towards a History of the Ottoman-Iranian Borderland and the Borderland Peoples, 1843–1881* (PhD Dissertation, New York University, 2006).

98   Victor Roudometof, "Nationalism, Globalization, Eastern Orthodoxy Unthinking 'the Clash of Civilizations' in Southeastern Europe," *European Journal of Social Theory* 2.2 (1999): 233–47.

99   Peter Sluglett, "The British, the Sunnis and the Shi'is: Social Hierarchies of Identity under the British Mandate," *International Journal of Contemporary Iraqi Studies* 4.3 (2010): 257–73.

100   The crucial adaptive "modern governmental" approach taken by "Westernized" Ottoman reformers was to pursue a "colonial Ottomanism" that, like their European counterparts of the era, sought to co-opt the "traditions" of "backward" "tribal" peoples and seek influence by capturing the loyalties of these colonial subjects' leaders. Hence the reference to "Tribal Schools" in Istanbul and the appointment of local "partners" to formal Ottoman government posts. The failure of these policies would necessarily reflect on how power would then be returned to "natives" in terms not entirely resembling those supposedly prevailing in "core" regions of the empire. My attempt at polemic here should not be considered personal and instead, as scholars, be taken as an invitation for debate taking into consideration my larger ethical concerns laid out in *Foundations of Modernity.*

101   Even during World War I and for years after, a violent struggle took place between those taking on the new radical ideologies that embraced "racial" separation as the only means to assure a homeland for the "nation," and those seeking to preserve a society whose "break-up" would constitute a disaster. The violence stemmed from the fact that there were few constituencies invested in this adaption of a broader "scientific" sociology. As we will see below, the need to impose a universal, homogeneous polity based on common, identifiable characteristics, was, and still is, utterly fictitious, and as such, the parameters are in constant renegotiation. Crucially for Anatolia, at the wrong place and wrong time, a perfect storm of operating logics converged, where strategic requirements linked with associations to loyalty entirely disconnected to any working models. This storm left a few powerful men, with a relative monopoly on violence, to attempt to create different realities on the

ground. Unfortunately, they took the rhetorical, conceptual, and bureaucratic form of "Turkification" as their framework for reconstituting a collapsed, post-Ottoman society. The result was mass murder and even genocide of not only Armenians, but also other identified "marginal" peoples, from Kurdish speakers, "Balkan Muslim refugees" and endless varieties of other "Christian" groups. Crucially for this last chapter, however, we must remember this genocidal calculus was entirely based on the operating logic of the Euro-American world, which, at selective moments, used "population politics" based on similar categories of distinction to bureaucratically, conceptually, and then physically eviscerate strategically "dangerous" peoples it was forced to engage. For the best new book on this process as it plays out in Diyarbakir province, see Üngör, *The Making of Modern Turkey*, 55–169.

Conclusion

1 Cf. Jeffery Lesser, "(Re)Creating Ethnicity: Middle Eastern Immigration to Brazil," *Americas* 53.1 (1996): 45–65, 58.

2 On the slurs that shaped the Ottoman refugee's life in Latin America see Gildas Brégain, "L'influence de la tutelle mandataire française sur l'identification des élites syriennes et libanaises devant la société argentine (1900–1946)," *Revue européenne des migrations internationales* 27.3 (2012): 177–99.

3 Maria Todorova, "The Trap of Backwardness: Modernity, Temporality, and the Study of Eastern European Nationalism," *Slavic Review* 64.1 (2005): 140–64; Asim Zubčević, "Pathology of a Literature: Some Roots of Balkan Islamophobia," *Journal of Muslim Minority Affairs* 16.2 (1996): 309–15; Jovo Bakić, "Extreme-Right Ideology, Practice and Supporters: Case Study of the Serbian Radical Party," *Journal of Contemporary European Studies* 17.2 (2009): 193–207 and Gökhan Saz, "Turkophobia and Rising Islamophobia in Europe: A Quantification for the Negative Spillovers on the EU Membership Quest of Turkey," *European Journal of Social Sciences* 19.4 (2011): 479–91.

4 Stark Draper, "The Conceptualization of an Albanian Nation," *Ethnic and Racial Studies* 20.1 (1997): 123–44 and Adrian Brisku, "Internalizing Europe: Albanian Perceptions of the Continent in Historical Perspective (1878–2008)," *Journal of Educational Media, Memory, and Society* 1.2 (2009): 97–124.

5 Nathalie Clayer, "Adapting Islam to Europe: The Albanian Example," *Islam und Muslime in (Südost) Europa im Kontext von Transformation und EU-Erweiterung* (2010): 53–69 and Nicola Nixon, "Always Already European: The Figure of Skënderbeg in Contemporary Albanian Nationalism," *National Identities* 12.1 (2010): 1–20.

6 For a comprehensive survey of Ottoman-era migrants histories in Latin America, see Abdeluahed Akmir (ed.), *Los árabes en América Latina: Historia de una Emigración* (Madrid: Siglo XXI de España Editores, 2009) and José Abu-Tarbush Quevedo, "De oriente próximo a Latinoamérica: la emigración árabe a través del Atlántico," *Política exterior* 24.133 (2010): 163–7. The documentation of such migrations is endless and largely forgotten. Ottoman Albanian migration to South America, for example, is still basically unstudied although considerable amounts joined their Ottoman compatriots in major cities like São Paulo, Montevideo, and Buenos Aires. For example, Ottoman officials reported that on just one boat,

700 Ottoman Albanians left Genova for an uncertain future in South America. The numbers were so significant that the Ottoman governing body managing migration was charged to investigate in order to find out both the final destination of this large group of Ottoman subjects and perhaps figure out why they literally "jumped ship" and abandoned their homeland. BBA I.HUS, 82/62 report issued 27 May 1900. Most likely, those Albanian-heritage grandchildren, scattered in Argentina, Chile, and Brazil today would grow up in a world that vilified the "Turk" and these migrants all did their best to erase any links to the old world.

7   Ethnographies of this settlement give-and-take in Brazil is quite rich and covers the entire twentieth century. Consider for the most recent developments in a resurgent Arabo-centric Brazil John Tofik Karam, *Another Arabesque: Syrian-Lebanese Ethnicity in Neoliberal Brazil* (Philadelphia: Temple University Press, 2007). For useful insights into how earlier communities assimilated into Brazil's major cities, see Taufik Kurban, *Os syrios e libaneses no Brasil* (São Paulo: Sociedade Impressora Paulista, 1933) and André Castanheira Gattaz, *História oral da imigração libanesa para o Brasil—1880–2000* (PhD Dissertation, Universidade de São Paulo, 2001).

8   Michael Humphrey, "Ethnic History, Nationalism and Transnationalism in Argentine Arab and Jewish Cultures," *Immigrants & Minorities* 16.1–2 (1997): 167–88 and Said Bahajin, "El modelo Latinoamericano en la Integración de los Inmigrantes árabes," *Ra Ximhai* 4.3 (2008): 737–73.

9   Douglas Kristopher Smith, *Discursos hegemónicos y corrientes alternativas en la colectividad palestina de Chile* (PhD Dissertation, Concordia University, 2012).

10 Alan Knight, "Racism, Revolution, and Indigenismo: Mexico, 1910–1940," in Richard Graham (ed.), *The Idea of Race in Latin America: 1870–1940* (Austin: University of Texas Press, 1990): 71–113.

11 Darío A. Euraque, "Nation Formation, Mestizaje and Arab Palestinian Immigration to Honduras, 1880–1930s," *Critique: Journal for Critical Studies of the Middle East* 4.6 (1995): 25–37 and Christina Civantos, "Custom-building the Fictions of the Nation: Arab Argentine Rewritings of the Gaucho," *International Journal of Cultural Studies* 4.1 (2001): 69–87. Crucially, as demonstrated by the path-breaking work of Steven Hyland Jr, in a number of settings, Ottoman subjects proved capable of mobilizing labor and commercial interests at different points of time to secure a seat in an otherwise "closed" Argentinian political economy. Hyland, "Arisen from Deep Slumber."

12 Christina Sue, "The Dynamics of Color: Mestizaje, Racism and Blackness in Veracruz, Mexico," in Evelyn Glenn (ed.), *Shades of Difference: Transnational Perspectives on How and Why Skin Color Matters* (Palo Alto: Stanford University Press, 2009): 114–28; Liz Hamui-Halabe, "Re-creating Community: Christians from Lebanon and Jews from Syria in Mexico, 1900–1938," *Immigrants & Minorities* 16.1–2 (1997): 125–45 and Andrew Grant Wood, "Introducing La Reina Del Carnaval: Public Celebration and Postrevolutionary Discourse in Veracruz, Mexico," *The Americas* 60.1 (2003): 87–108, 105.

13 Theresa Alfaro-Velcamp, *So Far from Allah, So Close to Mexico: Middle Eastern Immigrants in Modern Mexico* (Austin: University of Texas Press, 2007): 40–3, 66–95.

14 Camila Pastor de Maria y Campos, "Inscribing Difference: Maronites, Jews and Arabs in Mexican Public Culture and French Imperial Practice 1," *Latin American and Caribbean Ethnic Studies* 6.2 (2011): 169–87.

15 Abdeluahed Akmir, *La inmigración arabe en Argentina (1880–1980)* (Madrid: Universidad Complutense de Madrid 1991); Amarilio Junior, *As vantagens da*

imigração syria no Brasil (Rio de Janiero: Off. Gr. Da S.A.A. Noite, 1935) and Myriam Olguin Tenorio, *La inmigración arabe en Chile* (Santiago: Ediciones Instituto Chileno Arabe de Cultura, 1990).

16 Akram Fouad Khater, "Becoming 'Syrian' in America: A Global Geography of Ethnicity and Nation," *Diaspora: A Journal of Transnational Studies* 14.2 (2005): 299–331.

17 Alfaro-Velcamp, *So Far from Allah*, 56–8.

18 Alfaro-Velcamp, *So Far from Allah*, 45–67.

19 Jorge Nacif Mina, *Crónicas de un inmigrante libanés en México* (Mexico City: Instituto Cultural Mexicano Libanés, 1995): 61–3.

20 Luis Ramirez Carrillo, *Secretos de familia: Libaneses y elites empresariales en Yucatan* (Mexico City: Consejo Nacional para la Cultura y las Artes, 1994). For similar testimonials of Ottoman Arab successes in the business world in South America, see Mary Wilkie, *The Lebanese in Montevideo, Uruguay: A Study of an Entrepreneurial Ethnic Minority* (PhD Dissertation, University of Wisconsin, Madison, 1973) and Lois J. Roberts, *The Lebanese in Ecuador: A History of Emerging Leadership* (Boulder, CO: Westview Press, 2000): 41–6.

21 Lesser, "(Re) Creating Ethnicity," 49–55 and Alberto Tasso, *Aventura, trabajo y poder: Sirios e libaneses en Santiago del Estero, 1880–1980* (Buenos Aires: Ediciones Indice, 1988).

22 These Ottomans also, it must be stressed over and over again, included Jews. Liz Hamui de Halabe, *Los judíos de Alepo en México* (Mexico City: Maguén David, 1989).

23 Oliver T. Coomes and Bradford L. Barham, "The Amazon Rubber Boom: Labor Control, Resistance, and Failed Plantation Development Revisited," *Hispanic American Historical Review* (1994): 231–57; Greg Grandin, *Fordlandia: The Rise and Fall of Henry Ford's Forgotten Jungle City* (New York: Metropolitan Books, 2009) and John T. Karam, "A Cultural Politics of Entrepreneurship in Nation-Making: Phoenicians, Turks, and the Arab Commercial Essence in Brazil," *Journal of Latin American Anthropology* 9.2 (2004): 319–51.

24 Esther Regina Largman and Robert M. Levine, "Jews in the Tropics. Bahian Jews in the Early Twentieth Century," *The Americas* (1986): 159–70 and Louise Fawcett and Eduardo Posada-Carbo. "Arabs and Jews in the Development of the Colombian Caribbean 1850–1950," *Immigrants & Minorities* 16.1–2 (1997): 57–79.

25 Martha Diaz de Kuri and Lourdes Macluf, *De Libano a México, cronica de un pueblo émigrante* (Mexico City: Grafica Creatividad y Disno, 1995): 46–7.

26 Ran Aaronsohn, "Baron Rothschild and the Initial Stage of Jewish Settlement in Palestine (1882–1890): A Different Type of Colonization?" *Journal of Historical Geography* 19.2 (1993): 142–56.

27 David Barkin and John W. Bennett, "Kibbutz and Colony: Collective Economies and the Outside World," *Comparative Studies in Society and History* 14.4 (1972): 456–83.

28 Maria Cruz Heras, *La emigración libanesa en Costa Rica* (Madrid: Editorial Cantárabia, 1991) and Nancie González, *Dollar, Dove, and Eagle: One Hundred Years of Palestinian Migration to Honduras* (Ann Arbor: University of Michigan Press, 1992).

29 Colonization in the Ottoman lands was deemed strategically essential in that it helped both secure the vital trade routes through Suez and establish a stranglehold over the twentieth century's most vital commodity: oil. James A. Paul, "Great Power Conflict over Iraqi Oil—the World War I Era," Global Policy Forum (GPF), 2009; Helmut Mejcher, "Oil and British Policy towards Mesopotamia, 1914–1918," *Middle*

Eastern Studies 8.3 (1972): 377–91 and Edward Peter Fitzgerald, "France's Middle Eastern Ambitions, the Sykes-Picot Negotiations, and the Oil Fields of Mosul, 1915–1918," *The Journal of Modern History* 66.4 (1994): 697–725.

30   The dominating theme in Iraq was how the Colonial Office and the Bombay administration of the British Raj could effectively afford empire. In Iraq, the aggressive push to streamline the governing institutions, the tax collection apparatus, and finally the distribution of concessions to the right global capitalist interests constituted a major faction within the larger Mandate governing regime. The apparent contradictions would constantly incite indigenous responses, often with a reflective use of Ottoman-era associations that European administrators dismissed as "quaint" at their peril. Peter Sluglett, "Une mission sacrée pour qui? Quelques réflexions sur l'intégration nationale et le mandat britannique en Irak/Whose Sacred Trust? Some Thoughts on 'National Integration' and the British Mandate in Iraq," *Revue des mondes musulmans et de la Méditerranée* 117–18 (2007): 33–49 and Anthony B. Toth, "Conflict and a Pastoral Economy: The Costs of Akhwan Attacks on Tribes in Iraq, 1922–29," *Critique: Critical Middle Eastern Studies* 11.2 (2002): 201–27.

31   The French occupiers of Syria and Cilicia (until 1920 under French military administration) even tried to harness the Armenians to redraw the sociopolitical frontiers of Anatolia and Northern Middle East. Yücel Güçlü, "The Struggle for Mastery in Cilicia: Turkey, France, and the Ankara Agreement of 1921," *The International History Review* 23.3 (2001): 580–603. These brutalized remains of a genocidal campaign of forced migration by the late Ottoman regime under the military rule of Talat Pasha and company did not prove the most reliable surrogates for French Empire. Sam Kaplan, "Territorializing Armenians: Geo-texts, and Political Imaginaries in French-occupied Cilicia, 1919–1922," *History and Anthropology* 15.4 (2004): 399–423 and Ellen Marie Lust-Okar, "Failure of Collaboration: Armenian Refugees in Syria," *Middle Eastern Studies* 32.1 (1996): 53–68. Similar disappointed efforts to disaggregate Kurds, Assyrians, or Shiite from Sunnis, and Circassians from Arabs proved crucial to the creation of Pan-Arab, secular political movements who later manifested in the form of Baathist activism. James L. Gelvin, *Divided Loyalties: Nationalism and Mass Politics in Syria at the Close of Empire* (Berkeley: University of California Press, 1998): 97–125.

32   Philip S. Khoury, "The Tribal Shaykh, French Tribal Policy, and the Nationalist Movement in Syria between Two World Wars," *Middle Eastern Studies* 18.2 (1982): 180–93.

33   This aspect of the Mandate operations is perhaps best studied in the latest works on these issues by Daniel Neep, *Occupying Syria under the French Mandate: Insurgency, Space and State Formation* (Cambridge: Cambridge University Press, 2012): 39–65 and Benjamin White, "The Nation-State Form and the Emergence of 'Minorities' in Syria," *Studies in Ethnicity and Nationalism* 7.1 (2007): 64–85.

34   For complaints from sister Ottoman organizations about the poor treatment of Ottoman "Muslims" received from international organizations during the Balkan Wars of 1912–1913, see "Emraz-ı Sâriyeye Karşı Mücadele," *Magazine of the Red Crescent Society (OHAM)* no. 6 (17 Cemaziyelahir 1340 / 15 February 1922): 134–5.

35   Of course the degree to which Albanian delegations, as part of a recognized, independent government, were allowed to engage the League of Nations in sometimes formal ways, differed to the frustrations of Palestinians in México and Honduras petitioning the same offices for acknowledgment of their hitherto thwarted

efforts to be recognized as Palestinian citizens. LON R 19, Dossier No. 61497, dated 2 December 1927. One need only contrast the kind of attention afforded Albanian delegations to Paris and Geneva during the process of negotiating the final settlement of boundaries in a post-Ottoman Balkans and those of Palestinian peddlers in Honduras seeking passports from the new regime ruling their homelands in the 1920s. For detailed back-and-forth between League officials and Albanian delegates to the Paris Conference of 1921, see LON R 522, Doc. 11331, Dossier no. 1240, dated Paris, 2 March 1921.

36   It was clearly an issue of higher diplomatic priority for the League of Nations to selectively champion the cause of disgruntled, threatened peoples. For the case of Kosovar Albanians facing organized campaigns of land and property dispossession by Serbian colonists in the 1920s, they discovered the League of Nations no longer had any use for them. LON R552, Doc. 7533, Dossier 1240, dated Scutari, 28 September 1920. The result would be a major uprising that ultimately cost upwards of 40,000 lives and the expulsion of over 400,000 native Albanians (former Ottomans) to neighboring Albania or to Anatolia. AQSH F. 251, D 134. D. 6, dated 20 October 1925.

37   The pillaging got so bad in French Syria that Paris had to discipline its top official in the southern Druze region. Here, the nature of the crimes only gained strategic value once violence from indigenous populations got out of hand. For a candid assessment of Carbillet's performance in Jabal Druze by his successor, see AMAE-Nantes, 438, Delegué-Adjoint du Haut Commissaire au Sandjak de Dayr al-Zur à Envoyé Extraordinaire au Syrie et au Djebel Druse, dated 3 February 1927. See also Neel, *Occupying Syria*, 33–4.

38   On the role of passports in the nineteenth century to changing how communities interacted, see Leo Lucassen, "A Many-headed Monster: The Evolution of the Passport System in the Netherlands and Germany in the Long Nineteenth Century," in Jane Caplan and John Torpe (eds), *Documenting Individual Identity: The Development of State Practices in the Modern World* (Princeton: Princeton University Press, 2001): 235–55. The mechanics of regulating travel had very quickly helped enforce racial frontiers and thus enabled exploitative economies to funnel landless, desperate people to where they were needed to work. See Radhika Viyas Mongia, "Race, Nationality, Mobility: A History of the Passport," *Public Culture* 11.3 (1999): 527–55.

39   LON R.19, Doc. 59334, Dossier no. 2413, labeled Confidential, "Claims of Certain Palestinians in Honduras and San Salvador to Palestinian Citizenship," dated between 23 April and 10 June 1927. Members of the *Sociedad Fraternidad Palestina* organized for individuals wishing to obtain travel documents services to apply, through the British consular authorities, for Palestinian citizenship. Their applications were summarily refused, however, on the ground of the Palestinian petitioners were absent from the territories for more than ten years. Attempts to counterargue that the nature of their work as merchants required their long-term migration, along with the fact they owned much land in Palestine, should be reason enough to give them documents that allowed them the return home. The crucial weapon used to deny in a regular fashion such kinds of Palestinian requests for the documentation reflecting the change of regime from Ottoman to British was the actual protocols of the Treaty of Lausanne in 1923. The report to the LON highlights the "fact" that Article 34 of the Lausanne treaty granted the right of natives of any of ". . . the territories detached from Turkey [*sic*] habitually resident abroad to acquire the nationality of that

territory is made subject to the consent of the Government exercising authority . . ." In this respect, British had the "legal grounds" to deny Palestinian natives the right of return in an even earlier variation from the post-Nakba story. It gets worse as the underlying logic of the authorities was to declare that these Palestinians were "Turks" on the grounds their paper work originated from the now defunct Ottoman Empire. Here the selective reasoning demonstrates that there is no hardened doctrine, or law, to follow. Rather, it is always at the convenience of the purveyor. The underlying issue is British authorities were charged with maintaining an orderly transfer, as laid out in the Balflour Declaration, of indigenous lands to help create a European Jewish homeland/colony. In order for this to happen, natives would have to be systematically expelled. Ronald Sanders, *The High Walls of Jerusalem: A History of the Balfour Declaration and the Birth of the British Mandate for Palestine* (London: Holt, Rinehart and Winston, 1984).

40　Amazingly, Turkish Republican officials had also become very conscious of who were migrating to the core areas of the new post-Ottoman state. After completing the population exchanges with Greece and Bulgaria, and then signing agreements with Yugoslavia that would lead to the expulsion of upwards of 400,000 Muslim Slavs and Albanians from Yugoslavia by World War II, Ankara clamped down on possible immigration. Soner Çağaptay, "Citizenship Policies in Interwar Turkey," *Nations and Nationalism* 9.4 (2003): 601–19. Ankara, for instance, refused to honor the Ottoman documentation of people of Arab and Armenian decent, a reflection of the new kind of calculations involving territorial disputes with French Mandate Syria, ultimately leading to a League of Nations' administered referendum that gave residents of the Sancak of Alexandretta the right to choose under which regime to live. The subsequent battles over categories used in the ballots, the long process of registering and validating residents to be voters (to assure French, Arab, or Turkish interests did not flood the ballot box with imported voters) led to one of the uglier examples of race-centric policies and their destructive consequences to hitherto integrated, "mixed" communities. For details of the process that took place in the late 1930s, consult Sarah D. Shields, *Fezzes in the River: Identity Politics and European Diplomacy in the Middle East on the Eve of World War II* (New York: Oxford University Press, 2011).

41　This can also partially explain how violently the British authorities in Iraq uprooted Assyrians and spent the next 20 years trying to collectively deport them to other locations around the world. In 1920, some Assyrians had the temerity of demanding independence, in direct conflict with British interests around Mosul, which revolved around its oil wealth. As a reward, rather than developing a political and social order in Iraq that could replicate somewhat the Ottoman patterns of distributing responsibilities to various constituencies, the British authorities in Iraq were eagerly "marketing" to investment firms the fact that they had tens of thousands of "hard working, sturdy peasants" waiting to be deported. The nature of this campaign was to convince investors that these Assyrians were ideal for colonizing parts of Amazonia or Australia. LON C 1530, documents covering the 1930–8 period.

42　The nostalgic Ottomania that became a short "fad" in parts of the Balkans—the *rembetika* craze in Greece or the "re-Islamization" in Bulgaria—also touched grandee landowning families in Egypt, Tunisia, and Syria who have made new trans-Mediterranean claims to broaden their cosmopolitan claims. Nicholas G. Pappas, "Concepts of Greekness: The Recorded Music of Anatolian Greeks after 1922," *Journal of Modern Greek Studies* 17.2 (1999): 353–73; Talip Küçükcan,

"Re-claiming Identity: Ethnicity, Religion and Politics among Turkish-Muslims in Bulgaria and Greece," *Journal of Muslim Minority Affairs* 19.1 (1999): 49–68 and Ioanna Szeman, "'Gypsy Music' and Deejays: Orientalism, Balkanism, and Romani Musicians," *The Drama Review* 53.3 (2009): 98–116.

43   Fetime Myuhtar-May, "Pomok Christianization (Pokrastvane) in Bulgaria during the Balkan Wars of 1912–1913," in M. H. Yavuz and I. Blumi (eds), *War and Nationalism,* 316–60.

44   Mujeeb R. Khan, "The 'other' in the Balkans: Historical Constructions of Serbs and 'Turks,'" *Journal of Muslim Minority Affairs* 16.1 (1996): 49–63 and Paul Mojzes, *Balkan Genocides: Holocaust and Ethnic Cleansing in the Twentieth Century* (New York: Rowman & Littlefield Publishers, 2011).

45   Asim Zubčević, "Pathology of a Literature: Some Roots of Balkan Islamophobia," *Journal of Muslim Minority Affairs* 16.2 (1996): 309–15; Dimitris Livanios, "Beyond 'ethnic cleansing': Aspects of the Functioning of Violence in the Ottoman and post-Ottoman Balkans," *Southeast European and Black Sea Studies* 8.3 (2008): 189–203; and Hugh Poulton, "The Muslim Experience in the Balkan States, 1919–1991," *Nationalities Papers* 28.1 (2000): 45–66.

46   Vladimir Velebit, "Kosovo: A Case of Ethnic Change of Population," *East European Quarterly* 33 (1999): 177–94; Mojmir Križan, "New Serbian Nationalism and the Third Balkan War," *Studies in East European Thought* 46.1 (1994): 47–68 and Mile Bjelajać, "Migrations of Ethnic Albanians in Kosovo 1938–1950," *Balcanica* 38 (2007): 219–30.

47   A theme often repeated in Serbian historiography reports of Albanian irredentism and Muslim treachery would usually correspond with new campaigns to expel inhabitants in Kosovo and Macedonia to Turkey: Žviko Avramovski, "Treći Reich i 'Velika Albanija' posle kapitulacije Italije (1943–1944)," *Radovi Zavoda za hrvatsku povijest* 9.1 (1976): 93–213. See also documents relating to these sentiments that led to at least 300,000 Albanians expelled in the interwar period to Turkey and 400,000 more after World War II, in Robert Elsie, *Kosovo: In the Heart of the Powder Keg* (New York: East European Monographs, 1997): 207–32.

48   On some of the formal complaints issued by the Albanian state in the early 1920s, see for instance LON R 553, Doc. 15361, Dossier 1240, copy of letter from Hil Mosi to Secretary General of LON, dated Geneva, 6 August 1921. See also Milan Curčin, "Milan Rakić and the Idea of Kosovo," *The Slavonic and East European Review* 18.52 (1939): 170–4.

49   A notorious memorandum presented in Belgrade, 7 March 1937 by Serbia's most celebrated historian, Vaso Čubrilović, complained that these "Western" methods of resolving Serbia's (not Yugoslavia's) Albanian "problem" was leading nowhere, as Albanians were both "reproducing" too fast and entirely unassimilable. He advocated adopting "non-Western" methods to force them to leave the region. For a discussion of this document see Elsie, *Kosovo*, 400–24.

50   Another prominent "Yugoslav" human geographer in the period, Austrian-educated Jovan Cvijić proved especially influential in helping to shape the post-WWI "ethnic" borders in the Balkans. Jovan Cvijić, "The Geographical Distribution of the Balkan Peoples," *Geographical Review* 5.5 (1918): 345–61 and Jovan Cvijić, "The Zones of Civilization of the Balkan Peninsula," *Geographical Review* 5.6 (1918): 470–82.

51   In the CUP-dominated Ottoman Empire after a small group of positivist cum secularist ideologues led by Talat Pasha and Ziya Gökalp hijacked the party (and Ottomanism), the hitherto uncivil language of racial segregation and biological

boundaries became normal intellectual fare. Akçam, *From Empire to Republic*, 128–57.

52 Ulf Brunnbauer, "Fertility, Families and Ethnic Conflict: Macedonians and Albanians in the Republic of Macedonia, 1944–2002," *Nationalities Papers* 32.3 (2004): 565–98. On the colonization of Kosovo by upwards of 40,000 "Orthodox Slav peasants" in the interwar period as a means to institute the dispossession of Albanian properties and assure they would remain revenue-producing lands see Hugh Poulton, "Macedonians and Albanians as Yugoslavs," in D. Djokić (ed.), *Yugoslavism. Histories of Failed Idea, 1918–1992* (Madison: University of Wisconsin Press, 2003): 126; Sabrina P. Ramet, *Whose Democracy?: Nationalism, Religion, and the Doctrine of Collective Rights in Post-1989 Eastern Europe* (New York: Rowman & Littlefield Publishers, 1997): 144; and Ivo Banac, *The National Question in Yugoslavia: Origins, History, Politics* (Ithaca, NY: Cornell University Press, 1984): 297–300.

53 For British reports on the negotiations between Turkish and Yugoslav authorities in 1937 to finalize the transfer of "at least" 100,000 "Turks," see NAUK, FO 371/21221, report number 3921, dated Skopje, 23 February 1937. As for Bulgaria's "Muslims," there too, the generally hostile "minority" politics often differentiated between "native" Muslims (Pomoks) and "Turks" whose "natural" home was Turkey. Mary Neuburger, "Pomak Borderlands: Muslims on the Edge of Nations," *Nationalities Papers* 28.1 (2000): 181–98.

54 Indeed, the few discussions that were allowed to evoke the lost Balkans, men like the journalist Falih Atay, at once demonstrated in his travelogue how much of the "Turkish past" is gone in the Balkans and advised in no uncertain terms that refugees thinking of their past homelands "should forget" it entirely. See his discussion of a trip back from Italy through the Balkans, "Faşist Roma," Falih Rıfkı Atay, *Kemalist Tiran ve Kaybolmuş Makidonya* (Ankara: Hakimiyeti Milliye, 1931): 64.

55 Peter Loizos, "Ottoman Half-lives: Long-term Perspectives on Particular Forced Migrations," *Journal of Refugee Studies* 12.3 (1999): 237–63.

56 There was an inner group of ideologues in the late Ottoman Empire who embraced entirely the racial geographies au courant at the time—men like Ahmed Riza and Talat Pasha, for instance, would use the horrors of the period to try to enforce homogenization onto peoples still living an Ottoman experience. This did not, however, have to mean murder, but probably did almost exclusively mean by 1911 religious, thus ethnic, conversion. For an excellent explanation of the issues at stake see Bloxham, *The Great Game of Genocide*, 62–90.

57 Julian Go, "The 'New' Sociology of Empire and Colonialism," *Sociology Compass* 3.5 (2009): 775–88.

58 Julian Go, "'Racism' and Colonialism: Meanings of Difference and Ruling Practices in America's Pacific Empire," *Qualitative Sociology* 27.1 (2004): 35–58.

59 Uğur Ümit Üngör, "Geographies of Nationalism and Violence: Rethinking Young Turk 'Social Engineering,'" *European Journal of Turkish Studies* 7 (2008).

60 This is charted beautifully over a long duration in the case of Greek Macedonia by Anastasia N. Karakasidou, *Fields of Wheat, Hills of Blood*. See also Theodora Dragostinova, "Navigating Nationality in the Emigration of Minorities between Bulgaria and Greece, 1919–1941," *East European Politics and Societies* 23.2 (Spring 2009): 185–212.

61 There is something similar here to the way Žižek explores forms of death. Death is a "form" of "absence" that is not erasure but an "assembly of pain," Slavoj Žižek, *Living in the End Times* (London: Verso, 2010): 296–8.

62   French policies in Syria were especially egregious and disruptive of local life. The
      logics of border demarcation were variable, changing with time as well as place.
      For some peoples, the forging of the Republic of Lebanon helped them acquire a
      persona fixity and consecrated their "national" existence in 1920. On the other hand,
      the states of Damascus, Aleppo, and the 'Alawis were created at the same time as
      Lebanon. The three states, independent at first, were later federated in 1922. Just two
      years later, the configuration shifted again: the states of Aleppo and Damascus were
      dissolved to create a single state, including at the time the Sancak of Alexandretta.
      The Alawi state was not included in this new arrangement and was only united with
      the state of Syria in 1936. The same was true for the Jebel Druze area in the south,
      which had been a separate governorate until 1936. Both the 'Alawi State and the Jebel
      Druze were detached from Syria in 1930, only to be reunited in 1942 (as Alexandretta
      was disconnected from Aleppo). Khoury, *Syria and the French Mandate*, 57–9.
63   By relational history I wish to suggest that much of what we associate with the
      modern state apparatus develops in the context of intersecting interests taking the
      form of reciprocal or asymmetrical exchanges in a variety of socioeconomic and
      political settings, see M. C. Jacob and Ira Katznelson, "Agendas for Radical History,"
      Radical History Review 36 (September 1986): 26–47, especially 33–7. We also see this
      mutual formation of Europe and its colonies spelt out very well in Frederick Cooper
      and Ann Laura Stoler (eds), *Tensions of Empire: Colonial Cultures in A Bourgeois
      World* (Berkeley: University of California Press, 1989).
64   See Blumi, *Foundations* for discussion on meta-narrative and modern empire.

Bibliography

I Archival sources (listed by country)

ALBANIA
Arkivi Qendror Shtetëror (Tiranë)-AQSH

AUSTRIA
Haus, Hauf und Staatsarchiv (Vienna)-HHStA

FRANCE
Archives du Ministère des Affaires Étrangères (Paris)-AMAE
Centres des Archives diplomatiques de Nantes-AMAE

GERMANY
Politisches Archiv des Auswaertigen Amtes der Bundesrepublik Deutschland (Berlin)-PAAA

ITALY
Archivio Storico del Ministero degli Affari Esteri (Rome)-ASAME

PHILIPPINES
Philippines National Archive (Manila)-PNA

SINGAPORE
National Archives Singapore-NAS

SWITZERLAND
League of Nations Archives (Geneva)-LON

TURKEY
Başbakanlık Arşivi (Istanbul)-BBA

UNITED KINGDOM
Public Records Office (London)-NAUK
Indian Office Record (London)-IOR

UNITED STATES OF AMERICA
United State of America (Washington DC)-USNA

ZANZIBAR (Tanzania)
Zanzibar National Archives (Stone Town)-ZNA

II Published primary sources

Baron A. Meyendorff. *Correspondence diplomatique de M. de Staal* (Paris, 1929).
British North Borneo Chartered Company. *Handbook of the State of British North Borneo: Compiled from Reports of the Governor and Staff of North Borneo, with an Appendix Showing the Progress and Development of the State to the End of 1920* (Singapore: British North Borneo (Chartered) Company, 1921).

Carnegie Endowment. *Report of the International Commission to Inquire into the Causes and Conduct of the Balkan Wars* (Washington, DC: Carnegie Endowment for International Peace, 1914).
Great Britain, Foreign Office. *British and Foreign State Papers, 1877–1878* (vol. 69) and (vol. 72).
Kosova Vilayet Salnamesi (1305/1888).
Makedonya'daki Osmanlı Evraki, no. 29 (Ankara: T.C. Başbakanlık Devlet Arşivleri Genel Müdürlüğü Yayınları, 1996).

III Newspapers/Magazines

Albania (Rome)
Balkan (Sofia)
Bashkimi (Istanbul)
Bashkimi i Shqiptarëve (Cairo)
Dersaadet Ticaret Odası Gazetesi (Istanbul)
Dituria (Sofia)
Drita (Istanbul)
Drita (Bucharest)
La Nazione Albanese (Catanzaro)
Le Phare du Bosphore (Istanbul)
Le Siècle (Paris)
Mechveret Supplément Français (Istanbul)
Neue Freie Presse (Germany)
Osmanlı Supplément Français (Geneva)
Servet-i Fünun (Istanbul)
Shqiptetaret n'Egjypte (Cairo)
Tercüman-ı Hakikat
Toska (Cairo)

IV Unpublished sources: Dissertations and thesis

Arai, Kazuhiro. *Arabs who Traversed the Indian Ocean: The History of the al-'Attas Family in Hadramawt and Southeast Asia, c. 1600–c.1960* (PhD Dissertation, University of Michigan, 2004).
Ateş, Sabri. *Empires at the Margin: Towards a History of the Ottoman-Iranian Borderland and the Borderland Peoples, 1843–1881* (PhD Dissertation, New York University, 2006).
Betta, Chiara. *Silas Aaron Hardoon (1851?–1931): Marginality and Adaptation in Shanghai* (PhD Dissertation, University of London: School of Oriental Studies, 1997).
Bimanyu, Deogratias K. *The Waungwana of Eastern Zaire: 1880–1900* (PhD Dissertation, School of Oriental and African Studies, University of London, 1976).
Bishara, Fahad Ahmad. *A Sea of Debt: Histories of Commerce and Obligation in the Indian Ocean, c. 1850–1940* (PhD Dissertation, Duke University, 2012).
Can, Lâle. *Trans-Imperial Trajectories: Pilgrimage, Pan-Islam, and Ottoman-Central Asian Relations, 1865–1914* (PhD Dissertation, New York University, 2012).

Ertem, Özge. *Eating the Last Seed: Famine, Empire, Survival and Order in Ottoman Anatolia in the Late 19th Century* (PhD Dissertation, Florence: European University Institute, 2012).

Gattaz, André Castanheira. *História oral da imigração libanesa para o Brasil—1880-2000* (PhD Dissertation, Universidade de São Paulo, 2001).

Kocacık, Faruk. *Balkanlar'dan Anadolu'ya Yönelik Göçler* (PhD Dissertation, Hacettepe University, 1978).

Krause, Corinne Azen. *The Jews in Mexico: A History with Special Emphasis on the Period from 1850 to 1930* (PhD Dissertation, University of Pittsburgh, 1970).

Mandal, Sumit Kumar. *Finding their Place: A History of Arabs in Java under Dutch Rule, 1800-1924* (PhD Dissertation, Columbia University, 1994).

McDonnell, Mary. *The Conduct of the Hajj from Malaysia and its Socioeconomic Impact on Malay Society* (PhD Dissertation, Columbia University, 1986).

Pula, Besnik. *State, Law and Revolution: Agrarian Power and the National State in Albania, 1850-1945* (PhD Dissertation, University of Michigan, 2011).

Saracoğlu, Safa M. *Letters from Vidin: A Study of Ottoman Governmentality and Politics of Local Administration, 1864-1877* (PhD Dissertation, The Ohio State University, 2007).

Smith, Douglas Kristopher. *Discursos hegemónicos y corrientes alternativas en la colectividad palestina de Chile* (PhD Dissertation, Concordia University, 2012).

Wilkie, Mary. *The Lebanese in Montevideo, Uruguay: A Study of an Entrepreneurial Ethnic Minority* (PhD Dissertation, University of Wisconsin, Madison, 1973).

Yıldırım, Bülent. *Bulgaristan'daki Ermeni Komitelerinin Osmanlı Devleti Aleyhine Faaliyetleri (1890-1918)* (PhD Dissertation: Istanbul Universitesi Sosyal Bilimler Enstitüsü, 2010).

V Published non-primary sources

Aabakke, Vehmund. *Ethnic Rivalry and the Quest for Macedonia, 1870-1913* (Boulder: East European Monographs, 2003).

Aaronsohn, Ran. "Baron Rothschild and the Initial Stage of Jewish Settlement in Palestine (1882-1890): A Different Type of Colonization?" *Journal of Historical Geography* 19.2 (1993): 142-56.

Abaza, Mona. *Indonesian Students in Cairo: Islamic Education, Perceptions and Exchanges* (Paris: Cahier d'Archipel, 1994).

—. "Southeast Asia and the Middle East: Al-Manar and Islamic Modernity," in Claude Guillot, Denys Lombard, and Roderich Ptak (eds), *From the Mediterranean to the China Sea: Miscellaneous Notes* (Wiesbaden: Harrassowitz Verlag, 1998): 93-111.

Abbot, George F. "The Near Eastern Crisis," *The Quarterly Review* 210 (April 1909).

Abou-El-Haj, Rifa'at 'Ali. "Historiography in West Asian and North African Studies since Sa'id's Orientalism," in Arif Dirlik, Vinay Bahl, and Peter Gran (eds), *History after the Three Worlds: Post-Eurocentric Historiographies* (New York: Rowman & Littlefield Publishers, 2000): 67-84.

Abu-Manneh, Butrus. "The Islamic Roots of the Gülhane Rescript," *Die Welt des Islams* 34 (1994): 173-203.

Abu-Tarbush Quevedo, José. "De oriente próximo a Latinoamérica: la emigración árabe a través del Atlántico," *Política Exterior* 24.133 (2010): 163-7.

Adams, Julia. "Principals and Agents, Colonialists and Company Men: The Decay of Colonial Control in the Dutch East Indies," *American Sociological Review* 61.1 (1996): 12–28.

Adams, Sean Patrick. "Soulless Monsters and Iron Horses: The Civil War, Institutional Change, and American Capitalism," in Michael Zakim and Gary J. Kornblith (eds), *Capitalism Takes Command: The Social Transformation of Nineteenth-Century America* (Chicago: University of Chicago Press, 2012): 249–76.

Adanır, Fikret. *Die Makedonische Frage* (Wien: Franz Steiner Verlag, 1979).

Adas, Michael. "From Avoidance to Confrontation: Peasant Protest in Precolonial and Colonial Southeast Asia," *CSSH* 23.2 (1981): 217–47.

Akal, Emel. *Milli Mücadelenin Başlangıcında: Mustafa Kemal, Ittihat Terakki ve Bolşevizm* (Istanbul: Iletişim, 2012).

Akarlı, Engin. "The Tangled Ends of an Empire: Ottoman Encounters with the West and Problems of Westernization—an Overview," *CSSAAME* 26.3 (2006): 353–66.

Akçam, Taner. *From Empire to Republic: Turkish Nationalism and the Armenian Genocide* (London: Zed Books, 2004).

Akçuraoğlu, Yusuf. *Üç Tarz-ı Siyaset* (Istanbul: Matbaa-i Kadir, 1911).

Akhund, Nadine. "Muslim Representation in the Three Ottoman Vilayets of Macedonia: Administration and Military Power (1878–1908)," *Journal of Muslim Minority Affairs* 29.4 (2009): 443–54.

Akmir, Abdeluahed. *La inmigración arabe en Argentina (1880–1980)* (Madrid: Universidad Complutense de Madrid, 1991).

Akmir, Abdeluahed, ed. *Los árabes en América Latina: Historia de una emigración* (Madrid: Siglo XXI de España Editores, 2009).

Aktan, Reşat. "The Burden of Taxation on the Peasants," in Charles Issawi (ed.), *The Economic History of Turkey, 1800–1914* (Chicago: University of Chicago Press, 1980): 109–13.

Alavi, Seema. "'Fugitive Mullahs and Outlawed Fanatics': Indian Muslims in Nineteenth Century Trans-Asiatic Imperial Rivalries," *Modern Asian Studies* 45.6 (2011): 1337–82.

Alfaro-Velcamp, Theresa. *So Far from Allah, So Close to Mexico: Middle Eastern Immigrants in Modern Mexico* (Austin: University of Texas Press, 2007).

Allen, Richard B. "Satisfying the 'Want for Labouring People': European Slave Trading in the Indian Ocean, 1500–1850," *Journal of World History* 21.1 (2010): 45–73.

Altundağ, Şinasi. *Kavalalı Mehmet Ali Paşa Isyanı: Mısır Meselesi, 1831–1841* (Ankara: Türk Tarih Kurumu, 1988).

Amarilio, Junior. *As vantagens da imigração syria no Brasil: em torno de uma polêmica entre os Snrs. Herbert V. Levy e Salomão Jorge, no "Diário de São Paulo"* (Rio de Janiero: Off. Gr. Da S.A.A. Noite, 1935).

Anderson, Benedict. *Imagined Communities: Reflections on the Origin and Spread of Nationalism* (New York: Verso, 1983).

Anduze, Eric. *La franc-maçonnerie de la Turquie Ottomane, 1908–1924* (Paris: L'Harmattan, 2005).

al-Ansari, Muhammad Nur b. Muhammad Khayr. *Ta'rikh Harakat al-Irshad wa al-Islah wa-shaykh al-Irshadiyyin Ahmad Muhammad Surkitti fi Indunisiya* (Kuala Lumpur: International Islamic University, 2000).

Anscombe, Frederick F. *The Ottoman Gulf: The Creation of Kuwait, Saudi Arabia, and Qatar* (New York: Columbia University Press, 1997).

—. "Islam and the Age of Ottoman Reform," *Past and Present* 208 (August 2010): 159–89.

Antoljak, Stjepan. "Prilog historijatu borbe Albanaca za svoj alfabet," *Gjurmime Albanologjike* II.1 (1969): 23–57.

Arsan, Andrew Kerim. "Failing to Stem the Tide: Lebanese Migration to French West Africa and the Competing Prerogatives of the Imperial State," *CSSH* 53.03 (2011): 450–78.

Arslan, Ali. "The Vlach Issue during the Late Ottoman Period and the Emergence of the Vlach Community (Millet)," *Études Balkaniques* 4 (2004): 121–39.

Arslan, Ismail. *Selanik'in Gölgesinde bir Sancak: Drama, 1864–1913* (Istanbul: Bilge Kültür Sanat, 2010).

Asad, Talal. "Ethnographic Representation, Statistics and Modern Power," in Brian Keith Axel (ed.), *From the Margins: Historical Anthropology and its Futures* (Durham, NC: Duke University Press, 2002): 66–91.

Aslanian, Sebouh David. *From the Indian Ocean to the Mediterranean: The Global Trade Networks of Armenian Merchants from New Julfa* (Berkeley: University of California Press, 2011).

Atamian, Sarkis. *The Armenian Community: The Historical Development of a Social and Historical Conflict* (New York: Philosophical Library, 1955).

Atay, Falih Rıfkı. *Kemalist Tiran ve Kaybolmuş Makidonya* (Ankara: Hakimiyeti Milliye, 1931).

Ateş, Sabri. "The Margins of Empire: Kurdish Militias in the Ottoman Tribal Zone (review)," *CSSAAME* 32.2 (2012): 459–61.

Austen, Ralph. "The Islamic Red Sea Slave Trade: An Effort at Quantification," in Robert Hess (ed.), *Proceedings of the Fifth International Conference on Ethiopian Studies* (Chicago: University of Illinois Chicago Circle Press, 1979): 461–5.

Austin, Robert Clegg. *Founding a Balkan State: Albania's Experiment With Democracy, 1920–1925* (Toronto: University of Toronto Press, 2012).

Autheman, André. *La Banque impérial ottomane* (Paris: Comité pour l'histoire économique et financière de la France, 1996).

Avramovski, Žviko. "Treći Reich i 'Velika Albanija' posle kapitulacije Italije (1943–1944)," *Radovi Zavoda za hrvatsku povijest* 9.1 (1976): 93–213.

Aybar, Celal. *Osmanlı Imparatorluğunun Ticaret Muvazensesi, 1878–1913* (Ankara: Devlet Istatistik Enstitüsü, 1939).

Aydın, Bilgin. "Osmanlı devlet'inde tekkeler reform ve Meclis-i Meşayıh'ın Şeyhülislamlık'a bağlı olarak kuruluşu, faaliyetleri ve arşivi," *Istanbul Araştırmaları* 7 (1998): 93–109.

Aydin, Cemil. "The Politics of Conceptualizing Islam and the West," *Ethics & International Affairs* 18.3 (2004): 89–96.

Bacevich, A. J. "Disagreeable Work: Pacifying the Moros, 1903–1906," *Military Review* (June 1982): 50–1.

Bahajin, Said. "El modelo Latinoamericano en la Integración de los Inmigrantes árabes," *Ra Ximhai* 4.3 (2008): 737–73.

Bakić, Jovo. "Extreme-Right Ideology, Practice and Supporters: Case Study of the Serbian Radical Party," *Journal of Contemporary European Studies* 17.2 (2009): 193–207.

Ballinger, Pamela, and Jasna Apomega, Virginia R Dominguez, Charles Hale, Anastasia Karakasidou, lidija Nikoevi, Peter Skalnk, and Glenda Sluga. "'Authentic Hybrids' in the Balkan Borderlands," *Current Anthropology* 45.1 (2004): 31–60.

Banac, Ivo. *The National Question in Yugoslavia: Origins, History, Politics* (Ithaca, NY: Cornell University Press, 1984).

Bandžović, Safet. "Demografska deosmanizacija Balkana i kretanja bosanskohercegovačkih muhadžira (1878–1914)," *Bosna i Hercegovina u okviru Austro-Ugarske 1878–1918* (2011): 207–34.

Bang, Anne. *Sufis and Scholars of the Sea: Family Networks in East Africa, 1860–1925* (London: RoutledgeCurzon 2003).

—. "Authority and Piety, Writing and Print: A Preliminary Study of the Circulation of Islamic Texts in Late Nineteenth-and Early Twentieth-Century Zanzibar," *Africa* 81.1 (2011): 89–107.

Baptist, Edward E. "Toxic Debt, Liar Loans, Collateralized and Securitized Human Beings, and the Panic of 1837," in Michael Zakim and Gary J. Kornblith (eds), *Capitalism Takes Command: The Social Transformation of Nineteenth-Century America* (Chicago: University of Chicago Press, 2012): 69–93.

Bard, Solomon. *Traders of Hong Kong: Some Foreign Merchant Houses, 1841–1899* (Hong Kong: Urban Council, 1993).

Barkin, David and John W. Bennett. "Kibbutz and Colony: Collective Economies and the Outside World," *CSSH* 14.4 (1972): 456–83.

Barrows, David. "History of the Population," *Census of the Philippine Islands, 1903. Volume I: Geography, History, and Population* (Washington, DC: United States Bureau of Census, 1905).

Bayly, Christopher A. *Indian Society and the Making of the British Empire* (Cambridge: Cambridge University Press,1980).

—. *Rulers, Townsmen and Bazaars: North Indian Society in the Age of British Expansion, 1770–1870* (Cambridge: Cambridge University Press, 1988).

—. *The Birth of the Modern World, 1780–1914* (Oxford: Blackwell, 2004).

Beachey, Richard W. "The East African Ivory Trade in the Nineteenth Century," *Journal of African History* 8.2 (1967): 269–90.

Bennett, Norman. *The Zanzibar Letters of Edward D. Ropes Jr., 1882–1892* (Boston: Boston University, 1973).

—. *A History of the Arab State of Zanzibar* (London: Methuen, 1978).

—. *Arab versus European* (New York: Africana Publishing Company, 1986).

Betta, Chiara. "The Baghdadi Jewish Diaspora in Shanghai: Community, Commerce and Identities," *Sino-Judaica* 4 (2003): 81–104.

—. "From Orientals to Imagined Britons: Baghdadi Jews in Shanghai," *Modern Asian Studies* 37.4 (2003): 999–1023.

Bhacker, M. Reda. *Trade and Empire in Muscat and Zanzibar* (London: Routledge, 1992).

Bilenky, Serhiy. *Romantic Nationalism in Eastern Europe: Russian, Polish, and Ukrainian Political Imaginations* (Palo Alto: Stanford University Press, 2012).

Bingöl, Sedat. *Tanzimat Devrinde Osmanlı'da Yargı Reformu: Nizamiyye Mahkemeleri'nin Kuruluşu ve İşleyişi, 1840–1876* (Eskişehir: Anadolu Üniversitesi Yayınları, 2004).

Biolsi, Thomas. "The Birth of the Reservation: Making the Modern Individual among the Lakota," *American Ethnologist* 22.1 (February 1995): 28–53.

Birdal, Murat. *The Political Economy of Ottoman Public Debt: Insolvency and European Financial Control in the Late Nineteenth Century* (London: I.B. Tauris, 2010).

Bjelajać, Mile. "Migrations of Ethnic Albanians in Kosovo 1938–1950," *Balcanica* 38 (2007): 219–30.

Bjork, Katharine. "The Link That Kept the Philippines Spanish: Mexican Merchant Interests and the Manila Trade, 1571–1815," *Journal of World History* 9.1 (2005): 25–50.

Black, Ian. *A Gambling Style of Government: The Establishment of the Chartered Company's Rule in Sabah, 1878–1915* (Kuala Lumpur: Oxford University Press, 1983).

Blackhawk, Ned. *Violence over the Land: Indians and Empires in the Early American West* (Cambridge: Harvard University Press, 2006).

Blaisdell, Donald C. *European Financial Control in the Ottoman Empire* (New York: Columbia University Press, 1929).

Blok, Anton. "The Narcissism of Minor Differences," *European Journal of Social Theory* 1.1 (1998): 33–56.

—. "The Enigma of Senseless Violence," in Goran Aijmer and Jon Abbink (eds), *Meanings of Violence: A Cross-Cultural Perspective* (Oxford: Berg, 2000): 23–38.

Bloxham, Donald. *The Great Game of Genocide: Imperialism, Nationalism, and the Destruction of the Ottoman Armenians* (Oxford: Oxford University Press, 2005).

—. "Terrorism and Imperial Decline: The Ottoman-Armenian Case," *European Review of History—Revue européenne d'Histoire* 14.3 (2007): 301–24.

Bluhm-Warn, Jutta. "Al-Manar and Ahmad Soorkattie: Links in the Chain of Transmission on Muhammad 'Abudh's Ideas to the Malay-Speaking World," in Peter G. Riddell and Tony Street (eds), *Islam: Essays on Scripture, Thought and Society* (Leidin: Brill, 1997): 295–308.

Blumi, Isa. "Capitulations in the Late Ottoman Empire: The Shifting Parameters of Russian and Austrian Interests in Ottoman Albania, 1878–1912," *Oriente Moderno* 83.3 (2003): 635–47.

— "Contesting the Edges of the Ottoman Empire: Rethinking Ethnic and Sectarian Boundaries in the Malësore, 1878–1912," *IJMES* 35.2 (May 2003): 237–56.

—. "The Evolution of Red Sea Trade in the 19th Century Ottoman Yemen," *Journal of Turkish Studies Special Issue: In Memoriam Şinasi Tekin* 31.1 (2007): 157–75.

—. *Chaos in Yemen: Societal Collapse and the New Authoritarianism* (London: Routledge, 2010).

—. *Reinstating the Ottomans: Alternative Balkan Modernities, 1800–1912* (New York: Palgrave Macmillan, 2011).

—. *Foundations of Modernity: Human Agency and the Imperial State* (New York: Routledge, 2012).

Bonacich, Edna. "A Theory of Middleman Minorities," *American Sociological Review* 38.5 (1973): 583–94.

Borchard, Edwin. *State Insolvency and Foreign Bondholders: General Principles* (New Haven: Yale University Press, 1951).

Bosma, Ulbe. "The Cultivation System (1830–1870) and its Private Entrepreneurs on Colonial Java," *Journal of Southeast Asian Studies* 38.02 (2007): 275–91.

Boué, Ami. *La Turquie d'Europe* (Paris: Arhur Bertrand, 1840).

Bou-Nacklie, N. E. "Tumult in Syria's Hama in 1925: The Failure of a Revolt," *Journal of Contemporary History* 33.2 (1998): 273–89.

Bowen, Huw V. *The Business of Empire: The East India Company and Imperial Britain, 1756–1833* (Cambridge: Cambridge University Press, 2008).

Boyar, Ebru. *Ottomans, Turks and the Balkans: Empire Lost, Relations Altered* (London: Tauris Academic Studies, 2007).

Boztemur, Recep. "Religion and Politics in the Making of American Near East Policy, 1918–1922," *Journal for the Study of Religions and Ideologies* 4.11 (2010): 45–59.

Brah, Avtar. *Cartographies of Diaspora: Contesting Identities* (New York: Routledge, 1996).

Brantlinger, Patrick. "Victorians and Africans: The Genealogy of the Myth of the Dark Continent," *Critical Inquiry* 12.1 (1985): 166–203.

Brégain, Gildas. "L'influence de la tutelle mandataire française sur l'identification des élites syriennes et libanaises devant la société argentine (1900–1946)," *Revue européenne des migrations internationales* 27.3 (2012): 177–99.

Brisku, Adrian. "Internalizing Europe: Albanian Perceptions of the Continent in Historical Perspective (1878–2008)," *Journal of Educational Media, Memory, and Society* 1.2 (2009): 97–124.

Brockway, Thomas P. "Britain and the Persian Bubble, 1888–92," *The Journal of Modern History* 13.1 (1941): 36–47.

Brown, Beverly. "Muslim Influence on Trade and Politics in the Lake Tanganyika Region," *African Historical Studies* 4.3 (1971): 617–29.

Brown, Keith. *The Past in Question: Modern Macedonia and the Uncertainties of Nation* (Princeton: Princeton University Press, 2003).

—. *Loyal unto Death: Trust and Terror in Revolutionary Macedonia* (Bloomington: Indiana University Press, 2013).

Brown, Kevin S. and Jane K. Cowan. "Introduction: Macedonian Inflections," in Jane K. Cowan (ed.), *Macedonia—The Politics of Identity and Difference* (London: Pluto Press, 2000): 1–4.

Brown, Rajeswary A. "The Decline of Arab Capitalism in Southeast Asia," in Ahmed I. Abushouk and Ahmed I. Hassan (eds), *The Hadhrami Diaspora in Southeast Asia: Identity Maintenance or Assimilation?* (Leiden: Brill, 2009): 109–33.

Brubaker, Rogers. "The Aftermath of Empire and the Unmixing of Peoples," in Karen Barkey and Mark von Hagen (eds), *After Empire: Multiethnic Societies and Nation-Building: The Soviet Union and the Russian, Ottoman, and Habsburg Empires* (Boulder: University of Colorado Press, 1997): 155–80.

—. "Ethnicity without Groups," *Archives européenes de sociologie* XLIII.2 (2002): 163–89.

—. "The 'diaspora' diaspora," *Ethnic and Racial Studies* 28.1 (January 2005): 1–19.

Brunnbauer, Ulf. "Fertility, Families and Ethnic Conflict: Macedonians and Albanians in the Republic of Macedonia, 1944–2002," *Nationalities Papers* 32.3 (2004): 565–98.

Buelens, Frans and Stefaan Marysse. "Returns on Investments during the Colonial Era: The Case of the Belgian Congo," *The Economic History Review* 62.1 (2009): 135–66.

Burhanuddin, Jajat. "Aspiring for Islamic Reform: Southeast Asian Requests for Fatwas in al-Manar," *Islamic Law and Society* 12.1 (2005): 9–26.

Buzpinar, Ş. Tufan. "Abdulhamid II and Sayyid Fadl Pasha of Hadramawt: An Arab Dignitary's Ambitions, 1876–1900," *Journal of Ottoman Studies* 13 (1993): 227–39.

—. "Opposition to the Ottoman Caliphate in the Early Years of Abdülhamid II: 1877–1882," *Die Welt des Islams* 36.1 (1996): 59–89.

Byler, Charles. "Pacifying the Moros: American Military Government in the Southern Philippines, 1899–1913," *Military Review* (May–June 2005): 41–5.

Caccamo, Francesco. "L'Adriatico degli arbëreshë: il 'mare nostro' albanese e italiano," in Stefano Trinchese and Francesco Caccamo (eds), *Adriatico contemporaneo. Rotte e percezioni del mare comune tra Ottocento e Novecento* (FrancoAngeli: Milano, 2008).

Campos, Camila Pastor de Maria y. "Inscribing Difference: Maronites, Jews and Arabs in Mexican Public Culture and French Imperial Practice 1," *Latin American and Caribbean Ethnic Studies* 6.2 (2011): 169–87.

De Carolis, Adriana P. "La Hamalliyya di Nioro del Sahel: politica coloniale e identità islamica," *Africa* 45.2 (1990): 236–60.

Carrillo, Luis Ramirez. *Secretos de Familia: Libaneses y Elites Empresariales en Yucatan* (Mexico City: Consejo Nacional para la Cultura y las Artes, 1994).

Cassis, Youssef (ed.). *Finance and Financiers in European History, 1880–1960* (Cambridge: Cambridge University Press, 1992).

Chatty, Dawn. *Displacement and Dispossession in the Modern Middle East* (Cambridge: Cambridge University Press, 2010).

Cheong, Eang Weng. "The Decline of Manila as the Spanish Entrepôt in the Far East, 1785–1826: Its Impact on the Pattern of Southeast Asian Trade," *Journal of Southeast Asian Studies* 2.02 (1971): 142–58.

Chertier, Edmound. *Réformes en Turquie* (Paris: Dentu, Librairie-Editeur, 1858).

Chun, Allen J. "Pariah Capitalism and the Overseas Chinese of Southeast Asia: Problems in the Definition of the Problem," *Ethnic and Racial Studies* 12.2 (1989): 233–56.

Chung, Tan. "The Britain-China-India Trade Triangle (1771–1840)," *Indian Economic & Social History Review* 11.4 (1974): 411–31.

Civantos, Christina. "Custom-building the Fictions of the Nation Arab Argentine Rewritings of the Gaucho," *International Journal of Cultural Studies* 4.1 (2001): 69–87.

Clancy-Smith, Julia. *Mediterraneans: North Africa and Europe in an Age of Migration, c. 1800–1900* (Berkeley: University of California Press, 2010).

Clarence-Smith, William G. *The Economics of the Indian Ocean Slave Trade in the Nineteenth Century* (London: Routledge, 1989).

— "Middle Eastern Migrants in the Philippines: Entrepreneurs and Cultural Brokers," *Asian Journal of Social Sciences* 32.3 (2004): 425–57.

—. "Middle Eastern Entrepreneurs in South East Asia, c. 1750–c. 1940," in Ina Baghdiantz McCabe, Gelina Iarlaftis, and Ioanna P. Minoglou (eds), *Diaspora Entrepreneurial Networks: Four Centuries of History* (London: Berg, 2005): 217–44.

Clay, Christopher. "Labour Migration and Economic Conditions in Nineteenth-century Anatolia," *Middle Eastern Studies* 34.4 (1998): 1–32.

—. *Gold for the Sultan: Western Bankers and Ottoman Finance 1856–1881: A Contribution to Ottoman and to International Financial History* (London: I.B. Tauris, 2000).

Clayer, Nathalie. "The Albanian Students of the Mekteb-i Mulkiye: Social Networks and Trends of Thought," in Elisabeth Ozdalga (ed.), *Late Ottoman Society: The Intellectual Legacy* (London: Routledge/Curzon Press, 2005): 289–339.

—. *Aux origines du nationalisme albanais: La naissance d'une nation majoritairement musulmane en Europe* (Paris: Karthala, 2006).

—. "Adapting Islam to Europe: The Albanian Example," *Islam und Muslime in (Südost) Europa im Kontext von Transformation und EU-Erweiterung* (2010): 53–69.

Clayton, Daniel. "Colonizing, Settling and the Origins of Academic Geography," *The Wiley-Blackwell Companion to Human Geography* (2011): 50–70.

Cleary, Marc C. "Plantation Agriculture and the Formulation of Native Land Rights in British North Borneo," *The Geographical Journal* 158.2 (1992): 170–81.

Clifford, James. "Diasporas," *Cultural Anthropology* 9.3 (1994): 302–38.

Cole, Juan R. "Shaikh al-Ra'is and Sultan Abdülhamid II: The Iranian Dimension of Pan-Islam," *Histories of the Modern Middle East: New Directions*(2002): 167–85.

Colomb, Philip H. *Slave Catching in the Indian Ocean* (London: Longmans, 1873).

Coomes, Oliver T. and Bradford L. Barham. "The Amazon Rubber Boom: Labor Control, Resistance, and Failed Plantation Development Revisited," *Hispanic American Historical Review* (1994): 231–57.

Cooper, Frederick. *Planation Slavery on the East Coast of Africa* (New Haven: Yale University Press, 1977).

—. *Colonialism in Question: Theory, Knowledge, History* (Berkeley: University of California Press, 2005).

Cooper, Frederick and Ann Lauria Stoler (eds). *Tensions of Empire: Colonial Cultures in a Bourgeois World* (Berkeley: University of California Press, 1989).

Crampton, Jeremy W. "The Cartographic Calculation of Space: Race Mapping and the Balkans at the Paris Peace Conference of 1919," *Social & Cultural Geography* 7.5 (2006): 731–52.

Crews, Robert D. *For Prophet and Tsar: Islam and Empire in Russia and Central Asia* (Cambridge, MA: Harvard University Press, 2009).

Curčin, Milan. "Milan Rakić and the Idea of Kosovo," *The Slavonic and East European Review* 18.52 (1939): 170–4.

Cushman, Thomas. "Anthropology and Genocide in the Balkans: An Analysis of Conceptual Practices of Power," *Anthropological Theory* 4.1 (2004): 5–28.

Cvijić, Jovan. "The Geographical Distribution of the Balkan Peoples," *Geographical Review* 5.5 (1918): 345–61.

—. "The Zones of Civilization of the Balkan Peninsula," *Geographical Review* 5.6 (1918): 470–82.

Çadırcı, Musa. *Tanzimat Döneminde Anadolu Kentleri'nin Soysal ve Ekonomik Yapısı* (Ankara: Türk Tarih Kurumu, 1997).

Çağaptay, Soner. "Citizenship Policies in Interwar Turkey," *Nations and Nationalism* 9.4 (2003): 601–19.

Çakır, Coşkun. *Tanzimat Dönemi Osmanlı Maliyesi* (Istanbul: Küre Yayınları, 2001).

Çiçek, Nazan. *The Young Ottomans: Turkish Critics of the Eastern Question in the Late Nineteenth Century* (London: I.B. Tauris, 2010).

Çomu, Aslı Emine. *The Exchange of Populations and Adana, 1830–1927* (Istanbul: Libra Kitap, 2011).

Dakin, Douglas. *The Greek Struggle in Macedonia, 1897–1913* (Thessaloniki: Institute for Balkan Studies, 1993).

Dale, Stephen F. "The Mappilla Outbreaks: Ideology and Social Conflict in Nineteenth-Century Kerala," *The Journal of Asian Studies* 35.1 (1975): 85–97.

—. *Islamic Society on the South Asian Frontier: The Mappilas of Malabar, 1498–1922* (Oxford: Clarendon, 1980).

Darwin, John. "Imperialism and the Victorians: The Dynamics of Territorial Expansion," *English Historical Review* 112 (1997): 614–42.

Davidson, Roderick. "The Armenian Crisis: 1912–1914," *American Historical Review* 53.3 (April 1948): 481–505.

—. *Reform in the Ottoman Empire, 1856–1876* (Princeton: Princeton University Press, 1963).

Davis, Mike. *Late Victorian Holocausts: El Niño Famines and the Making of the Third World* (London: Verso, 2002).

Demirci, Sevtap. *British Public Opinion towards the Ottoman Empire during the Two Crises: Bosnia-Herzegovina (1908–1909) and Balkan Wars (1912–1913)* (Istanbul: The ISIS Press, 2006).

Dennis, Brad. "Patterns of Conflict and Violence in Eastern Anatolia Leading Up to the Russo-Turkish War and the Treaty of Berlin," in M. Hakan Yavuz (ed.), *War & Diplomacy: The Russo-Turkish War of 1877–1878 and the Treaty of Berlin* (Salt Lake City: University of Utah Press, 2012): 273–301.

Deringil, Selim. "The Struggle against Shiism in Hamidian Iraq: A Study in Ottoman Counter-Propaganda," *Die Welt des Islams* 30.1/4 (1990): 45–62.

—. "Legitimacy Structures in the Ottoman State: The Reign of Abdülhamid II (1876–1909)," *IJMES* 23.3 (1991): 345–59.

—. "'They Live in a State of Nomadism and Savagery': The Late Ottoman Empire and the Post-Colonial Debate," *CSSH* 45.3 (2003): 311–42.

—. *Conversion and Apostasy in the Late Ottoman Empire* (Cambridge: Cambridge University Press, 2012).

Dërmaku, Ismet. *Kuvendi i Lidhjes Shqiptare të Pejës "Besa Besë" 1899* (Prishtinë: NP, 1997).

—. *Nikolla N. Naço- Korça (1843–1913): Apostuli i Shqiptarizmit* (Prishtinë: NP, 2000).

Dirks, Nicholas B. *The Scandal of Empire: India and the Creation of Imperial Britain* (Cambridge, MA: Belknap Press, 2006).

Distler, Paul Antonie. "Exit the Racial Comics," *Educational Theatre Journal* 18.3 (1966): 247–54.

Dodani, Visar. *Memoret e Mija* (Constanţa: NP, 1930).

Dragostinova, Theodora. "Navigating Nationality in the Emigration of Minorities between Bulgaria and Greece, 1919–1941," *East European Politics and Societies* 23.2 (Spring 2009): 185–212.

—. *Between Two Motherlands: Nationality and Emigration among the Greeks of Bulgaria, 1900–1949* (New York: Cornell University Press, 2011).

Drakulić, Slobodan. "Anti-Turkish Obsession and the Exodus of Balkan Muslims," *Patterns of Prejudice* 43.3–4 (2009): 233–49.

Draper, Stark. "The Conceptualization of an Albanian Nation," *Ethnic and Racial Studies* 20.1 (1997): 123–44.

Durham, Mary Edith. *Through the Lands of the Serb* (London: E. Arnold, 1904).

—. "Some Montenegrin Manners and Customs," *The Journal of the Royal Anthropological Institute of Great Britain and Ireland* 39 (1909): 85–96.

Dwight, Harrison G. O. *Christianity in Turkey: A Narrative of the Protestant Reformation in the Armenian Church* (London: J. Nisbet, 1854).

Ediger, Volkan Ş. *Osmanlı'da Neft ve Petrol* (Istanbul: ODTü Yayıncılık, 2006).

Eldem, Vedat. *Osmanlı Imparatorluğunun Iktisadi Şartları Hakkında bir Tetkik* (Istanbul: Iş Bankası Yayınları, 1970).

Elsie, Robert. *Kosovo: In the Heart of the Powder Keg* (New York: East European Monographs, 1997).

Elson, Robert E. *Village Java under the Cultivation System, 1830–1870* (Sydney: Allen & Unwin, 1994).

Elteren, M. V. "Workers' Control and the Struggles Against 'Wage Slavery' in the Gilded Age and After," *The Journal of American Culture* 26.3 (2003): 188–203.

Emrence, Cem. *Remapping the Ottoman Middle East: Modernity, Imperial Bureaucracy and the Islamic State* (London: I.B. Tauris, 2011).

Engin, Vahdettin. *Rumeli Demiryolları* (Istanbul: Eren Yayincilik, 1993).

Enver Pasha, *Enver Paşa'nın Anıları (1881–1908)*, ed. H. E. Cengiz (Istanbul: Iletişim Yayınları, 1991).

Euraque, Darío A. "Nation Formation, Mestizaje and Arab Palestinian Immigration to Honduras, 1880–1930s," *Critique: Journal for Critical Studies of the Middle East* 4.6 (1995): 25–37.

Evered, Emine. *Empire and Education under the Ottomans: Politics, Reform and Resistance from the Tanzimat to the Young Turks* (London: I.B. Tauris, 2012).

Fabian, Johannes. *Time and the Other: How Anthropology Makes its Objects* (New York: Columbia University Press, 1983).

Fahmy, Khaled. *All the Pashas Men: Mehmed Ali, His Army and the Making of Modern Egypt* (Cairo: American University of Cairo Press, 2002).

Farah, Caesar E. "Great Britain, Germany and the Ottoman Caliphate," *Der Islam* 66.2 (1989): 264–88.

Farques, Phillippe. "Migration et identité: Le paradoxe des influences réciproques," *Esprit*, no. 361 (2010): 6–16.

Farrant, Leda. *Tippu Tip and the East African Slave Trade* (London: Hamilton, 1975): 78–86.

Farsy, Abdallah S. and Randall L. Pouwels. *The Shafi'i Ulama of East Africa, c. 1830–1970: A Hagiographic Account* (Madison: University of Wisconsin Press, 1989).

Fauzi, Nurulwahidah, Ali Mohammad, Ali and Saim Kayadibi. "The Religious-Intellectual Network: The Arrival of Islam in the Archipelago," *Ottoman Connections to the Malay World: Islam, Law and Society* (Kuala Lumpur: Islamic Book Trust, 2011): 1–31.

Fawaz, Leila. *Merchants and Migrants in Nineteenth Century Beirut* (Cambridge: Cambridge University Press, 1983).

Fawcett, Louise and Eduardo Posada-Carbo. "Arabs and Jews in the Development of the Colombian Caribbean 1850–1950," *Immigrants & Minorities* 16.1–2 (1997): 57–79.

Featherstone, Donald. "A Military Anomaly—the Army of the East India Company 1757–1857," *The RUSI Journal* 138.1 (1993): 48–52.

Federspiel, Howard M. *Sultans, Shamans, and Saints: Islam and Muslims in Southeast Asia* (Honolulu: University of Hawaii Press, 2007).

Fenner, R. Michael. "Hybridity and the 'Hadhrami Diaspora' in the Indian Ocean Muslim Networks," *Asian Journal of Social Science* 32.3 (2004): 353–72.

Ferguson, Niall. *The Ascent of Money: A Financial History of the World* (New York: Penguin, 2008).

Ferris, John. "'The Internationalism of Islam': The British Perception of a Muslim Menace, 1840–1951," *Intelligence and National Security* 24.1 (2009): 57–77.

Findley, Carter V. *Bureaucratic Reform in the Ottoman Empire: The Sublime Porte, 1789–1922* (Princeton: Princeton University Press, 1980).

—. "The Tanzimat," in Reşat Kasaba (ed.), *The Cambridge History of Turkey, vol. iv, Turkey in the Modern World* (Cambridge: Cambridge University Press, 2008): 11–37.

Firkatian, Mari. *Retaining Ethnic Identity: The Armenians in Bulgaria* (New York: Routledge, 2008).

Fitzgerald, Edward Peter. "France's Middle Eastern Ambitions, the Sykes-Picot Negotiations, and the Oil Fields of Mosul, 1915–1918," *The Journal of Modern History* 66.4 (1994): 697–725.

Fortna, Benjamin C. *Imperial Classroom: Islam, the State, and Education in the Late Ottoman Empire* (New York: Oxford University Press, 2002).

Fortune, Robert. *Three Years' Wanderings in the Northern Provinces of China: Including a Visit to the Tea, Silk, and Cotton Countries; with an Account of the Agriculture and Horticulture of the Chinese, New Plants, etc.* (London: J. Murray, 1847).

Foucault, Michel. *The Archaeology of Knowledge & the Discourse on Language*, trans. A. M. Sheridan Smith (London: Tavistock, 1972).

Frazee, Charles A. *The Orthodox Church and the Independent Greece 1821–1852* (Cambridge: Cambridge University Press, 1969).

Freitag, Ulrike. *Indian Ocean Migrants and State Formation: I Hadhramawt* (Leiden: Brill, 2003).

Fuccaro, Nelida. *Histories of City and State in the Persian Gulf: Manama since 1800* (Cambridge: Cambridge University Press, 2009).

Fulton, Robert. A. *Honor for the Flag: The Battle of Bud Dajo-1906 and the Moro Massacre* (Bend, OR: Tumalo Creek Press, 2011).

Gabaccia, Donna R. "Is Everywhere Nowhere? Nomads, Nations, and the Immigrant Paradigm in United States History," *The Journal of American History* 86.3 (1999): 1115–34.

Gauld, William A. "The 'Dreikaiserbündnis' and the Eastern Question, 1871–6," *English Historical Review* 40.CLVIII (1925): 207–21.

Gaunt, David and Jan Bet-Şawoce. *Massacres, Resistance, Protectors: Muslim-Christian Relations in Eastern Anatolia during World War I* (New York: Gorgias Press Llc, 2006).

Gavrilis, George. "The Greek-Ottoman Boundary as Institution, Locality, and Process, 1832–1882," *American Behavioral Scientist* 51.10 (June 2008): 1516–37.

Gawrych, George. *The Crescent and the Eagle: Ottoman Rule, Islam and the Albanians, 1874–1913* (London: I.B. Tauris, 2006).

Gaynor, Jennifer L. "Piracy in the Offing: The Law of Lands and the Limits of Sovereignty at Sea," *Anthropological Quarterly* 85.3 (2012): 817–57.

Gelvin, James L. *Divided Loyalties: Nationalism and Mass Politics in Syria at the Close of Empire* (Berkeley: University of California Press, 1998).

Gilbar, Gad G. "The Muslim Big Merchant-Entrepreneurs of the Middle East, 1860–1914," *Die Welt des Islams* 43.1 (2003): 1–36.

Gilbert, Erik. *Dhows and the Colonial Economic of Zanzibar, 1860–1970* (Athens: Ohio University Press, 2004).

Gilsenan, Michael. "Translating Colonial Fortunes: Dilemmas of Inheritance in Muslim and English Laws across a Nineteenth-Century Diaspora," *CSSAAME* 31.2 (2011): 355–71.

Gingeras, Ryan. "Between the Cracks: Macedonia and the 'Mental Map' of Europe," *Canadian Slavonic Papers* 50.3.4 (September–December 2008): 1–18.

—. *Sorrowful Shores: Violence, Ethnicity, and the End of the Ottoman Empire, 1912–1923* (New York: Oxford University Press, 2009).

—. "Last Rites for a 'Pure Bandit': Clandestine Service, Historiography and the Origins of the Turkish 'Deep State,'" *Past & Present* 206.1 (2010): 151–74.

—. "The Sons of Two Fatherlands: Turkey and the North Caucasian Diaspora, 1914–1923," *European Journal of Turkish Studies. Social Sciences on Contemporary Turkey*, 2011. [Online] Online since 30 November 2011, URL: http://ejts.revues.org/index4424.html (accessed on 12 January 2013).

Gladstone, William E. *Bulgarian Horrors and the Question of the East* (London: John Murray, 1876).

Glassman, Jonathon. *Feasts and Riot: Revelry, Rebellion, and Popular Consciousness on the Swahili Coast, 1856–1888* (Portsmouth, NH: Heinemann, 1995).

Gleeck, Lewis E. *American Business and Philippine Economic Development* (Manila: Carmelo and Bauermann, 1975).

Glenny, Misha. *The Balkans: Nationalism, War and the Great Powers, 1804–1999* (New York: Viking, 2000).

Go, Julian. "'Racism' and Colonialism: Meanings of Difference and Ruling Practices in America's Pacific Empire," *Qualitative Sociology* 27.1 (2004): 35–58.

—. "The 'New' Sociology of Empire and Colonialism," *Sociology Compass* 3.5 (2009): 775–88.

Goebel, Michael. "Von der hispanidad zum Panarabismus. Globale Verflechtungen in Argentiniens Nationalismen," *Geschichte und Gesellschaft* (2011): 523–58.

Goh, Daniel P. S. "States of Ethnography: Colonialism, Resistance, and Cultural Transcription in Malaya and the Philippines, 1890s–1930s," *CSSH* 49.1 (2007): 109–42.

Goldstein, Jonathan. "The Sorkin and Golab Theses and their Applicability to South, Southeast, and East Asian Port Jewry," *Jewish Culture and History* 4.2 (2001): 179–96.

—. "Singapore, Manila and Harbin as Reference Points for Asian 'Port Jewish' Identity," *Jewish Culture and History* 7.1–2 (2004): 271–90.

González, Nancie. *Dollar, Dove, and Eagle: One Hundred Years of Palestinian Migration to Honduras* (Ann Arbor: University of Michigan Press, 1992).

Gould, Andrew G. "Lords or Bandits? The Derebeys of Cilicia," *IJMES* 7.04 (1976): 485–506.

Gounaris, Basil C. "Railway Construction and Labour Availability in Macedonia in the Late Nineteenth Century," *Byzantine and Modern Greek Studies* 13.1 (1989): 139–58.

—. *Steam over Macedonia, 1870–1912: Socio-economic Change and the Railway Factor* (New York: East European Monographs, 1993).

—. "Social Cleavages and National 'Awakening' in Ottoman Macedonia," *Eastern European Quarterly* 24.4 (January 1996): 409–26.

Gowing, Peter G. *Mandate in Moroland: The American Government of Muslim Filipinos, 1899–1920* (Quezon City: University of Philippines System, 1977).

Grabill, Joseph L. *Protestant Diplomacy and the Near East: Missionary Influence on American Policy, 1810–1927* (Minneapolis: University of Minnesota Press, 1971).

Grandin, Greg. *Fordlandia: The Rise and Fall of Henry Ford's Forgotten Jungle City* (New York: Metropolitan Books, 2009).

Green, Abigail. "Nationalism and the 'Jewish International': Religious Internationalism in Europe and the Middle East c. 1840–c. 1880," *CSSH* 50.2 (2008): 535–58.

Grenouilleau, Olivier Petre (ed.). *From Slave Trade to Empire: European Colonisation of Black Africa, 1780s–1880s* (London: Routledge, 2004).

Grigoriadis, Ioannis N. "Redefining the Nation: Shifting Boundaries of the 'Other' in Greece and Turkey," *Middle Eastern Studies* 47.1 (2011): 167–82.

Gualtieri, Sarah "'Becoming' White: Race, Religion and the Foundations of Syrian/Lebanese Ethnicity in the United States," *Journal of American Ethnic History* (2001): 29–58.

— "Gendering the Chain Migration Thesis: Women and Syrian Transatlantic Migration, 1878–1924," *CSSAAME* 24.1 (2004): 67–78.

Le Guennec-Coppens, Françoise. "Changing Patterns of Hadrami Migration and Social Integration in East Africa," in U. Freitag and W. G. Clarence-Smith (eds), *Hadrami Traders, Scholars and Statesmen in the Indian Ocean, 1750s to 1960s* (Leiden: Brill, 1997): 157–74.

Guridy, Frank A. *Forging Diaspora: Afro-Cubans and African Americans in a World of Empire and Jim Crow* (New York: University of North Carolina Press, 2010).

Guy, Nicola. *The Birth of Albania: Ethnic Nationalism, the Great Powers of World War I and the Emergence of Albanian Independence* (London: I.B. Tauris, 2013).

Guzina, Ružica. *Opština u Srbiji, 1839–1918: Pravno-politička i sociološka studija* (Belgrade: Rad, 1976).

Güçlü, Yücel. "The Struggle for Mastery in Cilicia: Turkey, France, and the Ankara Agreement of 1921," *The International History Review* 23.3 (2001): 580–603.

Güran, Tevfik. *Osmanlı Devleti'nin Ilk Istatistik Yıllığı, 1897* (Ankara: T.C. Başbakanlık Devlet Istatistik Enstitüsü, 1997).

Hacisalihoğlu, Mehmet. *Die Jung Türken und die Mazedonische Frage, 1890–1918* (Munich: Oldenburg, 2003).

Hakan, Sinan. *Osmanlı Arşiv Belgelerinde Kürtler ve Kürt Direnişleri (1817–1867)* (Istanbul: Doz, 2007).

Halabe, Liz Hamui de. *Los judíos de Alepo en México* (Mexico City: Maguén David, 1989).

Halabi, Awad. "Liminal Loyalties: Ottomanism and Palestinian Responses to the Turkish War of Independence, 1919–22," *Journal of Palestine Studies* 41.3 (2012): 19–37.

Halaçoğlu, Ahmet. *Balkan Harbi Sırasında Rumeli'den Türk Göçleri (1912–1913)* (Ankara: TTK, 1995).

Hall, Richard C. *The Balkan Wars 1912–1913: Prelude to the First World War* (London: Routledge, 2000).

Hall, Stuart. "Cultural Identity and Diaspora," in Padmini Mongia (ed.), *Contemporary Postcolonial Theory: A Reader* (London: Arnold, 1996): 110–21.

Hamui-Halabe, Liz. *Los judíos de Alepo en México* (Mexico City: Maguén David, 1989).

—. "Re-creating Community: Christians from Lebanon and Jews from Syria in Mexico, 1900–1938," *Immigrants & Minorities* 16.1–2 (1997): 125–45.

Hanioğlu, Şükrü. *The Young Turks in Opposition* (New York: Oxford University Press, 1995).

—. *Preparation for a Revolution: The Young Turks, 1902–1908* (Oxford: Oxford University Press, 2001).

—. *A Brief History of the Late Ottoman Empire* (Princeton, NJ: Princeton University Press, 2008).

—. *Atatürk: An Intellectual Biography* (Princeton: University of Princeton Press, 2011).

Hansen, Lene. "Past as Preface: Civilizational Politics and the 'Third' Balkan War," *Journal of Peace Research* 37.3 (May 2000): 345–62.

Hanssen, Jens. *Fin de Siècle Beirut: The Making of an Ottoman Provincial Capital* (Oxford: Oxford University Press, 2005).

Harrison, Christopher. *France and Islam in West Africa, 1860–1960* (Cambridge: Cambridge University Press, 2003).

Hasimoto, Kohei. "Lebanese Population Movement, 1920–1939: Towards a Study," in Albert Hourani and Nadim Shehadi (eds), *The Lebanese in the World: A Century of Emigration* (London: I.B. Taurus, 1992): 65–107.

Hawkins, Michael. "Imperial Historicism and American Military Rule in the Philippines' Muslim South," *Journal of Southeast Asian Studies* 39.3 (2008): 411–29.

—. "Managing a Massacre: Savagery, Civility, and Gender in Moro Province in the Wake of Bud Dajo," *Philippine Studies* 59.1 (2011): 83–105.

Hegyi, Ottmar. "Minority and Restricted Uses of the Arabic Alphabet: The Aljamiado Phenomenon," *Journal of the American Oriental Society* 99.2 (1979): 262–9.

Heras, Maria Cruz. *La emigración libanesa en Costa Rica* (Madrid: Editorial Cantárabia, 1991).

Hertner, Peter. *The Balkan Railways, International Capital and Banking from the End of the 19th Century until the Outbreak of the First World War* (Sofia: Bulgarian National Bank, 2006).

Hincapie, Luz Mercedes. "Pacific Transactions: Nicolás Tanco Armero and the Chinese Coolie Trade to Cuba," *Journal of Iberian and Latin American Research* 16.1 (2010): 27–41.

Hirschkind, Charles. *The Ethical Soundscape: Cassette Sermons and Islamic Counterpublics* (New York: Columbia University Press, 2006).

Hirschon, Renée (ed.). *Crossing the Aegean: An Appraisal of the 1923 Compulsory Population Exchange between Greece and Turkey* (New York: Berghahn Books, 2003).

Ho, Engseng. *The Graves of Tarim: Genealogy and Mobility across the Indian Ocean* (Berkeley: University of California Press, 2006).

Hobsbawm, Eric. *The Age of Capital, 1848–1975* (New York: Mentor, 1979).

—. *The Age of Empire 1875–1914* (New York: Pantheon, 1987).

Hopper, Matthew S. "East Africa and the End of the Indian Ocean Slave Trade," *Journal of African Development* 13.1 (Spring 2011): 39–65.

Hoxie, Frederick E. "Retrieving the Red Continent: Settler Colonialism and the History of American Indians in the US," *Ethnic and Racial Studies* 31.6 (2008): 1153–67.

Hubka, Gustav. *Die Österreichisch-Ungarische Offiziermission in Makedonien: 1903–1909* (Wien: F. Tempsky, 1910).

Hudson, Michael. *Trade, Development and Foreign Debt: How Trade and Development Concentrate Economic Power in the Hands of Dominant Nations* (New York: ISLET, 2009).

Humphrey, Michael. "Ethnic History, Nationalism and Transnationalism in Argentine Arab and Jewish Cultures," *Immigrants & Minorities* 16.1–2 (1997): 167–88.

Hunt, Geoffrey. *Colorado's Volunteer Infantry in the Philippine Wars, 1898–1899* (Albuquerque: University of New Mexico Press, 2006).

Huntington, Ellsworth. "Railroads in Asia Minor," *Bulletin of the American Geographical Society* (1909): 691–6.

Hurley, Vic. *Swish of the Kris: The Story of the Moros* (New York: E. P. Dutton & Co., Inc., 2010).

—. *Jungle Patrol, the Story of the Philippine Constabulary (1901–1936)* (Dallas: Cerberus Books, 2011).

Hyland, Steven. "'Arisen from Deep Slumber': Transnational Politics and Competing Nationalisms among Syrian Immigrants in Argentina, 1900–1922," *Journal of Latin American Studies* 43.03 (2011): 547–74.

Hyman, Anthony. "Turkestan and Pan-Turkism Revisited," *Central Asian Survey* 16.3 (1997): 339–51.

Içduygu, Ahmet and B. Ali Soner. "Turkish Minority Rights Regime: Between Difference and Equality," *Middle Eastern Studies* 42.3 (May 2006): 447–68.

Iliffe, John. *A Modern History of Tanganyika* (Cambridge: Cambridge University Press, 1979).

Inalcık, Halil, Suraiya Faroqhi, Bruce McGowan, and Donald Quataert. *An Economic and Social History of the Ottoman Empire* (Cambridge: Cambridge University Press, 1997).

Iorachi, Constantin. *Citizenship, Nation and State Building: The Integration of Northern Dobrogea into Romania, 1878–1913* (Pittsburgh: University of Pittsburgh Press, 2002).

Ipek, Nedim. *Rumeli'den Anadolu'ya Türk Göçleri* (Ankara: Türk Tarih Kurumu Basımevi, 1994).

Ireland, Philip W. "The Baghdad Railway: Its New Rôle in the Middle East," *Journal of the Royal Central Asian Society* 28.3 (1941): 329–39.

Islamoğlu, Huri. "Property as a Contested Domain: A Reevaluation of the Ottoman Land Code of 1858," in Roger Owen (ed.), *New Perspectives on Property and Land in the Middle East* (Cambridge, MA: Harvard University Press, 2001): 3–61.

Ismail Kemal Bey. *The Memoirs of Ismail Kemal Bey* (London: Constable, 1920).

Issawi, Charles. *An Economic History of the Middle East and North Africa* (New York: Columbia University Press, 1982).

Jackson, Stanley. *The Sassoons* (London: Heineman, 1968).

Jacob, M. C. and Ira Katznelson. "Agendas for Radical History," *Radical History Review* 36 (September 1986): 26–47.

Jacob, Wilson Chacko. "Of Angels and Men: Sayyid Fadl b. 'Alawi and Two Moments of Sovereignty," *Arab Studies Journal*, vol. XX, no. 1 (Spring 2012): 40–72.

Jagodić, Miloš. *Naseljavange Kneze vine Srbije 1860–1861* (Belgrade: Istorijski institute, 2004).

JanMohamed, Abdul. "The Economy of Manichean Allegory: The Function of Racial Difference in Colonialist Literature," *Critical Inquiry* 12 (1985): 59–87.

Jelavich, Barbara. *Russia's Balkan Entanglements, 1806–1914* (Cambridge: Cambridge University Press, 1991).

Jelavich, Barbara and Charles Jelavich. *The Establishment of the Balkan National States, 1804-1920* (Seattle: University of Washington Press, 1977).

Johnson, Kevin. *The Huddled Masses Myth: Immigration and Civil Rights* (Philadelphia: Temple University Press, 2003).

Johnson, Walter. *Rivers of Dark Dreams: Slavery and Empire in the Cotton Kingdom* (Cambridge, MA: Harvard University Press, 2013).

Jonge, Huub de. "Discord and Solidarity among the Arabs in the Netherlands East Indies, 1890-1942," *Indonesia* 55 (1993): 73-90.

Kaiser, Hilmar. "Armenian Property, Ottoman Law and Nationality Policies during the Armenian Genocide, 1915-1916," in Olaf Farschid, Manfred Kropp, and Stephan Dähne (eds), *The First World War as Remembered in the Countries of the Eastern Mediterranean* (Beirut: Orient-Institut, 2006): 49-71.

Kaleshi, Hasan and Hans-Jürgen Kornrumpf. "Das Wilajet Prizren. Beitrag zur Geschichte der türkischen Staatsreform auf dem Balkan im 19. Jahrhundert," *Südostforschungen. Internationale Zeitschrift für Geschichte, Kultur und Landeskunde Südosteuropas* (München), 26 (1967): 176-238.

Kaligian, Dikran Mesrob. *Armenian Organization and Ideology Under Ottoman Rule, 1908-1914* (Piscataway: Transaction Publication, 2011).

Kamberović, Husnija. *Mehemed Spaho (1883-1939): Politička Biografija* (Sarajevo: Vijeće Kongresa bošnjačkih intelektualaca, 2009).

Kaplan, Sam. "Documenting History, Historicizing Documentation: French Military Officials' Ethnological Reports on Cilicia," *CSSH* 44.2 (2002): 344-69.

—. "Territorializing Armenians: Geo-texts, and Political Imaginaries in French-occupied Cilicia, 1919-1922," *History and Anthropology* 15.4 (2004): 399-423.

Kaptein, Nico J. G. "Arabophobia and Tarekat: How Sayyid 'Uthman Became Advisor to the Netherlands Colonial Administration," in Ahmed I. Abushouk and Hassan A. Ibrahim (eds), *The Hadhrami Diaspora in Southeast Asia: Identity Maintenance or Assimilation* (Leiden: Brill, 2009): 33-44.

Kara, Ismail. "Meclis-i Meşyaih, Ulema-Tarikat Münasebetleri ve İstanbul'da Şeyhlik Yapmış Beş Zatın Kendi Kaleminden Terceme-i Hali," *Kutadgubilig* (Istanbul) 1 (Ocak 2002): 185-214.

Kara, Mustafa. "Ikinci meşrutiyet devrinde dervişlerin sosyal ve kültürel etkinlikleri," in Ahmed Yaşar Ocak (ed.), *Osmanlı Toplumunda Tasavvuf ve Sufiler* (Ankara: Türk Tarih Kurumu, 2005): 533-8.

Karakasidou, Anastasia N. *Fields of Wheat, Hills of Blood: Passages to Nationhood in Greek Macedonia, 1870-1990* (Chicago: University of Chicago Press, 1997).

Karam, John Tofik. "A Cultural Politics of Entrepreneurship in Nation-Making: Phoenicians, Turks, and the Arab Commercial Essence in Brazil," *Journal of Latin American Anthropology* 9.2 (2004): 319-51.

—. *Another Arabesque: Syrian-Lebanese Ethnicity in Neoliberal Brazil* (Philadelphia: Temple University Press, 2007).

Karimullah, Kamran I. "Rival Moral Traditions in the Late Ottoman Empire, 1839-1908," *Journal of Islamic Studies* 24.1 (2013): 37-66.

Kark, Ruth. "Changing Patterns of Landownership in Nineteenth-century Palestine: The European Influence," *Journal of Historical Geography* 10.4 (October 1984): 357-84.

Kark, Ruth and Seth J. Frantzman. "Bedouin, Abdül Hamid II, British Land Settlement, and Zionism: The Baysan Valley and Sub-district 1831-1948," *Israel Studies* 15.2 (2010): 49-79.

—. "The Negev: Land, Settlement, the Bedouin and Ottoman and British Policy 1871–1948," *British Journal of Middle Eastern Studies* 39.1 (2012): 53–77.

Karpat, Kemal. *Ottoman Population, 1830–1914, Demographic and Social Characteristics* (Madison: University of Wisconsin Press, 1985).

—. *The Politicization of Islam: Reconstructing Identity, State, Faith, and Community in the Late Ottoman State* (Oxford: Oxford University Press, 2001).

Kasaba, Reşat. "Open-Door Treaties: China and the Ottoman Empire Compared," *New Perspectives on Turkey* 7 (1992): 77–89.

—. *A Moveable Empire: Ottoman Nomads, Migrants and Refugees* (Seattle: University of Washington Press, 2009).

Kempe, Michael. "'Even in the Remotest Corners of the World': Globalized Piracy and International Law, 1500–1900," *Journal of Global History* 5.03 (2010): 353–72.

Kerimoğlu, Hasan Taner. *Ittihat-Terakki ve Rumlar, 1908–1914* (Istanbul: Libra Kitap, 2009).

Kerr, Malcolm H. *Islamic Reform: The Political and Legal Theories of Muhammad Abduh and Rashid Rida* (Berkeley: University of California Press, 1966).

Khalid, Adeeb. *The Politics of Muslim Cultural Reform: Jadidism in Central Asia* (Berkeley: University of California Press, 1999).

Khan, Mujeeb R. "The 'Other' in the Balkans: Historical Constructions of Serbs and 'Turks,'" *Journal of Muslim Minority Affairs* 16.1 (1996): 49–63.

Khater, Akram. *Inventing Home: Emigration, Gender, and the Middle Class in Lebanon, 1870–1920* (Berkeley: University of California Press, 2001).

—. "Becoming 'Syrian' in America: A Global Geography of Ethnicity and Nation," *Diaspora: A Journal of Transnational Studies* 14.2 (2005): 299–331.

Khoury, Dina Rizk. *State and Provincial Society in the Ottoman Empire: Mosul, 1540–1834* (Cambridge: Cambridge University Press, 1997).

Khoury, Philip S. "The Tribal Shaykh, French Tribal Policy, and the Nationalist Movement in Syria between Two World Wars," *Middle Eastern Studies* 18.2 (1982): 180–93.

—. *Syria and the French Mandate: The Politics of Arab Nationalism, 1920–1945* (Princeton: Princeton University Press, 1987).

Khuri-Makdisi, Ilham. *The Eastern Mediterranean and the Making of Global Radicalism, 1860–1914* (Berkeley: University of California Press, 2010).

Kia, Merhdad. "Pan-Islamism in Late Nineteenth-century Iran," *Middle Eastern Studies* 32.1 (1996): 30–52.

Kieser, Hilmer L. "Dr Mehmed Reshid (1873–1919): A Political Doctor," in H. L. Kieser and D. J. Schaller (eds), *The Armenian Genocide and the Shoah* (Zurich: Chronos, 2002): 245–80.

King, Charles. "The Micropolitics of Social Violence," *World Politics* 56 (2004): 431–55.

King, E. H. "A Journey through Armenian Cilicia," *Journal of the Royal Central Asian Society* 24.2 (1937): 234–46.

Klein, Janet. *The Margins of Empire: Kurdish Militias in the Ottoman Tribal Zone* (Palo Alto: Stanford University Press, 2011).

Klich, Ignácio. "Criollos and Arabic Speakers in Argentina: An Uneasy Pas de Deux, 1888–1914," in Albert Hourani and Nadim Shehabi (eds), *The Lebanese in the World: A Century of Emigration* (London: I.B. Tauris, 1992): 243–83.

—. "Arab-Jewish Coexistence in the First Half of the 1900s' Argentina: Overcoming Self-Imposed Amnesia," in Ignacio Klich and Jeffrey Lesser (eds), *Arab and Jewish Immigrants in Latin America: Images and Realities* (London: Frank Cass, 1998): 1–37.

Knight, Alan. "Racism, Revolution, and Indigenismo: Mexico, 1910–1940," in Richard Graham (ed.), *The Idea of Race in Latin America: 1870–1940* (Austin: University of Texas Press, 1990): 71–113.

Knowlton, Charles. *Sírios e libaneses em São Paulo* (São Paulo: Editora Anhembi, 1961).

Knysh, Alexander D. *Islamic Mysticism: A Short History* (Leiden: Brill, 2000).

Kondo, Ahmet. "Kontributi i revistës 'Drita–Dituria' për përhapjen e ideve kombëtare dhe të njohurive shkencore (1884–1885)," *Studime historike* 3 (1970): 140–7.

—. *Çështja Kombëtare në Faqe të Shtypit të Rilindjes* (Tirana: 8 Nëntori, 1982).

Koponen, Juhani. "War, Famine, and Pestilence in Late Precolonial Tanzania: A Case for a Heightened Mortality," *International Journal of African Historical Studies* 21.4 (1988): 637–76.

Kovács, Béla and Gábor Timár. "The Austro-Hungarian Triangulations in the Balkan Peninsula (1855–1875)," *Cartography in Central and Eastern Europe* (2010): 535–44.

Krikorian, Mesrob K. *Armenians in the Service of the Ottoman Empire, 1860–1908* (London: Routledge, 1977).

Križan, Mojmir. "New Serbian Nationalism and the Third Balkan War," *Studies in East European Thought* 46.1 (1994): 47–68.

Kuneralp, Sinan and Gül Tokay (eds), *Ottoman Documents on the Origins of World War One, The Macedonian Issue, 1879–1912, Part 2 1905–1912* (Istanbul: Isis, 2011).

Kuran, Ahmed Bedevi. *Inkılap Tarihimiz ve Ittihad ve Terakki* (Istanbul: Tan Matbaası, 1948).

Kurban, Taufik. *Os syrios e libaneses no Brasil* (São Paulo: Sociedade Impressora Paulista, 1933).

Kuri, Martha Diaz de and Lourdes Macluf. *De Libano a México, cronica de un pueblo emigrante* (México City: Grafica Creatividad y Disno, 1995).

Kutuloğlu, Muhammad H. *The Egyptian Question (1831–1841): The Expansionist Policy of Mehmed Ali Paşa in Syria and Asia Minor and the Reaction of the Sublime Porte* (Istanbul: Eren, 1998).

Küçükcan, Talip. "Re-Claiming Identity: Ethnicity, Religion and Politics among Turkish-Muslims in Bulgaria and Greece," *Journal of Muslim Minority Affairs* 19.1 (1999): 49–68.

Lacam, Guy. *Un banquier au Yunnan dans les annees 1930* (Paris: L'Harmattan, 1994).

Laffan, Michael. *Islamic Nationhood and Colonial Indonesia: The Umma below the Winds* (London: RoutledgeCurzon, 2003).

— "'Another Andalusia': Images of Colonial Southeast Asia in Arabic Newspapers," *Journal of Asian Studies* 66 (2007): 689–722.

Lakshmi, L. R. S. *The Malabar Muslims: A Different Perspective* (Cambridge: Cambridge University Press, 2012).

Lambert, Andrew. *The Crimean War: British Grand Strategy against Russia, 1853–56* (Oxford: Ashgate, 2011).

Landau, John M. *The Politics of Pan-Islam: Ideology and Organization* (Oxford: Clarendon Press, 1990).

Lange-Akhund, Nadine. *The Macedonian Question, 1893–1908. From Western Sources* (New York: East European Monographs, 1998).

Langlois, Victor. "Réchid Pacha et les réformes en Turquie," *Revue de l'Orient, de l'Algérie et des Colonies* 7 (1858): 15–16.

Largman, Esther Regina and Robert M. Levine. "Jews in the Tropics. Bahian Jews in the Early Twentieth Century," *The Americas* (1986): 159–70.

Lascaris, Michael. "Greece and Serbia during the War of 1885," *The Slavonic and East European Review* 11.31 (1932): 88–99.

Lauzière, Henri. "The Construction of Salafiyya: Reconsidering Salafism from the Perspective of Conceptual History," *IJMES* 42.3 (2010): 369–89.

Lawson, Fred H. *The Social Origins of Egyptian Expansionism during the Muhammad 'Ali Period* (New York: Columbia University Press, 1991).

Lesser, Jeffery. "(Re)Creating Ethnicity: Middle Eastern Immigration to Brazil," *Americas* 53.1 (1996): 45–65.

—. "'Jews are Turks Who Sell on Credit' Elite Images of Arabs and Jews in Brazil," in Ignacio Klich and Jeffrey Lesser (eds), *Arab and Jewish Immigrants in Latin America: Images and Realities* (London: Frank Cass, 1998): 38–56.

Leur, Jacob C. Van. *Indonesian Trade and Society* (Hague: Van Hoeve, 1967).

Leustean, Lucian N. "The Political Control of Orthodoxy in the Construction of the Romanian State, 1859–1918," *European History Quarterly* 37.1 (January 2007): 61–80.

Levene, Mark. *Genocide in the Age of the Nation State: Vol. 2: The Rise of the West and the Coming of Genocide* (London: I.B. Tauris, 2013).

Li, Tania Murray. "Ethnic Cleansing, Recursive Knowledge, and the Dilemmas of Sedentarism," *International Social Science Journal* 173 (2002): 361–71.

—. "Centering Labor in the Land Grab Debate," *The Journal of Peasant Studies* 38.2 (2011): 281–98.

Livanios, Dimitris. "Beyond 'ethnic cleansing': Aspects of the Functioning of Violence in the Ottoman and Post-Ottoman Balkans," *Southeast European and Black Sea Studies* 8.3 (2008): 189–203.

Loffman, Reuben. "In the Shadow of the Tree Sultans: African Elites and the Shaping of Early Colonial Politics on the Katangan Frontier, 1906–17," *Journal of Eastern African Studies* 5.3 (2011): 535–52.

Loizos, Peter. "Ottoman Half-lives: Long-term Perspectives on Particular Forced Migrations," *Journal of Refugee Studies* 12.3 (1999): 237–63.

Lomnitz-Adler, Claudio. "Nationalism as a Practical System: Benedict Anderson's Theory of Nationalism from the Vantage Point of Spanish America," in Miguel Angel Centeno and Fernando Lopez-Alves (eds), *The Other Mirror: Grand Theory through the Lens of Latin America* (Princeton: Princeton University Press, 2001): 329–59.

Lorimer, J. G. *Gazetter of the Persian Gulf, Oman, and Central Arabia, vol. 1: Historical* (Calcutta: Superintendent Government Printing, 1915).

Lucassen, Leo. "A Many-headed Monster: The Evolution of the Passport System in the Netherlands and Germany in the Long Nineteenth Century," in Jane Caplan and John Torpe (eds), *Documenting Individual Identity: The Development of State Practices in the Modern World* (Princeton: Princeton University Press, 2001): 235–55.

Lüdke, Tilman. *Jihad Made in Germany: Ottoman and German Propaganda and Intelligence Operations in the First World War* (Berlin: LIT, 2005).

Lust-Okar, Ellen Marie. "Failure of Collaboration: Armenian Refugees in Syria," *Middle Eastern Studies* 32.1 (1996): 53–68.

Machado, Pedro. "A Forgotten Corner of the Indian Ocean: Gujarati Merchants, Portuguese India and the Mozambique Slave-Trade, c. 1730–1830," *Slavery and Abolition* 24.2 (2003): 17–32.

MacKenzie, David. *The Serbs and Russian Pan-Slavism, 1875–1878* (Ithaca, NY: Cornell University Press, 1967).

Mahon, Milena. "The Macedonian Question in Bulgaria," *Nations and Nationalism* 4.3 (1998): 389–407.

Majd, Mohammad Gholi. *The Great Famine and Genocide in Persia, 1917–1919* (New York: University Press of America, 2003).

Majuru, Adrian. *Bucureștiul albanez* (București: Ararat, 2002).

Makdisi, Ussama. "Reclaiming the Land of the Bible: Missionaries, Secularism, and Evangelical Modernity," *The American Historical Review* 102.3 (1997): 680–713.

—. *The Culture of Sectarianism, Community, History and Violence in Nineteenth-Century Ottoman Lebanon* (Berkeley: University of California Press, 2000).

Maksutoviçi, Gelcu. *Istoria Comunitatti Albaneze din Romania* (Bucharest: Kriterion, 1992).

Malkki, Liisa H. *Purity and Exile: Violence, Memory, and National Cosmology among Hutu Refugees in Tanzania* (Chicago: University of Chicago Press, 1995).

Mappa, Sophia (ed.). *Les deux sources de l'exclusion: Economisme et replies identitaires* (Paris: Karthala, 1981).

Marcovits, Claude. *The Global World of Indian Merchants, 1750–1947: Traders of Sind from Bukhara to Panama* (Cambridge: Cambridge University Press, 2000).

Mardin, Şerif. *The Genesis of Young Ottoman Thought: A Study in the Modernization of Turkish Political Ideas* (Syracuse, NY: Syracuse University Press, 2000).

Mareci, Harieta and Ștefah Purici. "Under Pressure for Change: Nation State Building and Identity Mutations in Modern Romania (1866–1890)," in Steven G. Ellis and Lud'a Klusáková (eds), *Imagining Frontiers, Contesting Identities* (Rome: Edizioni Plus, 2007): 175–88.

Martin, Brad G. "Muslim Politics and Resistance to Colonial Rule: Shaykh Uways B. Muhammad Al-Barawi and the Qadiriya Brotherhood in East Africa," *Journal of African History* 10.3 (1969): 471–86.

—. *Muslim Brotherhoods in 19th Century Africa* (Cambridge: Cambridge University Press, 1976).

Marx, Karl. *Capital: A Critique of Political Economy*, trans. Ben Fowkes, vol. 1 (New York: Penguin Classics, 1992).

Matossian, Bedross Der. "From Bloodless Revolution to Bloody Counterrevolution: The Adana Massacres of 1909," *Genocide Studies and Prevention* 6.2 (2011): 152–73.

Mavrogordatos, George. "Orthodoxy and Nationalism in the Greek Case," *West European Politics* 26.1 (2003): 117–36.

McCabe, Ina Baghdiantz, Gelina Harlaftis, and Ioanna Peplasis Minoglou (eds). *Diaspora Entrepreneurial Networks: Four Centuries of History* (Oxford: Berg, 2005).

McCarthy, Justin. *Death and Exile: The Ethnic Cleansing of Ottoman Muslims, 1821–1922* (Princeton: The Darwin Press, 1995).

McClellan, George B. "Capture of Kars, and Fall of Plevna," *The North American Review* (1878): 132–55.

McDougall, James. "Savage Wars? Codes of Violence in Algeria, 1830s–1990s," *Third World Quarterly* 26/1 (2005): 117–31.

McIntosh, Janet. *The Edge of Islam: Power, Personhood, and Ethnoreligious Boundaries on the Kenya Coast* (Raleigh: Duke University Press Books, 2009).

McKale, Donald M. "'The Kaiser's Spy': Max von Oppenheim and the Anglo-German Rivalry Before and during the First World War," *European History Quarterly* 27.2 (1997): 199–219.

McKeown, Adam. "Global Migration 1846–1940," *Journal of World History* 15.2 (2004): 155–89.

McMeekin, Sean. *The Berlin-Baghdad Express: The Ottoman Empire and Germany's Bid for World Power* (Cambridge, MA: Belknap Press, 2010).

McPherson, Jim. "The Savage Innocents: Part I, King of the Castle: Henry W. Savage and the Castle Square Opera Company," *The Opera Quarterly* 18.4 (2002): 503–33.

Meadows, Martin. "The Philippine Claim to North Borneo," *Political Science Quarterly* 77.3 (1962): 321–35.

Medlicott, William N. *The Congress of Berlin and After: A Diplomatic History of the Near Eastern Settlement, 1878–1880* (London: Methuen & Co. Ltd, 1938).

—. "The Powers and the Unification of the Two Bulgarias, 1885: Part II (Continued)," *English Historical Review* (1939): 263–84.

Meeker, Michael E. *A Nation of Empire: The Ottoman Legacy of Turkish Modernity* (Berkeley: University of California Press, 2002).

Mehta, Uday Singh. *Liberalism and Empire: A Study in Nineteenth-Century British Liberal Thought* (Chicago: Chicago University Press, 1999).

Meininger, Thomas E. *Ignatiev and the Establishment of the Bulgarian Exarchate (1864–1872): A Study of Personal Diplomacy* (Madison: University of Wisconsin Press, 1970).

Mejcher, Helmut. "Oil and British Policy towards Mesopotamia, 1914–1918," *Middle Eastern Studies* 8.3 (1972): 377–91.

Meyer, James J. "Immigration, Return, and the Politics of Citizenship: Russian Muslims in the Ottoman Empire, 1860–1914," *IJMES* 39.1 (2007): 15–32.

Midhat, Ali Hayder. *The Life of Midhat Pasha: A Record of His Services, Political Reforms, Banishment, and Judicial Murder, Derived from Private Documents and Reminiscences* (London: J. Murray, 1903).

Miers, Suzanne. "Slavery and the Slave Trade as International Issues 1890–1939," *Slavery and Abolition* 19.2 (1998): 16–37.

Mihăilescu, Vintilă. "Balkanisation of the Mind or the New Political Mysticism," *European Journal of Science and Theology* 8.1 (2012): 143–9.

Mikhail, Alan. *Nature and Empire in Ottoman Egypt: An Environmental History* (Cambridge: Cambridge University Press, 2011).

Milićević, Milan. *Kraljevina Srbija* (Belgrade: Drzavna stamparija, 1884).

Miller, Daniel G. *American Military Strategy during the Moro Insurrection in the Philippines, 1903–1913* (KS: Army Command and General Staff College Fort Leavenworth, 2009).

Miller, Herbert H. *Economic Conditions in the Philippines* (Boston: Ginn & Co., 1920).

Milligan, Jeffrey Ayala. "Democratization or Neocolonialism? The Education of Muslims under US Military Occupation, 1903–20," *History of Education* 33.4 (2004): 451–67.

Mills, Lennox A. *British Malaya, 1824–1867* (Kuala Lumpur: Oxford University Press, 1966).

Mina, Jorge Nacif. *Crónicas de un inmigrante libanés en México* (Mexico City: Instituto Cultural Mexicano Libanés, 1995).

Minoglou, Ioanna P. "Ethnic Minority Groups in International Banking: Greek Diaspora Bankers of Constantinople and Ottoman State Finances, c. 1840–81," *Financial History Review* 9.02 (2002): 125–46.

Mitchell, Timothy. *Colonising Egypt* (Berkeley: University of California Press, 1988).

— "Everyday Metaphors of Power," *Theory and Society* 19.5 (1990): 545–77.

Moaddel, Mansoor. *Islamic Modernism, Nationalism, and Fundamentalism: Episode and Discourse* (Chicago: University of Chicago Press, 2005).

Mobini-Kesheh, Natalie. "Islamic Modernism in Colonial Java: The al-Irshad Movement," in U. Freitag and W. F. Clarence-Smith (eds), *Hadrami Traders, Scholars, and Statesmen in the Indian Ocean, 1750s–1960s* (Leiden: Brill, 1997): 185–98.

—. *The Hadrami Awakening: Community and Identity in the Netherlands East Indies, 1900–1942* (Ithaca: Cornell University Press, 1999).

Mojzes, Paul. *Balkan Genocides: Holocaust and Ethnic Cleansing in the Twentieth Century* (New York: Rowman & Littlefield Publishers, 2011).

Mongia, Radhika Viyas. "Race, Nationality, Mobility: A History of the Passport," *Public Culture* 11.3 (1999): 527–55.

Montandon, George. *Frontières nationales: Détermination objective de la condition primordial necéssaire à l'obtention d'une paix durable* (Lausanne: Self-published Brochure, 1915).

Moore, Lyndon and Jakub Kaluzny. "Regime Change and Debt Default: The Case of Russia, Austro-Hungary, and the Ottoman Empire Following World War One," *Explorations in Economic History* 42.2 (2005): 237–58.

Moroni, Ileana. *O Ergatis, 1908–1909: Ottomanism, National Economy and Modernization in the Ottoman Empire* (Istanbul: Libra Kitap, 2010).

Morrison, Alexander. "Sufism, Pan-Islamism and Information Panic: Nil Sergeevich Lykoshin and the Aftermath of the Andijan Uprising," *Past & Present* 214.1 (2012): 255–304.

Moses, John A. "The Coolie Labour Question and German Colonial Policy in Samoa, 1900–1914," *The Journal of Pacific History* 8.1 (1973): 101–24.

Moumdjian, Garabet. "Rebels with a Cause: Armenian-Macedonian Relations and their Bulgarian Connection, 1895–1913," in M. H. Yavuz and I. Blumi (eds), *War and Nationalism: The Balkan Wars, 1912–1913, and their Sociopolitical Implications* (Salt Lake City: The University of Utah Press, 2013): 132–75.

Myuhtar-May, Fetime. "Pomok Christianization (Pokrastvane) in Bulgaria during the Balkan Wars of 1912–1913," in M. H. Yavuz and I. Blumi (eds), *War and Nationalism: The Balkan Wars, 1912–1913, and their Sociopolitical Implications* (Salt Lake City: The University of Utah Press, 2013): 316–60.

Naçi, Nuçi. *Korça dhe fshatrat për çark* (Sofia: Mbrothësia, 1901).

Naço, Nikolla N. *Viitorul Romanismului in Balcan: Scisoare Deschisa* (Bucuresti: Tipografia G.A. Lazareanu, 1905).

Nadi, Yunus. *Ihtilal ve Inkılab-ı Osmani* (Istanbul: Matbaa-ı Cihan, 1909).

Nadri, Ghulam. *Eighteenth-Century Gujarat: The Dynamics of its Political Economy, 1750–1800* (Leiden: Brill, 2008).

Nathan, Eze. *The History of Jews in Singapore, 1830–1945* (Singapore: Herbilu, 1987).

Neep, Daniel. *Occupying Syria under the French Mandate: Insurgency, Space and State Formation* (Cambridge: Cambridge University Press, 2012).

Ner, Marcel. "Les musulmans de l'Indochine française," *Bulletin de l'Ecole Française d'Eztreme Orient* 41.2 (1941): 151–202.

Neuburger, Mary. "Pomak Borderlands: Muslims on the Edge of Nations," *Nationalities Papers* 28.1 (2000): 181–98.

Newman, Daniel. "The European Influence on Arabic during the Nahda: Lexical Borrowing from European Languages (ta'rib) in 19th-century Literature," *Arabic Language and Literature* 5.2 (2002): 1–32.

Nicholls, David. "No Hawkers and Pedlars: Levantines in the Caribbean," *Ethnic and Racial Studies* 4.4 (1981): 415–31.

—. "Lebanese of the Antilles: Haiti, Dominican Republic, Jamaica, and Trinidad," in Albert Hourani and Nadim Shehadi (eds), *The Lebanese in the World. A Century of Emigration. The Centre for Lebanese Studies. London* (London: I.B. Tauris, 1992): 339–60.

Nicolini, Beatrice. "The Myth of the Sultans in the Western Indian Ocean during the Nineteenth Century: A New Hypothesis," *African and Asian Studies* 8.3 (2009): 239–67.

Nikolić-Stojančević, Vodosava. *Leskovac i oslobodjeni predeli Srbije, 1877–1878 godine: Etnicke, demografske, socijalno-ekonomske i kulturne prilike* (Leskovac: Narodni muzej, 1975).

Nimtz Jr, August. *Islam and Politics in East Africa: The Sufi Order in Tanzania* (Minneapolis: University of Minnesota Press, 1980).

Nixon, Nicola. "Always Already European: The Figure of Skënderbeg in Contemporary Albanian Nationalism," *National Identities* 12.1 (2010): 1–20.

Niyazi, Adjutant Major. *Hatırat-ı Niyazi Yahud Tarihçe-yi Inkılab-ı Kebir-i Osmaniden bir Sahife* (Istanbul: Sabah Matbaası, 1326 [1910]).

Nobuyoshi, Fujinami. "The Patriarchal Crisis of 1910 and Constitutional Logic: Ottoman Greeks' Dual Role in the Second Constitutional Politics," *Journal of Modern Greek Studies* 27.1 (2009): 1–30.

Nopcsa, Franz Baron. "Ergänzungen zu Meinen Buche über die Bauten, Trachten und Geräte Nordalbaniens," *Zeitschrift für Ethnologie* 59.3/6 (1927): 279–81.

Northrup, David. "A Church in Search of a State: Catholic Missions in Eastern Zaïre, 1879–1930," *Journal of Church and State* 30.2 (1988): 309–19.

O'Brien, Patrick K. "The Costs and Benefits of British Imperialism, 1846–1914," *Past and Present* 120 (1988): 163–200.

Oded, Arye. *Islam in Uganda: Islamization through a Centralized State in Pre-Colonial Africa* (London: Wiley, 1974).

O'Fahey, R. S. A. Hofheinz, and Bernd Radtke. "The Khatmiyya Tradition," in R. S. O'Fahey (ed.), *Arabic Literature of Africa, I: The Writings of Eastern Sudanic Africa to c. 1900* (Leiden: Brill, 1994): 178–227.

Okey, Robin. *Taming Balkan Nationalism: The Habsburg "Civilizing Mission" in Bosnia, 1878–1914* (Oxford: Oxford University Press, 2007).

Okyar, Osman. "A New Look at the Problem of Economic Growth in the Ottoman Empire (1800–1914)," *The Journal of European Economic History* 16.1 (1987): 7–50.

Onley, James. "The Raj Reconsidered: British India's Informal Empire and Spheres of Influence in Asia and Africa," *Asian Affairs* 40.1 (2009): 44–62.

Owen, Roger. *The Middle East in the World Economy* (London: I.B. Tauris, 1993).

Owen, Roger and Şevket Pamuk (eds). *A History of the Economies of the Middle East in the Twentieth Century* (London: I.B. Tauris, 1998).

Özden, Sezgin and Üstüner Birben. "Ottoman Forestry: Socio-economic Aspect and its Influence Today," *Ciência Rural* 42.3 (2012): 459–66.

Özkara, Sami. *Türkische Arbeiterbewegung 1908 im Osmanischen Reich im Spiegel des Batschafisberichte, der volkswirtschaftlichen und politischen Entwicklungen* (Franfurt/ Main: Verlag Peter Lang, 1985).

Özkaya, Yücel. *Osmanlı Imparatorluğu'nda Ayanlık* (Ankara: Türk Tarih Kurumu, 1994).

Özoğlu, Hakan. *Kurdish Notables and the Ottoman State: Evolving Identities, Competing Loyalties, and Shifting Boundaries* (New York: State University of New York Press, 2004).

Pagden, Anthony. *Peoples and Empires: A Short History of European Migration, Exploitation, and Conquest from Greece to the Present* (New York: Modern Library, 2001).

Page, Melvin E. "The Manyema Hordes of Tippu Tip: A Case Study in Social Stratification and the Slave Trade in Eastern Africa," *The International Journal of African Historical Studies* 7.1 (1974): 69–84.

Palairet, Michael. "Fiscal Pressure and Peasant Impoverishment in Serbia before World War I," *The Journal of Economic History* 39.03 (1979): 719–40.

—. *The Balkan Economies, 1800–1914: Evolution without Development* (Cambridge: Cambridge University Press, 1997).

Pamuk, Şevket. "The Ottoman Empire in the 'Great Depression' of 1873–1896," *Journal of Economic History* 44.1 (1984): 107–18.

—. *The Ottoman Empire and European Capitalism, 1820–1913, Trade, Investment and Production* (Cambridge: Cambridge University Press, 1987).

—. *A Monetary History of the Ottoman Empire* (Cambridge: Cambridge University Press, 2000).

Pamuk, Şevket and Jeffrey G. Williamson, "Ottoman de-industrialization, 1800–1913: Assessing the Magnitude, Impact, and Response," *The Economic History Review* 64 S1 (2011): 159–84.

Panayi, Panikos and Pippa Virdee (eds). *Refugees and the End of Empire: Imperial Collapse and Forced Migration in the Twentieth Century* (New York: Palgrave Macmillan, 2011).

Pappas, Nicholas G. "Concepts of Greekness: The Recorded Music of Anatolian Greeks after 1922," *Journal of Modern Greek Studies* 17.2 (1999): 353–73.

Paul, James A. "Great Power Conflict over Iraqi Oil-the World War I Era," *Global Policy Forum* (October 2009). Available at www.globalpolicy.org/component/content/article/185/40479.html (accessed on 20 October 2012).

Perry, Duncan M. *The Politics of Terror: The Macedonian Liberation Movements, 1893–1903* (Durham: Duke University Press, 1988).

—. "The Macedonian Revolutionary Organization's Armenian Connection," *Armenian Review* 42.5 (1989): 61–70.

Petmezas, Socrates D. "Bridging the Gap: Rural Macedonia from Ottoman to Greek Rule (1900–1920)," in Lorans Tanatar Baruh and Vangelis Kechriotis (eds), *Economy and Society on Both Shores of the Aegean* (Athens: Alpha Bank Historical Archives, 2010): 355–95.

Petropulos, John A. *Politics and Statecraft in the Kingdom of Greece 1833–1843* (Princeton, NJ: Princeton University Press, 1968).

Peyfuss, Max. *Die Aromunische Frage: Ihre Entwicklung von den Ursprüngen bis zum Bukarest (1913) une die Haltung Österreich-Ungarns* (Wien: Wiener Archiv fur Geschichte, 1972).

Philliou, Christine. "Communities on the Verge: Unraveling the Phanariot Ascendancy in Ottoman Governance," *CSSH* 51.01 (2009): 151–81.

Pieroni, Andrea, Maria Elena Giusti, and Cassandra L. Quave. "Cross-Cultural Ethnobiology in the Western Balkans: Medical Ethnobotany and Ethnozoology among Albanians and Serbs in the Pešter Plateau, Sandžak, South-Western Serbia," *Human Ecology* 39.3 (2011): 333–49.

Pierson, Gerald J. "US Consuls in Zanzibar and the Slave Trade, 1870–1890," *Historian* 55.1 (1992): 53–68.

Plummer, Brenda Gayle. "Race, Nationality, and Trade in the Caribbean: The Syrians in Haiti, 1903–1934," *The International History Review* 3.4 (1981): 517–39.

Plüss, Caroline. "Baghdadi Jews in Hong Kong: Converting Cultural, Social and Economic Capital among Three Transregional Networks," *Global Networks* 11.1 (2011): 82–96.

Polanyi, Karl. *The Great Transformation: The Political and Economic Origins of Our Time* (Boston: Beacon Press, 2001).

Porter, Jeremy R. "Plantation Economics, Violence, and Social Well-Being: The Lingering Effects of Racialized Group Oppression on Contemporary Human Development in the American South," *Journal of Human Development and Capabilities* 12.3 (2011): 339–66.

Poulton, Hugh. "The Muslim Experience in the Balkan States, 1919–1991," *Nationalities Papers* 28.1 (2000): 45–66.

—. "Macedonians and Albanians as Yugoslavs," in D. Djokić (ed.), *Yugoslavism. Histories of Failed Idea, 1918–1992* (Madison: University of Wisconsin Press, 2003).

Price, Richard. *Making Empire: Colonial Encounters and the Creation of Imperial Rule in Nineteenth-Century Africa* (Cambridge: Cambridge University Press, 2008).

Prifti, Kristaq. *Dervish Hima (1872–1928)* (Tirana: 8 Nentori, 1987).

—. *Le Mouvement national albanais de 1896 à 1900: La Ligue de Pejë* (Tiranë: Akademia Historike, 1989).

Provence, Michael. *The Great Syrian Revolt and the Rise of Arab Nationalism* (Austin: University of Texas Press, 2005).

Purvis, Martin. "Between Late-Lasting Empire and Late-Developing Nation-State: A Triestine Perspective on City-State Relations," *Social & Cultural Geography* 10.3 (May 2009): 299–317.

Quataert, Donald. "The Age of Reforms," in Halil Inalcik and Donald Quataert (eds), *An Economic and Social History of the Ottoman Empire* (Cambridge: Cambridge University Press, 1994): 759–933.

Quevedo, José Abu-Tarbush. "De oriente próximo a Latinoamérica: la emigración árabe a través del Atlántico," *Política exterior* 24.133 (2010): 163–7.

Quirino, Carlos. *Philippine Tycoon: The Biography of an Industrialist, Vincente Madrigal* (Manila: Madrigal Memorial Foundation, 1987).

Qureshi, M. Naeem. *Pan-Islam in British Indian Politics: A Study of the Khilafat Movement, 1918–1924* (New York: Oxford University Press, 2009).

Raccagni, Michelle. "The French Economic Interests in The Ottoman Empire," *IJMES* 11.3 (1980): 339–76.

Radtke, Bernd. *The Exoteric Ahmad Ibn Idris: A Sufi's Critique of the Madhahib and the Wahhabis* (Leiden: Brill, 2000).

Rafael, Vicente L. "White Love: Surveillance and Nationalist Resistance in the US Colonization of the Philippines," in Amy Kaplan and Donald E. Pease (eds), *Cultures of United States Imperialism* (Raleigh: Duke University Press, 1993): 185–218.

Rahimi, Shukri. *Lufta e Shqiptarëve për Autonomi, 1897–1912* (Prishtinë: Enti i Teksteve dhe i Mjeteve Mësimore i Krahines Socialiste Autonome të Kosovës, 1978).

Ramet, Sabrina P. *Whose Democracy?: Nationalism, Religion, and the Doctrine of Collective Rights in Post-1989 Eastern Europe* (New York: Rowman & Littlefield Publishers, 1997).

Raşid, Ahmed. *Tarih-i Yemen ve San'a'*, 2 vols (Istanbul: Basiret Matbassı, 1291/1874).

Ray, Benjamin. *Myth, Ritual and Kingship in Buganda* (London: Oxford University Press, 1991).

Reid, James J. *Crisis of the Ottoman Empire: Prelude to Collapse, 1839–1878* (Stuttgart: Franz Steiner Verlag, 2000).

Reill, Dominque Kirchner. *Nationalists Who Feared the Nation: Adriatic Multi-Nationalism in Habsburg Dalmatia, Trieste, and Venice* (Palo Alto: Stanford University Press, 2012).

Reiss, H. S. (ed.). *The Political Thought of the German Romantics* (Oxford: Basil Blackwell, 1955).

Rempel, Ruth. "Trade and Transformation: Participation in the Ivory Trade in Late 19th-Century East and Central Africa," *Canadian Journal of Development Studies/Revue canadienne d'études du développement* 19.3 (1998): 529–52.

Renault, François. "The Structures of the Slave Trade in Central Africa in the 19th Century," *Slavery and Abolition* 9.3 (1988): 146–65.

Reno, William. "Order and Commerce in Turbulent Areas: 19th Century Lessons, 21st Century Practice," *Third World Quarterly* 25.4 (2004): 607–25.

Reynolds, Michael A. "Buffers, not Brethren: Young Turk Military Policy in the First World War and the Myth of Panturanism," *Past & Present* 203.1 (2009): 137–79.

—. *Shattering Empires: The Clash and Collapse of the Ottoman and Russian Empires, 1908–1918* (Cambridge: Cambridge University Press, 2011).

Rezun, Miron. "The Great Game Revisited," *International Journal* 41.2 (1986): 324–41.

Ricklefs, M. C. "The Middle East Connection and Reform and Revival Movements among the Putihan in 19th Century Java," in Eric Tagliacozzo (ed.), *Southeast Asia and the Middle East: Islam, Movement, and the Longue Duree* (Paolo Alto: Stanford University Press, 2009): 111–34.

Riddel, Peter. *Islam and the Malay-Indonesian World: Transmission and Responses* (Honolulu: University of Hawai'i Press, 2001).

Roberts, Lois J. *The Lebanese in Ecuador: A History of Emerging Leadership* (Boulder, CO: Westview Press, 2000).

Robins, Nick. *The Corporation that Changed the World: How the East India Company Shaped the Modern Multinational* (London: Pluto Press, 2006).

Rockel, Stephen J. "Slavery and Freedom in Nineteenth Century East Africa: The Case of Waungwana Caravan Porters," *African Studies* 68.1 (2009): 87–109.

Roland, Joan G. "Baghdadi Jews in India and China in the Nineteenth Century: A Comparison of Economic Roles," in Jonathan Goldstein (ed.), *The Jews of China: Historical and Comparative Perspectives*, vol. 1 (Armonk: M.E. Sharpe, 1999): 141–53.

Rosaldo, Renato. *Culture and Truth: The Remaking of Social Analysis* (Boston: Beacon Press, 1993).

Roth, Cecil. *The Sassoon Dynasty* (London: Robert Hale Limited, 1941).

Roudometof, Victor. "Nationalism, Globalization, Eastern Orthodoxy Unthinking 'the Clash of Civilizations' in Southeastern Europe," *European Journal of Social Theory* 2.2 (1999): 233–47.

—. "The Social Origins of Balkan Politics: Nationalism, Underdevelopment, and the Nation-State in Greece, Serbia, and Bulgaria, 1880–1920," *Mediterranean Quarterly* 11.3 (2000): 144–63.

—. *Nationalism, Globalization and Orthodoxy: The Social Origins of Ethnic Conflict in the Balkans* (New York: Greenwood, 2001).

Rustom, Asad J. *The Royal Archives of Egypt and the Origins of the Egyptian Expedition to Syria, 1831–1841* (Beirut: American Press, 1936).

Sacre, Jacques Najm. *Directorio por familias de los descendientes libanese de México y Centroamérica* (Mexico City: Centro de Difusión Cultural de la Misión de México, 1981).

Safran, William. "Diasporas in Modern Societies: Myths of Homeland and Return," *Diaspora* 1.1 (1991): 83–9.

Sağlam, Mehmet Hakan. *Osmanlı Devleti'nde Moratoryum, 1875–1881: Rüstum-ı Sitte'den Dünyun-ı Umumiyye'ye* (Istanbul: Tarih Vakfi Yurt Yayınları, 2007).

Said Paşa. *Said Paşa'nin Hatıratı*, 2 vols (Istanbul: Sabah Matbaası, 1910).

Saleeby, Najeeb M. *Studies in Moro History, Law, and Religion* (Manila: Bureau of Public Printing, 1905).

—. *The History of Sulu* (Manila: Bureau of Printing, 1908).

—. *The Moro Problem: An Academic Discussion of the History and Solution of the Problem of the Government of the Moros in the Philippine Islands* (Manila: P.I., 1913).

Salt, Jeremy. *Imperialism, Evangelism and the Ottoman Armenians, 1878–1896* (London: Routledge, 1993).

Salzmann, Ariel. *Tocqueville in the Ottoman Empire: Rival Paths to the Modern State* (Leiden: E. J. Brill, 2004).

Sanders, Ronald. *The High Walls of Jerusalem: A History of the Balfour Declaration and the Birth of the British Mandate for Palestine* (London: Holt, Rinehart and Winston, 1984).

Sarkar, Sumit. *Beyond Nationalist Frames: Postmodernism, Hindu Fundamentalism, History* (Bloomington: Indiana University Press, 2002).

Sarkissian, Margaret. "Armenians in South-East Asia," *Crossroads: An Interdisciplinary Journal of Southeast Asian Studies* (1987): 1–33.

Sartori, Andrew. "The Categorical Logic of a Colonial Nationalism: Swadeshi Bengal, 1904–1908," *CSSAAME* 23.1 and 2 (2003): 271–85.

—. "The British Empire and its Liberal Mission," *Journal of Modern History* 78.3 (September 2006): 623–42.

Satyanarayana, Adapa. "'Birds of Passage': Migration of South Indian Laborers to Southeast Asia," *Critical Asian Studies* 34.1 (2002): 89–115.

Saydam, Abdullah. *Kırım ve Kafkas Göçleri, 1856–1876* (Ankara: Türk Kurumu Basımevi, 1997).

Saz, Gökhan. "Turkophobia and Rising Islamophobia in Europe: A Quantification for the Negative Spillovers on the EU Membership Quest of Turkey," *European Journal of Social Sciences* 19.4 (2011): 479–91.

Schaebler, Birgit. "Practicing Musha: Common Lands and the Common Good in Southern Syria under the Ottomans and the French," in Roger Owen and Martin P. Bunton (eds), *New Perspectives on Property and Land in the Middle East* (Cambridge, MA: Harvard University Press, 2001): 241–311.

Schoenberg, Philip Ernest. "The Evolution of Transport in Turkey (Eastern Thrace and Asia Minor) under Ottoman Rule, 1856–1918," *Middle Eastern Studies* 13.3 (1977): 359–72.

Scott, James C. *Seeing Like the State: How Certain Schemes to Improve the Human Condition Have Failed* (New Haven: Yale University Press, 1999).

—. *The Art of Not Being Governed: An Anarchist History of Upland Southeast Asia* (New Haven: Yale University Press, 2009).

Şener, Abdüllatif. *Tanzimat Dönemi Osmanlı Vergi Sistemi* (Istanbul: Işaret, 1990).

Seth, Mesrovb J. *History of the Armenians in India* (Delhi: Gian, 1988).

Sharkey, Heather J. "Ahmad Zayni Dahlan's al-Futuhat al-Islamiyya: A Contemporary View of the Sudanese Mahdi," *Sudanic Africa* 5 (1994): 67–75.

Shepard, F. D. "Personal Experience in Turkish Massacres and Relief Work," *The Journal of Race Development* 1.3 (1911): 316–39.

Sheriff, Abdul. *Slaves, Spices and Ivory in Zanzibar* (London: J. Currey, 1987).

Shields, Sarah D. *Fezzes in the River: Identity Politics and European Diplomacy in the Middle East on the Eve of World War II* (New York: Oxford University Press, 2011).

Shorrock, William I. "The Origin of the French Mandate in Syria and Lebanon: The Railroad Question, 1901–1914," *IJMES* 1.2 (1970): 133–53.

Silverstein, Brian. "Sufism and Governmentality in the Late Ottoman Empire," *CSSAAME* 29.2 (2009): 171–85.

Şimşir, Bilal N. *Rumeli'den Türk Göçleri*, 3 vols (Ankara: Türk Tarih Kurumuyu, 1989).

Skendi, Stavro. *The Albanian National Awakening, 1878–1912* (Princeton: Princeton University Press, 1967).

Slama, Martin. "Paths of Institutionalization, Varying Divisions, and Contested Radicalisms: Comparing Hadhrami Communities on Java and Sulawesi," *CSSAAME* 31.2 (2011): 331–42.

—. "Translocal Networks and Globalisation within Indonesia: Exploring the Hadhrami Diaspora from the Archipelagos North-East," *Asian Journal of Social Science* 39.2 (2011): 238–57.

Sluglett, Peter. "Une mission sacrée pour qui? Quelques réflexions sur l'intégration nationale et le mandat britannique en Irak/Whose Sacred Trust? Some Thoughts on 'National Integration' and the British Mandate in Iraq," *Revue des mondes musulmans et de la Méditerranée* 117-18 (2007): 33–49.

—. "The British, the Sunnis and the Shi'is: Social Hierarchies of Identity under the British Mandate," *International Journal of Contemporary Iraqi Studies* 4.3 (2010): 257-73.

Smythe, Donald. "Perishing and the Disarmament of the Moros," *Pacific Historical Review* 31.3 (1962): 241–56.

Sohrabi, Nader. *Revolution and Constitutionalism in the Ottoman Empire and Iran* (Cambridge: Cambridge University Press, 2011).

Sönmez, Banu İşlet II. *Meşrutiyette Arnavut Muhalefeti* (Istanbul: YKY, 2007).

Sowards, Steven W. *Austria's Policy of Macedonian Reform* (Boulder: East European Monographs, 1989).

Spasić, Milan. "Podaci o agrarnim odnosima hrišćana u oslobodjenim krajevima, okruga Topličkog i Vranjskog za vreme turske vladavine," in Duško Kečkemet (ed.), *Vranjic kroz vjekove* (Split: Institut za historijn radničkog pokreta Dalmacije, 1984): 263-370.

Stamatopoulos, Dimitris. "Ecumenical Ideology in the Orthodox Millet (19th–20th Century)," in Lorans T. Taruh and Vangelis Kechriotis (eds), *Economy and Society on Both Shores of the Aegean* (Athens: Alpha Bank, 2010): 201-47.

Stich, Heinrich. *Die welwirtschaftliche Entwicklung der Anatolischen Produktion seit Anfangs des 19 Jahrhunderts* (Kiel: Druck von C.H. Jebens, 1929).

Stojančević, Vladimir. *Srbi i Bulgari, 1804-1878* (Novi Sad: Prometej, 1995).

Stoler, Anne L. *Capitalism and Confrontation in Sumatra's Plantation Belt, 1870-1979* (New Haven: Yale University Press, 1986).

Storey, Moorfield. *The Moro Massacre* (Boston, MA: The Anti-Imperialist League, 1906).

Strakes, Jason E. "Between Two Masters: Khuzestan, Southern Iraq, and Dualities of State Making in the Arab/Persian Gulf," *The Arab World Geographer* 14.4 (2011): 336-61.

Strayer, Robert W. *The Making of Mission Communities in East Africa: Anglicans and Africans in Colonial Kenya, 1875-1935* (New York: Heinemann Educational Publishers, 1978).

Sue, Christina. "The Dynamics of Color: Mestizaje, Racism and Blackness in Veracruz, Mexico," in Evelyn Glenn (ed.), *Shades of Difference: Transnational Perspectives on How and Why Skin Color Matters* (Palo Alto: Stanford University Press, 2009): 114-28.

Sumner, Benedict H. *Russia and the Balkans, 1870-1880* (Oxford: Oxford University Press, 1937).

Suvla, Refii Ş. "The Ottoman Debt, 1850-1939," in Charles Issawi (ed.), *The Economic History of the Middle East, 1800-1914* (Chicago: Chicago University Press, 1966): 94-106.

Swietochowski, Tadeusz. *Russian Azerbaijan, 1905-1920: The Shaping of a National Identity in a Muslim Community* (Cambridge: Cambridge University Press, 2004).

Szeman, Ioanna. "'Gypsy Music' and Deejays: Orientalism, Balkanism, and Romani Musicians," *The Drama Review* 53.3 (2009): 98–116.

Tagliacozzo, Eric. "Trafficking Human Subjects in the Malay World, 1850-1910," in David Kyle and Rey Koslowski (eds), *Global Human Smuggling: Comparative Perspectives* (New York: The Johns Hopkins University Press, 2011): 87-107.

Talhamy, Yvette. "American Protestant Missionary Activity among the Nusayris (Alawis) in Syria in the Nineteenth Century," *Middle Eastern Studies* 47.2 (2011): 215–36.

Tarling, Nicholas. *Piracy and Politics in the Malay World* (Melbourne: F.W. Cheshire, 1963).

Tasso, Alberto. *Aventura, trabajo y poder: Sirios e libaneses en Santiago del Estero, 1880–1980* (Buenos Aires: Ediciones Indice, 1988).

Tatsios, Theodore G. *The Megali Idea and the Greek-Turkish War of 1897: The Impact of the Cretan Problem on Greek Irredentism, 1866–1897* (New York: Columbia University Press, 1984).

Tekeli, İlhan. "Involuntary Displacement and the Problem of Resettlement in Turkey from the Ottoman Empire to the Present," *Center for Migration Studies Special Issues* 11.4 (2012): 202–26.

Temo, Ibrahim. *Doktor Ibrahim Temo Ittihad ve Terakki Cemiyetinin Teşekkülü ve Hidemati Vataniye ve İnkılâbi Milliye Dair Hatıratım* (Mecidiye: Self-Published, 1939).

Tenorio, Myriam Olguin. *La immigración arabe en Chile* (Santiago: Ediciones Instituto Chileno Arabe de Cultura, 1990).

Thobie, Jacque. *Intérêts Français dans l'Empire Ottoman (1895–1914)* (Paris: La Documentation Française, 1977).

Timberg, Thomas A. "Baghdadi Jews in Indian Port Cities," *Jews in India* (New Delhi: Vikas Publishing House Private, 1986): 273–81.

Todorova, Maria. *Imagining the Balkans* (New York: Oxford University Press, 1997).

—. "The Trap of Backwardness: Modernity, Temporality, and the Study of Eastern European Nationalism," *Slavic Review* 64.1 (2005): 140–64.

Tokay, Gül. *Makedonya Sorunu: Jön Türk Ihtilalinin Kökenleri (1903–1908)* (Istanbul: AFA Yayınları, 1995).

—. "Macedonian Reforms and Muslim Opposition during the Hamidian Era 1878–1908," *Islam and the Christian-Muslim Relations* 14.1 (2003): 51–65.

Toksöz, Meltem. "Bir Coğrafya, Bir Ürun, Bir Bölge: Çukurova," *Kebikeç* 21 (2006): 97–110.

—. *Nomads, Migrants and Cotton in the Eastern Mediterranean* (Leiden: Brill, 2010).

Tolmacheva, Marina. "'They Came from Damascus in Syria': A Note on Traditional Lamu Historiography," *The International Journal of African Historical Studies* 12.2 (1979): 259–69.

Toth, Anthony B. "Conflict and a Pastoral Economy: The Costs of Akhwan Attacks on Tribes in Iraq, 1922–29," *Critique: Critical Middle Eastern Studies* 11.2 (2002): 201–27.

Toumarkine, Alexandre. *Les Migrations des populations musulmanes balkaniques en Anatolie (1876–1913)* (Istanbul: Isis Press, 1995).

Tregonning, Kennedy G. *A History of Modern Sabah, 1881–1963* (Singapore: University of Malaya Press, 1966).

Tregonning, Kevin G. "American Activity in North Borneo, 1865–1881," *Pacific Historical Review* 23.4 (1954): 357–72.

Trix, Frances. "Alphabet Conflict in the Balkans: Albanian and the Congress of Monastir," *International Journal of the Sociology of Language* 128.1 (1997): 1–24.

—. "The Stamboul Alphabet of Shemseddin Sami Bey: Precursor to Turkish Script Reform," *IJMES* 31.2 (1999): 255–72.

Trocki, Carl A. *Opium, Empire and the Global Political Economy: A Study of the Asian Opium Trade, 1750–1950* (London: Routledge, 1999).

Trotsky, Leon, in Trotskii, L. *The Balkan Wars, 1912–1913: The War Correspondence of Leon Trotsky.* D. Williams and G. Weissman (eds) (London: Monad Press, 1980): 231, 284.

Turda, Marius. "Whither Race? Physical Anthropology in Post-1945 Central and Southeastern Europe," *Focaal* 58 (2010): 3–15.

Turnbull, Constance M. "British Colonialism and the Making of the Modern Johor 1 Monarchy," *Indonesia and the Malay World* 37.109 (2009): 227–48.

Turović, Dobrosav. *Gornja Jablanica. Kroz istoriju* (Belgrade: Beograd Zavičajno udruženje, 2002).

Turton, E. R. "Kirk and the Egyptian Invasion of East Africa in 1875: A Reassessment," *The Journal of African History* 11.3 (1970): 355–70.

Twaddle, Michael. "The Muslim Revolution in Buganda," *African Affairs* 71.282 (1972): 54–72.

Uka, Sabit. *Dëbimi i Shqiptarëve nga Sanxhaku i Nishit dhe vendosja e tyre në Kosovë, 1878-1912,* 4 vols (Prishtine: Verana, 2004).

Üngör, Uğur Ümit. "Geographies of Nationalism and Violence: Rethinking Young Turk 'Social Engineering,'" *European Journal of Turkish Studies* 7 (2008) at: www.ejts.org/document2583.html

—. *The Making of Modern Turkey: Nation and State in Eastern Anatolia, 1913-1950* (Oxford: Oxford University Press, 2012).

—. "Rethinking the Violence of Pacification: State Formation and Bandits in Turkey, 1914-1937," *CSSH* 54.04 (2012): 746–69.

Vandiver, Frank E. *Black Jack: The Life and Times of John J. Pershing,* vol. 1 (College Station: TAMU Press, 1977).

Velay, André du. *Essai sur l'histoire financière de la Turquie* (Paris: A. Rousseau, 1903).

Verli, Marenglen. *Reforma agrare kolonizuese në Kosovë, 1918-1941* (Bonn: Ilira, 1992).

Viaene, Vincent. "International History, Religious History, Catholic History: Perspectives for Cross-Fertilization (1830-1914)," *European History Quarterly* 38.4 (2008): 578–607.

Vianello, Alessandra. "One Hundred Years in Brava: The Migration of the ʿUmar Bā ʿUmar from Hadhramaut to East Africa and Back, c. 1890-1990," *Journal of Eastern African Studies* 6.4 (2012): 655–71.

Vidal, José Montero y. *Historia de la Pirateria Malayo Mahometans en Mindanao, Jolo, y Borneo* (Madrid: Imprenta de M. Tello, 1888).

Vishesella, Nazmi. *Vuajtjet e Kombit Shqiptarë-Muhaxhirëve me Shekuj* (Ferizaj: DinoGraf, 2005).

Vitalis, Robert. "On the Theory and Practice of Compradors: The Role of ʿAbbud Pasha in the Egyptian Political Economy," *IJMES* 22 (1990): 291–315.

—. "The Graceful and Generous Liberal Gesture: Making Racism Invisible in American International Relations," *Millennium-London School of Economics* 29.2 (2000): 331–56.

—. "The Noble American Science of Imperial Relations and its Laws of Race Development," *CSSH* 52.4 (2010): 909–38.

Wallace, Alfred R. *The Malay Archipelago: The Land of the Orang-utan and the Bird of Paradise* (Singapore: Oxford University Press, 1986).

Wank, Solomon. "Foreign Policy and the Nationality Problem in Austria-Hungary, 1867-1914," *Austrian History Yearbook* 3.3 (1967): 37–56.

Ward, Kerry. *Networks of Empire: Forced Migration in the Dutch East India Company* (Cambridge: Cambridge University Press, 2008).

Warren, James F. "Sino-Sulu Trade in the Late Eighteenth and Nineteenth Century," *Philippine Studies: Historical and Ethnographic Viewpoints* 25.1 (1977): 50–79.

—. "Who Were the Balangingi Samal? Slave Raiding and Ethnogenesis in Nineteenth-Century Sulu," *Journal of Asian Studies* 37.3 (1978): 477–90.

—. *The Sulu Zone 1768–1898: The Dynamics of External Trade, Slavery, and Ethnicity in the Transformation of a Southeast Asian Maritime State* (Singapore: Singapore University Press, 1981).

—. "The Balangingi Samal: The Global Economy, Maritime Raiding and Diasporic Identities in the Nineteenth-Century Philippines," *Asian Ethnicity* 4.1(2003): 7–29.

—. *Rickshaw Coolie: A People's History of Singapore, 1880–1940* (Honolulu: University of Hawaii Press, 2003).

Watenpaugh, Keith D. *Being Modern in the Middle East: Revolution, Nationalism, Colonialism, and the Arab Middle Class* (Princeton: Princeton University Press, 2006).

Welsh, Frank. *A History of Hong Kong* (London: HarperCollins, 1977).

White, Benjamin. "The Nation-State Form and the Emergence of 'Minorities' in Syria," *Studies in Ethnicity and Nationalism* 7.1 (2007): 64–85.

White, Hayden. *Metahistory: The Historical Imagination in Nineteenth-century Europe* (Baltimore: Johns Hopkins University Press, 1975).

White, Richard. "Information, Markets, and Corruption: Transcontinental Railroads in the Gilded Age," *The Journal of American History* 90.1 (2003): 19–43.

Wild, Stefan. "Islamic Enlightenment and the Paradox of Averroes," *Die Welt des Islams* 36.3 (1996): 379–90.

Wilkinson, Henri R. *Maps and Politics: A Review of the Ethnographic Cartography of Macedonia* (Manchester: Manchester University Press, 1951).

Williams, Brian. G. "Hijra and Forced Migration from Nineteenth-century Russia to the Ottoman Empire. A Critical Analysis of the Great Tatar Emigration of 1860–1861," *Cahiers du monde russe. Russie-Empire russe-Union soviétique et États indépendants* 41.1 (2000): 79–108.

Willis, John M. "Debating the Caliphate: Islam and Nation in the Work of Rashid Rida and Abdul Kalam Azad," *The International History Review* 32.4 (December 2010): 711–32.

—. *Unmaking North and South: Cartographies of the Yemeni Past* (London: C. Hurst & Co., 2012).

Willmott, Bill. "Chinese Contract Labour in the Pacific Islands during the Nineteenth Century," *Journal of Pacific Islands Studies* 27.2 (2004): 161–76.

Wirthwein, Walter G. *Britain and the Balkan Crises, 1875–1878* (New York: Columbia University Press, 1935).

Wood, Andrew Grant. "Introducing La Reina Del Carnaval: Public Celebration and Postrevolutionary Discourse in Veracruz, Mexico," *The Americas* 60.1 (2003): 87–108.

Wood, Gillen D'Arcy. "The Volcano Lover: Climate, Colonialism, and the Slave Trade in Raffles's History of Java (1817)," *Journal for Early Modern Cultural Studies* 8.2 (2008): 33–55.

Wray, L. Randall. *Modern Money Theory: A Primer on Macroeconomics for Sovereign Monetary Systems* (New York: Palgrave Macmillan, 2012).

Wright, Leigh R. "Historical Notes on the North Borneo Dispute," *The Journal of Asian Studies* 25.03 (1966): 471–84.

—. *The Origins of British Borneo* (Hong Kong: Hong Kong University Press, 1970).

Wrigley, Christopher. *Kinship and State: The Buganda Dynasty* (Cambridge: Cambridge University Press, 1996).

Yang, Anand A. "Indian Convict Workers in Southeast Asia in the Late Eighteenth and Early Nineteenth Centuries," *Journal of World History* 14.2 (2003): 179–208.

Yasamee, Faruk A. K. *Ottoman Diplomacy: Abdülhamid II and the Great Powers, 1878–1888* (Istanbul: The Isis Press, 1996).

Yavuz, M. Hakan and Isa Blumi (eds), *War & Nationalism: The Balkan Wars (1912–1913) and Socio-Political Implications* (Salt Lake City: University of Utah Press, 2013).

Yazbak, Mahmoud. "From Poverty to Revolt: Economic Factors in the Outbreak of the 1936 Rebellion in Palestine," *Middle Eastern Studies* 36.3 (2000): 93–113.

Yetkin, Sabri. *Ege'de eşkıyalar* (Ankara: Türkiye Ekonomik ve Toplumsal Tarih Vakf, 1996).

Yoshihara, Kunio. *Philippine Industrialization: Foreign and Domestic Capital* (Singapore: Oxford University Press, 1985).

Young, George. *Corps de Droit Ottoman* (Oxford: Clarendon Press, 1905).

Young, Robert. *White Mythologies: Writing History and the West* (New York: Routledge, 1990).

Zarcone, Thierry. *Mystiques, philosophes et francs-maçons en Islam. Riza Tevfik penseur ottoman (1868–1949), du soufisme à la confrérie* (Paris: Jean Maisonneuve, 1993).

—. "Shaykh Succession in Turkish Sufi Lineages (19th and 20th Centuries): Conflicts, Reforms and Transmission of Spiritual Enlightenment," *Asian and African Studies* 7.1 (2007): 18–35.

Zardykhan, Zharmukhamed. "Ottoman Kurds of the First World War Era: Reflections in Russian Sources," *Middle Eastern Studies* 42.1 (2006): 67–85.

Zeidner, Robert F. "Britain and the Launching of the Armenian Question," *IJMES* 7.4 (1976): 465–83.

Zenner, Walter P. "Arabic-speaking Immigrants in North America as Middleman Minorities," *Ethnic and Racial Studies* 5.4 (1982): 457–77.

Zens, Robert. "Pasvanoğlu Osman Paşa and the Paşalık of Belgrade, 1791–1807," *International Journal of Turkish Studies* 8.1 and 2 (2002): 89–104.

Zubaida, Sami (ed.). *Race and Racialism* (London: Tavistock Publications, 1970).

Zubčević, Asim. "Pathology of a Literature: Some Roots of Balkan Islamophobia," *Journal of Muslim Minority Affairs* 16.2 (1996): 309–15.

Zürcher, Erik J. *The Unionist Factor: The Rôle of the Committee of Union and Progress in the Turkish National Movement, 1905–1926* (Leiden: Brill, 1984).

—. *Turkey: A Modern History* (London: I.B. Tauris, 1997).

—. "The Young Turks—Children of the Borderlands?" *International Journal of Turkish Studies* 9 (2003): 275–86.

Zürcher, Erik J. *The Young Turk Legacy and Nation Building: From the Ottoman Empire to Atatürk's Turkey* (London: I.B. Tauris, 2010).

Žižek, Slavoj. *Living in the End Times* (London: Verso, 2010).

Index